Alternatives to Imprisonment in England and Wales, Germany and Turkey

Öznur Sevdiren

Alternatives to Imprisonment in England and Wales, Germany and Turkey

A Comparative Study

Springer

Dr. Öznur Sevdiren
oznur.sevdiren@gmail.com

ISBN 978-3-642-17350-9 e-ISBN 978-3-642-17351-6
DOI 10.1007/978-3-642-17351-6
Springer Heidelberg Dordrecht London New York

Library of Congress Control Number: 2011922990

Cover design: WMX Design GmbH, Heidelberg, Germany

Printed on acid-free paper

Springer is part of Springer Science+Business Media (www.springer.com)

To my family

Acknowledgements

This study simply would not be possible without support and contribution of many people and institutions.

I am deeply indebted to my supervisor, Professor Thomas Weigend, for his guidance, perceptive criticism and invariable support. My thanks are also due to my second examiner, Professor Michael Walter, for his critical comments on my study. I should like to take this opportunity also to express my gratitude to numerous former and present members of the Institute of Foreign and International Criminal Law at the University of Cologne, in particular, to Michaela Noack.

I would like to extend my gratitude to DAAD (German Academic Exchange Service), University of Cologne and Friedrich-Ebert-Stiftung. The Friedrich-Ebert-Stiftung did not only provide financial assistance between January 2007 and Mai 2010, but also contributed a great deal to the publication of this book. My special thanks go to Josef Minzenbach. Thanks are also due to (PD.) Dr. Andreas Funke, a former holder of FES scholarship, for acting as an advisor during my doctorate at the University of Cologne.

Finally, as ever, I owe my deepest gratitude to my parents, Makbule and Ali; my sisters, Sevtap and Ülkü; and my brothers, Özgür and Inan for their incredible support and loving encouragement in the long years of researching and writing in London, Sheffield, Istanbul and Cologne. With my deepest love and gratitude, I dedicate this book to them.

Contents

List of Figures

List of Tables

Chapter 1
Introduction

This study attempts to shed light on the alternatives to imprisonment, as one dimension of arguably one of the central problems of Turkish penal policy: the over-reliance of imprisonment as a sentencing option and a corresponding inexorable increase in the prison population which hitherto has not exclusively, but mainly, been responded to with the enactment of amnesty laws and construction of new prison buildings. So far, this approach has resulted in a gloomy picture of penal justice. Currently, Turkish prisons accommodate one of the largest prison populations in Europe. After a steady increase over the decade, Turkey's prison population reached 116,340 in 2009, nearly four times greater than its level in 1992 (31,582).[1] In the same period, the imprisonment rate per 100,000 population increased dramatically from 54 by nearly 200% to 161. Although there are some puzzling statements on the official capacity of prisons, in the daily press constant reports have appeared indicating that the occupancy level has gone far beyond the actual capacity.[2] Not forgetting, when assessing the occupancy rate, except for a number of high security prisons, in contrast to many of its European counterparts, the Turkish prison system is still largely based on the dormitory system.[3]

In view of this state of affairs, a study of this kind is relevant in the greater context of penal reform in Turkey and more specifically for the introduction of a modern prison regime. However, the problem implies a universal phenomenon and, in any case, requires going beyond Turkey's own national boundaries. Remarkably, so far few comparative studies on non-custodial sanctions have been published

[1]See for the Turkish figures, the Turkish General Directorate of Penal Execution Institutions and Remand Houses the following web page http://www.cte.adalet.gov.tr (Access Date: March 2010), and the figures of the International Prison Studies, King's College London, the following web page: http://www.kcl.ac.uk/depsta/law/research/icps/worldbrief/wpb_country.php?country=119 (Access Date: March 2010).

[2]See e.g., *Cumhuriyet*, 25.8.2007, *Hürriyet*, 3.4.2007, *Radikal*, 26.7.2009, *Hürriyet*, 31.8.2009.

[3]For a critical English account on the theme, see, Green, P. (2002) Turkish Jails, Hunger Strikes and the European Drive for Prison Reform, *Punishment and Society*, vol. 4, no 1, pp. 97–101.

See Neziroglu, I. (2006) 'A Comparison of Law and Practice within the Turkish Prison System with Relevant International Prison Standards with Special Reference to F-Type High Security Prisons', *Turkish Studies*, vol. 7, no 3, pp. 421–450.

Ö. Sevdiren, *Alternatives to Imprisonment in England and Wales, Germany and Turkey*,
DOI 10.1007/978-3-642-17351-6_1,

and those available studies tend to deal with the subject through isolated country reports that are limited to providing information from an insider's perspective.[4] This study, in contrast, attempts to place recent (and possible future) developments in Turkish law and practice in a European context by comparing these developments with the experience in two major systems, namely England and Wales,[5] and Germany.

Somewhat paradoxically, in Turkey, despite the notorious record of high imprisonment rates and reportedly appalling prison conditions,[6] particularly during times of martial law, little has been systematically written about alternative ways of dealing with offenders. The recent reform of penal law, driven significantly by Turkey's desire to become a fully-fledged member of the European Union, has not changed this state of affairs. Apart from some passing statements that the avoidance of short-term imprisonment should be a goal of Turkish penal policy to the largest extent possible, the theme of prison alternatives has been marginal to the reform debate. Since that debate was preoccupied with such issues as the desirability of the death penalty, the limits of freedom of expression, the definition of sexual offences as well as with fundamental dogmatic issues in the theory of crime (*Verbrechenslehre*), it was perhaps inevitable that the reform debate was limited to the reiteration of the long-deplored drawbacks of short-term imprisonment without actually examining the merits of the Turkish system in this respect.

It is therefore not paradoxical that the result of the long-standing neglect of this topic has created some form of 'short-sightedness' or failure to recognise the fact that Turkish legislation does provide for a number of alternative modalities to imprisonment comparable to its European counterparts even though these alternatives play only a minor role in practice. Turkish commentators, relying heavily on German literature, seemed to take for granted the assumption that an extension of non-custodial sanctions was essential.[7]

Originally, this study started from the assumption that Turkey does not have a sufficient number of viable alternatives to imprisonment; it set out to discover new

---

[4]Jescheck, H.-H. (ed.) (1983–1984) *Die Freiheitsstrafe und ihre Surrogate im deutschen und ausländischen Recht*, vol. 1–3, Nomos, Baden Baden, Albrecht, H.-J. and Kalmthout, A., M. (eds.) (2002) *Community Sanctions and Measures in Europe and North America*, Max-Planck-Institut für ausländisches und internationales Strafrecht, Freiburg, see also, Dünkel, F. and Spiess, G. (1983) *Alternativen zur Freiheitsstrafe: Strafaussetzung zur Bewährung und Bewährungshilfe im internationalen Vergleich*, Max-Planck-Institut für ausländisches und internationales Strafrecht, Freiburg, van Kalmthout, A., M. (1989) *Sanction Systems in the Member-States of the Council of Europe*, Kluwer, Deventer, Zvekic, U. (1994) *Alternatives to Imprisonment* (United Nations Interregional Crime and Justice Research Institute), Nelson-Hall Publishers, Chicago, Tas-Junger, J. (1994) *Alternatives to Prison Sentences: Experiences and Developments*, Kugler Publications, Amsterdam.

[5]Hereinafter this study will refer to the jurisdiction of England and Wales as 'England'.

[6]See Neziroglu, *op. cit.*, pp. 421–450. For indication of relevant supranational case law concerning prison conditions in Turkey, see van Zyl Smit, D. and Snacken, S. (2009) *Principles of European Prison Law and Policy*, Oxford University Press, Oxford, pp. 126–175.

[7]See chapter 4.

ways to reduce the abundant use of imprisonment in Turkey. Yet, a close look at the theory and practice of prison alternatives made it possible to discover the shadowy existence of alternative measures to imprisonment in Turkey. The central theme of this study thus became the question whether and to what extent it is advisable to enrich the Turkish system by transplanting or importing ideas from other systems. In this context, particular attention is devoted to the question as to what extent non-custodial alternatives can be regarded as genuine substitutes for custody. Two jurisdictions have been chosen for closer study: Germany and England and Wales.

Germany is the one of the most influential countries with respect to its contribution to both Turkish public and private law in that the view can be shared that it is truly primarily Germanic legal traditions and culture that have influenced Turkish law up to the present.[8] As early as 1876, the first Ottoman Constitution was modelled closely after the Prussian Constitution of 1851.[9] In 1916, the German Civil Code was translated into Turkish, and consequently a discussion developed on whether the Ottoman Civil Code (*Mecelle*) met the standards of a modern civil code. After the proclamation of the republic, a commercial code was adopted based on significant influence from the Italian and German codes. The Turkish Criminal Procedure Code was adopted in 1929 from the German Code of Criminal Procedure.[10] More importantly, the German Penal Code and German doctrine had a substantial impact on the enactment of the new Turkish Criminal Procedure Code and Penal Code. The new Turkish Penal Code borrowed many concepts and institutions from the German law, among others are the formal distinction between penalties and measures, the day-fine system and the reformulation of the provisions on the suspended sentence.[11] Alongside, the contribution of German law to Turkish law, the choice of Germany has also been prompted by the fact that in this country although the sanction system based on a dualist system of imprisonment and fines, the use of prison sentences has been significantly reduced over more than a century.

In comparison to the influence of German law over Turkish law, English law has been less known in Turkish academic and legal circles. Since the beginning of the nineteenth century, Turkish law developed along the civil-law tradition.[12] Whereas

[8]Hoegen, E. and Brienen, M (2000) *Victims of Crime in 22 European Criminal Justice Systems*, Wolf Legal Production in cooperation with the Global Law Association, Nijmegen, pp. 960, Chapter 24.

[9]Bozkurt, G. (1996) 'Alman Arsiv Belgelerine Göre Alman Hukuku'nun Türk Hukuku'na Etkisi', *Ankara Üniversitesi Hukuk Fakültesi Dergisi*, vol. 45, no 4, pp. 29–40, p. 29.

[10]Law no 1412, date 4/4/1929, Official Gazette 20/4/1929, See Önder, A. (1974) Der Einfluss des deutschen Rechts auf das türkische Strafprozessrecht, *Annales de la Facultés de Droit d'Istanbul*, vol. 38, pp. 367–385 and (1981) Die türkische Strafprozessordnung, *Annales de la Facultés de Droit d'Istanbul*, vol. 44, pp. 178–196.

[11]See, Sözüer, A. (2007) Die Reform des türkischen Strafrechts, *Zeitschrift für die gesamte Strafrechtswissenschaft*, vol. 119, no 3, pp. 712–749.

[12]Alacakaptan, U. (1958) *Ingiliz Ceza Hukukunda Suc ve Cezalarin Kanuniligi Prensibi*, Ankara Üniversitesi Hukuk Fakültesi Yayinlari, Ankara.

the penal institutions, for which England was famous worldwide,[13] attracted attention in Turkey, much less consideration was given to English substantive criminal law. The concepts and traditions of the common law may have been regarded as too far removed from Turkish legal culture as to serve as an example for reform.[14]

For the study of alternatives to imprisonment the system of England and Wales has been chosen because this jurisdiction is internationally well known for its conception and innovative practice of various non-custodial alternatives.[15] Non-custodial sanctions such as the probation order and the community service order have a relatively long history in England and Wales. In contrast to some other countries, in England these penalties can be imposed as independent sanctions. Not surprisingly, English legal rules and practice in this regard have become a model for numerous European countries.[16] Even in a global context, the fact that in England a wide range of non-custodial sanctions are available has instigated academic curiosity. Notably, the establishment of a probation service in Turkey was informed substantially by experience gained in England. As will be touched on below, intergovernmental agreements exist between Turkey and England, the latter providing expertise in the establishment and development of a probation service. Such cooperation made the knowledge of the English experience even more valuable. In contrast to some of its counterparts, for example Germany, these penalties are established in their own right, i.e. the latter category of sanctions could be imposed as an independent sanction. Somewhat paradoxically though, the strategy of extending and strengthening non-custodial sanctions have some well-publicised disappointing results. A close look at the English system of sanctions therefore appeared indispensable for the present study.

As this brief overview reveals, the contrast between Germany and England in the context of this study cannot be merely reduced to their hitherto influence over Turkish law. What is even more interesting for this study is the distinct ways of managing offenders within the criminal justice system that these countries opted for. Indeed, at the risk of oversimplification, whilst the German system is characterised by an above mentioned system based on fines and imprisonment, the

---

[13]An English prison administrator and reformer, Ruggles-Brise, famously noted that "It is a remarkable fact, at least so far as my observation and experience goes that foreign countries look to England with anxiety and curiosity for the *practical* solution of the penal problem". Cited in Radzinowicz, L. (1991) 'Penal Regressions', *Cambridge Law Journal*, vol. 50, pp. 422–444, p. 439.

[14]On the penal establishments in England and Wales, see e.g., Gölcüklü, F. (1962a) 'Ingiltere ve Gal Eyaleti'nde Hürriyeti Baglayici Cezalar ve Cezaevi Sistemleri', *Ankara Üniversitesi Hukuk Fakültesi Dergisi*, vol. 17, no 1, pp. 159–202. From the same author on the English Judicial Mechanism, see (1955) 'Ingiliz Adli Teskilati', *Ankara Üniversitesi Siyasal Bilgiler Fakültesi Dergisi*, vol. 10, no 1, pp. 160–185.

[15]Bottoms, A., E. (1987) 'Limiting Prison Use: Experiences in England and Wales', *Howard Journal*, vol. 26, no 3, pp. 177–202, p. 177.

[16]For an early account, see Tak, P.J.P. (1986) Community Service Orders in Western Europe – A Comparative Survey – in Albrecht, H-J. and Schädler, W. (eds.) *Community Service*, Max-Planck-Institut für ausländisches und internationales Strafrecht, Freiburg.

English system is marked by the availability of a broad array of non-custodial sanctions. From this perspective, it is fair to suggest that the meaning and implications of such a 'contrast' is not only illuminating for the Turkish system (a system which has considerable similarities with the German system). Beyond this, overall such an "exercise in difference" may likely call on the somewhat axiomatic assumption that is still largely held that the extension of alternative sentences will necessarily bring a reduction in the use of imprisonment into question.[17]

1.1 The Scope

A major terminological question arose when trying to define the subject matter of this study and delineate its boundaries. At first glance, the term 'community sanctions and measures',[18] as used in documents of the Council of Europe as well as in comparative studies,[19] appeared to be particularly well suited. In one of the guiding documents of the Council of Europe, for example, that term is used to cover the following types of sanctions[20]:

1. Suspension of the enforcement of a sentence to imprisonment with imposed conditions
2. Probation as an independent sanction, imposed without the pronouncement of a sentence of imprisonment

[17]Frankenberg views comparative learning process as involving two stages: 'distancing' and 'differencing': He defines 'distancing' as "an attempt to break away from firmly held beliefs and settled knowledge and as an attempt to resists the power of prejudice and ignorance". And goes on to state that "from a distance old knowledge can be reviewed and new knowledge can be distinguished as it is in its own right. . .Mere distance, however, neither opens our eyes nor makes us see clearly. As long as foreign places only look like or unlike home, as long as foreign legal cultures only appear to be un-common or un-civil, and as long as they are treated as same or other, they do not speak for themselves. In order to break the unconscious spell that holds us to see others by the measure of ourselves without abandoning the benefits of criticism, travelling as well as comparison has to be an exercise in difference". Frankenberg, G. (1985) Critical Comparisons: Rethinking Comparative Law, *Harvard International Law Journal*, vol. 26, no 2, pp. 411–455.

[18]Other alternatives are 'community based penal measures', 'community-based penal measures', 'community-based dispositions', 'community care programmes', 'community corrections', 'community correctional programmes', 'supervision in the community', 'punishment in the community'. Vass, A. (1990) Alternatives to Prison: Punishment, Custody and the Community, Sage, London, p. xv.

[19]See e.g., most recently, Dünkel, F. and Pruin, I. (2009) 'Community Sanctions and the Sanctioning Practice in Juvenile Justice Systems in Europe' in Junger-Tas, J. and Dünkel, F. (eds.) *Reforming Juvenile Justice*, Springer, Dordrecht.

[20]*Recommendation No(2000)22 of the Ministers to Member States on Improving the Implementation of the European Rules on Community Sanctions and Measures (adopted by the Committee of Ministers on 29 November 2000 at the 731st meeting of the Ministers' Deputies) http://www.justizia.net/Docuteca/Ficheros.asp?intcodigo=1204&IdDoc=SP&Idio.ma=sp* (Access Date: December 2009).

3. High intensity supervision
4. Community service (i.e. unpaid work on behalf of the community)
5. Treatment orders/contract treatment for specific categories of offenders
6. Victim-offender mediation/victim compensation
7. Restriction of liberty of movement by means of, for example, curfew orders or electronic monitoring

The term 'community' in this document refers to the venue of execution of the sanction, emphasising that such sanctions are executed outside prison establishments. The implications of the term go beyond that, however. Inspired by recent theoretical and philosophical approaches in Anglo–Saxon literature,[21] the term 'community' is loaded to encompass various forms of voluntary involvement and assistance of 'community' members in the 'reintegration' of offenders into society. This perspective is clearly discernible in another guiding document including the rules on community sanctions and measures.[22] The following citation should elucidate the meaning given to this concept.

> (*Rule 44*) Justice cannot be effectively administered in isolation from the community it seeks to serve: this requires both the acceptance and the respect of the public. This level of confidence and commitment is most likely to be achieved if members of the public are encouraged and enabled to participate in the administration of justice. . ..
>
> (*Rule 45*). . ...The involvement of members of the local community greatly facilitates access to an extensive range of human and material resources and social support systems. Offenders are able to establish links with voluntary agencies, trade unions and staff associations, social and recreational clubs, religious groups, charitable bodies and other organisations and individuals with the capacity to provide them with assistance and support. The maintenance of links with the wider society is likely to enhance the prospects of an offender's social reintegration.

As emphasised by various commentators, such a community approach emphasising alternatives to the provision of services by the state, collective voluntarism as a source of resources, localism, and the involvement of non-criminal justice professionals, is deeply embedded in the cultural and political context of England.[23]

---

[21] E.g., Braithwaite, J. (1989) *Crime, Shame and Reintegration*, Cambridge University Press, Cambridge.

[22] *Recommendation (1992) 16 of The Committee of Ministers to Member States on the European Rules (adopted by the Committee of Ministers on 19 October 1982 at the 482nd meeting of the Ministers' Deputies) https://wcd.coe.int/com.instranet.InstraServlet?command=com.instranet.CmdBlobGet&InstranetImage=574882&SecMode=1&DocId=605174&Usage=2 (Access Date: December 2009).*

[23] See, Crawford, A. (1997) The Local Governance of Crime: Appeals to Community and Partnerships, Clarendon Press, Oxford, chapter 5, Brownlee, I. (1998) Community Punishment: A Critical Introduction, Harlow, Wesley Longman, pp. 56–59, Cavadino, M., Crow, I. and Dignan, J. (1999) *Criminal Justice 2000: Strategies for a New Century*, Waterside Press, Winchester, pp. 97–98, Worall, A. and Hoy, C. (2005) *Punishment in the Community: Managing Offenders and Making Choices*, Sage, London, pp. 57–70.

In stark contrast to England[24] where "the appeals to community connect with, and are nourished by anti-statism"[25] both Germany[26] and Turkey are countries in which the overall reliance on the state is strong, and an approach emphasising the role of 'the community' in the enforcement of non-custodial sanctions[27] has so far been largely absent. Noticeably, the term 'community' as an attribute of sanctions does not even translate easily into German[28] and Turkish. It is therefore fair to conclude that the term 'community sanctions and measures' does not denote the same meaning in all three countries featured in this study.

It is interesting to note that over time, the term 'community sanctions', may have lost some of its original meaning even on its native soil. As will be discussed, recent changes in English law have blurred the distinction between community and non-community sanctions.[29] Even, one of the authoritative definitions of 'community penalties' may thus no longer be accurate. In 2001, Bottoms *et al.* had defined 'community penalties' as:

> "Court ordered punishments structurally located between custody, on the one hand, and financial or nominal penalties (fines, compensation, and discharge) on the other. What distinguishes community penalties from fines and compensation is that they are personally restrictive, involving some active contact with a penal agent; but, unlike custodial sanctions, this contact takes place in a community-based setting".[30]

If one abandons the specific 'communal' element of 'community penalties' and simply defines them as 'intermediate punishments'[31] the question arises whether the term still extends to financial penalties. There is no doubt that fines must be included in any attempt to analyse the relationship between the use of non-custodial

---

[24]See, Raynor, P. (2001) Community Penalties and Social Integration: ‚Community' as Solution and as Problem in Bottom *et al.* (eds.), pp.183–199, Crawford, A. (2000) Contrasts in Victim Offender Mediation and Appeals to Community in France and England, in Nelken, D. (ed.) *Contrasting Criminal Justice*, Ashgate, Aldershot, pp. 205–229, p. 220.

[25]Crawford (2000), *op. cit.*, p. 220.

[26]Jung, H. (1999) Die "European Rules on Community Sanctions and Measures" in Feuerhelm, W., Schwind, H.-D. und Bock, M. (eds.) Festschrift für *Alexander Böhm zum 70. Geburtstag am 14. Juni 1999*, de Gruyter, Berlin, pp.69–79, Albrecht, H.-J. (2002)'Community Sanctions in the Federal Republic of Germany', in Albrecht and Kalmthout *op. cit.*, pp.243–270, p. 244, see also Lacey, N. and Zedner, L. (1995) Discourses of Community on Criminal Justice, *Journal of Law and Society*, vol. 22, pp. 301–325.

[27]In this context, see also Crawford (2000), *op. cit.*, p. 205.

[28]Jung, *op. cit.*, p. 72 'gemeinwesenorientiert'.

[29]Bottoms *et al.* (2004) *op. cit.*, p.13. In this context, see also, Roberts, J., V. (2004) *The Virtual Prison: Community Custody and the Evolution of Imprisonment*, Cambridge University Press, Cambridge.

[30]Bottoms, A., E., Gelsthorpe, L. and Rex, S. (eds.) (2001) Community Penalties: Change and Challenges, Willan Publishing, Cullompton, p. 1, see also Nellis, M. (2001) Community Penalties in Historical Perspective in Bottoms *et al.* (2001), pp. 16–40.

[31]Tonry, M. and Lynch, M. (1996) Intermediate Sanctions, *Crime and Justice*, vol. 20, pp. 99–144.

sentencing options,[32] since financial penalties have played a crucial role in reducing the use of imprisonment. It has been observed, for example, that in countries applying the unit or day-fine system, such as Austria, Switzerland, certain Scandinavian countries and France, short-term imprisonment has, to a considerable extent, been replaced by fines.[33] Accordingly, to disregard fines in this study would mean to neglect an indispensable element of the relationship between custody and its alternatives.

In the face of such conceptual difficulties, to use the term 'community penalties' for all non-custodial sanctions would be misleading. In lieu of this term, therefore, the terms 'alternatives to imprisonment' or, interchangeably, 'prison alternatives' and non-custodial sentences will be employed. A note of caution is in order, however. Although 'alternatives to imprisonment' is a convenient short-hand term that can be used with respect to all three jurisdictions treated here, it refers to a variety of diverse practices, ranging from programmes prior to court proceedings to early release arrangements.[34] For the sake of clarity and coherence, this study is primarily concerned with court ordered alternatives to imprisonment. Yet, pre-trial diversionary mechanisms will also be discussed at some point. This is because there is considerable evidence that, at least in England[35] and Germany,[36] such diversionary measures have significantly contributed to reducing the size of

---

[32]Harding, J. (2003) 'Which Way Probation? A Correctional or Community Justice Service?', *Probation Journal*, vol. 54, no. 4, pp. 369–373, Bottoms *et al.* (2004), p. 9, Hughes, G. (2001) 'The Competing Logics of Community Sanctions: Welfare, Rehabilitation and Restorative Justice', McLaughlin, E. and Muncie, J. (eds.) *Controlling Crime*, Sage, London, pp. 249–297, p. 291.

[33]Albrecht, A. and Kalmthout, A., M. (2002) 'Intermediate Penalties: European Developments in Conceptions and Use of Non-Custodial Criminal Sanctions' in Albrecht and Kalmthout *op. cit.*, pp. 1–11, p. 4.

[34]Vass, *op. cit.*, p. xv.

[35]See, for example, with regard to England, Gelsthorpe, L. and Morris, A. (1994) *Juvenile Justice 1945–1992* in Maguire, M., Morgan, R. and Reiner, R. (eds.) *the Oxford Handbook of Criminology*, Clarendon Press, Oxford, Young, J. and Matthews, R. (2003) *The New Politics of Crime and Punishment*, Cullompton, Willan, p. 82, Mair, G. (2004) Diversionary and Non-Supervisory Approaches to Dealing with Offenders in Bottoms *et al.* (2004) pp. 135–161, see also Allen, R. (1991) Out of Jail : The Reduction in the Use of Penal Custody for Male Juveniles 1981–1988, *Howard Journal*, vol. 30, no 1, pp. 30–52, pp. 33–36.

With regard to Germany, see Graham, J. (1987) *The Declining Prison Population in the Federal Republic of Germany*, Home Office Research Bulletin, no 24, London pp. 47–52 and (1990) Decarceration in the Federal Republic of Germany: How Practitioners are Succeeding Where Policy Makers Have Failed?, *British Journal of Criminology*, vol. 30, no 2., pp. 47–52.

See also, Mayerhofer-Ludwig, W. (1995) Sentence without Conviction Notes on Diversion from the Juvenile Court in the Federal Republic of Germany, pp. 108–109 in Albrecht, G. and Ludwig-Mayerhofer, W. (eds.) *Diversion and Informal Social Control*, de Gruyter, Berlin, Muncie, J. and Sparks, R. (1991) Expansion and Contraction in European Penal Systems in Muncie and Sparks (eds) *Imprisonnment European Perspectives*, Prentice Hall, New York, pp. 89–108, p. 101.

[36]See for example, Jeschek, H.-H. (1979) Die Krise der Kriminalpolitik, *Zeitschrift für die gesamte Strafrechtswissenschaft*, vol. 91, pp. 1060–1061, Feltes, T. (1982) Alternativen zur Jugendstrafe in Sievering, U., O. (ed.) Alternativen zur Freiheitsstrafe, Haag Herchen, Frankfurt, pp. 79–87, p. 83.

the prison population, and they also function as 'informal' sentencing disposals. Given the increasing quest for alternatives to imprisonment, the subject undoubtedly merits more attention than it has thus far received. Furthermore, the recent introduction of diversionary measures in Turkey makes their inclusion in this comparative study necessary.

A further caveat is necessary with reference to the comparison between the legal systems covered by this study. Both the German and the Turkish penal systems place great emphasis on the principle of culpability and therefore have resorted to a two-track sanctioning system. This system consists of punishments (e.g., imprisonment and fines meted out in accordance with the offender's individual guilt) and rehabilitative, protective and incapacitative measures, which are based on the degree of the offender's dangerousness as revealed by the offence and her/his previous criminal record.[37] English law lacks this distinction, and employ a unitary system of criminal sanctions.

Arguably, the concept of criminal measures suffers from grave doctrinal inconsistencies. Although the complexities of this topic cannot be treated here, a brief note on the legal nature of measures is necessary. When an offender cannot be punished because s/he has not acted with guilt, e.g., because s/he is insane, or when her/his guilt is reduced because s/he was drunk at the time of the offence, it may still necessary to protect the public from a recurrence of her/his criminal behaviour. Therefore, German and Turkish law provide for placement in a mental hospital or in a rehabilitation centre as a measure. Predicated upon the same notion of dangerousness as prohibition to exercise a certain profession or a temporary suspension of the offender's driver licence can be imposed if the offender would otherwise create a serious risk to health or safety. These measures can be imposed in addition to any penalty for the offender's culpable unlawful conduct. Whereas measures, in particular custodial measures in Germany and Turkey are regarded as (part of) the regular sentence under the Penal Code, in England such sanctions would be treated as 'alternatives' to a prison sentence.

These differences also pose serious difficulties for interpreting statistical data. Due to the two-track system existing in Germany and Turkey, exact statistical comparisons between the three jurisdictions are hardly possible because 'measures' are not qualified as non-custodial sanctions *per se*, and they may be imposed in conjunction with a custodial or non-custodial sentencing option. This is only one aspect of the challenge of comparing statistical data gathered from different countries. On a broader level, considering the substantial differences that exist with respect to the collecting and classifying statistical data in three jurisdictions

[37]On, 'Zweispurigkeit', see Jescheck, H.-H. and Weigend, T. (1996) *Lehrbuch des Strafrechts*, 5th edition, Duncker & Humblot, Berlin, p. 83, Streng, F. (2002) Strafrechtliche Sanktionen, 2nd edition, Kohlhammer, Stuttgart, p. 150, Schöch, H. (2008) On Section 61, in *Leipziger Kommentar* pp. 215–229 in Laufhütte, H. W, Rissing-van Saan, R. and Tidemann, K. (eds.) 12th edition, vol.3, pp. 215–402, pp. 215–229, Eser, A. (2001) Zur Entwicklung von Maßregeln der Besserung und Sicherung als zweite Spur im Strafrecht in Britz, G. (ed.) *Grundfragen des staatlichen Strafens*, Beck, München, pp. 213–236.

any attempt of comparative evaluation would require the expertise of research from the countries in question. Thus, in this study, no attempt will be made to provide an overall comparison. Instead, the statistical data of each jurisdiction will be discussed separately. Still significant differences exist between such categories as 'up to one year', 'up to six months' or the variety of custodial options under general, military and juvenile laws for the same country over a period of time.

On a theoretical level, the question of how to compare legal systems whose penal cultures and traditions have been shaped by distinct structural and cultural characteristics represents a persisting methodological problem, and this study cannot escape from it.[38] This study makes no pretence to conducting a comprehensive analysis of the ideological and cultural differences between the legal cultures involved but largely limits itself to explaining the present by giving an account of the past. The primary focus of this study is placed upon jurisdictional and legislative issues.

In this context, Chap. 1 provides a brief overview of the historical origins of alternatives to imprisonment in a broader perspective. This section serves various purposes. Firstly, it highlights the key trends and developments and thus aims at defining the historical origins of alternatives to imprisonment in the countries that are examined.[39] Secondly, Chap. 1 provides the requisite historical information needed to understand the genealogy of the ideas and institutions; as will be shown, the proposals of alternatives and the ensuing debates remain relevant even today. Thirdly, this chapter will help to understand the reasons why Turkey feels 'belated' and also 'exceptional' when compared with Western countries. Moreover, this chapter, though not supplying a fully-fledged discussion of the purposes of punishment, comprises an account of the various objectives attributed to punishment over time. Instead of conducting an abstract philosophical debate on punishment, this chapter points out the areas where different theories on the purposes of punishment are particularly relevant for the debate on alternatives to imprisonment.

Chapters 2, 3 and 4 are concerned with 'alternatives to imprisonment' in England, Germany and Turkey. In each of these chapters, a fairly comprehensive overview of the foundations and historical developments in these jurisdictions will be given, and subsequently the legislative scope and the use of imprisonment and its alternatives will be discussed. These chapters are followed by a summary section where a condensed outline of the main conclusions of this study will be provided as well as some reflections on their meaning for the recent penal reform in Turkey.

---

[38] Nelken, D. (2000) Just Comparing in Nelken (ed.), *op. cit.*, pp. 3–22 and (2007) Comparing Criminal Justice in Maguire, M., Morgan, R. and Reiner, R. (eds.) *The Oxford Handbook of Criminology, 4th edition*, Oxford University Press, Oxford.

[39] Truly, "foreign laws can (indeed) be understood correctly only with their history and with relevant criminological data". Weigend, T. (2006) 'Criminal Law and Criminal Procedure', *Elgar Encyclopaedia of Comparative Law*, Smits, J. (ed.), Edward Elgar Publishing, Cheltenham, pp. 214–227, p. 218.

1.2 A Brief Note on Terminology and Language

In the course of this study, the present author realised that to use terminology consistently for all three countries and for the historical past as well as the present presents a formidable challenge. For example, the classification of crimes, ('Vergehen', 'Verbrechen'), the nomenclature of various sanctions, and the translation of concepts such as 'Rechtsgut' which are deeply embedded in German and Turkish doctrine, has proved to be a difficult task. Except where a translation was simply not possible as with some Turkish words, the author has nevertheless attempted to use English terms rather than the original words, even though this may risk confusion.

In order to emphasise gender equality, instead of using the allegedly 'epicene' masculine form of pronouns, both male and female forms of third person singular personal and possessive pronouns have been used where necessary. This usage is in conformity with the wording of the new Turkish Penal Code, showing sensitivity to the feminist critique of the phraseology of the previous Penal Code.

Chapter 2
Some Reflections on the History and Development of Alternatives to Prison

2.1 Introduction

The interest vested in the examination of the historical development of non-custodial penalties is fairly limited in contradistinction to that of custodial penalties. Indeed, far less attention has been given to the gradual transformation that has been occurring in the modalities of punishment since the mid-nineteenth century. This is not to underestimate the existence of a body of literature on the history of individual punishments, most notably on the history of the probation order.[1] It seems fair, however, to suggest that a comprehensive historical analysis from a comparative perspective on the theme largely remains an unfulfilled task.

For two reasons such an historical analysis appears to be both feasible and essential. Firstly, as will be demonstrated below, on the whole the conceptualisation of alternatives to prison has to a great extent remained akin to its foundational forms. By virtue of this, a historical examination of the quest for alternatives and their legislative adoptions would potentially facilitate a greater understanding of the contemporary location of these sanctions. Secondly and equally importantly, the transformations which these penalties have undergone, both at philosophical and practical levels, may well likely indicate possible future directions of non-custodial sanctions.

This chapter therefore aims to take one modest step towards understanding the foundations of non-custodial modes of punishment, an arguably unduly neglected area of comparative penology. Two periods in this context will be under examination. Of these periods, the first is concerned with the early emergence of the concept of prison alternatives. Here, particular attention will be paid to the adoption of conditional suspension of the execution of imprisonment and probation as the most

---

[1]Timasheff, N., S. (1941) *One Hundred Years of Probation, 1841–1941,* Part I: Probation in the United States, England and the British Commonwealth Countries, and (1943) Part II: Probation in Continental Europe, Latin America, Asia, and Africa, Fordham University Press, New York; United Nations/Department of Economic and Social Affairs (1951) *Probation and Related Measures,* United Nations Publications, New York; Harris, R. (1995) Probation round the World: Origins and Development in Hamai, K., Ville, R., Harris, R., pp. 25–67; Hough, M. and Zvekic, U. (eds.) *Probation Round the World: A Comparative Study,* Routledge, London.

Ö. Sevdiren, *Alternatives to Imprisonment in England and Wales, Germany and Turkey,*
DOI 10.1007/978-3-642-17351-6_2, © Springer-Verlag Berlin Heidelberg 2011

innovative and practically sustainable forms of early prison alternatives. The second period focuses on the rapid proliferation of non-custodial penalties since the 1970s.

2.2 'Reforming' Prisons and Prisoners: Setting the Scene for the Concept of Alternatives to Imprisonment

The terms 'prison alternatives' and 'non-custodial penalties' have long been used interchangeably to reflect the common characteristic of an array of sanctions that are executed outside the prison realm. Historically, however, a further qualification ought to be made, since any insight into the historical development of such sanctions as public work, the fine reveals that sanctions of this kind in various forms existed in earlier periods of the history,[2] during which prisons were used to confine debtors and persons awaiting their trial and punishment.[3] In view of this fact, here no attempt is being made to cover the distinct origins of sanctions not containing custody. The chief concern of this section is, rather, to analyse the emergence of alternatives to imprisonment against the background of the birth of prison as a penal institution. As detailed below, for the concept of prison alternatives to evolve, first of all imprisonment needed to be inaugurated as a major form of punishment.

It was not until the early seventeenth century that confinement began to function more than a mere form of detention.[4] Gradually, by the early nineteenth century in virtually every European country, imprisonment became the dominant mode of punishment and in many cases replaced capital and corporal punishments. Several studies have attempted to explain the nature of this change occurring in the form of punishment within a broader context, according to which this transformation has been attributed to the social, economic and political needs of the period.[5] It is

[2]von Hentig, H. (1955) *Die Strafe*, vol. 2, Die modernen Erscheinungsformen, Berlin, Springer; Grebing. G. (1978) Die Geldstrafe in rechtsvergleichender Darstellung, in Jescheck, H.-H. and Grebing, G. (eds.) *Die Geldstrafe im deutschen und ausländischen Recht*, Nomos, Baden Baden, pp. 1185–1357, Albrecht, H-J. and Schädler, W. (1986) (eds.) *Community Service: a New Option in Punishing Offenders in Europe*, Max-Planck-Institut für ausländisches und internationales Strafrecht, Freiburg.

[3]Peters, E., M. (1995) Prison before the Prison: The Ancient and Medieval Worlds in Morris, N. and Rothman, D. J. (eds.) *The Oxford History of Prison*, Oxford University Press, Oxford, pp. 3–47.

[4]Spierenburg, P. (1996) Four Centuries of Prison History: Punishment, Suffering, the Body, and Power in Finzsch, N. and Jütte, R. (eds.) *Institutions of Confinement: Hospitals, Asylums, and Prisons in Western Europe and North America, 1500–1950,* Cambridge University Press, Washington, D. C., pp. 17–38, pp. 23–24.

[5]Rusche, G. and Kirchheimer, O. (1939) *Punishment and Social Structure*, Columbia University Press, New York; Rothman, D. (1971) *The Discovery of the Asylum: Social Order and Disorder in the New Republic*, Little Brown, Boston; and (1980) *Conscience and Convenience: the Asylum and*

beyond the scope of this chapter, however, to carry out such a macro analysis. This study is concerned with the consequences of the 'Great Confinement' into prisons in terms of a very narrowly defined area, its impulse in stimulating almost concurrently its alternatives.

In order to do so, first of all it must be noted that the need for incarceration of greater number of offenders led to a rapid proliferation of prisons across the Continent. In studying the newly emergent prisons in Europe, O'Brien highlights that these prisons displayed a remarkable similarity in relation to their prison regimes, construction, internal regimes, architecture, work systems and inmate cultures.[6] It may be by virtue of these similarities that reform initiatives came into existence simultaneously in various countries. However, reforming prisons was not as straightforward a task as it might once have been considered. As soon as the reform ideas entered into the field of application, they found themselves in conflict with the reality of the prisons of the period.

The reformers of this period envisaged a prison system that would be capable of regenerating the morality of prisoners and reintegrating the convict into the community as a useful, productive and law-abiding citizen.[7] Since the causes of crime were seen as 'oblivion of religious and moral principles, ignorance of duty, idleness and habits of drinking',[8] it was believed that through discipline, education and classification according to a 'moral diagnosis',[9] prison would enable inmates to resist criminal inclinations within and outside of prison. Such a system, in their view, was to enable the convict to acquire industrial, scholastic, moral and religious education, whereby particular importance was attached to moral instruction.[10] In accordance with this view, many of the reformers were in principle against the idea of a harsh, cruel and vindictive prison regime and of the opinion that corporal punishment-based prison discipline did not, in the long term, contribute to

its Alternatives in Progressive America, Little, Brown, Boston; Foucault, M. (1975) *Discipline and Punish: the Birth of the Prison*, Penguin, London; Ignatieff, M. (1978) *A Just Measure of Pain: the Penitentiary in the Industrial Revolution, 1750–1850*, Pantheon Books, New York; and (1981) State, Civil Society and Total Institutions: A Critique of Recent Social Histories of Punishment, *Crime and Justice*, vol. 3, pp. 153–192 and; Melossi, D. and Pavarini, M. (1981) The Prison and the Factory: Origins of the Penitentiary System, Macmillan, London.

[6]O'Brien, P. (1995) The Prison on the Continent: Europe, 1865–1965 in Morris and Rothman, *op. cit.*, pp. 199–226, pp. 199–200.

[7]Ruggles-Brise (1925), *op. cit.*, p. 20, Grünhut, M. (1948) *Penal Reform: A Comparative Study*, Clarendon Press, Oxford, pp. 96–98, at p. 68, Nutz, T. (2001) *Strafanstalt als Besseurungsmachine: Reformdiskurs and Gefängniswissenschaft,* Oldenbourg, München, pp. 69–97.

[8]Wines, E. C. (1873) *Report on the International Penitentiary Congress of London* (held July 3–13, 1872), Government Printing, Washington, pp. 98–100.

[9]*Ibid.*, p. 133, Carpenter, M. (1967) *Reformatory Prison Discipline*, reprinted from the 1872 edition, Patterson Smith, Montclair, p. ix.

[10]Tallack, W. (1889) *Penological and Preventive Principles*, reprinted in 1984, Garland Publishing, New York, pp. 62–65, Wines, *op. cit.*, p. 138.

the 'moral amendment' of the convicts.[11] Intriguingly, however, the translation of the idealised form of prison into practice, even in its very inception, appeared to be hard to achieve. In this sense, the very drive for the 'moral correction' of prisoners through a prison stay and through discipline soon led to a certain disillusionment as to the ability of the prison to fulfil such expectations. It began to be acknowledged that prison created the danger of further moral contamination and deviant careers.[12] Hence, the reformers of this period, while thinking about the ways in which prisons could become well-regulated, disciplined, humane and adequately sanitary, meanwhile questioned at the very outset their presumed reformatory function. One of the greatest hindrances in realising the latter function of prisons was, for many, the growing presence of habitual offenders in the establishments.

Indeed, at this period recidivism aroused great concern. Scholars and criminal justice practitioners demanded draconian penalties, a more rigorous imprisonment and the imposition of greater deprivations upon recidivists.[13] It was recorded that at this time recidivists or habitual criminals made up more than 50% of the prison population in Europe.[14] Offenders of this kind were seen as being "in a state of absolute antagonism to society",[15] affording no hopes of the improvement of their morals. In accordance with this point of view, it was thought that confining first offenders together with habitual and repeated offenders would constitute a serious obstacle to the rehabilitation of the former. One way of preventing this contagious effect of the prison might be the separation of the former from the latter kind of offenders. However, the classification on this basis was deemed insufficient for the purpose of the avoidance of contamination among prisoners. Neither was it seen in practice as fully achievable, since in many prisons the crowded state of the prison,

---

[11]Pears, E. (1872) *Prison and Reformatories At Home and Abroad: The Transactions of the International Penitentiary Congress*, Longmans, London, in fact, in the London Congress questions like 'ought corporal punishment to be admitted in the disciplinary code of a penitentiary system?' and 'should whipping be employed as a disciplinary punishment?' were also discussed. In response to these questions, some prison governors contended that 'there was a class of men who thought nothing of disgrace, but cared only for the stripes that they received.' See also p. 137, Wines, *op. cit.* p. 137, Ruggles-Brise (1925) *op. cit.*, p. 9, Grünhut (1948) *op. cit.*, pp. 65–72.

[12]Saleilles, for example, argued that "It is the promiscuous association within the prison, the contamination of its communal life, and the exposure to the vices of humanity, that make the habitual criminal". p. 105, Saleilles, R. (1911) *The Individualisation of Punishment*, reprinted in 1968, Patterson Smith, Montclair.

[13]Carpenter, *op. cit.*, pp. 9, Wines, *op. cit.*, pp. 141–142, von Liszt (1882/3) *Der Zweckgedanke im Strafrecht*, reprinted in 2002, Nomos Verlagsgesellschaft, Baden, pp. 42–47, Ruggles-Brise (1925) *op. cit.*, pp. 13–14 and 57–58, *Mitteilungen der Internationalen Kriminalistischen Vereinigung* (1891), vol. 2, Guttentag, Berlin, pp. 96–103, see also the report of von Lilienthal, Wie ist der Begriff der unverbesserlichen Gewohnheitsverbrecher im Gesetze zu bestimmen und welche Maßregeln sind gegen diese Verbrecher zu empfehlen?' in *Mitteilungen der Internationalen Kriminalistischen Vereinigung* (1891), vol. 2, pp. 64–75.

[14]Ruggles-Brise (1925), *op. cit.*, p. 15.

[15]Carpenter, *op. cit.*, p. ix.

and the regular changes of its inmates, made it difficult to introduce classification.[16] In this respect, the English historian Wiener's observation in the context of Britain that in this period "recidivism came increasingly to be interpreted as an evidence for the prison's ability either to deter or moralise criminals" may be generalised as being applicable across Europe.[17] This view was most evident within international discussion platforms such as International Penitentiary Congresses.[18]

Consequently, the debates on prison discipline, classification of offenders and creating a humane atmosphere in prisons turned out to provide the arguments for the necessity of keeping particular categories of offenders, first and petty offenders, out of prison. For the latter group of offenders, it came to be recognised that institutional confinement, due to its counter-productive effects, ought not to be a sanction of first resort. In a wider context, the state of prisons, particularly in terms of the inflated prison populations, posed a serious challenge to the operation and maintenance of prisons. Conditional release was one of the ways for diminishing such perceived effects of prisons while reducing the prison population. Nevertheless, by definition it only had a limited impact. Going one step further, the reformers of this age began to seek for alternative sentences which could replace custodial sentences in certain cases. However, without an accompanying shift in the perceptions of crime and punishment, such a change would certainly have been unthinkable.

2.3 The Intellectual Background of Alternatives to Imprisonment

The classical school regarded imprisonment as the most adequate method of punishment. Imprisonment was not merely a humane alternative to various forms of capital and corporal punishments, but also and more importantly a method of incapacitating offenders, while exerting more powerful and lasting deterrent effect on them.[19] This view is clearly reflected by Beccaria when he, having compared the death penalty with imprisonment, concluded that "it is not the terrible but fleeting sight of a felon's death which is the most powerful brake on crime, but the long-drawn-out example of a man deprived of his freedom".[20] In this sense, it may be

[16]Society for the Improvement of Prison Discipline and for the Reformation of Juvenile Offenders (1832) *The Eighth Report of the Committee of the Society for the Improvement of Prison Discipline and for the Reformation of Juvenile Offenders*, J. and A. Arch, London, pp. 132–156.

[17]Wiener, M, J. (1994) *Reconstructing the Criminal: Culture, Law and Policy in England, 1830–1914*, Cambridge University Press, Cambridge, p. 343, see also Ancel (1971), *op. cit.*, p. 6.

[18]For example, the Congress of Paris (1895), see Ruggles-Brise (1925), *op. cit.*, pp. 56–88.

[19]Beccaria, C. (1764) On Crimes and Punishments reprinted in 1995 in Bellamy, R. (ed.) *Beccaria On Crimes and Punishments and Other Writings*, Cambridge University Press, Cambridge, see the Purpose of Punishment, p. 31.

[20]Beccaria, *op. cit.*, the Death Penalty, p. 67.

plausibly argued that the institution of prison found its theoretical base and justifications in the writings of this school. It is therefore no coincidence that the alternatives to prison emanated from a lively scholarly debate severely questioning the assumptions of the classical school.

In this context, the notion of free will constituted a major point of conflict in newly emerging ideas about criminality. As opposed to what classical jurisprudence postulated; that criminal behaviour was a product of exercising free will and based on a pleasure-pain calculation, it was increasingly appreciated that there may be factors beyond the control of individual actors which may, to a lesser or greater degree, determine his/her choices and behaviours.[21] Once the idea of crime as rational choice began to be questioned, attention was paid to understanding the causes of criminal behaviour. The shift from studying crime to studying the causes of crime was then manifested by the statement that crime was conceived not merely as a judicial concept – as an abstract entity – but at the same time as a social and anthropological phenomenon.[22] It goes without saying that the advances made in the natural and social sciences functioned as an important catalyst for such a shift. And furthermore, the progress in the disciplines of medicine, psychiatry, psychology and sociology did not merely lend their concepts and methodologies to the efforts of understanding the deviant behaviour, but they also evoked a hope for the treatment and cures of deviance and criminality. It was thought that only after the causes of criminal behaviour were diagnosed, could efficient remedies be employed against them.[23] Different theories were put forward to explain the causes of crime.

Among these, the most provoking was perhaps the contribution of the Italian positivist school, established by Cesare Lombroso. Inspired by the evolutionary studies, Lombroso argued that the criminal is a distinct type from birth, a biological 'throwback', a result of *atavism* (explained as the reappearance of characteristics that were seen only in the distant ascendants).[24] The criminal, he argued, "must be a survivor of the primitive man and the carnivorous animal".[25] Certain physical features such as asymmetries in the face, deviation in head size were seen by the scholar as an atavistic 'stigmata'. In his subsequent studies Lombroso modified his argument by paying increasingly more attention to environmental factors such as

---

[21]von Liszt, F. (1905) *Strafrechtliche Aufsätze und Vorträge*, vol. 1 and 2, de Gruyter, Berlin, vol. 1, Die deterministischen Gegner der Zweckstrafe, p. 65.

[22]E.g., *Mitteilungen der Internationalen Kriminalistischen Vereinigung (1899), op. cit.*, vol. 7.

[23]von Liszt, *op. cit.,* vol. 2, Die gesellschaftlichen Faktoren der Kriminalität, p. 444, Ferri, E. (1901) The Positive School of Criminology reprinted in Grupp, S., E. (ed.) (1971) *Theories of Punishment*, Indiana University Press, Bloomington, pp. 229–242, p. 233.

[24]Lombroso, C. (1895) Atavism and Evolution, *Contemporary Review*, vol. 68, p. 42–49 reprinted in Horton, D., M. and Rich, E., K. (2004) The Criminal Anthropological Writings of Cesare Lombroso Published in the English Language (Periodical Literature During the Late 19th and Early 20th Centuries), Mellen, Lewiston.

[25]Lombroso, C. (1895) Criminal Anthropology: Its Origins and Application, *Forum,* vol. 20, pp. 33–49, in *ibid* p. 66.

climate, poverty, immigration and urbanisation.[26] With this alteration he distinguished three other criminal types alongside that of inborn or atavistic criminals: insane criminals, occasional criminals and criminals of passion. Lombroso's theory was further advanced through greater recognition of sociological factors in the causation of the crime by his disciples Ferri and Garofalo. Since the positivist school regarded criminality as a naturally occurring phenomenon and accordingly criminals as a special class of human, according to them, the concept of free will was nothing more than a "subjective illusion".[27] By focussing on criminals rather than crime as an abstract concept, the school declared one of its primary aims as preventing criminality, which meant that a scientific examination of criminality was deemed essential.

The groundbreaking ideas and influence of the Italian positivist school were met with a vigorous response across the Continent. Intriguingly, the response to the positivist school reflected a substantial agreement on their standpoints[28] and subsequently institutionalised under the roof of 'Internationale Kriminalistiche Vereinigung' in 1888. The leading figures of *Internationale Kriminalistiche Vereinigung* were von Liszt, Prins and van Hamel. Here a brief reference should particularly be made to the thoughts of von Liszt, who was one of the most prominent legal theoreticians of the Foundation, and who was therefore described as the soul of this influential organisation.[29]

Von Liszt, while acknowledging the significance of the positivist school in terms of widening the horizon of criminal law and introducing scientific methods to this discipline, firmly rejected the Lombrosian concept of inborn criminality or atavistic criminality. Instead, he considered criminal behaviour as a product of both individual dispositions of the offender (e.g. mental and physical deficiencies), which might be inherited or subsequently developed, and the social milieu and upbringing of the individual.[30] For him, social and biological factors ought not to be seen as contradictory in terms of determining criminality, since these factors in fact mutually complement one another.[31] In his view, however, social factors have a more decisive

---

[26]Lombroso, C. (1902) *Die Ursachen und Bekämpfung des Verbrechens*, Hugo Bermühler Verlag, Berlin.

[27]Ferri, E. (1896) *Das Verbrechen als soziale Erscheinung: Grundzüge der Kriminal-Soziologie*, Wigand, Leipzig, p. 21.

[28]von Liszt, *op. cit.*, vol. 2, Über den Einfluss der soziologischen und anthropologischen Forschungen auf die Grundbegriffe des Strafrechts, p. 77.

[29]Kitzinger, F. (1905) *Die Internationale Kriminalistische Vereinigung: Betrachtungen über Ihr Wesen und Ihre Bisherige Wirksamkeit*, Beck, München, p. 4, see also Bellmann, E. (1994) *Die Internationale Kriminalistische Vereinigung* (1889–1933), Lang, Franfurt am Main, Kesper-Biermann, S. (2007) *Die Internationale Kriminalistische Vereinigung*. Zum Verhältnis von Wissenschaftsbeziehungen und Politik im Strafrecht 1889–1932, Kesper-Biermann and Overath (eds.), pp. 85–107.

[30]von Liszt, *op. cit.*, vol. 1, Kriminalpolitische Aufgaben p. 309, Das Verbrechen als sozialpathologische Erscheinung, *op. cit.*, vol. 2, p. 232 and Die gesellschaftlichen Faktoren der Kriminalität, pp. 438–441.

[31]von Liszt, *op. cit.*, Das Verbrechen als sozialpathologische Erscheinung, p. 234.

role in determining the criminal career.[32] Critically, von Liszt distinguished three types of criminals: occasional criminals, persistent but corrigible criminals and incorrigible habitual criminals.

As this brief outline suggests, the ways in which criminals were classified presupposed the distinction between habitual and occasional offenders.[33] Such a differentiation of criminals constituted the foundation for the recognition that the punishment should fit the criminal and not the crime. In this regard the Italian positivist school rejected the use of the concept of punishment. On their account, since the offences of criminals are determined by factors external to their will, they cannot be held responsible for their criminal behaviour and thus they must be treated rather than punished. In this sense, it was contended that punishments "have the same relation to crime that medicine has to disease".[34] In a related but a distinct and legalistic vein, von Liszt developed the conception of purpose-oriented punishment, *Zweckstrafe*. Punishment, he argued, should no longer satisfy the collective vengeance of the public; it should not in this sense be conceived as an end itself. Rather, punishment should be adapted to bring about a certain result in a given case. This, according to him, could only be done by taking the nature and individual circumstances of the offender into account.[35] For the occasional offender, von Liszt argued that punishment ought to have a deterrent impact and in this sense it should function as a warning.[36] With regard to persistent but corrigible criminals, punishment should serve the re-socialisation of the offender. In this case, von Liszt proposed the use of indeterminate sentences indicating the minimum and maximum limit of the imprisonment term (which according to him should range from 1 to 5 years) without pronouncing the duration of imprisonment definitely. The duration of the sentence would then be meted out separately by the sentencing court according to the offender's rehabilitation. Finally, when it is ascertained that the criminal is incorrigible, the punishment (a life sentence) should be a measure taken for the sake of incapacitation, or in other words, a measure for the protection of society from the criminal, while preventing him/her from committing future crimes.

Overall, it seems plausible to suggest that despite the theoretical diversity among the positivist and modern schools, the agreement on differentiation of criminals and

---

[32] *Ibid.*, Kriminalpolitische Aufgaben, p. 312.

[33] See *e.g.*, *Mitteilungen der Internationalen Kriministaltistischen Vereinigung* (1897), *op. cit.*, vol. 5, p. 1, Satzungen der Internationalen Kriminalistischen Vereinigung.

[34] Ferri, E. (1901), p. 231, see also Lombroso, *op. cit.* p. 345–347.

[35] von Liszt, *op. cit.*, vol. 2, Die deterministischen Gegner der Zweckstrafe, p. 57, Der Zweckgedanke im Strafrecht pp. 39–49; von Liszt's argument created a lively academic debate, e.g. see, von Birkmeyer, K. (1909) *Studien zu dem Hauptgrundsatz der Modernen Richtung im Strafrecht*, Leipzig, Engelmann, p. 17.

[36] von Liszt, Der Zweckgedanke im Strafrecht, pp. 42–49.

their punishment at a practical level by implication induced a firm fight against recidivism.[37] In the face of the reality of prisons, as argued above, this consensus also implied the need for cutting down the 'clientele' of prison whose offending behaviour is rather occasional. Those offenders who were deemed to be amenable to correction were to be 'saved'.[38] The 'salvation' of these criminals, it was believed, required the establishment of alternative measures in order to remove them from prison. Such views furthermore gained a major boost through the meetings of the International Penitentiary Congresses and the *Internationale Kriminalistische Vereinigung*. This climate of opinion was categorically in favour of the legislative introduction of non-custodial alternatives, as will be discussed below.

2.4 The Legislative Developments: The Birth of Alternative Punishments

The end of the nineteenth century marks a milestone in the codified and non-codified penal laws of western countries, as alternatives to imprisonment were enacted for the first time in this period. Prior to a closer investigation into this development, it must be remembered that the adoption of these alternatives did not occur without disapproval,[39] since the new forms of punishment such as conditional suspension of punishment *per se* constituted a marked departure from the established principles of penal law. At this point, however, a distinction must be made, since the experiences of countries with civil and those with common law systems displayed significant differences.

Central to discussions in the civil law systems was the changing role of the judge, or in other words the extension of his discretionary power.[40] In the civil law

---

[37]E.g. the title of Berenger's Bill was "Bill on the progressive augmentation of sentences in cases of recidivism and on their mitigation for first offences", Ancel, M. (1971) *Suspended Sentence*, Heinemann, London (1971) p. 11.

[38]Lombroso (1895), *op. cit.*, pp. 33–49, reprinted in Horton and Rich, *op. cit.* p. 79 Lombroso argued that "all efforts should be concentrated upon occasional criminals. They are the only ones for whom much can be done".

[39]Kirchenheim (1890) Bedingte Bestrafung, *Gerichtssaal*, vol. 43, pp. 51–70, Appelius, H. (1891) *Die Bedingte Verurteilung und die anderen Ersatzmittel für Kurzzeitige Freiheitsstrafen: eine Kritik der neusten Reformbestrebungen auf dem Gebiet des Strafrechts,* 4th edition, Keßler, Cassel, Wach, A. (1899) Die bedingte Verurteilung, *Deutsche Juristen-Zeitung*, vol. 4, no 6, pp. 117–120. See also, Grünhut (1948) *op. cit.*, pp. 104, Ancel (1971), *op. cit.*, p. 12, Ruggles-Brise, E. (1911) An English View of the American Penal System, *Journal of Criminal Law and Criminology*, vol. 2, no. 3, pp. 356–369. He noted that "at the present time complaints (in France, Belgium and Italy) are loud that 'sursis de l'exceution de la peine' means only immunity for the malefactor, and that the arm of law is being weakened by its operation". p. 364

[40]For example, the Paris Congress 1895, Ruggles-Brise, E. (1925) *Prison Reform at Home and Abroad: A Short History of the International Movement since the London Congress 1872,* Macmillan, London, pp. 59–64.

tradition, influenced by the classical school, which viewed an unguided discretion of the judge as 'always contrary to public safety',[41] the latter concept was then in general interpreted as causing inevitable arbitrariness, favouritism, and accordingly breach of equality before the law.[42] In accordance with this philosophy, the function of the judge was that of an "automatic dispenser",[43] limited to pronouncing the sentence laid down objectively by the law. As such the judge had no right to decide whether or not the sentence which s/he pronounced should be executed.[44] This was seen as an essential prerequisite of justice. Hence, extending the discretion of the judge at the sentencing stage would, according to some accounts, cause unwarranted privilege of grace and mercy, while lessening the deterrent effect of punishment.[45]

Of equal significance was another controversy related to the notion of proportionality. The classical theory of penal justice comprised of a strict equivalence between crime and punishment, and demanded for what Beccaria called a 'mathematical exactness'[46] in fixing corresponding scale of punishment. Thus, if two individuals incur different punishments for the same offence "it would seem as though equity had been disregarded, and that caprice had replaced justice".[47] However a growing body of opinion increasingly questioned the idea of 'equal punishments for equal crimes'. Many believed that not only the gravity of the offence, but also the personality and the unique circumstances of the offender must also be taken into account in determining the punishment.[48]

Clearly, such tensions between the established principles and the proposed methods determined the way in which early prison alternatives were introduced into legislation. Thus, on the Continent the reform initiatives, as Ancel observed, gained recognition only insofar as they were presented as "a limited exception to the traditional rules of penal law".[49] That limited exception was deemed to be justifiable by many continental scholars only in respect of those petty and first offenders who incurred a sentence of short-term imprisonment.[50] The underlying belief of the legislative enactments was that short-term imprisonment was ineffective and had a detrimental impact upon the individual. Most vocal in 'the crusade

[41]Beccaria, Of Detention Awaiting Trial, p. 73.

[42]Kirchenheim (1890), *op. cit.*, p. 53.

[43]Ancel (1971), *op. cit.*, p. 5.

[44]Kirchenheim (1890), *op. cit.*, for a discussion, see Saleilles *op. cit.*, pp. 57–61.

[45]Groß, A. (1907) *Für den Bedingten Straferlass: Rechtsvergleichend-Kritische Untersuchung*, A. Hödler, Wien, *op. cit.*, p. 56, Kirchenheim, *op. cit.*, p. 60.

[46]Beccaria, the Proportion between Crimes and Punishments, *op. cit.*, p. 19.

[47]Saleilles, *op. cit.*, p. 13.

[48]*Ibid.*, pp. 57–61 and 187–188, Garland, D. (1985) *Punishment and Welfare: A History of Penal Strategies*, Aldershot, Gower, pp. 86–87.

[49]Ancel (1971), *op. cit.*, p. 22.

[50]For example, see Mitteilungen der Internationalen Kriminalistischen Vereinigung (1889) vol.1, p. 2, von Liszt, *op. cit.*, Die Reform der Freiheitsstrafe, p. 513.

against short-term imprisonment'[51] is von Liszt with the statement that a short prison sentence is "worthless, indeed harmful. It does not deter, it does not improve, it contaminates".[52]

On the other hand, the existing non-custodial sanctions appear to have failed to achieve the desired impact in law in action.[53] The fine, as the major non-custodial sentence, was often, in the face of the inability of the offenders to pay, far from being an alternative to short-term imprisonment. Although there were enthusiastic arguments for imposing a fine after a thorough assessment of the defendant's income and resources,[54] in the absence of such measures in sentencing, default detention was often unavoidable, as will be touched upon later in Chaps. 3 and 4. In this respect, it may be argued that the attempts to reduce the use of default detention also gave the stimulus to alternative modes of punishment.

Other existing non-custodial penalties such as forced work, judicial reprimand and home detention were rarely applied in practice.[55] A special mention here ought to be made to work as a sanction. The origin of using work as a sanction, as academic studies suggest, goes back far beyond this period, in particular with regard to Germany. However, as an alternative to prison, it was not until this period that the question was raised as to the feasibility and desirability of forced labour or labour sentences as a replacement for short-term imprisonment.[56] In many respects, forced labour was deemed unsuitable to substitute short-term imprisonment, and was even found 'chimerical'[57] in its application. First of all, it was theoretically dismissed by the suggestion that this sanction relates essentially to the assets of an individual, which does not contain any limitation of personal freedom. Secondly, the applicability of this sanction in practice was deemed to be limited to only a small number of offender categories. Thirdly, it was believed that the enforcement of it in terms of inspection, control and so on would entail drastic costs. Fourthly, the stigmatising effect of work as a penal sanction was seen potentially as an undesirable consequence of the execution of this type of punishment. Lastly, the danger that the 'moral infection' that the gathering of convicts would cause was regarded as a possible counter-productive effect of forced labour, which was deemed practically no less harmful than in the case of short-term imprisonment.

---

[51]von Liszt, *op. cit.,* vol. 1, Kriminalpolitische Aufgaben, p. 347.

[52]*Ibid.*, p. 382.

[53]*Ibid.*

[54]von Liszt ,Welche Maßregeln können dem Gesetzgeber zur Einschränkung der kurzzeitigen Freiheitsstrafe empfohlen werden?, in Mitteilungen der Internationalen Kriminalistischen Vereinigung (1889), p. 45, Mitteilungen der Internationalen Kriminalistischen Vereinigung (1892), vol. 3, pp. 143–157.

[55]See, e.g., von Liszt, *op. cit.,* vol. 1, Kriminalpolitische Aufgaben, pp. 347–382.

[56]von Liszt in *Mitteilungen der Internationalen Kriminalistischen Vereinigung*, vol. 1, p. 46, Kitzinger, *op. cit.*, p. 144, Zürcher, Ist Zwangsarbeit ohne Einsperrung geeignet, für gewisse Fälle an die Stelle der kurzzeitigen Freiheitsstrafe zu treten?' in *Mitteilungen der Internationalen Kriminalistischen Vereinigung*, (1891), vol. 2, pp. 76–82, pp. 76–77.

[57]Baron Mackay (Holland) in the London Congress in Ruggles-Brise, E. (1925), *op. cit.,* p. 28.

Turning back to the above-mentioned legislative development, the overwhelming use of short-term imprisonment proved beyond any doubt that forced labour, reprimand and other alternative sentences were of little significance in practice.[58] It was not until the introduction of the conditional sentence (*condamnation conditionelle*) or the conditional suspension of the execution of the sentence that a practically sustainable alternative was created to substitute for short-term imprisonment.[59] In effect this made the establishment of this institution one of the most significant developments in the realm of penology.

France was the first country where the suspended sentence was brought before parliament by an official draft in 1884.[60] The draft emphasised the importance of avoiding the effects of short-term imprisonment on an offender "who has not been previously prosecuted and whose moral character, despite his offence, has remained sufficiently intact for society to have nothing to fear from his liberty".[61] However, it was not until 1891 that the draft was enacted. According to this law, the conditional suspension of the execution of both fines and imprisonment was possible and could be granted to those offenders who were not previously sentenced to imprisonment or a more severe penalty. The duration of the period of suspension was 5 years. The suspension was to be revoked, if the offender, during the term of suspension, was to be sentenced to imprisonment, otherwise no conviction was deemed to have taken place.

In the meantime, as early as 1888, Belgium had adopted a law,[62] the origin of which could be traced back to the French draft.[63] The Belgian law determined the ambit of application of the conditional sentence more restrictively than the French law of 1891. As opposed to the French draft in its original form, the suspension could be made only with regard to prison sentences not exceeding 6 months and only granted to offenders who had not incurred a sentence for felonies (*crimes*) or misdemeanours (*delits*). Further, the Belgian law empowered the judge to determine the duration of the period of suspension within a maximum limit of 5 years.

As this brief description of the French and Belgian laws shows, the Belgian law did not differ from the French law much. Due to the similarities between the law of the aforementioned countries in terms of purpose and principles, the respective legislation of these countries was later seen as constituting a pattern in the creation

[58]See e.g., Zürcher, *op. cit.*, pp. 76–82.

[59]Conditional sentence is defined as "a penalty which consists of the threat of execution. Conditional sentence is a true sentence comprising a penalty whose execution is suspended and an admonition which is a moral punishment". Ancel (1971), *op. cit.*, p. 16.

[60]Gruber, L. (1903) Die bedingte Verurteilung in Frankreich, *Gerichtssaal*, vol. 62, pp. 292–306.

[61]Cited in Ancel (1971), *op. cit.* p. 18.

[62]See Belgisches Gesetz vom 31 Mai 1888 über bedingte Entlassung und bedingte Strafurteile, *Gerichtsaal*, vol. 41, pp. 246–250.

[63]Ancel (1971), *op. cit.*, p. 15.

of the suspended sentence.[64] In the years immediately following the introduction of the French and Belgian laws, as an alternative to imprisonment the suspended sentence began to be presented in international meetings, most notably at the third International Penitentiary Congress in 1885 in Rome and the fourth Congress in St. Petersburg in 1890.[65] The dissemination and exchange of the ideas soon inspired the adoption of the suspended sentence or the conditional execution of punishment with local modifications in Europe with the following chronology: Luxemburg (1892), Portugal (1893), Norway (1894), Italy (1904), Bulgaria (1904), Denmark (1905), Sweden (1906), Spain (1908), Hungary (1908), Greece (1911), the Netherlands (1915) and Finland (1918).[66]

Germany, despite its influential proposition of the conditional suspension of imprisonment was initially an exception to this tendency.[67] In German states, by this time a distinctive method, the so-called conditional pardon, as will be further elucidated in Chap. 4, functioned as a prison surrogate. Saxony was the first German state where a law concerning conditional pardon 'bedingte Begnadigung' was enacted. Subsequently, this law constituted an example for the other states. The principle purpose of this measure was based on the need of diverting juvenile and petty offenders from the prison. Hence in the final analysis it theoretically differed little from related measures in other countries, considering the fact that it also envisaged a suspension of a prison sentence or under certain circumstances also the suspension of the prosecution. Practically, however, the German conditional pardon was an administrative measure. Its application was at the discretion of the public prosecutor and only after (her)/his inquiry into the circumstances of the offender as to the suitability of an application of the conditional pardon could s/he refer the case to the Ministry of Justice. The ultimate decision was entrusted to the Minister of Justice. In practice, the new measure was mainly applicable to young offenders whose prison sentences were not longer than 6 months.[68]

Concomitant with the legislative developments occurring on the Continent, in the common law countries too, statutory enactments were made to provide a legislative basis for the previous ad hoc practice of releasing of offenders on the condition of good behaviour. In fact, as distinct from civil law countries, with regard to a small number of offenders prison had long not been the sole device,

[64]United Nations (1951) *op. cit.*, p. 66.

[65]Frede, L. (1932) *Die Beschlüsse der Internationalen Gefängnis-Kongresse 1872–1930*, Frommann, Jena, Teeters, N., K. (1949) *Deliberations of the International Penal and Penitentiary Congresses: Questions and Answers, 1872–1935*, Temple University Book Store, Philadelphia, Schmidt, E. (1935) 'Zum internationalen Kongreß für Strafrecht und Gefängniswesen: Die internationalen Gefängniskongresse: Ein Rückblick auf ihre Arbeit, *Zeitschrift für die gesamte Strafrechtswissenschaft*, vol. 55, pp. 177–200, Henze, M. (2007) Die internationalen Gefägnis-kongresse 1872–1935 in Keser-Biermann and Overath, *op. cit.*

[66]Trought, T. W. (1927) *Probation in Europe*, Basil Blackwell, Oxford.

[67]von Liszt, *op. cit.*, vol. 1, Kriminalpolitische Aufgaben, p. 412 and Die Reform der Freiheits-strafe, p. 524.

[68]Groß, *op. cit.*, p. 57.

since over time common law accommodated a number of measures enabling the courts to suspend sentences conditionally. There is no space here for a detailed analysis of these institutions, but very briefly the primary institutions that are frequently cited as the forerunners of probation are the 'judicial reprieve', 'the recognizance or binding over on good behaviour' and 'the benefit of clergy'. Of these measures, the benefit of clergy enabled clergy to claim exemption from or mitigation of punishment in the secular (as opposed to ecclesiastical) courts, while the judicial reprieve suspended the imposition of the sentence in order to allow the defendant to apply to the Crown for a pardon. Finally and perhaps more importantly, recognizance for keeping the peace and good behaviour at the very outset functioned as a release from custody without bail while awaiting the trial. Here the offender promised to pay a bond or bail, with or without guarantee, and was returned to the court if s/he violated any of the specified conditions. At the beginning of the nineteenth century, the measure of recognizance on the subject of good behaviour was applied increasingly. In some localities of the common law jurisdictions, such as Birmingham and Boston, in addition to suspension of sentence, some form of supervision and guidance was also provided for. Such a practice of a combination of the conditional suspension of sentence and the supervision certainly pointed to the birth of a distinct method of dealing with offenders, which was subsequently referred to as 'probation', the "more adventurous and adaptable sister"[69] of the continental suspended sentence.

As a "simultaneous social invention occurring in England and the United States",[70] the institution of probation revealed a number of commonalities. In both countries, a selection of appropriate cases was initially made, whereby particular categories of offenders were deemed more suitable for such supervision and/or treatment e.g. juveniles, inebriated offenders. The intellectual background of the probation order and its distinct origin in comparison to the continental 'conditional sentence' will be analysed in Chap. 3 in detail, a brief overview on the emergence of probation at this point is still however deemed necessary. Certain courts in these two common law jurisdictions assumed the power of suspending sentences in combination with the placement of the defendant under the supervision of a guardian. In the course of the supervision, conducted on an informal basis, periodical inquiries were to be made into the conduct of the offenders, and if the offender failed to comply with the obligations prescribed, the decision suspending the sentence might be revoked. Alongside these legal similarities, it can be maintained that a clear religious zeal, what has been metaphorically expressed as 'saving the souls',[71] was an underlying motivation in both countries.

---

[69]Radzinowicz in Ancel (1971), *op. cit.*, p. vii.

[70]Timasheff, *op. cit.*, p. 1.

[71]Whitehead, P. (1990) *Community Supervision for Offenders*, Gower Publishing, Aldershot, see Chapter 1: From Saving Souls to the Decline of Rehabilitation, pp. 1–18.

In the United States[72] the probation practice of the courts gained a legal basis as early as in 1878, when the state of Massachusetts passed a law empowering the mayor of Boston to appoint a paid probation officer with jurisdiction in Boston's criminal courts. Despite the fact that this law regulated only the selection of probation officers, it had marked policy implications, leading to a widespread adoption of probation laws in the United States. In England, the legislative development took place relatively slower. The first step was taken with the passing of the Summary Jurisdiction Act. The Act stipulated that the court could conditionally discharge an offender as long as the offender was of good behaviour and 'agreed' to appear for sentencing if required. The 1887 Probation of First Offenders Act later gave a greater statutory recognition of the institution of probation by extending the application of the measure to a certain number of offences other than summary offences. Accordingly, this Act, after considering the special circumstances of the offender and offence, allowed the court to release the offender on probation of good conduct, provided that s/he was previously not convicted of an offence punishable with 2 years imprisonment. However, it was not until the enactment of the 1907 Probation of Offenders Act that probation became an established practice of the English courts. With this Act the previously informal practice of the guardianship of a member of community was refined and defined as personal supervision and individual guidance, whereby the role of the probation officer was delineated as 'advising, assisting and befriending the offender while monitoring, instructing and reporting'. Thus, as opposed to civil law countries, the probation order was not formed solely as a device of the suspension of the execution of sentence, but more importantly as a special method of punishment offering a rehabilitative treatment to the offenders.

With its very innovative nature, the probation order in due course gave rise to similar institutions of mixed nature on the Continent such as the French institution of *liberté surveillée* in the continental European countries.[73] In this respect Max Grünhut may be agreed with in retrospect, when he regarded the rise of probation as "the most remarkable feature of the recent history of criminal law".[74] However, it would be misleading to see the subsequent developments tracing the Anglo–American institution of probation in the continental European countries as a 'smooth' process of 'reception'.

Many continental legal scholars from the inception of the probation order were of the opinion that the latter conflicts with the ideas on which the continental law

---

[72]On the early legislative developments in the United States, see Parsons, H., C. (1918) Probation and Suspended Sentence, *Journal of American Institute of Criminal Law and Criminology*, vol. 8, no. 5, pp. 694–708.

[73]United Nations (1951), *op. cit.*, pp. 66–67; Dünkel, F. (1983) Strafaussetzung zur Bewährung und Bewährungshilfe in Internationalen Vergleich: Ein Überblick in Dünkel, F. and Spiess, G., *Alternativen zur Freiheitsstrafe*, Max-Planck-Institut für internationales und ausländisches Strafrecht, Freiburg, p. 400, Harris, *op. cit*, pp. 63–66.

[74]Grünhut (1948) *op. cit.*, p. 297.

systems are based, as will be further elaborated in the discussion in the chapter concerned with Germany.[75] As touched upon above, with the introduction of the suspension of sentences the judge was empowered to grant a suspension, when particular criteria specified by law were met. For many, this constituted the maximum limit of the discretionary power that a judge might have. It would then therefore be inconceivable to enable the judge or any other person to give instructions or orders to the defendant whose sentence was suspended as in common law jurisdictions. Nor would it be acceptable for any kind of non-compliance to such instructions or obligations to automatically lead to a revocation of the suspended sentence.[76] On the Continent, suspended sentences or conditional sentences formed, in their inception, a particular form of 'leniency', as the related document of the United Nations indicated.[77] At the heart of the recognition of this method of dealing with certain offenders was the view that these offenders are capable of rehabilitating themselves.[78] In this sense, a conditional sentence was to function as a warning against future offending behaviour rather than a measure of rehabilitation on its own.

This perception, however, underwent a dramatic change in course of the spreading of juvenile courts and welfare laws, for at that time it came to be recognised that the offending behaviour of juveniles indicated a need for educational measures.[79] In accordance with this view, with regard to juvenile justice, the individualised dispositions comprising a supervision element began to find a place in the legislation of numerous European countries.[80] The field of juvenile justice in this sense functioned as an experiment for adult supervision.

---

[75]For a summary of the discussions and the proposals at the time, see, Ancel, M. (1954) Probation in Relation to European Penal Systems and Modes of Criminal Procedure, pp. 33–48 and Nuvolone, P. (1954) Probation and Related Measures in European Legal Systems: A Comparative Survey, pp. 15–32, in United Nations, *European Seminar on Probation, 20–30 October 1952*, United Nations Publications, London.

[76]Ancel (1954), *op. cit.*, p. 36.

[77]United Nations/Department of Social Affairs, (1954) *Practical Results and Financial Aspects of Adult Probation in Selected Countries*, United Nations Publications, New York, p. 79.

[78]The Belgian Minister Le Jeune in the course of the discussions taking place during the adoption of the conditional suspension of the execution of a sentence indicated that "those for the benefit of whom the conditional sentence has been created, have *no need of the assistance of protective supervision*. They will reform by themselves". (Emphasis added.) Cited in United Nations (1951), *op. cit.*, p. 64.

[79]Grünhut (1948) *op. cit.*, p. 301, United Nations (1951), *op. cit.*, p. 70, Harris, *op. cit.*, p. 55.

[80]Trought, *op. cit.*, pp. 185–186. See on the changing perceptions in this context in France, e.g. Germain, C. (1954) Post-war Prison Reform in France, *Annals of the American Academy of Political and Social Science*, vol. 293, pp. 139–151, pp. 150–151. Germanin noted that "during very recent years it has become clear that it would be useful to have a special type of suspension, to which there would be attached both a control over conduct and aid by guidance for certain individuals who, not being subject to a mandatory punishment, need both control and help during a probationary period if they are to be saved from recidivism".

In a further step, a number of European countries recognised probationary supervision in relation to adult justice. It was increasingly acknowledged that this measure would be instrumental to the rehabilitation of offenders.[81] On the other hand, in the hope of reducing the reliance on custodial sentences in England, the suspended sentence was statutorily introduced as an independent measure. Faced with similar problems in dealing with offenders, the convergence between common and civil law jurisdictions (and the Nordic jurisdictions), in terms of creating alternative modes of punishment to imprisonment, was further intensified, as will be discussed below.

2.5 The Proliferation of Prison Alternatives: 2nd Period

A comparative penological survey of the post-war western countries reveals that since the emergence of the concept of non-custodial penalties, there appears to have been a slow expansion in the number and variety of non-custodial penalties until the 1970s. During the course of the 1970s, a wide variety of alternative penalties and measures began to be introduced. These new sanctions and measures include the conditional dismissal of cases at the prosecution stage; sanctions of restricting and withdrawing rights, compensation and notably public work at the sentencing stage, and intermittent custody and house arrest at the execution stage.[82] Thus, here too, one could talk of an emergence of new patterns, a new trend that is perceptible in the introduction of new measures among western countries. Clearly, each country reacted in this context in proportion to its needs and available resources. It would be an interesting task to highlight these differences with reference to the economic, social, cultural and legal characteristics of European countries, and perhaps this remains a challenging assignment for the researchers. The scope of this study at this point is less ambitiously defined; this section is concerned with the causes of a common pattern that occurred for a second time in western countries.

At the risk of oversimplification, the causes of this trend can be seen as the growth of prison population and related fiscal problems, the loss of the belief in the rehabilitation paradigm and the discovery or perhaps rediscovery of the victim as an actor in criminal justice. In fact, all these factors are dialectically interrelated, and as such a demarcation of these themes will, to a certain extent, be artificial. Nevertheless, for the purpose of clarity, a separate examination of these causes under these three headings seems necessary.

---

[81] United Nations (1951), *op. cit.*, p. 204.

[82] See, Rentzmann, W. and Robert, J., P (1986) *Alternative Measures to Imprisonment*, Council of Europe, Strasbourg.

2.5.1 Expanding and Inflating Prison

From the 1970s onwards, the rapid growth of the size of the prison population was one of the important preoccupations of penal policy, even in those countries where the increase in the reception into custody remained relatively stable.[83] This trend was on the grounds of both humanitarian and economic considerations and posed a serious challenge for western penal systems.

The prison population growth was and has often been linked with the increase in crime rates.[84] Indeed, the 1970s were characterised in Western Europe by a rapid increase in the recorded level of crime. At this point, however, one has to be cautious about the extent to which those crime rates brought corresponding increases in imprisonment rates with them, since subsequent cross-national research has demonstrated that imprisonment rates do not directly flow from the volume of officially discovered crime.[85] Even studies comparing crime rates in specified categories of serious offences which are likely to incur custodial sentences have not been able to show that any consistent relationship between those rates and prison populations exists. For example, between 1950 and 1975 recorded crime in the Netherlands increased by 300%, whereas the prison population fell by 50%.

Even if the increased level of crime was only partially responsible for the increase in imprisonment rates, it clearly influenced the public attitudes towards crime and as such led to, as Junger-Tas rightly puts it, 'a public outcry for stiffer sentencing'.[86] The policy response was then in proportion to the public demand for harsher penalties for the increasing level of the threat of crime, in particular with regard to certain offence types; drug-related offences, sexual offences and

---

[83] See, Changes in prisoner numbers in Council of Europe member states since 1970 excluding Austria, Iceland, the Netherlands and Turkey, Council of Europe (1987) *Prison Information Bulletin, no 9, p. 18,* Changes in prisoner numbers since 1970 in Turkey *Source: Council of Europe Prison Information Bulletin (1987) No 9,* p. 19.

[84] For the results of the First and Second United Nations Crime and Operations of Criminal Justice Statistics, see HEUNI (1985) *Criminal Justice Systems in Europe and North America*, Helsinki, p. 2., van Dijk, J. (1993) More than a Matter of Security: Trends in Crime Prevention in Europe in Heidensohn, F. and Farrel, M. (eds.) *Crime in Europe*, Routledge, London, pp. 26–54.

[85] Young, W. (1986) Influences upon the Use of Imprisonment: A Review of Literature, *Howard Journal*, vol. 25, issue 2, pp. 125–135, Young, W. and Brown, M. (1993) Cross National Comparisons of Imprisonment in Tonry, M. (ed.) *Crime and Justice,* vol. 17, pp. 1–49, Muncie, J. and Sparks, R. (1992) *op. cit.*, pp. 89–106, see for a slightly revised approach, Aebi, M., F. and Kuhn, A. (2000) Influences on the Prisoner Rate: Number of Entries into Prison, Length of Sentences and Crime Rate, *European Journal on Criminal Policy and Research*, vol. 8, issue 1, pp. 65–75.

[86] Junger-Tas, J. (1994), *op. cit.*, p. 44, see also, van Dijk, J. (1979) The Extent of Public Information and the Nature of Public Attitudes Towards Crime in Public Opinion and Crime and Criminal Justice (Reports presented to the Thirteenth Criminological Research Conference, 1978), Council of Europe, Strasbourg, pp. 7–39, Snacken, S. and Beyens. K. (1994) Sentencing and Prison Overcrowding, *European Journal on Criminal Policy and Research*, vol. 2, no 1, pp. 84–99, p. 92.

terrorism. During the seventies many European countries increased the maximum penalties applicable to the respective crime types in their legislation. The 'law and order' legislation at the time was also backed by the judiciary, who pronounce more frequent and longer terms of imprisonment. Consequently, the increase in the length of sentences drastically enlarged the size of the prison population.[87]

The almost exploding prison population led to two immediate results. One consequence was the massive increase in prison expenditure in virtually all western countries. During the 1970s the economic costs of imprisonment, as Robert and Rentzmann phrases, 'skyrocketed' at such a speed that the financial considerations became a key factor in the promotion of non-custodial alternatives in Europe.[88] Coupled with an economic climate that was generally worsening, there was broad recognition of the need to establish new alternatives to prison.

The consensus was particularly clearly expressed by Resolution 76 (10) adopted by the Committee of Ministers of the Council of Europe on 'Some Alternative Penal Measures to Imprisonment'.[89] Based on the available research at the period, it was concluded that imprisonment has a higher unit cost than almost any alternative measure of punishment. This was, it is indicated, due to the fact that the cost of prison entailed various spending on the construction, personal and security costs, physical health services, rehabilitative services, supervision of inmates and finally the increased social spending needed to support the families of the incarcerated people.[90] It was further pointed out that prisons also indirectly had an impact on the other areas of public spending due to its greater budgetary allocation. Indeed, the increased expenditure on the construction, maintenance and operation of prisons meant, in the practice, the curtailment of resources in the other areas of public expenditure. For example, Rutherford suggests that the spending on the English prison system over the 5-year period up to 1978–1979 rose by 36%, compared with 15% hospital services and 9% on education.[91]

Hence, non-custodial sanctions were deemed far more cost-effective than custody, even though it was appreciated that a full cost comparison between prison and its alternatives is a complex matter. At this point in time there already was the recognition that a real saving can only occur if the construction of new prisons and corresponding staff recruitment can be halted or if existing institutions can be closed and staff numbers reduced.[92] Over time, the merits of non-custodial penalties in terms of their economical advantages proved to be difficult to substantiate, since the

---

[87]This was also confirmed by the Fifth United Nations Survey, see Kangaspunta, K., Joutsen, M. and Ollus, N. (1998) Crime and Criminal Justice in Europe and North America 1990–1994, HEUNI, Helsinki, see also, Tournier, P. (1994) The Custodial Crisis in Europe: Inflated Prison Populations and Possible Alternatives, *European Journal on Criminal Policy and Research*, vol. 2, no 4, pp. 89–100.

[88]Robert and Rentzmann, *op. cit.*, p. 2.

[89]Council of Europe (1976) *op. cit.*

[90]*Ibid*, pp. 44–51.

[91]Rutherford, A. (1984) *Prisons and Process of Justice*, Heinemann, London, p. 90.

[92]Council of Europe (1976), *op. cit.*, p. 45.

existing institutions were only exceptionally closed. In many countries, subsequently substantial prison buildings and capacity enlargement programmes were launched.[93] Nevertheless, the view that the administration of alternatives is considerably 'cheaper' than the administration of imprisonment with the reference to the long term prospects has remained a major justification for non-custodial sanctions.[94]

Returning to the direct results of prison overcrowding, the second direct consequence of the dramatic increase in the size of the prison population was overly crowded prisons in a number of countries, most notably in the United States and England.[95] The detrimental effects of overcrowding have been manifested in a number of ways in the respective countries.[96] Research has shown, for example, that prison overcrowding causes a drastic deterioration in living conditions of prisons in terms of space and facilities. This has further detrimental impacts on the physical and mental well-being of the inmates and staff, while the lack of space potentially restricts the educational activities taking place in penal establishments. In addition, it has been well-established that overcrowded prisons are a potential source of inter-personal violence and the risk of disturbances, as was the case in English prison disturbances in the early 1980s.[97] Offering greater capacity in prisons, non-custodial alternatives were and have been seen as a remedy to prevent prison overcrowding.

2.5.2 *The Shift from 'Doing Good' to 'Doing Less': Prison Under 'Attack'*

As argued in the earlier pages of this chapter, the birth of the notion that offenders could be 'cured' of criminal tendencies, which later became known as the treatment

---

[93]van Swaaningen, R. and de Jonge, G. (1995) The Dutch Prison System and Penal Business Management in Ruggiero, V., Ryan, M. and Sim, J. (eds.) *Western European Penal Systems: A Critical Anatomy*, Sage, London, pp. 26–27.

[94]See *e.g.*, Rentzmann and Robert, *op, cit.;* Schädler, W. (1988) The Interest of the State in the Effectiveness of Alternatives to Imprisonment, in HEUNI, Alternatives to Custodial Sanctions (Proceedings of the European Seminar held in Helsinki, Finland, 26–28 September, 1987), Helsinki; Bishop, N. (1988) *Non-Custodial Alternatives in Europe*, HEUNI, Helsinki.

[95]van Zyl Smit, D. and Dünkel, F. (1991) *Imprisonment Today and Tomorrow: International Perspectives on Prisoners' Rights and Prison Conditions*, Kluwer, Deventer; Peters, Sesar, K. (1994) Overcrowding- Not only Crisis in the Custodial System, *European Journal on Criminal Policy and Research*, vol. 2, no 4, pp. 107–116, pp. 107–111; Kensey, A. and Tournier, P. (1999) Prison Population Inflation, Overcrowding and Recidivism: the Situation in France, *European Journal on Criminal Policy and Research*, vol. 7, issue 1, pp. 97–119.

[96]Gaes, G. (1985) The Effects of Overcrowding in Prison, *Crime and Justice*, vol. 6, pp. 94–146, Kuhn, A. (1994) 'What can we do about prison overcrowding?', *European Journal on Criminal Policy and Research*, vol. 2, issue 7, pp. 107–116.

[97]Cavadino, M. and Dignan, J. (1997) The Penal System: An Introduction, 2nd edition, Sage, London, p. 120.

model, dates back to the early attempts to uncover the aetiology of crime. From this point onwards, in Anglo–American countries the rehabilitation paradigm, as a philosophical source of treatment model, exerted a considerable influence on penal policy-making, in terms of the execution of both custodial and non-custodial sentences (such as probation orders).[98] Conversely, with the notable exceptions of the Nordic countries (in particular Sweden and Denmark)[99] and the Netherlands,[100] with indeterminate sentences not being available to the courts on a comparable scale, in many European countries the treatment model never dominated the policy-making as such.[101] In these countries, the rehabilitation, or more accurately re-socialisation philosophy,[102] was also incorporated into law, but despite its legislative pronouncement from the very outset it was subordinated to the aims of retribution and general deterrence. Paradoxically, however, the 'obsolescence' of the rehabilitative thinking produced internationally recognisable trends in varied degrees in the countries in which it had hitherto ascendancy in penal thought. Below, a very condensed summary of the grounds for the loss of confidence in rehabilitative thinking will be provided.

From the end of the 1960s towards the end of the 1970s, the treatment model began to be subjected to a burgeoning criticism.[103] One important thrust of this criticism was concerned with the rights of the offenders involved in those 'rehabilitative' processes. In this context indeterminate sentencing as the most substantiated form of rehabilitative thinking most notably in the United States came

---

[98]Whitehead, *op. cit.*; May, T. (1991) *Probation: Politics, Policy and Practice*, Open University Press, Milton Keynes, Crow, I. (2001) *The Treatment and Rehabilitation of Offenders*, Sage, London.

[99]Finland may partly be seen as an exception in this context, see *e.g.*, Lappi-Seppälä, T. (2001) Sentencing and Punishment in Finland: The Decline of the Repressive Ideal, in Tonry, M. and Frase, R., S. (eds.) *Sentencing and Sanctions in Western Countries*, Oxford University Press, Oxford, pp. 92–150, pp. 92–93.

[100]van Swaaningen, R. and Beijerse, J. (1983) From Punishment to Diversion and Back again: the Debate on Non-Custodial Sanctions and Penal Reform in the Netherlands, *Howard Journal*, vol. 32, issue 2, pp. 136–156; Downes, D. (1998) The Buckling of the Shields: Dutch Penal Policy 1985–1995, in Weiss, R., P. and South, N. (eds.) *Comparing Prison Systems: Toward a Comparative and International Penology*, Gordon & Breach, Amsterdam, pp. 143–174, pp. 144–149.

[101]Kaiser, G. (1977) Resozialisierung und Zeitgeist in Rüdiger, H. and "Kienapfel, D. (eds.) *Kultur, Kriminalität, Strafrecht, Festschrift für Thomas Würtenberger zum 70. Geburtstag am 7.10.1977*, Duncker & Humblot, Berlin, pp. 359–372, at p. 366; Weigend, T. (1982) "Neoklassizismus" – ein transatlantisches Missverständnis, *Zeitschrift für die gesamte Strafrechtswissenschaft*, vol. 94, pp. 801–814, p. 812.

[102]For a comparative examination of the difference between the notion of rehabilitation in Anglo-Saxon countries and 're-socialisation' in the academic writing in Germany see Lazarus, L. (2004) *Contrasting Prisoner's Rights: A Comparative Examination of England and Germany*, Oxford University Press, Oxford.

[103]Bishop, N. (1974) Aspects of European Penal Systems in Blom-Cooper, L. (ed.) *Progress in Penal Reform*, Clarendon Press, Oxford, pp. 83–100, pp. 97–98, Ryan, M. and Sim, J. (1998) Power, Punishment and Prisons in England and Wales 1975–1996 in Weiss and South, *op. cit.*, pp. 175–206, Mathiesen, T. (2000) *Prison on Trial*, 2nd edition, Waterside Press, Winchester.

increasingly under attack. It was believed that indeterminate sentencing leaves an unwarranted discretion on the hands of executive bodies, and this often led to a lengthy custody in the name of treatment, since it was the psychological assessment of the offender as to the amenability to treatment that determined the duration of custody in prison. Instead, it was maintained that it should no longer be the rehabilitative needs of the offender that determine the severity of punishment, but the gravity of the offence. On the other hand, the allegedly unjustified interventions of social work professionals for the rehabilitation of juvenile offenders constituted another important strand of the criticism. It was posited that the interventions of social work professionals often take a form in which the rights of juveniles are infringed, while the 'net' is widened and the use of institutional responses to juvenile crime is promoted. It must also be mentioned that on the other side of the political spectrum, the treatment approach was also seen as too soft in dealing with offenders.

However, it was not until the publication of Martinson's classic essay of the empirical analysis of the effectiveness of various forms of treatment programmes in terms of recidivism[104] that the rehabilitative approach was questioned widely by the academic community as well as criminal justice practitioners. In this study, by reviewing 231 studies between 1945 and 1967 Martinson concluded that none of these treatment methods in fact made any 'appreciable effect' on recidivism'.[105] He furthermore suggested that not only treatment programs that were taking place in custodial establishments, but also those of non-institutional programs such as probation, parole and intensive supervision gave no indication as to their effectiveness in preventing recidivism. However, Martinson acknowledged that treatment programmes in non-custodial settings had the advantage of being cost effective and thus he concluded that "the implication is clear: *if we can't do more for (and to) offenders, at least we can safely do less*" (emphasis in original).[106]

The main argument of Martinson's study, 'nothing works', despite critical evaluations[107] was taken as a widely accepted indictment of the failure of the prison system to rehabilitate its subjects in those countries where the sentencing system was characterised by the ideal of rehabilitation. Interestingly, to a significant extent, this period marks in many European countries the legislative entrenchment of the principle of re-socialisation in major western European countries such as

[104]Martinson, R. (1974) What works? - Questions and Answers about Prison Reform, *Public Interest*, vol. 35, pp. 22–54.

[105]*Ibid.* p. 25.

[106]*Ibid.*, p. 48.

[107]Some argued that rehabilitative measures in fact have never been given a chance to prove their effectiveness. For example, Cullen and Gilbert argued "the pre-eminence of rehabilitation was more myth than reality". Cullen, F., T. and Gilbert, K. E., (1982) *Reaffirming Rehabilitation*, Anderson, Cincinnati, p. 7.

France (1972, 1975), Germany (1976), and Italy (1975).[108] In two respects, however, these developments were not able in practice to facilitate rehabilitative optimism in the countries in question. Firstly, in these countries the notion of rehabilitation, despite its official encouragement, was not wholly affirmed by practice and as such remained an official discourse[109] or even a myth[110] rather than an operational principle of the penal justice system. Secondly, and equally importantly, the academic writing in these countries was and has been heavily influenced by the negative findings of the effectiveness literature elsewhere. This state of affairs, as it was in other countries, however, did not bring about a dramatic renunciation of the offender rehabilitation. The belief that offenders can be 're-socialised' still retained its power,[111] but it was/has been increasingly appreciated that prison in its present form is not able to facilitate a suitable atmosphere for achieving this.

Thus, losing one of its primary justifications, as Pavarani suggests, prison was bound to be "an instrument of incapacitation for those who cannot be otherwise controlled".[112] This approach meant in practice what is often termed in the literature a strategy of bifurcation or 'la politique de dualisation',[113] the central aspect of which is to incarcerate serious offenders, while dealing with less serious offenders through non-custodial penalties. Rooted in a critique of rehabilitative measures and the rise of labelling theories,[114] as will be dealt with in the following section,

---

[108]Faugeron, C. (1991) Prisons in France: Stalemate or Evolution? in van Zyl Smit and Dünkel, *op. cit.*, pp. 249–273, p. 250, Dünkel, F. and Rössner, D. (1991) Federal Republic of Germany in *ibid.*, pp. 203–248, p. 215, Fachiotti, V. (2002) Alternatives to Imprisonment in the Italian Criminal Justice System, p. 331 and Kensey, A. (2002) Community Sanctions and Measures in France in Albrecht and Kalmthout *op. cit.*, pp. 209–242, p. 210.

[109]Gallo, E. (1995) The Penal System in France. from Correctionalism to Manageralism in Ruggiero, Ryan and Sim, *op. cit.*, pp. 71–92, pp. 74–78; Feest, J. and Weber, H.-W. (1998) Germany: Ups and Downs in Resort to Imprisonment- Strategic or Unplanned Outcomes in Weiss and South, *op. cit.*, pp. 233–261, pp. 234–239, Pin, X. and Lombard, F. (2001) Frankreich in Eser, A., and Walther, S. (eds.) *Wiedergutmachung in Kriminalrecht: Internationale Perspektiven*, Max-Planck-Institut für internationales und ausländisches Strafrecht, Freiburg, pp. 1–127, pp. 9–10.

[110]Ruggiero, V. (1998) The Country of Cesare Beccaria: the Myth of Rehabilitation in Italy, in Weiss and South, *op. cit.*, pp. 207–232, p. 208.

[111]See *e.g.*, Redondo, S., Sanchez-Meca, J. and Garrido, V. (2002) Crime Treatment in Europe: A Review of Outcome Studies in McGuire, J. (ed.) Offender Rehabilitation and Treatment: Effective Programmes and Policies to Reduce Re-offending Crime, John Wiley, Chichester.

[112]Pavarani, M. (1994) The New Penology and Politics in Crisis, the Italian Case in Ruggiero, *British Journal of Criminology* vol. 34, special issue, pp. 49–61, pp. 55.

[113]Sim, J., Ruggiero, V. and Ryan, M. (1995) Punishment in Europe: Perceptions and Commonalties in Ruggiero, Ryan and Sim, *op. cit.*, pp. 1–23, p. 3–8; Cavadino and Dignan, *op. cit.*, p. 187, Ashworth, A. (2002) European Sentencing Tradition: Accepting Divergence or Aiming for Convergence? in Tata, C. and Hutton, N. (eds.) *Sentencing and Society: International Perspectives*, Ashgate, Aldershot, pp. 225–226, p. 231.

[114]Dean-Myrda, M., C. and Cullen, F., T. (1985) Panacea Pendulum: An Account of Community as a Response to Crime in Travis, L., F. (ed.) *Probation, Parole and Community Corrections*, Waveland Press, Prospect Heights, pp. 9–29, pp. 19–20.

a second implication of the loss of confidence in rehabilitation at the policy level was the increasing importance attached to the diversion of juveniles from custody and residential institutions.[115] If, it was maintained, everything was equally ineffective, non-custodial sanctions at the very least are generally less expensive and socially less damaging.[116] Since the existing forms of non-custodial sanctions, in particular probation and suspended sentences, were also discredited on the ground that they had also no significant effect in reducing recidivism, there was a growing interest in introducing new forms of non-custodial sanctions. This tendency was furthermore underpinned by the increasing attention paid to crime victims, which will be discussed later in this chapter.

2.5.3 The Emergence of Diversion: Right Time and Right Place?

The notion of diversion in its 'contemporary' sense entered into the discourse of criminal justice in the 1960s in the United States. This decade in the United States was characterised by a widespread social unrest, periodical economic recessions, and a sharp rise in violent and juvenile offences.[117] The growth in juvenile crime was then in part attributed to the perceived ineffectiveness of traditional practises of both juvenile welfare and justice.[118] The existing practices were not merely found to be ineffective in controlling delinquency, but more significantly, they were also

---

[115]Kerner, H.-J. (1983) Statt Strafe: Diversion, Zur Einführung in die Thematik in Kerner (ed.) *Diversion statt Strafe?: Problems und Gefahren einer neuen strafrechtlicher Sozialkontrolle*, Kriminalistik Verlag, Heidelberg, pp. 1–13, pp. 1–5, van Swaaningen, and Beijerse, *op. cit.*, pp. 136–139, Muncie, J. (1999) *Youth and Crime: A Critical Introduction*, Sage, London.

[116]Crow, *op. cit.*, p. 31, Vass (1990), *op. cit.*, p. 9.

[117]The President's Commission on Law Enforcement and Administration of Justice (1967) *The Challenge of Crime in a Free Society*, U.S. Government Printing Office, Washington, pp. 18–31, Austin, J. and Krisberg, B. (1981) Wider, Stronger and Different Nets: The Dialectics of Criminal Justice Reform, *Journal of Research in Crime and Delinquency*, vol. 18, no. 1, pp. 165–196, p. 166, 167, Sarri, R. (1983) Paradigms and Pitfalls in Juvenile Justice Diversion, in Morris, A. and Giller, H. (eds.) *Providing Criminal Justice for Children*, Edward Arnold, London, pp. 52–73, pp. 52–53, Davidson, W., S., Redner, R., Amdur, R., L. and Mitchell, C., M. (1990) *Alternative Treatments for Troubled Youth The Case of Diversion from the Justice System*, Plenum Press, New York, at pp. 6–7, Feld, B. (1993) Criminalising the American Juvenile Court, *Crime and Justice*, pp. 197–280, pp. 204–206, Krisberg, B. (2004) *Juvenile Justice: Redeeming Our Children*, Thousand Oaks, California, pp. 50–51.

[118]Brantingham, P., L. and Blomberg, T., G. (1979) Introduction in Brantingham, P. L., and Blomberg, T., G. (eds.) *Courts and Diversion*, Beverly Hills, pp. 7–14, p. 7, Lemert, E. (1981) Diversion in Juvenile Justice: What hath been wrought? *Journal of Research on Crime and Delinquency*, vol. 18, no.1, pp. 34–46, p. 37, Sarri, *op. cit.*, pp. 52–53, Jannsen, H. (1983) Diversion: Entstehungsbedingungen, Hintergründe und Konsequenzen einer veränderten Strategie sozialer Kontrolle, Oder: Es gibt viele zu Packen, tun wir es ihnen an, in Kerner, H.-J. (ed.) *Diversion statt Strafe? Probleme und Gefahren einer neuen Strategie sozialer Kontrolle*, Kriminalistik Verlag, Heidelberg, pp. 15–54, p. 22–32.

regarded as failing to give a proportionate and fair response to offenders of minor offences.[119] The juvenile court, in this context, was seen as bearing primary responsibility in creating a setting in which juveniles were declined their rights and ended up in custody for indefinite periods of time largely for the so-called status offences such as truancy, running away from home (which would not constitute a crime if committed by an adult). In effect, this criticism constituted a fundamental attack on the philosophical premises of the juvenile court, which was originally conceived as focussing on the 'needs' and 'best interests' of the juvenile through informal, flexible and discretionary procedures.[120]

Such sustained critical scrutiny of the conventional conception and practices of the juvenile court gained substantial momentum with two landmark decisions of the Supreme Court: *Kent* and *Gault*.[121] In both decisions, the Supreme Court of the United States took a critical position of the hitherto procedures and recognised certain elementary procedures in juvenile court proceedings.[122] Having also been questioned judicially, the redefinition of the mission of the court was inevitable.[123] Paradoxically, the scepticism towards the informal procedures of juvenile courts gave rise to 'informal' methods of dealing with juvenile offenders at the pre-court stage. In 1967, the President's Commission on Law Enforcement and the Administration of Justice gave signals of this change in the policy towards juvenile offenders. In a well-known passage of the report, the Commission indicated that:

> The formal sanctioning system and pronouncement of delinquency should be used only as a last resort. In place of the formal system, dispositional alternatives to adjudication must be developed for dealing with juveniles, including agencies to provide and coordinate services and procedures to achieve necessary control without unnecessary stigma.... The range of conduct for which court intervention is authorised should be narrowed, with greater emphasis upon *consensual and informal means* of meeting the problems of difficult children".[124] (Emphasis added.)

---

[119]Singer, S., I. (1996) Recriminalising Delinquency, Cambridge University Press, Cambridge, p. 39–44, Feld, B. (1998) The Juvenile Court in Tonry, M. (ed.) *The Handbook of Crime and Punishment*, Oxford University Press, New York, pp. 509–540, pp. 512–513.

[120]Mack, J. (1909) The Juvenile Court, *Harvard Law Review*, vol. 23, no 2, pp. 104–122, Mennel, R. (1972) Origins of the Juvenile Court: Changing Perspectives on the Legal Rights of Juvenile Delinquents, *Crime and Delinquency*, vol. 18, no. 1, pp. 68–78, Feld, 1993, *op. cit.*, pp. 200–204, Vito, G., F. and Wilson, D., G. (1985) *The American Juvenile Justice System*, Sage, London, pp. 47–49.

[121]Feld, B. (1987) The Juvenile Court Meets the Principle of the Offence: Legislative Changes in Juvenile Waiver Status, *Journal of Criminology and Criminal Law*, vol. 78, no. 3, pp. 471–533, pp. 478–480.

[122]*Kent v. United States*, 383 U.S., 541, 556, (1966), *In re Gault*, U.S. 1 (1967).

[123]Krisberg, B. (2006) Rediscovering the Juvenile Justice Ideal in the United States in Muncie, J. and Goldson, B. (eds.) *Comparative Youth Justice*, Sage, London, pp. 6–18, p. 7.

[124]The President's Commission on Law Enforcement and Administration of Justice (1967) Task Force Report: *Juvenile Delinquency and Youth Crime*, US Government Printing Office, Washington, p. 21.

This report had a profound impact upon policy-making,[125] but certainly, its impact upon policy ought to be understood as a result of the complex interplay between various factors. The unique structural and political situation of the United States has been mentioned above. Beside and as a result of this favourable conjuncture, in a broader perspective, what Stanley Cohen famously described the 'destructuring' ideas[126] ('away from the state', 'away from the expert', 'away from the institution' and 'away from the mind') of the 1960s gave further justification to diversion programmes.[127]

Here particularly relevant is the widespread reception of labelling theory as a sociological analysis and perhaps critique of crime and deviance.[128] It is indeed in this period that 'labelling approaches' began to attract a great deal of attention from different quarters. Clearly, there is no one single theory of labelling, rather there were (and have been) divergent constructions of the 'labelling process'. Hence, an overview of the theory runs a high risk of oversimplifying the significant differences between various sources of the labelling approach.[129] What appear to be highly pertinent for the purpose of this study are those theories that give particular attention to the effects of the so-called 'labelling process' on the subsequent deviant behaviour. Of these, the approach of Edwin Lemert is particularly noteworthy.[130] This is not solely because Lemert introduced such crucial concepts as primary and secondary deviance in criminal sociology, but also because his ideas appear to have exerted great influence on policy-making at the time in

---

[125]Kury, H. (1981) Diversion – Möglichkeiten und Grenzen am Beispiel Amerikanischer Programme in Kury, H. and Lerchenmüller, H. (eds.) *Alternativen zu klassischen Sanktionsformen*, Studienverlag, Bochum, pp. 165–245, pp. 170–171, Sarri, *op. cit.*, p. 53.

[126]Cohen (1985), *op. cit.*, pp. 30–39.

[127]Jannsen, *op. cit.*, p. 208.

[128]Klein, M. (1979) Deinstitutionalisation and Diversion of Juvenile Offenders: A Litany of Impediments, in Morris, N. and Tonry, M. (eds.) *Crime and Justice*, vol. 1, University of Chicago Press, pp. 145–201, p. 146, Kirchhoff, G., F. (1981) Diversionprogramme in den USA – Diversion zwischen Entdeckung und Verurteilung im Juvenile Justice System in Kury, and Lerchenmüller, *op. cit.*, pp. 253–255, Farrington, D., Ohlin, L., E. and Wilson, J. (1986) *Understanding and Controlling Crime – Toward a New Strategy*, Springer, New York, pp. 111–119, Krisberg, B. (2006) Rediscovering the Juvenile Justice Ideal in the United States, in Muncie. and Goldson, *op. cit.*, pp. 6–18, p. 7.

[129]There are, however, a number of valuable attempts to provide an overview on the theme; see for example Hawkins, R. and Tiedeman, G. (1975) *The Creation of Deviance*, Charles E. Merrill Publishing, Columbus, pp. 43–67, Gove, W: (1980) *The Labelling of Deviance: Evaluating a Perspective*, 2nd Edition, Sage Publications, Beverly Hills, pp. 9–33, Lilly, R., Cullen, F. and Ball, R., A. (2002) *Criminological Theory: Context and Consequences*, 3rd edition, Sage Publications, The Irony of State Intervention, at pp. 105–125, Anderson, J., F. and Dyson, L. (2002) *Criminological Theories: Understanding Crime in America*, University Press of America, Lanham, see Chapter 11, Labelling Theories, pp. 201–213, Burke, R., H. (2002) *An Introduction to Criminological Theory*, Willan, Cullompton, pp. 136–146.

[130]Gove, *op. cit.*, p. 10, Krisberg, B. (2006), *op. cit.*, p. 7.

question. Very generally, primary deviance, Lemert suggested, emerges as a result of a variety of socio-cultural and psychological sources.[131] It is occasional in nature and does not affect the self-concept of the individual.[132] By contrast secondary deviance, which in his view occurs when these initial deviant activities are noticed by the society and thus subjected to 'societal reaction', has far-reaching consequences for the individual's self-concept. This is because, Lemert argued, with each act of 'primary deviance' the deviant becomes "more stigmatised through name calling, labelling, or stereotyping".[133] The result of this process, according to Lemert, is stage by stage the acceptance of the deviant identity; reorganising her/his life according to the status of deviance.[134] This very assumption that the labelling process generates further delinquent activity appears to be the conclusion of other labelling theorists who followed distinct lines in explaining the impact of the labelling process upon the individual. Consequently, theorising the potentially damaging effects of 'official labelling', the labelling approach favoured *per se* the avoidance or minimisation of the interventions of criminal justice agencies at the level of policy formulation.[135]

Underpinned powerfully by the labelling approach as such, diversion in the United States consequently became a national strategy, in particular with the enactment of the federal Juvenile Justice and Delinquency Prevention Act of 1974, a strategy which was quick to bring about certain disenchantment.[136] At the end of 1970s, it became clear in many respects that the goals of diversion programmes were largely unrealised. Research studies demonstrated that these programmes did not limit themselves to juveniles who would otherwise have proceeded to a juvenile court, but also targeted those offenders who "are normally counselled and released by the police, if indeed they have any dealings with the police".[137] For many, the conclusion was that rather than reducing or minimising social control, diversion measures widened the net of social control.[138]

---

[131]Lemert, E. (1967) *Human Deviance, Social Problems and Social Control*, Prentice Hall, New Jersey, p. 17.

[132]Lemert, E. (1951) Social *Pathology – A Systematic Approach to the Theory of Sociopathic Behaviour*, McGraw-Hill, New York, p. 75.

[133]Lemert 1967, *op. cit.*, pp. 76–77.

[134]*Ibid.*

[135]Some proponents of labelling approach went even further to demand 'non-intervention' in all but serious cases, see for example, Schur, M., E. (1973) *Radical Non-Intervention* (Rethinking the Delinquency Problem), Prentice Hall, London.

[136]Zimring, H. (2005) *American Juvenile Justice*, Oxford University Press, New York, pp. 43–44.

[137]Klein, *op. cit.*, p. 165.

[138]Austin and Krisberg, *op. cit.*, p. 40, Curran; D., J. (1988) Destructuring, Privatisation and Juvenile Diversion: Compromising Community-Based Corrections, *Crime and Delinquency*, vol. 34, no 4, pp. 363–378, Polk. K. (1987) When Less Means More: An Analysis of Destructuring in Criminal Justice, *Crime and Delinquency*, vol. 33, no. 2, pp. 358–378.

Interestingly, though, diversion as an idea and set of programmes began to be imported at this time, when the idea was already discredited on the ground of its 'unintended' consequences in its 'native' soul.[139] Nevertheless, the American experience in this context was an important foundation for many European countries, as will be exemplified in part below in discussing diversion measures in the countries featured in this study.

2.5.4 *The Appearance of the Victim in the Punishment Discourse*

The disillusionment with the rehabilitative approach did not solely give rise to the renaissance of retributive ideas, but it also created a fertile ground for victim-oriented developments to flourish. It is in this period that the victim began to be recognised as a most neglected actor in the criminal justice system in western countries.[140] The shift in the perceptions understandably had far more consequences in the common law jurisdictions than in those of civil law. Until then, as opposed to the civil law countries where the victim has generally enjoyed the right to participate in proceedings, to present civil claims therein and under certain circumstances to initiate prosecution, in the common law countries the role of the victim in criminal proceedings was traditionally limited to that of witness.[141]

In changing the victim policy, the United States served as a beacon for other common law jurisdictions. Underpinned by an influential victim 'lobby' or 'movement',[142] a significant step in improving the rather passive role of victims in the criminal justice system was taken by enactment of certain procedural measures. A second and more directly relevant development to non-custodial measures and sanctions was the initiation of experimental victim-offender reconciliation

[139]Blau, G. (1985) Diversion unter nationalem und internationalem Aspekt in Kury, H. (ed.) *Kriminologische Forschung in der Diskussion: Berichte, Standpunkte und Analysen*, Carl Heymanns, Köln, pp. 311–339, p. 322 and (1987) Diversion und Strafrecht, *Jura*, vol. 9, no. 1, pp. 25–34, p. 28 Heinz, W. (1992) Diversion im Jugendstrafverfahren der Bundesrepublik Deutschland in Heinz, W. and Storz, R., Bundesministerum der Justiz, Forum Verlag, Bonn, p. 8.

[140]Dignan, J. and Cavadino, M. (1996) Towards a Framework for Conceptualising and Evaluating Models of Criminal Justice from a Victim's Perspective, *International Review of Victimology*, vol. 4, pp. 153–182, p. 155.

[141]However, on the Continent too, these traditional methods were in practice only of limited importance. See for example, HEUNI (1989) *Changing Victim Policy: the United Nations Victim Declaration and Recent Developments in Europe* (Report on the Meeting of an ad hoc Expert Group Meeting, Helsinki 17–20 November 1988), Helsinki.

[142]At the very outset, numerous objections with regard to the appropriateness of the use of the term 'victim movement' have been raised. For example, Pointing and Maguire suggest that the term 'victims movement' gives a misleading impression of unity, p. 2 in Pointing, J. and Maguire, M. (eds.) (1988) Introduction: the Rediscovery of the Crime Victim, in *Victims of Crime: A new Deal?*, Open University Press, Milton Keynes, also see Reeves, H. and Wright, M.(1995) Victims: Towards a Reorientation of Justice in Ward, D. and Lacey, M. (eds.) *Probation Working for Justice*, Whiting and Birch, London, pp. 73–85, pp. 74–79.

programmes.[143] These programmes started as an alternative to probation for juvenile offenders, and later transformed into pre-sentence programmes which allowed the victim and offender to make a sentencing proposal.

In Europe, victim-offender mediation programmes first appeared in the beginning of 1980s.[144] By this time increasing awareness on the rights and needs of victims, both on national and international level, already shaped public policy markedly. This trend is clearly perceptible in the relevant recommendations of the Council of Europe, the introduction of state compensation schemes[145] and the promotion of victim support schemes.[146] Victim-offender mediation programmes on the Continent arguably emanated as a consequence of the considerations of diverting offenders, particularly young offenders, from the court procedures and the severity of sentencing measures.[147] The priority of diversion was not only justified by the perceived ability of these measures in preventing the stigmatising effect of formal court procedures, but also by reference to the need for reducing the caseloads of criminal justice.[148]

---

[143] The first victim-offender mediation programme was developed in 1974 in Kitchener/Ontario. Peachey, D., E. (1989) The Kitchener Experiment, Wright, M. and Galaway, B. (eds.) *Mediation and Criminal Justice: Victims, Offenders and Community*, Sage, London.

[144] On the early experiments carried out in Europe, see Messmer, H. and Otto, H.-U. (1992) (eds.) *Restorative Justice on Trial: Pitfalls and Potentials of Victim-Offender Mediation- International Research Perspectives*, Kluwer, Dordrecht, Jung, H. (1998) Mediation/Paradigmwechsel in der Konfliktregelung, pp. 913–926 in Scwind, H.-D., Kube, E. and Kühnè, H.-H. (eds.) *Festschrift für Hans Joachim Schneider zum 70. Geburtstag am 14 November 1998*, de Gruyter, Berlin.

[145] Council of Europe/European Committee on Crime Problems (1978) *Compensation for Victims of Crime*, Strasbourg, Greer, D. (1996) *Compensating Crime Victims: a European Survey*, Max-Planck-Institut für ausländisches and internationales Strafrecht, Freiburg.

[146] van Dijk, J. (1988) Ideological Trends within the Victims Movement: An International Perspective in Maguire, M. and Pointing, J., *op. cit.*, pp. 127–137, Shapland, J. and Maguire, M. (1990) The Victim Movement in Europe in Lurigio, A., J., Skogan, W., G. and Davis, R., C. (eds.) *Victims of Crime: Problems, Policies and Programmes*, Sage, Newbury Park, pp. 205–225, Fattah, E. and Peters, T. (eds.) (1998) *Support for Crime Victims in a Comparative Perspective*, Leuven University Press, Leuven, Weitekamp (2001) *op. cit.*, pp. 145–160, Miers, D. and Willemsens, J. (eds.) (2004) *Mapping Restorative Justice Developments in 25 European Countries*, European Forum for Victim-Offender Mediation and Restorative Justice, Leuven, Mestitz, A. (2005) A comparative perspective on Victim-Offender Mediation with Young Offenders throughout Europe in Mestitz, A. and Ghetti, S. (eds.) Victim-*Offender Mediation with Youth Offenders in Europe*, Springer, Dordrecht, pp. 3–22, Pelikan, C. and Trenczek, T. (2008) Victim offender mediation and Restorative Justice: the European Landscape in Sullivan, D. (ed.) *Handbook of Restorative Justice*, Routledge, London, pp. 63–90.

[147] See *e.g.*, Hartmann, A. and Kilchling, M. (1998) The Development of Victim/Offender Mediation in the German Juvenile Justice System from the Legal and Criminological Point of View in Walgrave, L. (ed.) *Restorative Justice for Juveniles: Potentials, Risks and Problems*, Leuven University Press, Leuven, pp. 261–282, Trenczek, T. (2003) Within or outside System? Restorative Justice Attempts in the Penal System in Weitekamp, E., G. and Kerner, H.-J. (eds.) *Restorative Justice in Context: International Practice and Directions*, Willan, Devon, pp. 272–284.

[148] See *e.g.*, Verrest, P. (2000) The French Public Prosecution Service, *European Journal of Crime, Criminal Law and Criminal Justice*, vol. 8, no 3, pp. 210–244, pp. 211, Albrecht, H-J. (2000)

The development of victim-offender mediation programmes, and other schemes that were inspired by indigenous and informal justice practices, most notably in Canada and New Zealand, in due course stimulated a vast body of literature on what has come to be termed as 'restorative justice'. Given the contentious nature of the philosophy behind this concept,[149] this study does not seek here to discuss different constructions of the notion of restorative justice. Suffice to say that the term "restorative justice" does not indicate a "unitary" concept[150] but rather a "shorthand convenient term"[151] that describes a variety of divergent practices in which victim orientation is noticeable. The challenge of the basic philosophy of restorative justice is suggested to be in its conception of crime, as crime is not seen as a mere violation of law or the interests of the state, but as a violation of human relations.[152] Accordingly, the innovative pledge of restorative justice is explained with the 'restoration' of 'harm' that is caused by the crime through a process whereby the offender is held accountable for her/his crime and the victim is given a voice to participate in decisions that affect them. Such a process involving both the offender and victim, it is believed, provides a more satisfactory experience to the individual victims on the one hand, and offers greater reintegration possibilities to offenders on the other hand.[153]

The promises that are attributed to this new 'paradigm' have certainly made restorative justice an important philosophical source of creating new forms of alternative sanctions and measures. Also considering the savings on cost and administrative efficiencies that this perspective inherently brings about, restorative justice as a new panacea seems to reshape existing methods and induce new forms of non-custodial sanctions and measures.

Criminal Prosecutions: Developments, Trends and Open Questions in the Federal Republic of Germany, *European Journal of Crime, Criminal Law and Criminal Justice*, vol. 8, no 3, pp. 245–256.

[149]For critical evaluations on the theme, see Haines, K. (1998) Some Principled Objections to a Restorative Justice Approach to Working with Juvenile Offenders in Walgrave, L. (ed.) Restorative Justice for Juveniles: Potentials, Risks and Problems for Research, Leuven University Press, Leuven, pp. 93–113, Levrant, S., Cullen, F. T., Fulton, B. and Wozniak, J., F. (1999) Reconsidering Restorative Justice: The Corruption of Benevolence Revisited?, *Crime and Delinquency*, vol. 45, pp. 3–27.

[150]Shapland, J. (2003) Restorative Justice and Criminal Justice: Just Responses to Crime in von Hirsch, A., Roberts, J., V., Bottoms, A., Roach, K. and Schiff, M. (eds.) *Restorative Justice and Criminal Justice: Competing or Reconcilable Paradigms?* Hart Publishing, Oxford, pp. 195–218, p. 197.

[151]Dignan, J. with Lowey, K. (2000) *Restorative Justice Options for Northern Ireland: A Comparative Review*, Criminal Justice Review Commission/Northern Ireland Office, Belfast, p. 3.

[152]Zehr, H. (1990) *Changing Lenses: A New Focus for Crime and Justice*, Herald Press, Scottdale.

[153]Bazemore, G. and Colleen, M. (2002) Restorative Justice and the future of Diversion and Informal Social Control in Weitekamp and Kerner, *op. cit.*, pp. 143–176, p. 143, Pavlich, G. (2002) Deconstructing Restoration: the Promise of Restorative Justice in Weitekamp, G., M. and Kerner, H.-J. (eds.) *Restorative Justice Theoretical Foundations*, Willan, Cullompton, pp. 90–109, p. 90, Weitekamp, E., G. (2001) Mediation in Europe: Paradoxes, Problems and Promises in Morris and Maxwell, *op. cit.*, pp. 145–160.

2.6 Conclusions

The foregoing discussion of the history of prison alternatives appears to reveal that the changes in the perceptions of crime and punishment played a critical role in the making of and expanding of the scope of prison alternatives. Indeed, the philosophical justification of imprisonment, alongside 'deterrence' and 'retribution', on the grounds of 'reform' or 'rehabilitation', should be regarded as the principal source of inspiration of early prison alternatives. In conjunction with the new ideas on the very nature of criminality and the distinction of criminals, the notion of rehabilitating criminals soon gave a foundation to the differential treatment of offenders. Early prison alternatives, in this sense, ought to be seen as a direct outcome of such a change of view in dealing with offenders. Interestingly, another crucial development that has affected prison alternatives emerged as a result of increasing scepticism on the ability of prisons to rehabilitate its inmate populations. As has been argued above, the decline of the rehabilitation paradigm created a strong case for non-custodial sanctions. Finally, in this chapter it has been highlighted that the recognition of the notorious status of crime victims in criminal justice and their 'location' in the punishment discourse has made alternatives to prison continue to grow.

The examination of non-custodial sentences in a historical context is also indicative of the fact that the exchange and dissemination of ideas have had a profound impact upon law-making. This has been the case from the very origin of alternative sanctions to the present. Even if recently the legal influences of the United States upon European jurisdictions appears to be reversed considerably,[154] as has been shown, in many respects the penological developments occurring in the United States in the 1970s and 1980s were widely followed by European countries. Matti Joutsen, therefore, is right to call the United States a powerhouse of empirical (and to a lesser extent, theoretical) criminology, and victimology-related sciences.[155] On the other hand, this chapter has provided sufficient evidence to argue that in the realm of non-custodial sanctions, there is a certain form of convergence between European countries. By comparing three jurisdictions in terms of non-custodial measures and sanctions that are, at any rate, geographically located in Europe, the following chapters are likely to further explain and exemplify such interaction and convergence occurring within Europe.

---

[154]See, for example, Tonry, M., H. (2006) *Thinking about Crime: Sense and Sensibility in American Penal Culture*, Oxford University Press, Oxford. See for an early account on the theme, Weigend, T. (1980) Continental Cures for American Ailments: European Criminal Procedure as a Model for Law Reform, *Crime and Justice*, vol. 2, pp. 381–428.

[155]Joutsen, M. (1991) Changing Victim Policy: International Dimensions in Kaiser, G., Kury, H. and Albrecht, H.-J., *Victims and Criminal Justice*, vol. 52/2, Max-Planck-Institut für internationales and ausländisches Strafrecht, Freiburg, pp. 765–797, p. 785, also Downes, D. (2001) Mass Incarceration in the United States- a European Perspective in Garland, D. (ed.) *Mass Imprisonment- Social Causes and Consequences*, Sage, London; Cavadino, M. and Dignan, J. (2006) *Penal Systems: A Comparative Approach*, Sage, London.

Chapter 3
Alternatives to Imprisonment in England: Destined to Fail?

3.1 Non-custodial Sanctions for 'Surplus' Populations of Prisons: The Foundation

In England, the origin of alternatives to imprisonment can be traced back to the late nineteenth century in the adoption of probation as a supervisory sanction in the community for both juveniles and adults. The core features of the development of probation, both with regard to England and the United States, were dealt with in some detail earlier in this study. In this section, an attempt will be made to highlight the relation between the development of supervision in the community and the efforts to control the number of prisoners from a broader perspective.

In order to do so, first and foremost it must be underlined that the creation of the probation order in England derived its stimulus to a considerable extent from the rising concern about a perceived increase in drunkenness, idleness and moral degeneration.[1] The Church of England Temperance Society's police court missionaries, who were generally cited as the founders of modern probation practice,[2]

---

[1] King, J., F., S. (1969) *The Probation and After-Care Service*, 3rd edition, Butterworths, London, Jarvis, F., V. (1972) *Advise, Assist and Befriend: A History of Probation and After-Care Service*, National Association of Probation Officers, London, pp. 1–8, Young, P. (1976) A Sociological Analysis of the Early History of Probation, *British Journal of Law and Society*, vol. 3, no. 1, pp. 44–58, Bochel, D. (1976) *Probation and After Care: Its Development in England and Wales*, Scottish Academic Press, Edinburgh, McWilliams, W. (1983) The Mission to the English Police Courts 1876–1936, *Howard Journal*, vol. 22, pp. 129– 47, May (1991) *op. cit.*, pp. 6–21, Raynor, P. and Vanstone, M. (2002) *Understanding Community Penalties. Probation, Policy and Social Change*, Open University Press, Buckingham, pp. 15–20, Vanstone, M. (2004) *Supervising Offenders in the Community: a History of Probation Theory and Practice*, Ashgate, Aldershot, pp. 7–8, Newburn, p. 82, Whitehead, P. and Statham, R. (2006) *The History of Probation: Politics, Power and Cultural Change*; 1876–2005, Shaw & Sons, Crayford, pp. 4–6, Cavadino, M. and Dignan, J. (2007) *The Penal System*, Sage, London p. 146, Raynor, P. (2007) Community Penalties: Probation 'What Works', and Offender Management in Maguire, M., Morgan, R. and Reiner, R. (eds.) *the Oxford Handbook of Criminology*, 4th edition, Oxford University Press, pp. 1066–1099, p. 1066.

[2] See e.g., Jarvis, *op. cit.*, 2–8, May, *op. cit.*, p. 862, Vanstone (2004), *op. cit.*, pp. 7–8, see also a rather different view on the theme Whitehead and Statham, *op. cit.*, pp. 4–11.

Ö. Sevdiren, *Alternatives to Imprisonment in England and Wales, Germany and Turkey*,
DOI 10.1007/978-3-642-17351-6_3,

devoted their attention mostly, as their name suggests, but not exclusively, to inebriated offenders. Under the considerable influence of missionary work, probation practice therefore developed as a challenging modality of *treatment* aiming to 'improve the character and moral fibre of the offender'. Arguably, this fact explains the rather distinctive pattern of the development of 'alternatives to imprisonment' here.

Indeed, in England, notwithstanding the fact that the reduction of imprisonment was a demand of progressive thought,[3] an intellectual (doctrinary) movement against short-term imprisonment did not take place as it did in the other major European countries. England was also represented in the international congresses of the day, in which prison alternatives, *inter alia* constituted an important theme. However, perhaps due to the fact that at the time academic criminology and/or penology was in an embryonic form, the dissemination and reception of these ideas appears not to have occurred on the same scale as in many other European countries.[4]

One consequence of this is that probation as an alternative measure of sentencing had at the very outset a less discursive relation with custody and its adverse effects than its continental counterpart, the *sursis*. The English probationer was regarded as a person, usually a juvenile, who was deemed to require special assistance.[5] In contrast, the clientele of the *sursis* in various forms in Continental Europe were generally composed of persons who were deemed to be 'occasional offenders', and who required no special attention. Both the probation order and the *sursis* were, in the final analysis, substitutes for short-term imprisonment, although their different objectives, which might be imperfectly formulated as 'avoidance of imprisonment' and 'reformation of the individual', assumed markedly different weight in the conceptualisation of each of these court disposals. In England, at the centre of the probation order lay the task to 'advise, assist and befriend' the offender in a non-custodial setting, which gained greater prominence later with the appointment of probation officers within the jurisdiction of each court.[6]

---

[3]On the official attitude towards imprisonment and its alternatives, see for example Bochel, *op. cit.*, pp. 1–32, see also Rutherford, A. (1986), *op. cit.*, pp. 123–127.

[4]Ruggles-Brise noted that "England has not participated to any great extent in these controversies of the criminological schools, which have been so active and have excited so much interest on the Continent of Europe, and in America, during the last fifty years. It may almost be said that there is no school of criminology in England.", Ruggles-Brise, E. (1925), *op. cit.*, p. 16, Mannheim, H. (1939) *The Dilemma of Penal Reform*, George Allen and Unwin Ltd., London, in Preface by Carr-Saunders, A., M., pp. 7–9, Radzinowicz, L. and Hood, R. (1990) *The Emergence of Penal Policy in Victorian and Edwardian Penal Policy*, Clarendon Press, Oxford, part 1 'Searching for the Roots of Crime', chapter 1 'English Reactions to Positivism', pp. 3–27, also Radzinowicz, L. (1961) *In Search of Criminology*, Heinemann, London, pp. 167–175, Garland, D. (1988) British Criminology before 1935, *British Journal of Criminology*, vol. 28, no 1, pp. 131–147.

[5]May, *op. cit.*, p. 862, Bailey, J. (1987) *Delinquency and Citizenship: Reclaiming the Young Offender 1914–1948,* Clarendon Press, Oxford, pp. 36–37.

[6]The 1925 Criminal Justice Act, see Jarvis, *op. cit.*, pp. 33–44.

As the ongoing analysis suggests, even though the probation order *per se* was an important contribution in the attempts to abate the overwhelming use of the short-term prison sentence, it emanated without rigorously questioning the place of the short-term imprisonment in the penal system. Probation was born, rather, as a means of helping and supporting certain sectors of criminals. Conceived in this manner, it was initially used moderately.[7] Hence it is not difficult to understand in retrospect that the introduction of probation did not halt the search for ways to limit the use of imprisonment. The gradual incorporation of the latter into the penal system was soon followed by the creation of a number of statutory restrictions and the extension and improvement of the existing sentencing options. Before going on to consider the relevant legislation, at this point it is essential to emphasise the contribution of the emergence of juvenile justice in the development of the notion of alternatives to imprisonment.

Clearly, the premise that juvenile offenders should be treated differently had some obvious repercussions for the criminal justice system as a whole. The institutional segregation of juvenile and adult offenders, i.e. the reformatory initiatives of the 19th century as an early crystallisation of this notion, was driven by the goal to prevent the 'contamination' of juveniles by adult prisoners.[8] Although the paramount consideration here was that penal establishments designed for juveniles could reform them more effectively, by the same token, it was apparently an acknowledgement that prisons did have adverse effects upon the juvenile offender. One step further was the enactment of certain procedural modifications with respect to juvenile offenders. Such developments paved the way for the juvenile court. In effect, unlike its many contemporaries in the western world, the first English juvenile court was a modified version of an ordinary criminal court, the paramount consideration of which was the 'deeds' of juvenile offenders, rather than their 'needs'. However, despite the fact that the English juvenile court did not initially have special sentencing measures, as was the case for the German juvenile court, for example, the move towards its establishment alone constituted a considerable recognition of the distinctive nature of juvenile offending and the responses required to it. Not surprisingly, imprisonment in this emerging scene of juvenile justice attracted an increasing amount of attention, in that the

---

[7]Bailey, *op. cit.*, p. 37.

[8]Morris, A., Giller, H., Szwed, E. and Geach, H. (1980) *Justice for Children*, Macmillan, London, Morris, A. and Giller, H. (1987) *Providing Criminal Justice for Children*, Edward Arnold, London, Parsloe, P. (1978) *Juvenile Justice in Britain and the United States The Balance of Needs and Rights*, Routledge & Kegan Paul, London, pp. 103–121, Matthews, R. and Young, J. (2003) *The New Politics of Crime and Punishment*, Willan, Cullompton, pp. 72–74, Haines and Drakeford (1998) *op. cit.*, Newburn, T. (2002) Young People, Crime, and Youth Justice in Maguire, M., Morgan, R. and Reiner, R. (eds.) *the Oxford Handbook of Criminology*, 3rd edition, Oxford University Press, Oxford, pp. 531–578, Pitts, J. (2005) The Recent History of Youth Justice in England in Bateman, T. and Pitts, J. (eds.) *The RHP Companion to Youth Justice*, Russel House Publishing, Dorset, pp. 2–11, Morgan, R. and Newburn, T. (2007) Youth Justice in Maguire *et al.* (2007) *op. cit.*, pp. 1061–1099, Morgan (2007), *op. cit.*, pp. 201–223.

contagious atmosphere of prisons was frequently cited as an argument against the incarceration of juveniles.

In a changing climate such as this, and with evidence that a significant part of the prison population had either received a sentence for a non-indictable offence or had been imprisoned for fine default,[9] it was inevitable that official circles contemplated reducing the abundant use of short-term imprisonment. The increase in the number of probation orders in this sense appears to not have had any significant impact during the first decade of the last century. A number of solutions were proposed including abolishing imprisonment for debt, an extension of the use of probation for young adult offenders, allowing time for offenders to pay fines and giving courts the power to suspend sentences for petty offences of up to 1 month.[10]

Apart from suspended sentences, all of these translated into practice to a considerable extent. The 1914 Criminal Justice Administration Act, the full title of which markedly included the phrase 'an act to diminish the number of cases committed to prison'[11] made the courts of summary jurisdictions' option to allow time for payment an *obligation* (previously laid at the discretion of the court by the Summary Jurisdiction Act 1879[12]), unless one of the reasons specified by the Act applied.[13] Section 2 of the latter Act stated that the time allowed should be not less

[9]Rutherford, *op. cit.*, p. 124. Hendrick notes that crimes were largely of non-indictable variety such as drunkness, malicious mischief, loitering, begging and dangerous play. Hendrick, H. (2006) Histories of Youth Crime and Justice in Goldon, B. and Muncie, J. (eds.) *Youth Crime and Justice*, Sage, London, pp. 3–16, p. 7.

Parsloe cited a letter written to the Queen Victoria, which tried to prove the abundant use of imprisonment in relation to juvenile offenders, by indicating that "...many of these cases were trifling offences, as for instance, a boy of nine year old for throwing stones; several boys of eleven and twelve years for damaging grass by running about in the fields; a girl of thirteen for being drunk; several boys of twelve and thirteen for bathing in a canal, and similarly playing at pitch and toss; a boy of nine for stealing scent; a boy of thirteen for threatening a woman, three boys of eleven for breaking windows; a boy of ten for wilfully damaging timber.", *op. cit.*, p. 131.

[10]Fox, L. W. (1950) The Criminal Justice Act and Prison Administration, *Journal of Criminal Science*, vol. 2, Macmillan & St. Martin's Street, London, pp. 1–22, Radzinowicz and Hood, *op. cit.*, pp. 770–775, Rutherford (1984), *op. cit.*, p. 124.

[11]The full title was "an act to diminish the number of cases committed to prison, to amend the law with respect to the treatment of punishment of young offenders, and otherwise to improve the administration of criminal justice". For an introductory comments on the provisions regarding imprisonment for fine default see Sanders, E., C. (1915) *The Criminal Justice Administration Act, 1914*, Butterworth: Shaw & Sons, London, see also Fox, *op. cit.*, at pp. 46–49.

[12]As regards the collection and enforcement of fines the Act of 1879 authorised courts of summary jurisdictions when imposing a fine to:
–allow time for payment, or
–direct payment by instalments, or
–take security for payment, or
–postpone the issue of a warrant of commitment upon such conditions, if any, as the court might think fit.

[13]Section 1 of the Criminal Justice Administration Act 1914, with the heading '*obligation to allow time for payment of fine*', stated that "(1) A warrant committing a person to prison *(a)* in respect of non-payment of a sum adjudged to be paid by a conviction *(b)* of a court of summary jurisdiction

than seven days. Innovatively, the Act furthermore provided that in fixing the amount of the fine, the court of summary jurisdiction was required to take the means of the offender into account.[14] At a time in which imprisonment for fine default accounted for a significant part of the prison population, by virtue of these provisions the Act was a bold step towards reducing the frequency of imprisonment for non-payment of fines.[15] The impact of this Act can be better understood by comparing the figures of imprisonment for fine default. In 1910, the number of offenders sent to prison in default of payment of fines was 85,000, whereas in 1921, this figure fell to 15,000.[16]

A second and equally important development for the present discussion was the enactment of the 1908 Children Act. The Children Act prohibited *imprisonment*[17] of juveniles under 14 (classified as 'children') under any circumstances.[18] It strictly limited the use of *prison* sentences for juveniles under 16 (classified as 'young persons') to those cases where the court took the view that the juvenile was "of so unruly or depraved a character to be sentenced to *punitive detention*". The effect of these provisions on juvenile sentencing was remarkable. In 1904–1905 the number of juveniles under 16 sentenced to imprisonment was 572, while in 1925 it was only 8.[19]

These lines of development were further embodied in a landmark piece of legislation, the Criminal Justice Act 1948. The 1948 Act placed a number of further restrictions on the use of imprisonment. According to the 1948 Act, the magistrates' courts could no longer impose a sentence of imprisonment on juveniles under the age of 17,[20] and at the higher courts, those under 15. The Act also urged sentencers not to imprison those under 21 unless they were of the opinion that no other method

(c) shall not be issued forthwith *(d)* unless the court which passed the sentence *(e)* is satisfied *(f)* that he is possessed of sufficient means *(g)* to enable him to pay the sum forthwith, or unless upon being asked by the court whether he desires that time should be allowed for payment, he does not express any such desire, or fails to satisfy the court that he has a fixed abode *(h)* within its jurisdiction or unless the court for any other special reason *(i)* expressly directs *(j)* that no time shall be allowed".

[14]Section 5 of the Criminal Justice Administration Act 1914.

[15]Mannheim, H. (1955) *Group Problems in Crime and Punishment and Other Studies in Criminology and Criminal Law*, Patterson Smith, Montclair, pp. 246–248, Rutherford (1986), *op. cit.*, p. 124.

[16]Fox, *op. cit.*, p. 66, see also Cordes, E. (1950) Fines and their Enforcement, *Journal of Criminal Science*, vol. 2, pp. 46–64. The provisions of the Criminal Justice Administration Act 1914 in this respect were strengthened by the Money Payments (Justice Procedure) Act 1935. The latter Act provided that when imposing the fine, magistrates should not fix the period of imprisonment in case of default, which was the case previously, unless they have special reasons to do so, e.g. the gravity of offence. The Act also required magistrates to make enquiries into the offender's ability to pay, before the committal to prison due to fine default. It also empowered magistrates to place offenders in fine default supervision until the fine had been paid.

[17]Hence, 'borstal detention' for this matter is irrelevant to the respective section of the Act.

[18]Section 102 of the Children Act.

[19]Bailey, *op. cit.*, p. 58.

[20]Criminal Justice Act 1948, s. 17 (1).

of dealing with the offender was appropriate.[21] Equally significant was the introduction of a number of non-custodial sanctions. Of these disposals, absolute and conditional discharge were to be used in cases where the court, taking the nature of the offence and the character of the offender into account, felt that "it is inexpedient to inflict punishment and that a probation order is not appropriate".[22] Attendance centre orders[23] were designed for those aged 12–20. The idea was in a contemporary sense 'punishment by the deprivation of leisure time' without removing the juvenile from her/his home. The attendance centre order was to be applied to those juveniles who were deemed to have not "yet become anything in the nature of a habitual criminal".[24] A further opportunity to avoid imprisonment in suitable cases provided by the Act concerned the extension of the range of indictable offences that are punishable by fines. Prior to the 1948 Act, unlike courts of summary jurisdiction, which had a general power to impose a fine for both misdemeanour and felony, higher courts (courts of assize and quarter sessions) had no authority to fine for felony.[25] Regardless of the court of conviction, the Act made it possible to fine the offender in lieu of imprisonment except for those felonies for which the sentence is fixed by law, e.g. murder.

Another significant legislative development which deserves a mention here was the enactment of the First Offenders Act 1958.[26] This Act adopted the approach to the restriction of imprisonment of juvenile offenders envisaged by the Criminal Justice Act 1948 for adults. It provided that a court of summary jurisdiction could only impose a prison sentence on a first offender when it was deemed that there was no other suitable method of dealing with her/him. In order to secure compliance with this provision, the Act required magistrates to give reasons for the decision of imprisonment.

As this brief outline suggests, in the period under review the English legislator endeavoured to restrict the use of *imprisonment* with statutory criteria, in particular in relation to juvenile offenders. Meanwhile, the creation of such non-custodial sanctions as absolute and conditional discharges and attendance centre orders was a crucial development at a time when imprisonment for non-indictable offences was commonplace, as mentioned above. However, it would be an exaggeration to see these developments as eventually making a prison sentence an *ultimum remedium* for offences of a certain gravity. Neither had imprisonment at this period in time

[21]Criminal Justice Act 1948, s. 17 (2).

[22]Section 7(1), 7(3) of the 1948 Criminal Justice Act.

[23]See, McClintock, F., H. with Walker, M., A., and Savill, N., C. (1961) *Attendance Centres (An Enquiry by the Cambridge Institute of Criminology on the Use of Section 19 of the Criminal Justice Act, 1948)*, Macmillan, New York, Tutt, N. and Gelsthorpe, L. (1986) The Attendance Centre Order, *Criminal Law Review*, pp. 146–153, Mair, G, (1991) Part *Time Punishment The Origins and Developments of Senior Attendance Centre*, HMSO, London.

[24]Cited in Tutt and Gelsthorpe, *op. cit.*, p. 147.

[25]Section 13 of the Criminal Justice Act 1948, Fox, *op. cit.*, pp. 52–53.

[26]Walker, N. (1972) Crime and Penal Measures in Halsey, A., H. (ed.) *Trends in British Society since 1900,* Macmillan & St. Martin, London, Hawkins, p. 73.

faced a crisis of legitimacy in terms of its ability to 'rehabilitate'.[27] It is true that in the official documents and the papers of such influential non-governmental organisations as the Howard League for Penal Reform, short-term imprisonment was criticised.[28] However, these critics appear to have often directed their criticisms against the existing enforcement method(s) of short-term imprisonment, rather than the notion of the short-term imprisonment in general. This approach may be illustrated with a citation from the Advisory Council on alternatives, which undertook a large-scale inquiry into alternatives to imprisonment:

> The short sentence has a definite and necessary place in our criminal law. . .There is (thus) nothing inherently wrong in a short sentence being the only sentence of imprisonment open to magistrates' courts. . .*Nor is there any reason why a short sentence should not be socially and penally useful.*[29] (Emphasis added.)

Certainly, in England the belief in the rehabilitative capacity of imprisonment was a reflection of the time period in question. As commentators often emphasise, the changes in the contours of the penal policy at the time bore strong affinities with welfare legislation, i.e. the establishment of the National Health Service, an enlarged social insurance scheme and a new statute concerning education.[30] The new approach is therefore sometimes called 'penal welfarism',[31] a concept that was developed by David Garland.[32] Central to 'penal welfarism' was (is) the recognition that by ameliorating deprivation, unequal opportunity and unemployment, the incidence of crime could be reduced. Notably, at this time, the crime figures indeed displayed relative stability. Between 1948 and 1953, the number of adults found guilty of indictable offences, as recorded by Vass, was around 100,000 for each year.[33] On the other hand, despite a fluctuating prison population, the number of short-term prison sentences decreased substantially.[34]

In the realm of non-custodial sanctions the figures also were encouraging. It has been already noted that the use of the probation order was initially fairly limited. In 1919, under 10,000 people were placed on probation; this rose to 25,000 in 1936 and to 35,000 by 1943.[35] Within this time, the combination of a medical approach involving such concepts as assessment, diagnosis, treatment and social work

---

[27]There were, however, some opposing views. See Fox, *op. cit.*, p. 65.

[28]See Webber, G. (1957) Recent Trends in Criminal Justice, *Current Legal Problems*, vol. 10, pp. 127–151, pp. 149–151.

[29]Home Office (1957) *Alternatives to Short-Terms of Imprisonment* (A Report of the Advisory Council on the Treatment of Offenders), HMSO, London, p. 4.

[30]Vass (1990), *op. cit.*, p. 8.

[31]Bottoms *et al.* (2004), *op. cit.*, p. 2.

[32]Garland, D. (1985) *op. cit.*, critically, Zedner, L. (2002) Dangers of Dystopias in Penal Theory, *Oxford Journal of Legal Studies*, vol. 22, pp. 341–366.

[33]Vass, *op. cit.*, p. 9.

[34]Mannheim (1955) *op. cit.*, p. 248. See Sutherland, E., H. (1934) The Decreasing Prison Population of England, *Journal of Criminal Law and Criminology*, vol. 24, pp. 880–900.

[35]Newburn (2003), *op. cit.*, p. 88.

techniques formed the English style of probation practice[36]: in the words of Bottoms, probation was then "more secularised and scientificised".[37]

The fine, too, displayed an upward trend. Rutherford notes that following the 1948 Act, the fine became the most often used sanction for dealing with serious offences, e.g., violence against persons, in England, accounting for approximately half of sentences for serious offences.[38] The consideration of the means of the offender, the option to pay in instalments and the allowance of time reduced the default imprisonment substantially further. The number of persons sent to prison in default of payment of fines fell from 85,000 in 1910 to 15,000 in 1921. In 1947 it had fallen to 2,952.[39] Despite a rather hesitant beginning in the 1950s, the number of attendance centres increased considerably.[40]

This picture in many respects was regarded as having promising implications for the further development of the penal policy. Assuming that "every offender offers a hope of reclamation",[41] rehabilitation was no longer a mere adjunct to other aims such as incapacitation or deterrence ascribed to prisons, but in itself became an underlying rationale of the prison stay, at least in the rhetoric.[42] It was believed imprisonment oriented towards rehabilitation would reduce offending behaviour, while reintegrating those individuals as law-abiding citizens into 'mainstream' society. Those who did not require any rehabilitative intervention were a marginal sector of the prison population. It is worthwhile at this point to mention once again the Report of the Advisory Council, which reflected the *Zeitgeist* of the period. In line with the general approach the Council listed, those who should be removed from the domain of prison as the following: fine defaulters, chronic alcoholics, women convicted of child neglect, husbands who had defaulted on a maintenance order, and offenders of petty forms of larceny or assault.[43] Notably, the Advisory Council argued, in dealing with them, there was no need to extend the available non-custodial penalties.[44] What should be done was to improve the practice of existing sanctions, rather than import such sanctions as the suspended sentence

---

[36]McWilliams, B. (1981) The Probation Officer at Court: From Friend to Acquaintance, *Howard Journal of Criminal Justice*, vol. 20, pp. 97–106, Cavadino *et al.* (2000), *op. cit.*, p. 102.

[37]Bottoms, A., E. (1980b) An Introduction to 'the Coming Crisis' in Bottoms, A., E. and Preston, R., H. (eds.) *The Coming Penal Crisis: A Criminological and Theological Exploration*, Scottish Academic Press, Edinburgh, pp. 1–24, pp. 1–2, see also Jarvis, *op. cit.*, pp. 59–60.

[38]Rutherford (1986), *op. cit.*, p. 152.

[39]Fox, *op. cit.*, pp. 65–66.

[40]Mair (1991) *op. cit.*, pp. 41–51.

[41]Webber, *op. cit.*, p. 151.

[42]See for example also the White Paper, Home Office (1959) *Penal Practice in a Changing Society: Aspects of Future Development (England and Wales)*, HMSO, London.

[43]Alternatives to Short Term Imprisonment: Report of the Advisory Council on the Treatment of Offenders, HMSO, London, 1957 (reprinted in 1968).

[44]In fact, as early as in the White Paper 'Penal Practice in a Changing Society' "a fundamental re-examination of penal method' was deemed necessary for the prevention of crime.

from continental jurisdictions. For almost a decade, this opinion also reflected the official view and hence no extension of the repertoire of sanctions took place.

3.2 The Extension of Non-custodial Sanctions

In the 1960s, the widely shared belief that traditional measures provided sufficient alternatives to imprisonment began to change.[45] A white paper entitled *The War against Crime in England and Wales* was indicative of this shift, when it demanded a fundamental review of the penal system in order to address such questions as whether new sentences were advisable, the extent to which the existing sentences were effective, and how they might be developed.[46] The emerging scepticism may be explained, from a macro perspective, against the background of the questioning of the assumptions about a welfare state, more specifically, of the role of the state in various spheres of public policy and the administration of public expenditure.[47] Penal justice, one of the main areas of public policy, was much less susceptible to changes. In relation to juvenile justice, there were even significantly distinct trends at the time in question, though short-lived, as will be seen below. Still, however, it is possible to observe that the perceptions of the post-war penal welfare period underwent a gradual transformation. It was in this period that the Home Office most authoritatively announced that "rising standards in material prosperity, education and social welfare have brought no decrease in the high rate of crime".[48]

This is not the place to assess the extent to which criticism towards the penal welfare approach in the case of the English experience was justifiable, but a crude reading of the crime and prison figures gave ample evidence to those who argued that penal welfarism 'malfunctioned'. As Fig. 3.1 shows, the number of indictable offences grew steadily. In 1950 the number of indictable offences was 461,435,

[45]Hood, R. (1974) Criminology and Penal Change: A Case Study of the Nature and Impact of Some Recent Advice to Governments in Hood (ed.) *Crime, Criminology and Public Policy*, pp. 375–417, Young, W. (1979) *Community Service Orders: the Development and Use of a new Penal Measure*, Heinemann, London, pp. 6–8, Garland, D. and Young, P. (1983) 'Towards a Social Analysis of Penality' in Garland, D. and Young, P. (eds.) *The Power to Punish. Contemporary Penality and Social Analysis*, Heinemann, London, Bailey, *op. cit.*, Vass, *op. cit.*, pp. 8–10, Bottoms, A. and Stevenson, S. (1994) 'What Went Wrong? Criminal Justice Policy in England and Wales 1945–1970' in Downes, D. (ed.) *Unravelling Criminal Justice*, Macmillan, Basingstoke, pp. 1–45, Downes, D. and Hansen. K. (2007) 'Welfare and Punishment in Comparative Perspective' in Armstrong, S. and McAra, L. (eds.) *Perspectives on Punishment: The Contours of Control*, Oxford University Press, Oxford.

[46]Home Office (1964) The War Against Crime in England and Wales 1959–1964, HMSO, London, particularly para. 54, Mair, G. and Canton. R. (2007) Sentencing Community Penalties and the Role of Probation Service in Gelsthorpe, L. and Morgan, R. (eds.) *Handbook of Probation*, Willan, Cullompton, pp. 248–291, p. 251.

[47]Vass, *op. cit.*, p. 9–10. For a detailed analysis see, Hale, C. (1989) Economy, Imprisonment and Punishment, Contemporary Crises, vol. 13, pp. 327–349.

[48]Home Office (1959) para. 1. See Bottoms and Taylor, *op. cit.*, p. 220.

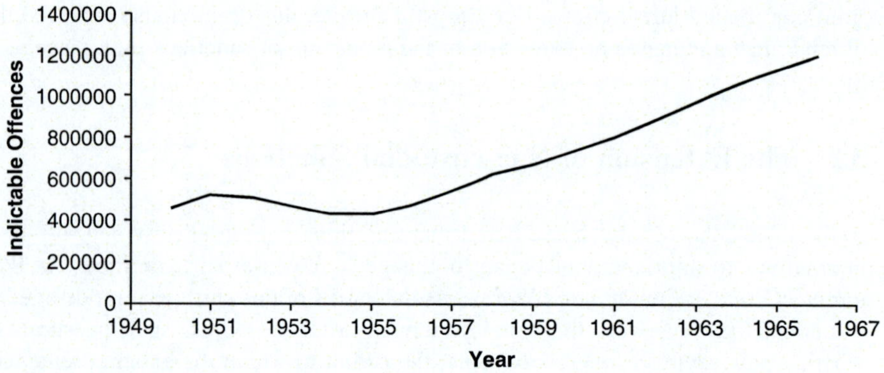

Fig. 3.1 Indictable offences known to the police and cleared up 1950–1966[49]

whereby in 1966 this figure was 1,199,859.[50] During this time, indictable offences recorded by the police per 100,000 population grew from 1,094 in 1950 to 2,732 in 1966.[51]

Furthermore, by 1966 the number of offenders found guilty of indictable offences at all courts was 201,458 – twice the level of 1950, which was 116,021.[52] The increase in violent crime was particularly noteworthy. The number of crimes of violence against persons increased from 3,839 to 16,036.[53] Again, by the mid 1960s the prison population had reached a total of three times its pre-war level and the absolute numbers of receptions under sentence into penal establishments rose from 32,865 in 1948 to 49,258 in 1968.[54]

The corollary of mounting crime, first and foremost, was a greater concern for the phenomenon of crime. Until then, criminal justice policy, as was widely recognised, was entrusted to experts from governmental circles and the lobbying function of professional associations, penal reform bodies and trade unions.[55] The 1960s witnessed the move of crime and justice issues to political discourse.[56] In this decade the 'political' differences in dealing with the soaring crime rates and the treatment of offenders became more apparent than ever before. While, as observed

[49] Home Office (1968) *Criminal Statistics, England and Wales 1967*, p.x.

[50] Home Office (1967) *Criminal Statistics England and Wales 1966*, Home Office, London, p.x.

[51] Home Office (1979) *Criminal Statistics England and Wales 1978*, p. 40.

[52] Home Office (1967) *Criminal Statistics, England and Wales 1966*, p. xii.

[53] *Ibid.*, see also Walker, N., D. (1965) *Crime and Punishment in Britain*, Edinburgh University Press, pp. 18–22.

[54] Young (1978), *op. cit.*, p. 6, Brownlee, *op. cit.*, p. 8.

[55] Bottoms and Stevenson, *op. cit.*, p. 6, Rutherford (1996) Principled Pragmatism in Rutherford, A. (ed.) *Transforming Criminal Policy*, pp. 85–123, p. 85.

[56] Downes, D. and Morgan, R. (1997) Dumping the 'Hostages to Fortune'? The Politics of Law and Order in Post-War Britain in Maguire, M., Morgan, R. and Reiner, R. (eds.) *the Oxford Handbook of Criminology*, 2nd edition, Clarendon Press, Oxford, pp. 87–134.

by Downes and Morgan, such demands as 'harsher penalties' and 'the priority given to victims interests' became a pre-eminent part of the vision of the Conservative Party. The Labour Party, too, gradually declared its position on more crime and law enforcement matters.[57] Hence at some point, such issues increasingly became one of the key topics of election campaigns.[58]

The period under examination was marked also by a powerful entry of the problem and concept of 'prison overcrowding' into the official discourse.[59] For much of the twentieth century and until then, placing more than one prisoner in a cell designed for one person was "virtually unknown",[60] as prisons were never full at capacity. In 1950, the number of inmates sharing cells, however, went up to 2,500 prisoners, accounting for 12% of the prison population. At the end of 1967, the population of the general local prisons (usually occupied by short-term prisoners) exceeded their capacity by about 40%.[61] The potential effects of such an excess in numbers was enunciated in the Home Office documents as early as this period. In these documents, prison overcrowding was viewed as a potential cause for insecure prisons[62] and a hindrance making it difficult for the essential custodial and rehabilitative task to be carried out by the prison service.[63] Another development, though less visible, was the gradual evaporation of the belief in the rehabilitative ability of the prison.[64] A qualification must be made in this regard. Despite the provision in Prison Rule 1 making rehabilitation the primary objective of the prison system[65] and its frequent official pronouncement, it would be misleading to overstate the significance attached to the treatment orientation in the enforcement of imprisonment, certainly not anything comparable with the United States.[66] Unlike the United

---

[57]*Ibid.*

[58]*Ibid.*, p. 189, see also Raynor and Vanstone (2004), *op. cit.*, pp. 69–71.

[59]Home Office (1965) The Adult Offender, HMSO, Cmnd. 2852, para. 28, Home Office (1969) *People in Prison (England and Wales)*, HMSO, Cmnd 4214, Hawkins, K. (1975) Alternatives to Imprisonment in McConville, S. (ed.) *The Use of Imprisonment:Essays in the Changing State of English Penal Policy*, Routledge & Paul, London, pp. 66–87, pp. 70–72, Cylotte, M. (1989) *The Crisis of Prison Overcrowding*, Social Work Monographs, Norwich, p. 3. (House of Commons Estimates Committee), Mair and Canton, *op. cit.*, p. 251, Soothill, K. (2007) Prison Histories and Competing Audiences 1776–1966 in Jewkes, Y. (ed.) *Handbook of Prisons*, Willan, Cullompton, pp. 27–48, pp. 44–45.

[60]Rutherford (1984), *op. cit.*, p. 53.

[61]Hawkins, *op. cit.*, p. 73, Sparks, R. (1971) The Use of Suspended Sentences, *Criminal Law Review*, pp. 384–401, p. 384.

[62]Home Office (1969), *op. cit.*, p. 239, Hawkins, *op. cit.*, p. 70, Newburn (2003), *op. cit.*, p. 18.

[63]Hawkins, *op. cit.*, pp. 69–70.

[64]Young, *op. cit.*, pp. 4–8, Worrall and Hoy, *op. cit.*, pp. 21–23.

[65]The primary objective of the prison system is to "encourage and assist (prisoners) to lead a good and useful life".

[66]Bottoms, A., E. and Taylor, M., H. (1980) Retrospect and Prospect in Bottoms and Preston, *op. cit.*, pp. 214–230, p. 214–222, Ryan, M. (1983) *The Politics of Penal Reform*, Longman, London, pp. 42–45, Nellis, M. (2001) Community Penalties in Historical Perspective in Bottoms *et al.* (2001), *op. cit.*, p. 18, Crow, *op. cit.*, pp. 25–26.

States, indeterminate sentences for treatment purposes in England[67] were available at the time solely in the context of the juvenile law: borstal training and preventive detention (two different forms of juvenile custody, which contained discretionary release and a period of supervision on licence, i.e. supervision after release).[68] However, the results of the declining in faith in the rehabilitative ideal in the United States in the long term had more severe consequences in England than in many other European countries. In fact, even before Martinson's seminal 'nothing works' essay, in 1970, the highly influential Report of the Advisory Council on the Penal System 'Non-Custodial and Semi-Custodial Penalties', for example, regarded imprisonment as "inappropriate and harmful for many offenders for whom it is used".[69]

Consequently, in conjunction with other factors which have been outlined above, the gradual decline in rehabilitation in England from the end of the 1960s towards the 1980s had immediate important implications for non-custodial sanctions. Recognising the somewhat exceptional position of juvenile justice, two trends in this era may be distinguished in this respect. The first was the adoption of new non-custodial sentences such as the suspended sentence, community service, compensation orders, and, with their unique characteristics, parole and the deferment of sentence.[70] A second 'trend' was the explicit conceptualisation and reconceptualisation of non-custodial sanctions as alternatives to custody. This pattern was most clearly epitomised by the shift in the mission of the probation order. Until then the probation order was regarded primarily as a measure of rehabilitation, a model of treatment, but at this time, its potential in terms of reducing custody acquired significant weight in policy documents and in academic writing alike.[71] Probation

---

[67]Walker noted that "since the effect of a 'life' sentence is that the offender is released when the Home Secretary thinks fit; and since the Home Secretary does not usually give him more than one year's notice of the date of his release, the life sentence is in practice an indeterminate sentence". So too was according to him, the sentence of detention during Her Majesty's Pleasure imposable for offenders under the age of 18 who are convicted of murder. Walker (1965), *op. cit.*, p. 151.

[68]Borstal detention introduced by the Prevention of Crime Act of 1908. It could be imposed between six months (for male offenders and three months for females) and three years, which were to be followed by a period of supervision. Preventive detention was adopted for serious habitual offenders.

[69]In the late 1970s pessimism about the effectiveness of rehabilitative treatment reached its peak. A quotation from the Interim Report of the Advisory Council on the Penal System epitomises the shift in the perceptions clearly:

"A steadily accumulating volume of research has shown that, if reconviction rates are used to measure the success of the failure of sentencing policy, there is virtually nothing to choose between different lengths of custodial sentence, different types of institutional regime and even between custodial and non-custodial treatment..." p. 3 of Home Office (1977) *The Length of Prison Sentences (Interim Report of the Advisory Council on the Penal System)*, HMSO, London, See also, Brody, S., R. (1976) The Effectiveness of Sentencing, Home Office Research Study no 35, HMSO, London.

[70]Home Office 1970, para. 8, for a discussion of alternatives to imprisonment in the early 1970s, see Hawkins, *op. cit.*, pp. 66–87.

[71]See e.g., Raynor and Vanstone, *op. cit.*, p. 55, May, T. (1991) Under Siege: Probation in a Changing Environment in Reiner, R. and Cross, M. (eds.) *Beyond Law and Order: Criminal Justice Policy and Politics into the 1990s*, Macmillan, Basingstoke.

began to be viewed as a penalty "aiming to increase its market share and reduce imprisonment, rather than a 'treatment' aiming to change people".[72] Probation with requirements (probation day centres, see below) as a new sentencing option served in its own right, for example, to realise the prioritised objective of reducing the recourse to imprisonment further.

Moving on to the sentencing scene of juvenile justice, here the scope of non-custodial sanctions such as supervision orders was also consequently extended, and the existing penalties were increasingly identified over time as alternatives to imprisonment. Examples included intensive treatment schemes in relation to supervision orders and the attendance centre order. However, the commonalities of juvenile and adult justice at the period in question in this regard should not be overemphasised. The supervision order, for example, was introduced by the Children and Young Persons Act 1969, which has been seen as the apogee of the welfare philosophy in England in relation to juveniles.[73] In line with the overall philosophy of the Act, behind the supervision order there was a good deal of faith in its rehabilitative capability and as such reliance upon social work.[74]

At this point, mention must also be made to the emergence of diversion as a 'brand' new idea. Notably, in England and Wales, the notion of diverting certain offenders from the formal criminal justice system emanated from a rigorous debate about the juvenile court. However, the context in which the discussion took place bore little resemblance to the United States. At the centre of discussion in England was the recognition that the English juvenile court was a modified criminal court, with certain special procedural arrangements.[75] It was believed, despite the obligation of the juvenile court to take the welfare of the juvenile into account, both juvenile and adult courts focussed essentially on the offence, rather than the offender. The demand was then for many a welfare-oriented tribunal, which would diagnose the causes of the offending behaviour with the help of social workers and accordingly take the necessary steps to solve such problems of the juvenile. It was this "de-criminalised"[76] version of the juvenile court embodied in the Children and Young Persons Act of 1969 which paved the way for the English version of diversion. Indeed, by the establishment of juvenile liaison panels in

---

[72]Mair (2007), *op. cit.*, p. 1069.

[73]Farrington, D. (1984) England and Wales in Klein, M., W. (ed.) *Western Systems of Juvenile Justice*, p. 71, Muncie, J. (2004) *Youth and Crime: A Critical Introduction*, 2nd edition, Sage, London, pp. 254–255, Morgan and Newburn (2007), *op. cit.*, p. 293.

[74]Pickford, J. (2000) A New Youth Justice for A New Century in Pickford, J. (ed.) *Youth Justice, Theory and Practice*, Cavendish, London, p. xxx, Crow, *op. cit.*, p. 10.

[75]Morris, A. and McIsaac, M. (1978) *Juvenile Justice*, Heinemann, London, pp. 1–31, Morris *et al.* (1980), *op. cit.*, pp. 3–15, Giller, H. (1999) From Centre Stage to Spear Carrier: The Repositioning of the English Juvenile Court, *European Journal on Crime Policy and Research*, vol. 7, no. 3, pp. 395–403, p. 395, Crawford, A. and Newburn, T. (2003) *Youth Offending and Restorative Justice: Implementing Reform in Youth Justice*, Willan, Cullompton, p. 7.

[76]Bottoms, A. E. (1974) On the Decriminalisation of the English Juvenile Court in Hood, R. (ed.) Crime, Criminology and Public Policy, London, Heinemann reproduced in Muncie *et al.* (2002) pp. 257–302.

which the police, in consultation with social services, decide whether or not to prosecute apprehended juveniles (for the 14 to 17 age group), this Act was the first piece of legislation which endorsed a policy of diversion.[77] The Act envisaged the juvenile court as "a last resort of referral",[78] to which only those cases were to be referred, where a voluntary and informal agreement could not be reached between social workers, the juvenile and her/his parents.

The ascendancy of the logic of welfare in juvenile justice was affected dramatically by the above-identified decline of the 'penal welfare' approach and concomitant factors. Given this state of affairs, it was not surprising that the welfare provisions of the 1969 Act were highly vulnerable. Since the 1969 Act was only partially implemented,[79] the model that it envisioned with respect to the pre-court stage, for example, was never fully realised. Nevertheless, even though the 1969 Act was partially implemented, the treatment and training of juveniles, at the very least discursively remained to provide vigorous justification for both custodial and non-custodial interventions until the new era beginning in the 1980s.

Noting the peculiar position of juvenile justice in this respect, the new alternatives to prison at this period can now be addressed. This discussion does not contain the compensation order introduced by the Criminal Justice Act 1972[80] as an ancillary order, where injury, loss or damage occurred as a result of the offence.[81] It may be combined with a custodial sentence or any other non-custodial sentence, thus the compensation order in its own cannot theoretically be an alternative to imprisonment. In view of this fact, what effect the introduction of compensation orders has had, if any, on the use of custodial sentences has remained largely unidentified.[82]

---

[77]Farrington, D., P. and Bennett, T. (1981) Police Cautioning of Juveniles in London, *British Journal of Criminology*, vol. 21, no 2, pp. 123–135, p. 123, Pratt, J. (1986) Diversion from the Juvenile Court A History of Inflation and a Critique of Progress, *British Journal of Criminology*, vol. 26, no. 3, pp. 212–233, p. 222–223, Muncie, J. (1999) *Youth and Crime: A Critical Introduction*, Sage, London, p. 268, Davies, M., Croall, H. and Tyrer, J. (2005) *Criminal Justice*, 3rd edition, Pearson Longman, Harlow, p. 218, Gelsthorpe, L. and Padfield, N. (2003) Youth Justice: Discretion in Pre-Court Decision-Making in Gelsthorpe, L. and Padfield, N. (eds.) *Exercising Discretion: Decision-Making in the Criminal Justice System and Beyond*, Cullompton, Willan, pp. 29–49, p. 30.

[78]Gelsthorpe and Morris (1994), *op. cit.*, pp. 949–993, p. 957.

[79]Gelsthorpe and Morris (2002) Restorative Justice, the Last Vestiges of Welfare in Muncie *et al.* (2002) pp. 238–254, pp. 239, Muncie (2004) *op. cit.*, p. 254. This was primarily due to a complex political and ideological battle on administering juvenile justice between the two major parties in England: the Labour Party and Conservative Party, see Newburn (2002), *op. cit.*, p. 551.

[80]For the origin of the compensation order, see Chapter 2.

[81]Before the enactment of the compensation order by the Criminal Justice Act 1972, there exist provisions concerning compensation in a number of statutes for example, the Larceny Act 1861, Malicious Damage Act, Gardens and Hothouses Act 1826. For a brief history in this context, see e.g. Softley, P. (1978) Compensation Orders in Magistrates' Courts, HMSO, London, pp. 1–5.

[82]Rutherford (1986), *op. cit.*, p. 157.

3.2.1 *Suspended Sentence*

The suspended sentence was a clear example of a measure designed to avoid imprisonment. It was hoped that it would not merely reduce the number of short-term prison sentences, but make it possible for courts to reserve probation for offenders in need of that kind of treatment.[83] In fact, as mentioned above, the introduction of the suspended sentence was discussed already throughout 1950s, but rejected on the ground that nothing could be gained to add the suspended sentence alongside probation.[84] Intriguingly, however, a decade later, pressures within the English penal system made an adoption of a distinct version of the suspended sentence possible.

The Criminal Justice Act 1967[85] introduced two types of suspended sentences: discretionary and mandatory suspended sentences. A discretionary suspended sentence was to be considered in cases where a sentence of imprisonment not exceeding 2 years could be held in suspension during a period specified in the order, the operational period, the duration of which ranged from between one to no more than 3 years.[86] Suspension was mandatory in relation to sentences of imprisonment of 6 months, unless:

1. The offence was one of assault, violence, possession of firearms and so forth, or indecency with or to a person under 16,
2. The offender was on probation or conditional discharge when the act was committed, or was being dealt with for breach of one of these orders,
3. The offender had previously been sentenced to imprisonment, borstal, corrective training or a suspended sentence,
4. The court proposed to pass a sentence of imprisonment on the offender for another offence, which the court was not required to suspend.

The suspended sentence was only to take effect if the offender was subsequently convicted of an imprisonable offence committed within the operational period.[87] On such a conviction the (reconvicting) court was obliged to order that the offender serve the full suspended term, unless, after consideration of all circumstances including the facts of the subsequent offence, the court took the view that "it would be unjust to do so".[88] Intriguingly, in the latter case, the court might substitute a lesser length, make it longer or, alternatively, make no order.

Facing vociferous criticism of the judiciary on the ground that it unduly confined their discretion, the Criminal Justice Act 1972 abolished the mandatory suspended

[83]Radzinowicz in Ancel (1971), *op. cit.*, p. vi, foreword.

[84]See above.

[85]The Criminal Justice Act 1967, Sections 39–42.

[86]With the Criminal Justice Act 1972, the maximum 'operational' period for the suspended sentence was reduced from three years to two years.

[87]The Criminal Justice Act 1967, Section 39(1).

[88]*Ibid.*, Section 40(1).

sentence.[89] Meanwhile, the 1972 Act introduced the suspended sentence supervision order available to the Crown Court. The related provision read that suspended sentences exceeding 6 months for a single offence could have an additional supervision requirement attached, which unlike probation supervision consisted of merely being informed of the whereabouts of the offender.[90]

Introduced with the hope of reducing the prison population, the practice of the suspended sentence appeared to have been far from achieving such an aim. Research evidence suggested that courts imposed the suspended sentence not only in place of imprisonment, but also where they would previously have imposed a fine or probation. A research study by Home Office for example found that

> courts have used the suspended sentence both to replace immediate imprisonment and as a sentence in its own right... It has been estimated that only somewhere between 40 and 50% (of people given suspended sentences passed up to 1970) would, but for the new provisions, have been sentences to imprisonment for the original offence.[91]

By analysing sentencing trends in the years 1967–1969, in an early essay, Sparks emphasised that the decline in the proportionate use of immediate imprisonment after the introduction of the suspended sentence (about 7%) in 2 years was also accompanied with a decline in the use of the fine and probation orders at both higher courts (assizes and quarter sessions) and magistrates' courts.[92] Intriguingly, Sparks estimated that a quarter of all those given suspended sentences in 1969 would have been fined before the 1967 Act came into force, and 15% put on probation. Sparks' conclusion, too, was that "instead of being used as an alternative to imprisonment a suspended sentence was often used for offenders who would not have been sent to prison before the 1967 Act".[93]

Furthermore, Bottoms identified two patterns in his various studies concerning suspended sentences. According to Bottoms, courts tended to impose suspended sentences containing longer terms of imprisonment than what they might ordinarily have imposed for a sentence of immediate imprisonment, particularly as far as magistrates' courts were concerned.[94] Bottoms argued that this was because courts endeavoured to 'balance' the perceived leniency of the suspended sentence with the imposition of a longer sentence. A second problematic issue according to Bottoms, was the sentencers' very conception of the suspended sentence. Bottoms argued that courts were keen to use suspended sentences, where they felt that the threat of

---

[89]Bottoms (1980a), *op. cit.*, pp. 8–10.

[90]Criminal Justice Act 1972, Section 12(3).

[91]Oatham, E. and Simon, F. (1972) Are Suspended Sentences Working, *New Society,* no. 3 (August), pp. 233–235, p. 233.

[92]Sparks, *op. cit.*, p. 387.

[93]*Ibid.*

[94]Bottoms, A., E. (1981) The Suspended Sentence in England 1967–78, *British Journal of Criminology*, vol. 21, no 1, pp. 1–26, p. 8, see also Bottoms, A., E.(1980) *The Suspended Sentence After Ten Years: a Review and Reassessment*, University of Leeds, Centre for Social Work and Applied Social Sciences, pp. 2–4.

imprisonment would function effectively as a special preventive disposal. In this sense, the consideration whether or not an individual offence warranted imprisonment in the first place was not as important as the potential deterrent effect of the suspended sentence.

Attempts were made to overcome such documented 'misconception' amongst sentencers as to the exact role of the suspended sentence. Chief among was the guidance provided in *O'Keefe* by the Court of Appeal.[95] In this case, the Court emphasised that before meting out a suspended sentence courts should first consider whether any non-custodial sentencing options appropriate. After the elimination of such options as absolute discharge, conditional discharge, probation order and fines, they ought to consider whether imprisonment is necessary in a given case. Only after ascertaining that imprisonment is necessary and after the fixation of the imprisonment term should courts consider whether to impose an immediate or suspended custodial sentence.

The *O'Keefe* guidance was given a legislative base in the Criminal Justice Act 1972 and subsequently consolidated in the Powers of Criminal Courts Act 1973. The subsequent amendment of legislation enacted the principle that an offender shall not be dealt with by means of a suspended sentence unless the case appears to the court to be one in which a sentence of imprisonment is warranted. The Criminal Law Act 1977 empowered courts to partially suspend prison sentences not exceeding 2 years with the condition that the first part would actually be served.[96] Nevertheless, all these subsequent modifications and enactments, as will be seen below, did not change the fate of the suspended sentence in England as "Sword of Damocles".[97] It was even argued that the frequent breach of such sentences as suspended sentence may have actually increased the size of the prison population.[98]

3.2.2 Parole

Another major innovation in the 1967 Act for the reduction of the prison population was providing the opportunity for early release on parole licence,[99] which deserves

[95]Bottoms (1981), *op. cit.*, p. 9.

[96]It was not until 1982 that the partially suspended sentence was implemented. The Criminal Justice Act 1991 repealed it. See Bottoms (1980a) *op. cit.*, pp. 14–16.

[97]Bottoms (1979), *op. cit.*, p. 444.

[98]For the suspended sentence e. g. Bottoms (1979), *op. cit.*, pp. 438–439, Home Secretary Roy Jenkins famously concluded in 1970 that "The accumulated evidence is not encouraging. If the main object of the suspended sentence was to reduce the prison population, there are considerable doubts as to whether it has achieved this effect. It may have even increased the size of the prison population". cited in Bottoms (1979), *op. cit.*, p. 438.

[99]Hawkins, *op. cit.*, pp. 74–76, Nuttall, C., P. with Barnard, E., E., Fowles, A., J., Frost, A., Hammond, W., H., Mayhew, P., Pease, K., Tarling, R. and Weatheritt, M. (1977) *Parole in England and Wales*, Home Office Research Study no 38, HMSO, London, Home Office (1981) *Review of Parole in England and Wales*, HMSO, London, Morgan, N. (1983) The Shaping of

a mention here. In England, the practice of early release began with the 'ticket of leave' in which convicts under a sentence of *transportation* were allowed to work.[100] This was followed by a system of remission, by the Prison Act 1898. Under this system, a prisoner would receive a deduction from her/his sentence on the basis of good behaviour ('industry and good conduct') for all determinate sentences except for a custodial sentence involving 31 days or less. The maximum remission was one-quarter for male prisoners and one-third for female prisoners. This was subsequently changed to one-third for all inmates.[101] Although 'remission' was not designed as an entitlement, rather a measure of prison discipline subject to good behaviour, in practice it was in effect automatically meted out.[102]

Unlike remission, parole was conceived for all purposes as a privilege, which found its official justification with reference to the notion of rehabilitation.[103] A White Paper preceding the 1967 Act, for example, proposed the use of parole in relation to those offenders who had reached "a recognisable peak in their training".[104] The 1967 Act provided that a minimum period of 12 months' imprisonment or one third of the sentence, whichever was longer, needed to have been served before parole could be considered. The release was to be accompanied by a period of supervision. Eligibility of parole was in the first instance to be examined by a local review committee attached to each prison. This committee consisted of the prison governor or her/his deputy and not less than three other persons who were (are) appointed by the Home Secretary. The eligible cases were then to be referred to the Parole Board, established by the respective Act, which consisted of experts including high court judges and the local review committees. Finally, upon the recommendations of the Parole Board, the Home Secretary was to decide on whether or not to grant parole.

The 1967 Criminal Justice Act did not spell out the criteria for parole selection; only some time later (in 1975) were official guidelines stipulating the criteria drawn up. The criteria listed six groups of factors affecting parole decisions: the nature of the offence, criminal history, prison behaviour and response to the treatment, medical treatment, home circumstances and employment prospects, and co-operation with parole supervision.

Parole in England and Wales, *Criminal Law Review*, pp. 137–151, Bottomley, K. (1984) Dilemmas of Parole in a Penal Crisis, *Howard Journal*, vol. 23, no. 1, pp. 24–40 and (1990) Parole in Transition: A Comparative Study of Origins, Developments and Prospects for the 1990s, *Crime and Justice*, vol. 12, pp. 319–374.

[100]Cavadino and Dignan, *op. cit.*, p. 182. For a summary see, Witmer, H., L. (1927) The History, Theory and Results of Parole, *Journal of Criminal Law and Criminology*, vol. 18, no. 1, pp. 47–61.

[101]Since early in the Second World War, Walker (1965), *op. cit.*, p. 154.

[102]Cross, R. (1971) *Punishment, Prison and the Public*, Stevens, London, p. 90.

[103]Home Office (1981), *op. cit.*, pp. 1–3, Bottomley (1990) *op. cit.*, pp. 347–349.

[104]Home Office (1965), *op. cit.*, p. 4.

At the outset, the parole system was applied rather cautiously.[105] Bottomley records that on April 1 1968, only 8.5% of the 4,764 prisoners eligible on that day were recommended for release on licence. In 1972, 30.3% of all eligible cases considered by the local review committees were finally released on parole.[106] In the same year, with the Criminal Justice Act 1972 the Home Secretary was empowered to release prisoners on licence on the anonymous recommendation of the local review committee, without first seeking the advice of the Parole Board.[107] This procedural modification meant in practice an extension of the application field of parole.[108] A more significant growth in terms of paroling rate in fact occurred when the Home Secretary (Roy Jenkins) in 1975 advocated a more liberal approach in granting parole.[109] The extension of the application of parole was accompanied with a marked decline in the prison population from 39,700 in 1971 about 36,000 in 1974.[110] The extent to which parole had an impact upon this decline is still to be researched, but the view that 'parole works' in reducing the prison population prevailed in official circles. Ironically though, parole, as a method of shortening prison sentences for long-term prisoners, did not greatly alleviate prison overcrowding, since prison overcrowding existed largely in local prisons, where short-term prisoners and persons on remand custody were accommodated.[111]

As the desire to reduce the prison population increasingly became the centre piece of the English penal policy at the end of the 1970s, the fact that parole was working fairly well inspired new efforts to extend its use. Most significantly, a review of parole by the Home Office proposed automatic release under supervision for those serving between 6 months and 3 years after serving one-third of their sentence.[112] Such a regulation, it was believed, might be "an invaluable contribution" to the efforts to relieve "the chronic and severe pressures on the prison system".[113] However, due to strong criticism of the judiciary it was dropped by the Home Secretary. This setback was followed by a lowering of the parole threshold in the early 1980s. However, parole and remission remained the 'safety valve' of the prison system, and as will be seen below, from this point onwards the policy of 'back-door' options continued to be on the policy-makers agenda.[114]

---

[105] Bottomley (1990) *op. cit.*, p. 347, Morgan, *op. cit.*, p. 148.

[106] Bottomley (1990) *op. cit.*, p. 348.

[107] The Criminal Justice Act 1972, Section 35.

[108] Home Office (1981), *op. cit.*, p. 6, Bottomley (1984), *op. cit.*, p. 26.

[109] Home Office (1981), *op. cit.*, p. 6, Bottomley (1984), *op. cit.*, p. 26, Bottoms (1987), *op. cit.*, p. 195.

[110] Hawkins, *op. cit.*, p. 76.

[111] Newburn (2003), *op. cit*, p. 22.

[112] Home Office (1981), *op. cit.*

[113] *Ibid.* para. 60.

[114] *Ibid.*, p. 7.

3.2.3 Community Service Order

The community service order was proposed for the first time in the above-mentioned report, 'Non-Custodial and Semi-Custodial Penalties' of the Advisory Council on the Penal System.[115] The report viewed community service as a penalty appealing to different penal philosophies: retribution, reparation and rehabilitation.[116] Significantly and most pertinently here, the respective report raised the question whether to community service as being limited to imprisonable offences.[117] It reflected the view that courts should use community service principally as an alternative to short custodial sentences. However, according to the report, the application of community service should not be confined to the latter category of cases, but might be used in warranted cases involving a non-imprisonable offence (e.g. non-imprisonable traffic offences) or in lieu of a fine or probation.[118]

Following the recommendation of the Advisory Council, the Criminal Justice Act 1972 conceived community service as applicable for offences punishable by imprisonment[119] for offenders aged 17 and over.[120] Under this Act, community service was unpaid work between 40 and 240 h, which was to be consented to by the offender. The breach of community service order, i.e. a failure to attend work or failure to work as instructed, could lead to the committal of the offender to the court. In the latter case, the court could impose a fine, and allow the offender to continue, or sentence her/him for the offence for which the community sentence had been imposed.

In absence of any further explicit criteria, the phrase 'imprisonable offence' led to discussions about whether community service was an alternative to a prison sentence like the suspended sentence, the application of which required the real likelihood of imprisonment in a given case, or whether it was another kind of non-custodial sanction, which could also serve as an alternative to a fine or probation.[121]

---

[115]The Advisory Council on the Penal System (1970) *Non-Custodial and Semi-Custodial Penalties*, Home Office, London, paras, 33–34. For a detailed analysis on the subject see, Young, W. (1979) *op. cit.*, Chapter 3.

[116]The Advisory Council on the Penal System, *op. cit.*, para.37.

[117]*Ibid.*

[118]*Ibid.*

[119]Section 1(1) of the Murder (Abolition of Death Penalty) Act 1965 provides that "a person convicted of murder shall be sentenced to imprisonment for life". In England, life imprisonment since the abolition of the death penalty is the mandatory sentence for murder.

[120]The Criminal Justice Act 1982 extended community service to 16-year-olds, with the upper limit reduced to 120 hours for this age group.

[121]Pease, K. (1975) *Community Service Orders*, Home Office Research Study no 29, HMSO, London, Pease, K. (1980) Community Service and Prison: Are They Alternatives?, in Pease, K. and McWilliams, W. (eds.) *Community Service by Order*, Scottish Academic Press, Edinburgh, Young, W. (1979) *op. cit.*, see also Pease, K. (1985) Community Service Orders in Tonry, M. and Morris, N. (eds.) *Crime and Justice*, vol. 6, University of Chicago Press, Chicago. Vass, *op. cit.*,

The wording of 'offences punishable by imprisonment', thus, from the very beginning, proved to be even notionally far from securing a uniform understanding of the place of the community sentence in what has been termed as a sentencing 'tariff'. The confusion was particularly intensified with the press reports and the pronouncements of the Home Office officials, which with great enthusiasm viewed the community sentence as an alternative to a short custodial sentence.[122]

Surrounded by this ambiguity, the use of community service initially displayed a significant disparity in the experimental schemes. A survey of the perceptions of the probation officers (who were to provide sentence recommendations to the court) in the experimental areas revealed that in some of these areas, community service was seen exclusively as an alternative to custody, whereas in others it had a wider use.[123] The ambiguity was even greater after the gradual national implementation of community service throughout the country in 1973.[124] From their analysis of available data concerning primarily the pre-sentence reports and cases involving a breach of the community service order, Pease and Williams estimated that only about half of community service orders functioned as an alternative to an immediate custodial sentence.[125] Young, studying the sentencing practices of courts in a certain area regarding community sentence orders in relation to age, the offence in question, criminal record and the court's approach, drew the conclusion that:

> In each court the sentence was imposed upon offenders who had committed crimes of widely differing degrees of seriousness... While some were similar to those sentenced to imprisonment, others were at a stage where such a sentence would have been *unlikely*.[126] (Emphasis added.)

In view of this state of affairs, the Court of Appeal, in some of its rulings, aimed to eradicate the difference between the original conception of community sentences as an alternative to a short custodial sentence and its practice as a mere non-custodial sentence.[127] The Court encouraged the use of this measure in cases which might otherwise have been dealt with by imprisonment. Nevertheless, even the guidance of the Court of Appeal did not alter the position of community service in the eyes of the sentencers, and it remained by and large "an alternative disposal, yet not an alternative to custody".[128]

---

p. 83, Willis, A. (1977) Community Service as an Alternative to Imprisonment, *Probation Journal*, 24, 120–122, Wayne, L. (1993) The History of Change in Whitfield, D. and Scott, D. (eds.) *Paying Back Twenty Years of Community Service*, Waterside Press, Winchester, pp. 18–29, Oldfield, M. (1993) Assessing the Impact of Community Service – Lost Opportunities and the Politics of Punishment in Whitfield, D. and Scott, D. (eds.) *Paying Back Twenty Years of Community Service*, Waterside Press, Winchester, pp. 30–50.

[122] Pease and Williams, *op. cit.*, pp. 35–37.

[123] *Ibid.*, pp. 31–36.

[124] Young, W. (1979), *op. cit.*, p. 297.

[125] Pease and Williams, *op. cit.*, p. 35.

[126] Young, W. (1979) *op. cit.*, p. 135.

[127] Pease (1985), *op. cit.*, pp. 66–67.

[128] Oldfield, *op. cit.*, p. 46.

3.2.4 Probation with Day (Training) Centre Requirement

The Criminal Justice Act 1972 empowered courts to require an offender to attend a 'day training centre' as a condition of the probation order. The intention behind such a provision was initially to create a suitable alternative measure to custody for petty and 'socially inadequate offenders'.[129] This special type of probation supervision, as opposed to the 'ordinary' version, involved training in social and personal skills on a daily basis for 60 working days in facilities known as 'probation day training centres'. Claiming to be oriented towards the rehabilitation and reintegration of offenders into society in a rapidly changing climate, the new disposal had from the very beginning a less advantageous position compared with its other non-custodial counterparts.

Four experimental day training centres were set up (in Liverpool, London, Sheffield and Pontypridd). From their inception, the high operational costs of the probation day centres constituted a great challenge for criminal justice policy-making.[130] Courts were not particularly keen to make use of the new provision. Hence, the experiment with probation day centres progressed with a low rate of referrals from courts.[131] Outside the experimental scheme, in some probation areas, day training centres were established, which exhibited notably significant differences in terms of their ultimate aims and the ways in which they dealt with their offending clients. Perhaps due to the distinct aims which pervaded in the *raison d'être* of day centres, their practice also displayed a variety of different forms in terms of services, operation styles and organisation structures. Research demonstrated that where probation day centres facilitated a relatively neutral approach towards offenders, the requirement was used in accordance with the original intention of the legislature, namely as an alternative to prison.[132] Where rehabilitative considerations were prioritised, it was observed that the day centre requirement was imposed on those who would have probably not received custodial sentences otherwise but who were deemed to be in need of 'care and support.'[133] Academic critics soon levelled criticism at the 'net-widening' effects of day centres.

While such practices of probation day centres, coupled with ostensibly intrusive practice of probation day centres (sometimes called a 'day prison centre')[134] were

[129]Later, it was amended by the Powers of Criminal Courts Act 1973. Vass, A. and Weston, A. (1990) Probation Day Centres As An Alternative to Custody: A Trojan Horse Examined, *British Journal of Criminology*, vol. 30, no 2, pp. 189–206, Brownlee, *op. cit.*, p. 12.

[130]See Vass and Weston, *op. cit.*

[131]*Ibid.*

[132]Fairhead, S. (1981) *Day Centres and Probation*, Home Office Research Unit Paper No. 4, Home Office, London, p. 25.

[133]*Ibid.*

[134]Vass and Weston, *op. cit.*, Vanstone describes day training centres as "expurgated form of prison.", Vanstone, M. (1993) A "Missed Opportunity" Reassessed: the Influence of the Day Centre Experiment on the Criminal Justice System and Probation, *British Journal of Social Work*, vol. 23, pp. 213–229, p. 216.

under constant criticism, this did not prevent courts from adding further conditions to probation orders in due course. It was also subject to judicial objections, on the grounds that it is not legally admissible to impose further requirements other than what the legislation allows such as abstention from alcohol under the 1907 Act and conditions of residence under the Criminal Justice Administration Act 1914. The Criminal Justice Act 1982 made provisions for probation with conditions. The Act enacted both positive conditions – e.g. presenting oneself to a specified person(s) at a specified place(s), attending a day centre, or performing specified activities and negative conditions – e.g. refraining from certain activities-.[135] The stipulation of positive and negative conditions by the 1982 Act appears to have been unable to dismiss the confusion, and did little to clarify the position of probation day centres in the sentencing tariff. This remained largely the case until the restructuring of the probation order by the Criminal Justice Act 1991, as will be seen below.

3.2.5 Supervision Order

Introduced by the 1969 Children and Young Persons Act, the supervision order was underpinned by the assumption that personal and social problems and educational deficiencies of the juvenile are key factors in the commission of an offence, and accordingly addressing such issues to prevent offending and/or re-offending of juveniles.[136] By its design, the supervision order in this statute was hence conceived not merely as a punitive disposal for those who offended, but also a preventive measure for those who were thought to be "at the risk of offending". In essence, the supervision order was by and large a form of probation for younger offenders.[137] The difference was that the supervision order was generally administered by social workers employed by *local authorities* and only exceptionally by the *probation service*. Again, unlike probation, the supervision order did not require the consent of the person subject to the order.

As will be seen below, what proved to be more significant in due course was a requirement enabling the supervisor to direct the supervised person to participate in activities for a period of up to 90 days.[138] This requirement has come to be known as 'intermediate treatment'. The term 'intermediate treatment' was not used by the Children and Young Persons Act 1969. It was used for the first time in a white paper called *Children in Trouble* which preceded the 1969 Act.[139] The

[135]The Criminal Justice Act 1982 Schedules X I 4A and 4B.

[136]Bottoms, A., Brown, P., McWilliams, B., McWilliams, W., Nellis, M. with Pratt, J. (1990) *Intermediate Treatment and Juvenile Justice: Key Findings and Implications from a National Survey of Intermediate Treatment Policy and Practice*, HMSO, London, pp. 9–10.

[137]*Ibid.*

[138]Section 12(2) of the Children and Young Persons Act 1969.

[139]Home Office (1968) *Children in Trouble*, Cmdn. 3601, HMSO, London, para. 25–29.

white paper used the term ‘intermediate treatment’ for those activities which allow “the child to remain in *his own home*”, hence without removal from home and placement of care institutions, but which “bring [the child] also into contact with a *different environment*”.[140] With this innovative disposal, it was envisaged that intermediate treatment facilities would eventually replace juvenile custodial institutions and attendance centres.[141] In the first circular on intermediate treatment by the Department of Health and Social Security (hereafter DHSS) in 1969, this rather vaguely defined term was clarified by suggesting that the term could be used

> “narrowly to describe treatment undertaken by a supervised person under the supervisor’s direction or more broadly to describe arrangements for helping juveniles in trouble or at risk of getting into trouble”.[142]

The content of early intermediate treatment programmes accordingly displayed a wide variety of activities and tasks, including recreational, educational and socially constructive activities within a non-custodial setting.

The scope of the provision governing intermediate treatment and supervision orders was generally broad, and so was initially the practice of intermediate treatment schemes.[143] Despite such huge claims as replacing detention and attendance centres, in the first decade intermediate treatment was developed mainly for low-risk offenders or alternatively for non-offenders who were deemed to be at risk. In various schemes, the category of juveniles ‘at risk’ was furthermore ambiguously defined to include juveniles who were having ‘problems with school e.g. chronic truancy or with families’, those who were deemed to be ‘in need of creative leisure pastimes’ and those ‘having poor relationships with adults and peers’ and/or having a ‘poor self image’.[144] A report from DHSS in 1977 revealed that out of 28 existing schemes, only three exclusively dealt with offenders, and the rest dealt with a mixture of juvenile offenders and non-offenders.[145]

Consequently, as this brief description of intermediate treatment schemes in the 1970s shows, they concentrated less on those who were really at risk of custody, and focussed more on juveniles who were deemed to be at risk. Hence Muncie may be agreed with when he observes that intermediate treatment schemes were initially “widening the net”, rather than acting as alternatives to custody.[146] However,

---

[140] *Ibid.*, para. 25.

[141] Morris and Giller, *op. cit.*, p. 184, Matthews and Young (2003) *op. cit.*, p. 78, Newburn (2002) *op. cit.*, p. 644.

[142] Cited in Bottoms (1981) *op. cit.*, p. 94.

[143] Paley, J. and Thorpe, D. (1974) *Children: Handle with Care* (A Critical Analysis of the Development of Intermediate Treatment), National Youth Bureau, Leicester.

[144] Thorpe, D. (1982) Intermediate Treatment: Problems of Theory and Practice in Bailey, R. and Lee, P. (eds.) *Theory and Practice in Social Work*, Basil Blackwell, Oxford, pp. 78–97, pp. 84–85.

[145] *Ibid.*

[146] Muncie (2004), *op. cit.*, p. 260, see also Haines and Drakeford, *op. cit.*, p. 40.

significant changes occurred in the 1980s which altered the scope and content of intermediate treatment schemes, and consequently their position as alternatives to custody, which will be dealt with later in this chapter.

3.2.6 *Deferment of Sentence*

Deferment of sentence was introduced with the Criminal Justice Act 1972[147] and later re-enacted in the Powers of Criminal Courts Act. Section 1 of the Powers of Criminal Courts Act 1973 gave both the Crown Courts and magistrates' courts the power to defer passing sentence on an offender for a period up to 6 months, where having regard for the nature of the offence and the character and circumstances of the offender, it would be "in the interests of justice" to exercise that power.[148] Thereby, after the period of deferment in passing a sentence, the court was to consider the reparation efforts or any change in the circumstances of the offender. In order to make use of the power to defer passing a sentence, the consent of the offender was required. In fact, this disposition was by no means unfamiliar to English law. Binding over to come up for judgement when called upon, with the condition of keeping the peace and being of good behaviour, was an established measure of common law, as demonstrated in Chap. 2. Due to the similarity of the deferred sentence to this old power of common law, and in some way, to probation and conditional discharge, from the very beginning there were doubts about the exact nature of deferred sentence, and even whether it is necessary to adopt such a measure. It was argued, for example, that deferment was an alternative to neither custodial nor non-custodial measures; it was simply a postponement of the court's decision, while in another account the deferred sentence was seen as "a halfway between an adjournment and a non-custodial measure".[149]

In the Advisory Council's report in 1970, preceding the enactment of this sentencing option, it was stated that deferment was not primarily an alternative to imprisonment but an additional penal sanction.[150] Originally deferment of sentence in this report was envisaged with some formal obligations which were to be pronounced by the court in written form and given to the defendant. Notwithstanding the recognition that some form of misuse might occur, the right of appeal was regarded as a safeguard. The recommendation of the Council was not adopted, on

[147] Section 22 of the Criminal Justice Act 1972.

[148] Section 1 of the Powers of Criminal Courts Act 1973.

[149] Wasik, M., cited in Jones, S. (1983) Deferment of Sentence, An Appraisal Ten Years On, *British Journal of Criminology*, vol. 23, no 4, pp. 381–393.

[150] The Advisory Council, *op. cit.*, para. 65.

the grounds that it was neither necessary nor desirable. Central to this rejection was the idea that there would be no way to ensure that these obligations were not breached.[151] In practice, the deferred sentence was generally used to allow the convict to pay compensation to repair the damage caused by the crime.[152] It was deemed sufficient to see the defendant's reaction to the conviction, and whether or not s/he would try to undertake a reparative activity, participate in a course or find employment.

Little is known about the extent to which a deferred sentence was imposed in cases where the court would otherwise have probably considered a custodial sentence, as there have been few studies shedding light on the use of this 'measure'. Even in studies dealing with deferment of sentence it was acknowledged that it was hard to assess how far those offenders whose sentences were initially deferred were at risk of a custodial sentence.[153] However, there was some evidence that in some cases deferment of sentence eventually resulted in avoiding the use of a custodial disposal. In a research study, it was found that two-thirds of the "high risk" group for whom a custodial sentence was likely to be given (because it had been recommended in the social inquiry report) did not receive a custodial penalty after deferment.[154] In another research study, it was also found that the deferred sentence was generally used for offenders aged between 17 and 25 who had previous convictions and whose offence for which the sentence was deferred was usually "some kind of dishonest appropriation of property", though generally of a small amount.[155] A related feature of the decisions of deferment of sentence that was highlighted by research was that many of those offenders whose sentences were initially deferred had previously had 'contact' with the probation service.[156] This finding was then interpreted as showing that deferment of sentence was not generally applied to first-time and inexperienced offenders, but rather that repeated offenders were more likely to be subject to deferment of a sentence. Finally, it was found that if the offender did not reoffend during the period of deferment, s/he almost always received a non-custodial sentence.[157] Thus overall, the conclusion drawn from the afore-mentioned research studies was that deferment of sentence affected the use of imprisonment to a certain degree.

---

[151]Jones, *op. cit.*, p. 382.

[152]*Ibid.*, p. 390.

[153]Corden, J. and Nott, D. (1980) The Power to Defer Sentence, *British Journal of Criminology*, vol. 20, no 4, pp. 358–367, p. 366.

[154]*Ibid.*

[155]See Jones, *op. cit.*, p. 384.

[156]Corden and Nott, *op. cit.*, p. 366.

[157]*Ibid.*

3.3 The 'Impact' of Proliferation of Prison Alternatives in the Sentencing Figures

The extension of non-custodial sanctions was the product of endeavours to combat the growing numbers of the prison population. However, as has been demonstrated above, despite such an overarching goal behind the policy of proliferation, from the outset there was controversy about the exact nature of these punishments In each case, courts appear not to have applied the sentencing options in the way in which the legislature intended, and the resulting situation was accordingly highly complex. During this period, as the Fig. 3.2 shows, the use of immediate custodial sentences increased dramatically, standing at 43,000 in 1979.[158] Logically, one reason for this state of affairs was an increase in the total number of offenders sentenced by the court.[159] In 1970 all offenders found guilty in all the courts was 1,674,100. Over the decade this figure increased steadily, and in 1979 it reached 2,211,700.[160]

Another reason that is more relevant for the present discussion was the growth in the proportionate use of imprisonment. In fact, between 1970 and the mid-1970s the use of the sentence of *imprisonment* declined as a proportion of the total number of persons sentenced. However, from this time onwards the proportionate use of

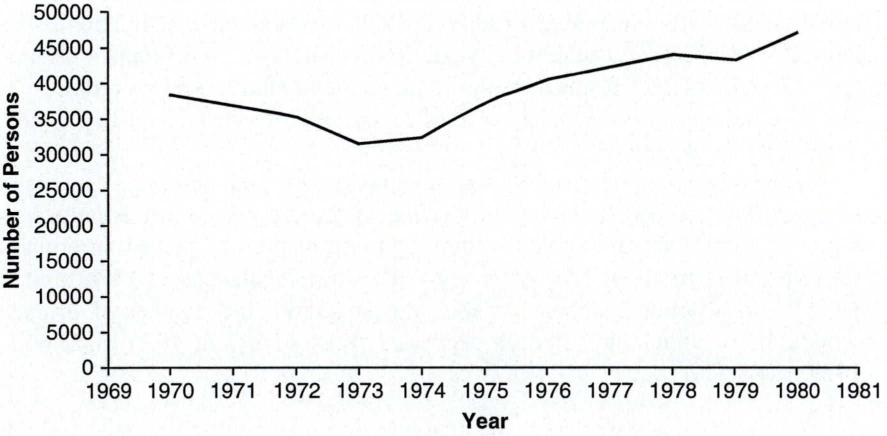

Fig. 3.2 Total number of persons sentenced to immediate imprisonment[161]

[158] Home Office (1970) *Criminal Statistics, England and Wales* 1969, p. xxii and Home Office (1980) *Criminal Statistics, England and Wales 1979*, p. 113.

[159] Home Office (1982) *Criminal Statistics, England and Wales 1981*, p. 138.

[160] Home Office (1981) *Criminal Statistics, England and Wales 1980*, pp. 82–83.

[161] Home Office (1982) *Criminal Statistics, England and Wales 1981*, pp. 162–163 and Home Office (1980) *Criminal Statistics England and Wales 1979*, p. 136.

imprisonment increased.[162] Bottomley and Pease calculated that the use of prison sentences for indictable offenders, for example, increased from 1 in 13 in 1973 to 1 in 11 in 1983.[163]

The aforesaid changes occurred both in relation to indictable and summary offences in magistrates' courts and the Crown Court, and with regard to both male and female offenders. The use of other custodial measures; borstal training (introduced by the Children Act 1908 and was applicable for 16–21-year-olds) and *detention* (introduced by the Criminal Justice Act 1948 in the form of 'short-sharp-shock' confinement) was also on the increase. Between 1969 and 1979 the number of juveniles who received a detention centre order at all courts went up from 6,652 to 11,635. In the same period, the sentence of borstal training rose from 2,943 to 7,770.[164]

What is striking is the fact that in the mid-1970s, all newly introduced measures which were promoted principally as alternatives to custody – suspended sentence, community service, and probation with day requirements – were in operation, and resorting to them was on the increase. The number of persons given suspended sentences, following a decline due to the removal of the mandatory suspended sentence, fell sharply in 1973 to about 26,000 from an average of about 32,000 a year in the period of 1971–1972. Rising each year on average by 5% from 1973 to 197 the number of persons given suspended sentences increased to 34,227 in 1979.[165]

Furthermore, from 1975, after its national implementation, the use of the community service order increased steadily. In 1979, it was given over 15,356 times for indictable offences.[166] In the same year, 7% of male and 2% of female offenders aged 17 and under 21 respectively were given a community service order.[167] The use of community service for males aged 21 and over reached 3% in 1979, and for females its use accounted for 1%.

Another change which was without doubt related to the increasing 'popularity' of a new type of penalties was the decline in the use of the probation order as Fig. 3.3 shows. During the 1970s, the proportion of persons placed on probation steadily fell from about 13% of persons of all ages sentenced in 1970 to 4% in 1979.[168] In absolute numbers, as the graphic shows, the number of offenders sentenced for indictable offences decreased from 44,700 in 1970 to 23,600 in 1979.[169]

---

[162]See e.g., Bottomley, K. and Pease, K. (1986) *Crime and Punishment: Interpreting Data*, Open University Press, Milton Keynes, pp. 85–86.

[163]*Ibid.*, p. 85.

[164]Matthews and Young (2003), *op. cit.*, p. 79.

[165]Home Office (1982) *Criminal Statistics 1981*.

[166]Home Office (1980) *Criminal Statistics 1979*, p. 113.

[167]*Ibid.* p. 126.

[168]Home Office (1981) *Criminal Statistics 1980*, p. 152.

[169]*Ibid.*, p. 153.

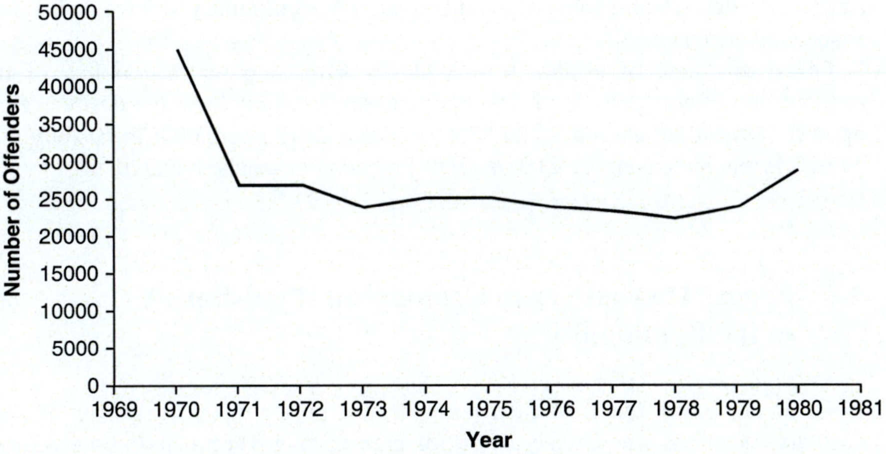

Fig. 3.3 Offenders received probation order for indictable offences[170]

The volume of the decline in the use of the probation order, as Rutherford reported, was most dramatic in relation to young adult males. In 1970, 12% of all young adult males sentenced for indictable offences were placed on probation. By 1978 this percentage had fallen to 6%, its lowest value of the decade.[171] A parallel decline in juvenile supervision in the community also took place during the 1970s. Thorpe et al. noted that 3,500 fewer supervision orders in 1977 were made than probation orders on juveniles in 1969.[172]

Similarly, the proportionate use of the fine displayed some fluctuation in this period. It has been already noted that in the late 1960s, following the introduction of the suspended sentence, the use of the fine had declined. It was plausibly argued by Sparks that the decline of the fine could be attributed to the tendency of the courts to impose a suspended sentence on certain offenders who would otherwise have received a fine. After the legislative guidance on the use of the suspended sentence, the fine reached its level prior to the introduction of the suspended sentence in the mid-1970s.[173] However, since the late 1970s, there was (and has been) a steady decline in the use of fines. In 1973, the proportionate use of fines for males aged 17–20 years for indictable offenders accounted for 59%, yet in 1979 it declined to 54%. Again, in 1973, the proportionate use of the fine for male offenders aged 21 and over amounted to 55%, in 1979 this number stood at 53%. The decline in the use of the fine was in part attributed to the appeal of the

[170]Home Office (1981) *Criminal Statistics 1980*, p. 158.

[171]Rutherford, *op. cit.*, p. 153.

[172]Thorpe, D., Smith, D., Green, C. and Paley, J. (1980) *Out of Care*, Allen and Unwin, London, p. 29.

[173]Bottomley and Pease, *op. cit.*, p. 89.

newly-introduced non-custodial penalties such as community service orders and suspended sentences.[174]

Given this state of affairs, it was hardly surprising that the policy of the proliferation of non-custodial sentencing measures did not have the desired effect upon the prison population.[175] In 1969, average daily population in custody was 34,667, while increasing by 21% in 1979 this number reached 42,220.[176]

3.4 From 'Alternatives to Custody' to 'Punishment in the Community'

Towards the end of the 1970s, the failure of the policy of the expansion of non-custodial sanctions was already taken for granted in governmental and academic circles. The problems associated with the growth in prison numbers appear to have deteriorated.[177] Prison overcrowding at this period was further exacerbated. The physical conditions were due to overcrowding, reportedly were much less tolerable.[178] A series of prison disturbances and the industrial actions of prison staff also came out as a protest against overcrowding in prisons.[179] At the beginning of the new decade, prisons were increasingly viewed as inhuman and inadequate in their capacity, as insecure due to a spreading wave of prison disturbances and staff unrest and as increasingly ineffective in rehabilitating inmate populations.[180] It then became commonplace to use the term 'crisis' to describe this state of the prisons.[181] Various 'crisis' management strategies emerged to relieve the problem of overcrowding in prisons and perceived consequences for the prison system.

---

[174]Home Office (1981) *Criminal Statistics 1980*, p. 124, Bottomley and Pease, *op. cit.*, p. 89.

[175]Rutherford (1984) *op. cit.*, pp. 55–56, Brownlee, *op. cit.*, p. 10.

[176]Home Office (1980) Statistics of the Criminal Justice System England and Wales 1969–79, HMSO, London, p. 59.

[177]See for example, Parliamentary All-Party Penal Affairs Group (1980) *Too Many Prisoners*, Barry Rose Publishers, Chichester.

[178]Sim, J. and Fitzgerald, M. (1982) British Prisons, Blackwell, Oxford, 2nd edition, pp. 15–20.

[179]*Ibid.*, p. 19.

[180]Evans, P. (1980) *Prison Crisis*, George Allen & Unwin, London, pp. 12–20, Ryan, *op. cit.*, pp. 62–70, Willis, A. (1986) Alternatives to Imprisonment: an Elusive Paradise in Pointing, J. (ed.) *Alternatives to Custody*, Blackwell, Oxford, pp. 18–38, Stern, V. (1989) *Bricks of Shame: Britain's Prisons*, Penguin, London, pp. 36–58, Brake, M. and Hale, C. (1992) *Public Order and Private Lives: The Politics of Law and Order*, Routledge, London, pp. 136–157, Dunbar and Langdon, *op. cit.*, pp. 22–25, Newburn, *op. cit.*, pp. 27–29, Sparks, R. (2002) Prisons, Punishment and Penality in McLaughlin and Muncie, *op. cit.*, pp. 201–256, Scot, D. (2007) The Changing Face of the English Prison: A Critical Review of the Aims of Imprisonment in Jewkes, *op. cit.*, pp. 49–72, pp. 52–54.

[181]The early account of the perceived components of the crisis, see Fitzgerald and Sim, J. (1981), *op. cit.*

In order to find a balance between the number of prisoners and the available prison accommodation, one strategy was to launch a prison-building programme.[182] The prison-building programme initiated in this period was the largest since the nineteenth century.[183] The capacity of prisons was significantly increased and new prisons were opened, but the existing prisons still could not keep up with the growth in prison population. Prison privatisation was then proposed as a solution to cope with the challenges that the expansion of prisons would bring with it.[184]

A second method was the extension of the scope of the parole system. The Criminal Justice Act 1982 lowered the minimum threshold for the eligibility of parole. Section 33 of the Act allowed the minimum qualifying period for parole to be revised from time to time; for certain offences an early release specified by the Home Secretary was made possible. Furthermore, the Home Secretary was empowered to reduce the 12-month minimum period which an offender was required to serve before s/he could be considered for release on licence. In 1984, the threshold for parole eligibility was lowered from 12 to 6 months. In 1987, the remission period was increased to one-half for offenders serving sentences of less than 12 months.

A third way to alleviate the 'crisis' was the enactment of statutory criteria regulating the imposition of custody for juvenile offenders. The Criminal Justice Act 1982[185] stipulated that with regard to persons under 21 years of age, custodial sentences should only be imposed where the gravity of the offence so required, or although the offence was not serious enough to justify the use of custody, either the court was of the opinion that public protection required a custodial sentence, or the offender had failed to respond to other non-custodial measures previously.[186] The 1982 Act was also significant for its placement of a number of legal safeguards against the use of custody. The Act required that the reason for the decision to imprison be stated. Further, it urged courts to obtain a 'social inquiry report' in every case in which custody was being considered in order to determine that there was no other way of dealing with the offender. A court which considered a report unnecessary was obliged to give reasons. The Act also required that any offender sentenced to custody must have been offered an opportunity to be legally represented.

A rather distinct and more influential crisis management strategy was the proliferation of intensive intermediate schemes and the narrowing of their

---

[182]Evans, *op. cit.*, pp. 16–17, Vass, *op. cit.*, pp. 18–19, Brake and Hale, *op. cit.*, p. 145, Hale, *op. cit.*, p. 336. See, Rutherford, A. and Morgan, R. (1981) *No More Prison Building*, Howard League for Penal Reform, London.

[183]At the end of the 1975 only eight prisons had been built since 1914. Morgan and Liebling, *op. cit.*, p. 1137.

[184]Matthews, *op. cit.*, p. 129, Ryan and Sim, *op. cit.*, pp. 185–193.

[185]Criminal Justice Act, Section 1(4), on a detailed account on the theme see, Burney, E. (1985) All Things to All Men: Justifying Custody under the 1982 Act, *Criminal Law Review*, pp. 284–293.

[186]Criminal Justice Act 1988 revised the criteria.

remit.[187] To recapitulate, it was noted above that intermediate treatment programs were conceived under the auspices of the Children and Young Persons Act 1969, and they targeted both juvenile offenders and non-offenders. The subsequent development of intermediate schemes was patchy so much and so long that as Jones and Kerslake highlighted,[188] the concept itself "has had to fight for its survival".[189] At the beginning of the 1980s, however, the idea of supervision of juvenile offenders in the 'community' attracted more interest than ever before to the belief that intermediate schemes might reduce the number of juveniles committed to care and custody.[190]

What is noteworthy in this regard is the enthusiastic engagement of a group of academics from Lancaster University, Norman Tutt, David Thorpe and David Smith, the ideas of whom were strongly informed by managerial techniques, most notably from 'systems management'.[191] At the risk of oversimplification, the central premises of 'system management' in their account may be outlined as inter-agency cooperation, monitoring and 'gate-keeping' procedures. It was the assumption of the aforesaid scholars that through the cooperation of various agencies having a stake in juvenile justice with clear objectives, and targets and strategies for dealing with juvenile offenders, the use of custody could be reduced. The philosophy behind this managerial approach towards juvenile justice was the recognition that less severe intervention methods should be preferred and, by virtue of this, its pioneers continuously advocated the use of diversion and intermediate treatment schemes.[192] Interestingly, both of these ideas came to prominence at a time when a 'law and order' policy through the newly instituted 'short, sharp and shock' detention centres (involving hard physical work, fewer privileges, more inspection and so on) was gaining growing popularity. However, this concurrence was more than a coincidence, as it was the intention of the government at the same time to reduce the cost of custody.[193]

In the 1980s, a series of legislative and administrative steps created a suitable atmosphere in favour of supervision in the community.[194] The Criminal Justice Act

---

[187]Haines and Drakeford, *op. cit.*, pp. 37–61, Bottoms *et al.* (1990), *op. cit.*, pp. 2–6 and 11–23.

[188]Jones, R., L. and Kerslake, A. (1979) *Intermediate Treatment and Social Work*, Heinemann, London.

[189]Crow, *op. cit.*, p. 10, Muncie (2004), *op. cit.*, p. 260.

[190]Burney, E. (1985) Sentencing Young People: What Went Wrong with the Criminal Justice Act 1982?, Gower Publishing, Aldershot. Smith, R. (2007) *Youth Justice: Ideas, Policy and Practice*, Willan, Cullompton, pp. 14–17, Cavadino and Dignan, *op. cit.*, p. 295.

[191]Cavadino, Crow and Dignan, *op. cit.*, p. 45.

[192]Most importantly, see for example Paley and Thorpe (1976) *op. cit.*

[193]Pitts, J. (1986) Thinking About Intermediate Treatment, *Youth and Policy*, no 17, pp. 1–8, Coleman, J., C. and Warren-Adamson, C. (1992) *Youth Policy in the 1990s: The Way Forward*, Routledge, London, p. 175, Hendrick, *op. cit.*, p. 189, Goldson, B. (2006) Penal Custody: Intolerance, Irrationality and Indifference, pp. 139–156 in Goldson, B. and Muncie, J. (eds.) *Youth, Crime and Justice: Critical Issues*, Sage, London, p. 141.

[194]Pitts, J. (1986), *op. cit.*, p. 1.

1982 reshaped the existing form of the supervision order by clearly defining its scope with the removal of non-offenders. As mentioned above, it added positive and negative requirements such as participating in or refraining from certain activities. The Act adopted a 'supervised activities requirement' as an alternative option to intermediate treatment, which enabled magistrates to specify the content of programme to be undertaken by the juvenile offender.[195] In 1983, a circular of the DHSS gave administrative impetus to intermediate treatment schemes. This circular emphasised the significance of the cooperation of various agencies in dealing with serious and persistent offenders, and pledged to finance the establishment of new intermediate treatment schemes.[196]

These schemes affected, and were affected by the attitudes of those social workers engaging with 'high-risk' offenders. One of the most significant features of the 1980s was the remarkable rejection by social workers of juvenile imprisonment.[197] Rutherford summarises this development by suggesting that:

> "The once ambiguous, if not ambivalent, attitudes about custody held by social workers during the early 1980s, have been replaced by unequivocal opposition".[198]

Indisputably, the change in the attitudes of social workers and criminal justice professionals in general should be understood against the background of the changing views on treatment in custodial institutions and its adverse effects, as was dealt with earlier in this study. The point here is to emphasise that the government of the day's approach in encouraging intensive intermediate schemes in order to sustain a policy of diversion from custody was widely shared among criminal justice professionals throughout much of the 1980s. Courts were observed to be making an increasing number of supervision orders, in line with the policy of promoting intensive community programmes.[199]

The impact of the policy of diversion from custody in conjunction with the statutory restriction of juvenile custody was substantial.[200] In 1980, the number of offenders sentenced to immediate custody for indictable offences was 63,000. In 1990, this figure dropped to 48,000. The decline in the number of persons sentenced to immediate custodial sentences was most remarkable in relation to juvenile offenders. Indeed, the numbers of persons under 18 years of age sent to immediate custody (either detention centre or borstal training) fell from 7,900 in 1981 to 1,700 in 1990.[201] This decline, as has been discussed earlier in this study, was among

---

[195] Section 12(3c)(a) of the Criminal Justice Act 1982.

[196] Muncie (2004) *op. cit.*, p. 269, Smith, R. (2007) *op. cit.*, pp. 15–17.

[197] Smith, R. (2007) *op. cit.*, pp. 18–19.

[198] Rutherford, A. (1989) The Mood and Temper of Penal Policy, *Youth and Policy*, no. 27, pp. 27–31, p. 29.

[199] Smith, R. (2007), *op. cit.*, p. 13.

[200] Tilley (2005) p. 360, Smith, R. (2007), *op. cit.*, pp. 22–27.

[201] Allen (1991), *op. cit.*, pp. 30–2, Matthews and Young, *op. cit.*, p. 82.

other things also intertwined with the increasing cautioning practice, which will be discussed in the following section.[202]

3.4.1 The Triumph of Diversion: More Diversion, Less Imprisonment?

It was already noted that the Children and Young Persons Act 1969 envisioned a diversionary approach from both courts and prisons. The Act was never fully realised, but even the circumscribed implementation of the Act gave a considerable boost to what established itself in the practice for some time without having a statutory base[203]: police cautioning.[204] At the very outset, the increasing importance of police cautioning as a strategy of diversion was met with certain cynicism on the ground that it caused some form of net-widening, as some believe that cautioning replaced previous practices of informal warning of the police.[205] The criticism was in part justified by the fact that the increasing use of cautioning did not lead to an immediate reduction in the number of persons brought to court.[206] Yet, despite rather pessimistic net-widening expectations initially, in the 1980s England witnessed a major movement of diversion and has therefore been described as a 'decade of diversion', at least as far as juvenile offenders were concerned.[207] An overview of the English literature leads one to discern three separate developments which point to the creation of a 'diversion-friendly' atmosphere at the time in question.

Chief among these appears to have been the official encouragement of police cautioning which was heralded in government documents, consultative documents and circulars to the police during the 1980s.[208] In these various documents it was

---

[202] Bateman, T. (2001) Custodial Sentencing of Children: Prospects for Reversing the Tide, *Youth Justice*, vol. 1, no.1, pp. 28–39, p. 29.

[203] Ditchfield, J., A. (1976) *Police Cautioning in England and Wales*, Home Office Research Study no. 37, HMSO, London, p. 1.

[204] Pratt, *op. cit.*, p. 223, Evans, R. and Wilkinson, C. (1990) Variations in Police Cautioning Policy and Practice in England and Wales, *Howard Journal*, vol. 29, no 3, pp. 155–176, p. 155, Gelsthorpe and Morris (1994), *op. cit.*, pp. 967–968, Davies, Croall and Tyrer, *op. cit.*, p. 219.

[205] Ditchfield, *op. cit.*, p. 12, Farrington and Bennet, *op. cit.*, p. 134.

[206] Morris, A. and Giller, H. (1987) *Understanding Juvenile Justice*, Croom Helm, London, pp. 143–144.

[207] Dignan, J. (1992) Repairing the Damage: Can Reparation be Made to Work in the Service of Diversion?, *British Journal of Criminology*, vol. 32, no. 4, pp. 453–472, p. 453, see also Newburn, T. and Souhami, A. (2005) Youth Diversion in Tilley, N. (ed.) *the Handbook of Crime Prevention and Community Safety*, pp. 355–386, p. 356, Newburn, T. (2002) Young People, Crime and Youth Justice in Maguire, Morgan and Reiner (eds.), *op. cit.*, 3rd edition, pp. 553–555.

[208] Gelsthorpe and Morris (1994), *op. cit.*, p. 997, Allen, R. (2002) Alternatives to Prosecution in McConville, M and Wilson, G.(eds.) *The Handbook of Criminal Justice Process*, Oxford University Press, pp. 167–181, p. 175, Davies, M., Croall, H. and Tyrer, J. (2005) *Criminal Justice*, 3rd edition, p. 219.

established and continuously affirmed that criminal proceedings should not be instituted, unless deemed absolutely necessary. This position was stronger with respect to first time minor offenders for whom the filing of prosecution was regarded as unlikely to be 'justifiable' unless there were exceptional circumstances. The Home Office Circular 14/1985 was of particular significance in this connexion. This circular also aimed to establish a set of criteria which, it was envisaged, would eventually reduce the widespread diversity among different police forces, what is sometimes called 'justice by geography'.[209] The criteria included offence seriousness, previous convictions, dramatic mitigating circumstances, wishes of the victim and so forth.

A second development peculiar to this decade was the establishment of multi-agency diversion panels composed of representatives from the police, social services, education, the youth services and the voluntary sector, in various localities. These diversion panels offered a range of educational, recreational and therapeutic 'alternatives to prosecution'[210] to which a juvenile could be diverted as a condition of her/his police caution. Since these panels set such priorities as diverting juveniles from prosecution and/or imprisonment, where possible, multi-agency panels working in the diversion schemes has been seen as the utmost impulse of the expansion of cautioning practices and the declining number of juveniles receiving custodial sentences in the 1980s.[211] Among these schemes, the Northamptonshire Multi-Agency Diversion was cited as particularly influential in stimulating an 'anti-custodial' ethos within and outside the scheme.[212]

And finally a third development, which has suffered the absence of in-depth research studies, was the increasing use of adult cautioning in some police forces.[213] As early as in 1983 the Metropolitan Police in London began using cautions for "drunkenness offenders" on a regular basis. The 1985 circular (affirmed in the 1994 circular at p. 2) was indicative of the greater importance of adult cautioning in practice. In order to structure the increasing use of adult cautioning, the circular listed certain categories of adult offenders as particularly eligible for cautions: the elderly or infirm, young adults (those between the ages of

[209]Laycock, G. and Tarling, R. (1985) Police Force Cautioning: Policy and Practice, *Howard Journal of Criminal Justice*, vol 24, no 2, pp. 81–92, Sanders, A. (1989) The Limit to Diversion from Prosecution, *British Journal of Criminology*, vol. 28, no 24, pp. 513–532, p. 567, Evans and Wilkinson, *op. cit.*, pp. 155–176.

[210]Fox, D., Dhami, M., K. and Mantle, G. (2006) Restorative Final Warnings: Policy and Practice, *Howard Journal of Criminal Justice*, vol. 45, no.2, pp. 129–140, p. 130, Crawford, A. (1996) Alternatives to Prosecution: Access to, or Exits from, Criminal Justice in Young, R. and Wall, D., S. (eds.) *Access to Criminal Justice: Legal Aid, Lawyers and the Defense of Liberty*, Blackstone, London, pp. 313–344, p. 319.

[211]Haines and Drakeford, *op. cit.*, pp. 55–56, Crawford, A. and Newburn, T. (2003), *op. cit.*, p. 10, Newburn and Souhami, *op. cit.*, pp. 357–358.

[212]Haines and Drakeford, *op. cit.*, pp. 47–50.

[213]Dignan, *op. cit.*, pp. 467–468, Evans, R. and Ellis, R. (1997) Police Cautioning in the 1990s, Home Office Research and Statistics Directorate No. 52, London. As noted already in 1990 by Evans and Wilkinson, available research on police cautioning is mainly concerned with juveniles, p. 156.

17 and 20), persons at risk, and those persons suffering from some kind of malady such as mental illness or impairment. The effect of this circular was most visible with respect to young adults.[214]

Given the extent of all such government activity and local initiatives, it was not surprising that England in the 1980s was marked substantially by diversion. Notably, this decade witnessed some significant changes in the attitude of the courts and size of the prison populations, which led to many to conclude that the decline in the use of custody is also attributable to the growth in cautioning.[215] Indeed, the numbers of juveniles aged 17 or under who were 'found guilty or cautioned' fallen from 204,600 in 1983 to 129,500 in 1993.[216] The number of juvenile offenders sentenced to immediate custody was significantly reduced. In 1983 a total of 13,500 fourteen-to seventeen-year-old males were sentenced to custody for indictable offences, compared to 3,300 in 1993.[217]

However, the optimistic view on the impact of diversionary schemes has been very usefully questioned by Matthews in his discussion of the reasons of such decline in the numbers of juvenile offenders receiving custodial disposals.[218] Matthews demonstrated that the changing use of cautioning did not correspond with changes in the use of custody at the time under consideration; he highlighted that it was in fact in the second half of the 1980s that the level of custody dropped most sharply when the level of cautioning was being reduced.[219] And furthermore, recognising the fact that the use of cautioning was uneven across England, Matthew emphasised that there was no evidence which indicates that custody rates were significantly lower in localities where cautioning was more widespread.[220] Even in the heydays of diversion, Matthews emphasised that police cautioning was only rarely used for more serious offenders. Accordingly, the effect of police cautioning on the juvenile custody rates was therefore small.

3.4.2 The Criminal Justice Act 1991

Towards the end of the 1980s, informed markedly by the neo-classicist theories stressing the importance of proportionality between 'the seriousness of the

[214]Evans and Wilkinson, *op. cit.*, p. 160.

[215]Muncie, *op. cit.*, p. 267, Gelsthorpe and Morris (1994), *op. cit.*, p. 968, Mair, *op. cit.*, p. 138.

[216]Allen (1991), *op. cit.*, pp. 28–29.

[217]Allen (1991), *op. cit.*, pp. 30–31. See also Muncie (1999), *op. cit.*, p. 270.

[218]Matthews, R. (1995) The Diversion of Juveniles from Custody: the Experience of England and Wales 1980–1990 in Albrecht, G. and Ludwig-Mayerhofer, W. (eds.) *Diversion and Informal Social Control*, de Gruyter, Berlin.

[219]*Ibid.*

[220]On this theme, see also Evans and Wilkinson, *op. cit.*, pp. 157–161.

offence'[221] and the severity of the punishment,[222] a rather distinct strategy was formed to cope with the prison population growth and its adverse effects: the policy of making non-custodial sanctions 'tough and demanding'.[223] Underlying this strategy was the belief that non-custodial sentences were as mere alternatives to prison and not appealing for sentencers and the public to the desired extent.[224] The record of community service, suspended sentences, probation and related measures were, in this respect, regarded as delivering evidence that the magnitude of the strategy of promoting non-custodial sanctions as alternatives to prison was far from achieving any notable impact in reducing the numbers of prisoners. Having recognised this, the policy-making targeted the conceptualisation of non-custodial sentences as alternatives to custody. It was the assumption that if non-custodial sentences were to secure the confidence of sentencers and the public, it needed to be established that the imposition of these sentences did not constitute avoidance of "the real punishment".[225] Hence it was believed that non-custodial sentences should have their own place in the sentencing tariff without being classified under the rubric of 'alternatives'. The new term for non-custodial sentences, 'punishment in the community', which was then translated into legislation as 'community sentences', therefore did not solely represent a discursive shift in the English policy-making, but also signified a fundamental change in the nature of non-custodial sentencing. With the new phrase, the intention was to emphasise that non-custodial penalties are forms of punishment which are executed in the 'community' and which therefore must be imposed in proportion to the seriousness of the offence. The Criminal Justice Act 1991 Act reflected this approach in numerous ways.[226]

---

[221]Von Hirsch defines the seriousness of the offence as containing two elements: the extent of the harm caused or risked by the offender and the offender's culpability in relation to that harm. According to him "harm refers to the injury done or risked by the criminal act. Culpability refers to the factors of intent, motive, and circumstance that determine how much the offender should be held accountable for his act". Von Hirsch, A. (1986) *Past or Future Crimes*, Manchester University Press, Manchester, p. 64.

[222]See, for example, von Hirsch, A. and Wasik, M. (1988) Non-Custodial Penalties and the Principle of Desert, *Criminal Law Review*, September, pp. 555–572.

[223]Wasik, M, (1992) Sentencing: a Fresh Look at Aims and Objectives in Stockdale, E. and Casale, S. (eds.) *Criminal Justice under Stress*, Blackstone, London, pp. 119–141, Brake and Hall, *op. cit.*, p. 151, Hoy, C. and Worrall, A. (2005) Punishment in the Community: Managing Offenders, Making Choices, Willan, Cullompton, p. 40, Ashworth, A. (1992b) Criminal Justice Act 1991: Part 2: Non-Custodial Sanctions, *Criminal Law Review*, April, pp. 242–251, p. 243, Cavadino, Crow and Dignan, *op. cit.*, pp. 96–129, May, T. (1994) Probation and Community Sanctions in Maguire, M., Morgan, R. and Reiner, R. (eds.) *the Oxford Handbook of Criminology*, Clarendon Press, Oxford, pp. 875–877, pp. 861–887. Dunbar and Langdon, *op. cit.*, pp. 86–98.

[224]Ashworth (1992b), *op. cit.*, p. 243, Brownlee, *op. cit.*, p. 14.

[225]Hudson, B. (1993) *Penal Policy and Social Justice*, Macmillan, Basingstoke, p. 31, Ashworth, A. (1992b), *op. cit.*, p. 243.

[226]See Ward, R., W. and Ward, M., S (1993) *Community Sentences: Law and Practice,* Blackstone, London, Wasik, M. and Taylor, R. (1994) *Guide to the Criminal Justice Act 1991*, 2nd edition, Blackstone, London, particularly chapter 2.

It is beyond doubt that the most significant step in trying to assimilate the principle of proportionality was the enactment of a general custody threshold by the Criminal Justice Act 1991,[227] akin to that which the 1982 Act provided for juveniles. Section 1(2) of the Act stated that a court must not pass a custodial sentence on an offender unless it is of the opinion that the offence in question, or its combination with associated offences was so serious that no other form of penalty would be justified. The custody criteria for violent or sexual offences were distinctively defined. The Act stipulated that the court was not bound by the seriousness of the criteria as provided for in Section 1(2), where it took the view that that a longer term of custody would be adequate to protect the public from serious harm from her/him. In this sense, the 1991 Act was founded fundamentally on a *bifurcatory* approach, reserving custody for serious offenders and diverting less serious offenders from custody,[228] which confirmed the international trends identified in Chap. 2. Notably, the Act did not repeat the other justification of custody, 'a failure to respond to non-custodial sentences', in the Criminal Justice Act 1982 Act. It also provided that the consideration of previous convictions of the offender in the sentencing decision was limited to cases in which previous offences disclosed the features of the current offence which make it more serious.[229] Again, the court was required to state its reasons for imposing a custodial order and to explain why it formed that view, and was also normally required to consider a pre-sentence social inquiry report prior to sentencing.[230]

The 1991 Act also defined a threshold for community sentences, which under the Act was the probation order, the community service order, the combination order, the curfew order, the supervision order and the attendance centre order. It provided that a community sentence may only be imposed if the court considered the combination of the offence and one other offence associated with it sufficiently serious to justify the use of the community sentence.[231] This was again an attempt to establish a hierarchy between penalties with reference to seriousness, and in this way, theoretically, the provision drew a line between the use of community sentences and financial penalties. At the same time, by providing that the restriction on liberty imposed by a particular order must be proportionate to the gravity of the

[227]Criminal Justice Act 1991 s. 1(2).

[228]For a detailed account on the subject see e.g., Ashworth, A. (1992a) Sentencing Reform Structures in Tonry, M. (ed.) *Crime and Justice*, vol.16, pp. 180–241 p. 194–195.

[229]Section 29 of the Criminal Justice Act 1991 stipulated that "(1) An offence shall not be regarded as more serious for the purposes of any provision of this Part by reason of any previous convictions of the offender or any failure of his to respond to previous sentences. (2) Where any aggravating factors of an offence are disclosed by the circumstances of other offences committed by the offender, nothing in this Part shall prevent the court from taking those factors into account for the purpose of forming an opinion as to the seriousness of the offence".

[230]*Ibid*, Section 1(4), (5) and (3).

[231]*Ibid*, Section 6(2).

offence, the principle of proportionality was qualified as the primary consideration in deciding on a particular community order.[232]

Another illustration of the influence of neo-classicist thinking or the 'just-desserts' approach was the placement of the probation order into the sentencing framework.[233] Indeed, until then the probation order was not a sentence in itself. As explicitly provided in the statute,[234] *instead* of sentencing, a court might make a probation order. In this sense, it was rather

> "a form of conditional liberty, an expression of the court's mercy in a deserving case, or a form of social work with offenders to help them overcome personal difficulties linked with offending".[235]

With the 1991 Act, the probation order became strictly a sentence of the court based on the proportionality principle, reflecting the culpability of the offender. According to the 1991 Act, the order could be imposed with the purpose of securing the rehabilitation of the offender or preventing her/him from committing further offences.

Under the 1991 Act, one or more community orders could be combined. However, alongside this provision, it was deemed necessary to create an order which would be particularly suitable for some of the *persistent petty offenders* who might otherwise have received a custodial sentence.[236] The combination order, introduced by Section 11 of the 1991 Act in accordance with the general policy of 'toughening' community sentences, was an attempt to convince sentencers that even in relatively more serious cases, public protection and deterrence could still be achieved without resorting to custody.[237] Indeed, the combination order was arguably the most intrusive sentence in its content. It was made up of community service of up to 100 h and a probation order of 1–3 years, and was available for offenders over the age of 16 who were convicted of an imprisonable offence.

Another crucial innovation that was introduced by the 1991 Act was the curfew order. Section 12 of the Act empowered courts to require an offender to remain at home or at another specified place for between 2 and 12 h per day for offenders aged 16, with a 6-month maximum period. Notably, despite opposition from professional and penal reform groups, the Act recognised electronic monitoring as a form of curfew.[238] At this point it must be noted that in England, the debate over electronic

[232]*Ibid.* Section 6(2)(a) and 6(2)(b).

[233]Ashworth (1992b), *op. cit.*, p. 247, Whitehead and Statham, *op. cit.*, pp. 123–126.

[234]Section 3 of the Criminal Justice Act 1948.

[235]Raynor and Vanstone, *op. cit.*, p. 1.

[236]Home Office (1991) *Crime, Justice and Protecting the Public*, Cm. 965, HMSO, London.

[237]Newburn (2003) *op. cit.*, p. 103, Cavadino and Dignan, *op. cit.*, p. 145.

[238]On this topic, see Ball, R., A. and Lilly, J., R. (1988) Home Incarceration with Electronic Monitoring in Scott, E., J. and Hirschi, T. (eds.) *Controversial Issues in Crime and Justice*, Sage, London, Nellis, M. (1991) The Electronic Monitoring of Offenders in England and Wales, *British Journal of Criminology*, vol. 31, no 2, pp. 165–185, Whitfield, D. (1997) *Tackling the Tag: the Electronic Monitoring of Offenders*, Waterside Press, Winchester.

monitoring predated the late 1980s. Electronic monitoring was first recommended in a report prepared for the House of Commons Home Affairs Committee,[239] and in a green paper (Punishment, Custody and Community),[240] favourable remarks on electronic monitoring were expressed. The first schemes used electronic monitoring as an alternative to remand or as a condition of bail. Despite the provision allowing curfew to be enforced through electronic monitoring, it was not until 1996 that electronic monitoring curfews were used as a sentencing option.[241] As will be seen below, less than a decade later electronic monitoring acquired major pre-eminence in the penal policy.

In line with the overall philosophy of the 1991 Act, the Act also introduced unit fines for *magistrates*' courts into the new sentencing framework.[242] In discussing the figures, it was noted above that since the late 1970s, the use of the fine began to decline. Inspired by the day-fine systems in the Continent, in 1988 the Home Office launched an experimental scheme at four magistrates' courts (called 'means-related fines'). It was the belief of the promoters of the unit fine schemes that if the seriousness of the offence could be separately assessed and financial penalties could be directly related to means, many problems associated with assessment of the amount of fines and their enforcement might be ameliorated.[243] This, it was believed, would reverse the decline in the use of a fine, while ensuring that fines for similar offences have an "*equal impact*" [244] upon offenders with different financial incomes and resources. This experiment was successful in terms of apparent improvements occurring in the fine enforcement and reducing the rate of imprisonment for fine defaults.[245] Encouraged by the experiment, the unit fine system was incorporated into the Criminal Justice Act 1991. Under the Act, in the first step, the courts were to assess the seriousness of the offence by also taking into consideration any aggravating and mitigating circumstances.[246] The seriousness of the offence was then reflected by the units – which could range from one to 50.[247] The second step was to determine the value of each unit, calculated according to 'the offender's *weekly* disposable income', the minimum value for a unit being £4 and the maximum being £100.[248] The weekly disposable income was the income after

[239] Newburn, *op. cit.*, p. 104.

[240] Mair, G. and Nee, C. (1990) *Electronic Monitoring: the Trials and their Results*, Home Office Research Study 120, HMSO, London.

[241] Nellis, M. (2004) Electronic Monitoring and the Community Supervision of Offenders in Bottoms *et al.* (2004), *op. cit.*, p. 228. Curfew orders were nationally rolled out in December 1999.

[242] Ashworth (1992b), *op. cit.*, pp. 244–246.

[243] For the problems of fine enforcement see, Prison Reform Trust (1990) *Tackling the Fine Default*, London, Gibson, B. (1990) *Unit Fines*, Waterside Press, Winchester.

[244] Ashworth (2005), *op. cit.*, p. 303.

[245] Moxon, D, Sutton, M. and Hedderman, C. (1990) *Unit Fines: Experiments in Four Courts*, Research and Planning Unit Paper, Home Office, London, Gibson, pp. 25–43.

[246] The Criminal Justice Act 1991, Section 18 (2)(a).

[247] *Ibid.*, Section 18(4).

[248] *Ibid.*, Section 18 (2)(b).

basic expenditures had been deducted.[249] The unit fine system came into force on 1 October 1992, although its life-span was surprisingly short, as will be touched upon below.

3.5 The Repositioning of Custody: "Prison Works"

By providing criteria for the use of custody, extending the range of non-custodial sanctions and giving a statutory base for unit fine schemes with the intention to eliminate imprisonment for fine defaults, the Criminal Justice Act 1991 was a significant attempt to limit the number of prisoners.[250] However, the 1991 Act, as a pillar of decarceration policies in England, was met with strong opposition from the judiciary and the media soon afterwards.[251] Unit fines, symbolising the philosophy of the Act, were at the forefront of the discussions, as many believed that far from securing equality in the enforcement of fines, unit fines caused unduly unfair outcomes. Certain sectors of the English media appeared to be particularly keen to show anomalies which the unit fine system ostensibly caused among offenders having different income levels.[252] The custody threshold of the Act, too, was subject to criticism from its very beginning. The Court of Appeal saw this restriction as "a wholly unnecessary straitjacket on judges",[253] meaning that it unduly fettered the discretionary power of sentencers. Most famously, a Court of Appeal judge (Lord Justice Lawton) argued against the statutory restriction that "courts can recognise an elephant when they see it, but may not find it necessary to define it".[254]

The opposition against the 1991 Act was fruitful in its consequences; the core features of this Act were hastily repealed with the enactment of the Criminal Justice Act 1993. Most significantly, the latter Act abolished the unit fine system.[255] It also

[249]Moxon, Sutton and Hedderman, *op. cit.*, p. 36.

[250]Brownlee, *op. cit.*, pp. 15–24, Cavadino, Dignan and Crow, *op. cit.*, p. 108, Cavadino, P. (1992) Reflections on the Criminal Justice Act 1991, *Criminal Justice Matters*, Autumn, p. 7,Worrall and Hoy, *op. cit.*, p. 43.

[251]Dunbar and Langdon, *op. cit.*, pp. 144, Worrall and Hoy, *op. cit.*, pp. 40–56, Ashworth and Gibson (1994) *op. cit.*, p. 101, Thomas, D. (2003) Judicial Discretion in Sentencing in , Gelsthorpe, L. and Padfield, N. (eds.) *Exercising Discretion: Decision Making in the Criminal Justice System and Beyond*, Willan, Cullompton, pp. 50–73, pp. 61–62, Ashworth, A. and Player, E. (2005) Criminal Justice Act 2003: The Sentencing Provisions, *Modern Law Review*, vol. 68, no 5, pp. 822–838, Koffman, L. (2006) The Rise and Fall of Proportionality: the Failure of the Criminal Justice Act 1991, *Criminal Law Review*, April, pp. 281–299.

[252]Hough, M. and Ashworth, A. (1996) Sentencing and the Climate of Opinion, *Criminal Law Review*, pp. 776–787, pp. 778–779, Ashworth, A. (2005) *Sentencing and Criminal Justice*, Cambridge University Press, Cambridge, pp. 305–306 and pp. 144–146.

[253]Cited in Wasik, M. (2004), *op. cit.*, p. 294.

[254]Cited in von Hirsch, A. and Asworth, A. (1997) Recognising Elephants: the Problem of the Custody Threshold, *Criminal Law Review*, pp. 187–200, p. 187.

[255]The unit fine system was abolished by section 65 of the 1993 Criminal Justice Act.

reversed the custody criteria.[256] Under the 1991 Act, a custodial sentence was warranted by reference to the seriousness of the offence for which the offender had been convicted. Hence, under the 1991 Act, sentencers were required to disregard previous convictions other than 'one other offence' associated with the offence in question, unless the previous offence disclosed features of the current offence which made it more serious. The 1993 Act made it possible for all existing previous convictions and non-compliance with previous sentences to be taken into account in considering the seriousness of any offence.

Unquestionably, such a rapid renunciation of the 1991 Act cannot be understood without reference to the unprecedented rise in the politicisation of crime and justice issues.[257] As was noted above, increasing importance attached to crime and justice issues in the hope of electoral benefit had its roots much earlier. However, this era, with its infamous incidents such as the killing of the 2-year-old James Bulger by two 10-year-old juveniles, was a turning point in which the importance of such concepts as 'the distinctive nature of juvenile crime', 'treatment of juvenile offenders', 'diversion' and 'the prevention of the adverse effect of imprisonment' gradually lost the significance that they once occupied in official rhetoric.[258]

As far as diversion is concerned, in the face of what English scholars call a 'moral panic' fuelled by some notorious cases and escalating crime rates, the official support for diversion practices based on minimum intervention was already in retreat in the mid 1990s.[259] The first signal of this change was a Home Office Circular in 1994 aiming to reduce multiple cautioning. An influential report of the Audit Commission Misspent Youth, made a strong case against the cautioning practices of police by pointing to repeat cautioning, the problems of inconsistent usage and the perceived failure to provide early intervention.[260] It was within this climate that diversion came to be seen as in need of re-conceptualisation.[261] This

---

[256]See for a detailed account, Ashworth, A. (1995), *op. cit.*, and Ashworth and von Hirsch (1997) *op. cit.*

[257]Raynor and Vanstone, *op. cit.*, p. 67, see also Pitts, J. (2003) Changing Youth Justice, *Youth Justice*, vol. 3, no 1, pp. 5–20.

[258]Nellis (2001), *op. cit.*, p. 29, Hoy and Worrall, *op. cit.*, pp. 47–48, Smith, R. (2007), *op. cit.*, pp. 29–31, see also, Pitts (2003) Youth Justice in England and Wales in Matthews and Young, *op. cit.*, pp. 86–95, Muncie, J. and Hughes, G. (2002) Modes of Youth Governance: Political Rationalities, Criminalisation and Resistance in Muncie *et al.* (2002), pp. 1–18, Morgan, R. (2007) Children and Young Persons in Gelsthorpe and Morgan (2007), *op. cit.*, pp. 201–222, p. 206, Cavadino and Dignan (2007) *op. cit.*, p. 67–71.

[259]Hughes, G, Pilkington, A. and Leisten, R. (1998) Diversion in a Culture of Severity, *Howard Journal*, vol. 37, no 1, pp. 16–33, pp. 17–18, Haines (1998), *op. cit.*, pp. 102–103, Muncie (1999), *op. cit.*, p. 249, Crawford, A. (2006) Institutionalising Restorative Justice in a Cold, Punitive Climate in Aertsen, I., Daems, T. and Robert, L. (eds.) *Institutionalising Restorative Justice*, Willan, pp. 120–150, pp. 122–125, see also Cavadino, Dignan and Crown, *op. cit.*, pp. 190–196.

[260]Audit Commission (1996) *Misspent Youth: Young People and Crime*, Audit Commission, London.

[261]Home Office (1997) *No More Excuses: A New Approach to Tackling Youth Crime in England and Wales*, HMSO, London.

re-conceptualisation, in spite of its punitive features and 'no more excuse'[262] rhetoric, somewhat paradoxically, was made with what had at that time come to determine the language of policy documents: restorative justice.[263] This shift was purely reflected in the advent of the Crime and Disorder Act 1998.[264] In order to provide an "effective and graduated intervention",[265] the Act replaced cautioning with a much more restrictive statutory regime comprising the distinct categories of statutory police reprimand for a first offence and a final warning for a second offence. The measures, influenced dramatically by the concept of restorative justice in England, unlike other jurisdictions where such measures have broader scope in terms of offence categories and eligible offenders,[266] are of moderately limited

---

[262]*Ibid.*

[263]The affinity between restorative justice and the newly-introduced measures is probably most visible in the establishment and operation of final warning schemes in Thames Valley Police Force (Thames Valley police force covers the English counties of Oxfordshire, Berkshire and Buckinghamshire.). See, e.g., Young, R. and Hoyle, C. (2002) New Improved Police-Led Restorative Justice? Action Research and the Thames Valley Police Initiative in von Hirsch, A., Roberts, J., Bottoms, A., E., Roach, K. and Schiff, M. (eds.) *Restorative Justice and Criminal Justice: Competing or Reconcilable Paradigms*, Hart Publishing, Oxford, Young, R. and Goold, B. (1999) Restorative Police Cautioning in Aylesbury – from Degrading to Reintegrative Shaming Ceremonies, *Criminal Law Review*, pp. 126–138, Young, R. (2001) Just Cops Doing 'Shameful' Business? :Police-led Restorative Justice and the Lessons of Research in Morris, A. and Maxwell, G. (eds.) *Restorative Justice for Juveniles*, Hart Publishing, Oxford, pp. 7–42.

This scheme was adopted from the Australian conferencing practised in Wagga Wagga in New South Wales, where it is closely associated with the theory of re-integrative shaming (See, Young and Goold, *op. cit.*, p. 127, see also see Johnstone, G. (1999) Restorative Justice, Shame and Forgiveness, *Liverpool Law Review*, vol. 21, pp. 197–216.) developed by Australian criminologist John Braithwaite. By challenging the labelling theory Braithwaite argues that the most effective way to control crime is to induce a sense of shame in offenders for their offences, provided that this shaming is followed by efforts to 'reintegrate' shamed persons into the community. The theory further postulates that *reintegrative* shaming is best achieved not by the police or the courts but those people who the offenders most 'care about', such as parents, partners and friends, as Braithwaite argues that people are generally far more concerned with the opinions of families and friends. Braithwaite (1989), *op. cit.* Based on this theory, the above-mentioned English final warning scheme aims to give the opportunity to all parties to contribute to decision-making through a conference the outcome of which is expected to be reintegration into the community *through*, somewhat oddly, '*shaming*'.

[264]Dignan, J. (1999) The Crime and Disorder Act and the Prospects of Restorative Justice, *Criminal Law Review*, pp. 48–60, Crawford, and Newburn, *op. cit.*, pp. 11–17, Newburn and Souhami, *op. cit.*, p. 365; for a critical view on the theme see, Morris, A. and Gelsthorpe, L. (2000) Something Old, Something Borrowed, Something Blue, but Something New? A Comment on the Prospects for Restorative Justice under the Crime and Disorder Act 1998, *Criminal Law Review*, pp. 18–30.

[265]Giller, H. (2004) *Final Warnings Interventions*, Youth Justice Board, London.

[266]For instance in New Zealand where except murder and manslaughter all other charges against a juvenile aged 14–17 are dealt with by way of family conferencing, Masters, G. and Warner Roberts, A. (1999) Family Group Conferencing for Victims, Offenders and Communities in Liebmann, M. (eds.) *Mediation in Context*, Jessica Kingsley Publishers, London, pp. 140–154, p. 142, McElrea, F., W., M. (1998) The New Zealand Model of Family Group Conferencing, *European Journal on Criminal Policy and Research*, vol. 6, no. 4, pp. 527–543.

significance in terms of the aims that are assigned to a diversionary approach. As one informed commentator suggests, restorative justice has on the whole become "an ideal vehicle through which early intervention is provided".[267] Given that the attention is paid to early intervention rather than diversion of the juvenile offender, there is increasing danger that these measures widen the net[268] and are accordingly less likely to divert offenders from custodial disposals.

Exactly, at this point, with regard to diverting offenders from custody, the policy makers reacted even "tougher". It was in this period that the Conservative Home Secretary, Michael Howard, most vocally announced that the success of the criminal justice system would no longer be measured with a reduction in the prison population, and claimed that:

> "Prison works. It ensures that we are protected from murderers, muggers and rapists – and it will make many who are tempted to commit crimes think twice".

Such political encouragement of prison sentences was soon translated into the criminal policy. In several respects, the approach towards juvenile offenders was subject to change. There is value in highlighting these changes.

The 1994 Act extended the duration of '*detention in a young offender institution*' for offenders aged 15–17 years old from 12 to 24 months.[269] The Act further allowed for 'long-term detention' for juveniles aged 10–13, and empowered the courts to impose long-term sentences on 10 to 13-year-olds for a wider range of offences than was previously possible, e.g. for sexual assault. Most notably, the latter Act provided the *secure training order* for persistent offenders. [270] The secure training order was designed for 12 to 14-year-olds who had been convicted of three imprisonable offences and who had failed to comply with the requirements of supervision while on remand or under sentence. The first half of a secure training order was to be served in newly constructed secure training centres, and following the release from the centre the offender was to remain under compulsory supervision for the rest of the sentence. The order was to last for a fixed term of at least 6 months and at most 2 years, as determined by the court. Meanwhile, the power to detain juveniles classified as 'young offenders' (15–17 years old) in a young offender's institution was extended from 12 months to 2 years. With these

[267] Haines (1998) *op. cit.*, p. 103.

[268] Darrel, Dhami and Mantle, *op. cit.*, p. 137.

[269] Prior to the Criminal Justice and Public Order Act 1994, two types of custodial sentences existed. Of these, '*detention in young offender institution*' could be imposed on males between 14 and 20 years, and females between 15 and 20. Subject to a number of exceptions, the minimum term of custody was 21 days, and the maximum 12 months. Alongside this option, the long-term detention of juveniles, which was governed by Section 53 of the Children and Young Persons Act 1933, was to deal with those aged 14 and above who had been convicted of murder or manslaughter.

[270] Muncie *et al.* (2002) p. 394, Cavadino, Crow and Dignan, *op. cit.*, pp. 24–25, Cavadino, P. (1995) The Criminal Justice and Public Order Act 1994 and Young Offenders, *Youth and Policy*, vol. 48, pp. 71–83.

provisions the 1994 Act, as Goldson suggests, "effectively reversed the decarcerative provisions of youth justice law and policy – in respect of children aged 12–14 years – that dated back to the Children Act 1908".[271]

The *de jure* policy of greater incarceration of juveniles was sustained in the Crime and Disorder Act 1998. A single sentence of '*detention and training orders*' was introduced in 1998 to replace the secure training order and detention in a young offender institution for juveniles aged 12–17 years. The new sentence contained a custodial term accompanied by a period of supervision in the 'community'. The Act also included the possibility of the extension of the power of courts to impose a detention and training order for 10–11-year-olds, provided that the Home Secretary extends the application of the order to this age group and the court is of the opinion that such a sentence is the only way of protecting the public from further offences by that offender. The Act also relaxed the above-mentioned criteria for custody of offenders under 15 in relation to 'persistence' with the provision that a custodial sentence is warranted where the court is of the opinion that s/he is a persistent offender. The impact of the changes was dramatic. Between 1993 and 1998, the number of juvenile offenders under sentence in custodial institutions increased by 60%, from 5,081 to 8,500.[272]

3.6 A Mixed Approach towards Non-custodial Sanctions

Despite the 'tough' approach which reversed the approach of parsimony in the use of custody, the 'alternatives to custody' rhetoric has maintained its place in the juvenile justice agenda, but in a different guise.[273] The design and implementation of non-custodial sanctions are now heavily dominated by attempts to reduce re-offending, as the Crime and Disorder Act 1998 requires. And even such new alternative programmes to custody as 'intensive supervision and surveillance programmes' do not necessarily rule out custody. The intensive supervision and surveillance programmes[274] (which have been given a statutory base by the

[271]Goldson (2006) *op. cit.*, p. 143, see also Smith, R. (2007), *op. cit.*, p. 33–37, Cavadino, P. (1995) pp. 71–83, Gibson, B. (1995) Young People, Bad News, Enduring Principles, *Youth and Policy*, vol. 48, pp. 64–70, pp. 67–68.

[272]Pitts, *op. cit.*, p. 87.

[273]Smith, R. (2007), *op. cit.*, p. 41.

[274]The ISSP was launched by the Youth Justice Board in July 2001 in 80 areas, and extended to all areas in October 2003. For a detailed account on the background, aims and implementation strategies of intensive supervision and surveillance programmes, see Moore, R. (2004) Intensive Supervision and Surveillance Programmes for Young Offenders: the Evidence Base So Far in Burnett, R. and Roberts, C. (eds.) *What Works in Probation and Youth Justice: Developing Evidence-Based Practice*, Willan, Cullompton, Stephenson, M., Giller, H. and Brown, S. (2007) *Effective Practice in Youth Justice*, Willan, Cullompton, pp. 210–230.

Criminal Justice and Immigration Act 2008) are designed to deal with 'hardcore' persistent and serious juvenile offenders.[275] These programmes may be a part of a detention and training order, as a condition of bail, or alternatively an adjunct to a community sentence. They are available for those juvenile offenders who are appearing in court either charged with or convicted of an offence, and who have been charged or warned for an imprisonable offence on four or more separate occasions within the last 12 months, or have previously received at least one community or custodial sentence, or are at risk of custody in view of the fact that the current charge is so serious that an adult could be sentenced to 14 years imprisonment or more. An intensive supervision and surveillance programme, as the name suggests, contains supervision including electronic tagging or tracking and participation in educational and vocational training, offender behaviour programmes, and recreational activities.[276]

Similarly, in relation to adult offenders, the reduction of the custodial population has appeared to no longer be an overarching imperative which shapes sentencing legislation and decisions. The success of the penal justice system is indeed no longer measured with reference to the reduction of custody. The success is rather to be found in the effectiveness of a sentence. This shift is epitomised clearly in the recent revival of interest in short-term imprisonment. The present official position is no longer the emphasis on the counter-productive effects of short-term imprisonment upon offenders and the need to divert a certain category of offenders from short-term prison stays. Rather it is the extent to which effective short-term imprisonment could be designed to deal with "persistent offenders with multiple problems and high risks" more adequately.[277] In a very influential Home Office consultation paper, known as the Halliday Report and which will be touched upon below,[278] a reformation of short-custodial sentences, referring to custodial sentences of less than 12 months, was proposed. The suggestion was that all such sentences should consist of a period in prison (maximum 3 months) and a period of compulsory supervision in the community, subject to conditions and requirements of the breach. Failure to comply with these may lead to a return to prison.

Against this background, the Criminal Justice Act 2003 introduced two new forms of short custodial sentences: custody plus and intermittent custody, and also

[275]Persistent young offenders who at the time of appearing in court have previously been charged, warned or convicted on four or more separate occasions in the preceding 12 months and have previously received at least one community or custodial sentence.

[276]See Moore, *op. cit.*, McNeill, F. (2006) Community Supervision: Context and Relationships in Goldson and Muncie, *op. cit.*, pp. 125–138, p. 126.

[277]Home Office (2001) *Making Punishments Work* (Report of a Review of the Sentencing Framework for England and Wales), Home Office Communication Directorate, London, p. ii.

[278]The review of the sentencing framework in England and Wales was chaired by John Halliday, see Clarkson, C., M., V., and Baker, E. (2002) Making Punishments Work? An Evaluation of the Halliday Report on Sentencing in England and Wales, *Criminal Law Review*, February, pp. 81–97.

restructured the suspended sentence, custody *minus*.[279] Under the Criminal Justice Act 2003, custody plus comprised a custodial period of at least two weeks and not more than 13 weeks, and after the custodial element, a period of supervision no shorter than 26 weeks had to be undertaken by the convict. The court could impose one or more of a wide range of requirements with which s/he had to comply. Intermittent custody was designed for a term ranging from 14 to 90 days, in which it was aimed to enable the offender to continue employment and educational activities, while spending a part of the day in prison.[280] While intermittent custody was piloted in a number of probation areas,[281] custody plus remained solely in the statute book, without any practice. In 2006, both custody plus and intermittent custody were deferred on the grounds that they could not yet be adequately resourced. Despite them being temporarily[282] withdrawn, the inception of both custody plus and intermittent custody may well reveal the new directions of the English penal policy.

With these sentences, in particular with the custody plus, by combining custody and supervision elements, the edges of community and custodial sentences are "blurring",[283] while the reality and the danger of net-widening[284] is growing. It remains to be seen when these sentences, if ever, will be implemented, but the emphasis on short-term imprisonment, with some form of supervision, seems to be a discursive move back to the earlier days of the English penal system.

Significant changes have occurred not only in the realm of custodial sentences, but the Criminal Justice Act 2003 also significantly changed the structure of non-custodial sentences. The Act sustained the policy of toughening non-custodial

---

[279]Thomas, D. (2004) *op. cit.*, pp. 702–711, Roberts, J. and Smith, M., E. (2004) Custody Plus and Custody Minus in Tonry, M. (ed.) *Confronting Crime: Crime Control Policy under new Labour*, Willan, Cullompton, pp. 182–210, Morgan and Alison, pp. 1100–1138, p. 1100, Ashworth (2005) *op. cit.*, Ashworth and Player (2005), *op. cit.*, pp. 822–838.

[280]Explanatory Notes of the Criminal Justice Act 2003.

[281]See e.g., Penfold, C., Hunter, G. and Hough, M . (2006) The Intermittent Custody Pilot: A Descriptive Study, Home Office Online Publication, accessible from the following link http://www.homeoffice.gov.uk/rds/pdfs06/rdsolr2306.pdf (Access Date: October 2009).

[282]Mair notes that "whether this is a temporary delay or a more indefinite postponement remains unclear" p. 399, Mair, G. (2007) Research on Community Penalties in Doing Research on Crime and Justice in King, R., D. and Wincup, E. (eds.) *Doing Research in Crime and Justice*, Oxford University Press, pp. 399–430.

[283]Bottoms and Rex, *op. cit.*, pp. 12–13, Hughes, G. (2001) Competing Logics of Community Sanctions: Welfare, Rehabilitation and Restorative Justice in McLaughlin and Muncie, *op. cit.*, pp. 257–301, Rex, S. (2005) Reforming Community Penalties, Sage, London, pp. 12–15, Harding (2003), *op. cit.*, pp. 369–373.

Harding argues that "custody, under this model, becomes the norm and community penalties become more difficult to market. First these measures will not reduce prison expansion, but add to it; second, we will create a new round of net-widening; and finally we perpetuate values that support imprisonment. Seductive seamlessness raises the spectre of custody as the first resort of the courts rather than the last". p. 371.

[284]Tonry, *op. cit.*, pp. 10–11, Bateman, T. (2005) Reducing Child Imprisonment: a Systemic Challenge, *Youth Justice*, vol. 5, no 2, pp. 91–104, pp. 93–94.

sentences. Correspondingly, the 'alternatives to imprisonment' discourse has occupied less and less of a place in their promotion. In order to fill the resultant lacuna in the face of worsening overcrowding in prisons and growing costs of prisons,[285] the Act appears to pay more tribute to another approach, the policy of 'back door measures'. Notably, under the new arrangements, after serving one-half of their sentences, all offenders serving determinate sentences[286] will be on licence under supervision with requirements until the end of their term of imprisonment. However, even before this regulation, since 1999, alongside the early release arrangements, 'home detention curfew' (introduced by the Crime and Disorder Act 1998) has existed to enable an earlier release for offenders serving less than 4 years. The 2003 Act also expanded the application of the home detention curfew.[287] Under the present scheme, prisoners serving sentences of between 3 months and 1 year can be released up to 90 days before the sentence expires, provided that they are assessed as low-risk offenders and are subject to a home curfew enforced by electronic tagging.[288]

3.6.1 Interim Appraisal

As discussed above in detail, the inexorable growth in the English prison population from the 1960s onwards had given principal impulse to the quest for viable front-door sentencing options e.g. suspended sentences and community service and back-door options e.g. parole and home detention curfew. Contrary to the intentions behind these initiatives, the adoption of new non-custodial measures had proved to fail to exert an appreciable effect on the incarceration rate. The dramatic decline in the use of the fine and the probation order showed that the growth of the use of community sentences took place at the expense of these disposals. At the end of the 1980s, in the face of increasing prison population and overpopulated prisons, the failure of 'alternatives to custody' was increasingly acknowledged. In many quarters, the failure was attributed to the assumption that these sentences were not regarded as sufficiently 'punitive' both by sentencers and public at large alike.

In order to increase the credibility of 'alternatives to custody', two main approaches were developed. One was the repositioning of alternatives to custody as community sentences that were accompanied with a substantial neo-classical rhetoric of the desert based sentencing. A second way, which aimed at reversing the decline in the use of fine, was the introduction of the unit fine system into the magistrates' courts. The unit fine system was abandoned soon after its national implementation

[285] In 2005, 33 of the 142 prisons were crowded, which meant that their capacity was exceeded by 30 per cent or more, see Morgan and Alison, *op. cit.*, p. 1101.

[286] Apart from those are under life sentence and imprisonment for dangerousness.

[287] The Crime and Disorder Act 1998 provided the release of short-term prisoners (those serving less than four years) up to two months before their normal release date subject to 'home curfew detention'.

[288] Release on home detention curfew has been entrusted to the discretion of the prison governor.

due to the belief that it led to great differences in the amount of fines imposed for 'similar' offences and that it unduly restricted the discretion of sentencers.

The effect of the reformulation of alternatives to custody as community sentences was, in any case, far from being a success story because, as was shown, during that time the prison population had been growing. Commentators emphasised that rather than an increase in the level of crime or in the number of offenders coming before the courts, the growth in the prison population can be attributed to the increasing severity of the sentencing.[289] Indeed, as Cavadino and Dignan highlights, between 1995 and 2005, crime generally decreased by nearly 44%.[290] In the same period, the total number of offenders sentenced to immediate custody (including detention in a young offender institution) went up by 27% from 79,500 in 1995 to 101,200 in 2005.[291] The proportionate use of custody was also on the increase; the figure is more equivocal when one considers the proportionate use of custody for indictable offenders. At magistrates' courts, the proportionate use of custody was 9% in 1995, while at the Crown Court, the proportionate use of immediate custody was 56% in 1995. In 2005, the proportion of the use of custody accounted for 60% at the Crown Court, whereas in magistrates' courts it was 14%.[292]

Overall, extending the numbers of available non-custodial sanctions has not had the impact on custodial levels that had been hoped for. Despite the growth in the use of community sentences (for example between 1995 and 2005 the total number of community sentences rose from 129,900 to 204,000[293]) the research demonstrated that overall offenders, who a decade ago might have received a fine, are now likely to receive a more onerous community penalty, and those who might have received community penalties are now more likely to be imprisoned.[294] In the last section, the numerical meaning of these trends will be further elaborated on with reference to the most recent available statistical data. First, however, an account of the current sentencing framework is essential.

3.7 Current Non-custodial Sanctions: The Context

If a conclusion can be drawn from all the above, it can be said without any hesitation that regardless of the intention of the legislature, throughout recent history, the approach of the English judiciary to any non-custodial sanction has

[289] See, Home Office (2001*), op. cit.*, pp. 79–81, Hough, M., Jacobson, J. ad Millie, A. (2003) *The Decision to Imprison, Sentencing and the Prison Population*, Prison Reform Trust, London, pp. 23–28.

[290] Cavadino and Dignan (2007), *op. cit.*, p. 101.

[291] Home Office (2007) Sentencing Statistics 2005, HMSO, p. 27.

[292] Home Office (1996) Criminal Statistics, England and Wales 1995, HMSO, p. 145, Home Office (2007) Sentencing Statistics, pp. 30–31.

[293] Home Office (2007), *op. cit.*, p. 51.

[294] See for a detailed study on this theme, Hough *et al.* (2003), pp. 7–39.

substantially determined its fate. The great influence of the courts can be explained with reference to the extent of the discretionary power conferred to courts at the sentencing stage.[295] Indeed, the wide degree of judicial discretion with respect to the form and length of sentence has long been the fundamental characteristic of English sentencing law. Conventionally, two primary constraints on the exercise of discretion existed: maximum statutory limits and the appellate review.[296] Notably, with the so-called *guideline judgments*, the Court of Appeal has clarified general issues in relation to a number of serious crimes such as aggravating and mitigating circumstances, and developed what English scholars call 'tariff'; the array of penalties varying for the degrees of seriousness of the offence. It would exceed the scope of this study to deal with these themes. What is crucial here for the purpose of this study is to emphasise the significance of sentencing discretion with respect to non-custodial sanctions. It must be underlined that it is not only the margin of discretion which judges have been vested with which displays a difference in comparison to other countries featured in this study, but the way in which discretion has been justified and sustained.

In searching for the philosophical premises of broad sentencing discretion, one finds the notion of judicial independence. While judicial independence, in countries adherent to civil law, connotes the constitutional principle that judicial decision-making must be free from the influence of the executive, its construction in England goes well beyond that understanding. Here the meaning of judicial independence was construed until very recently much more broadly as embracing the minimisation of the intervention of the legislature on sentencing policy.[297] Indeed, for much of the twentieth century, it was the firm conviction of the English judiciary that any constraint on discretion other than the determination of maximum penalties would be an infringement on judicial independence. Not surprisingly, any attempt to fetter judicial discretion was met with strong criticism by the judiciary.[298]

Gradually, with the increasing importance attached to the avoidance of disparities and inconsistencies in sentencing decisions, sentencing has become the subject of

---

[295] For a detailed account see, e.g., Ashworth (1992a) *op. cit.*, Tonry, M. (2004) *Punishment and Politics: Evidence and Emulation in the Making of English Criminal Control Policy*, Willan, Cullompton, pp. 92–146, Wasik, M. (2004) What Guides Sentencing Decisions in Bottoms *et al.* (2004) *op. cit.*, pp. 290–312, see also Thomas, D. (2003) Judicial Discretion in Sentencing in Gelsthorpe, L. and Padfield, N. (eds.) *Exercising Discretion: Decision Making in the Criminal Justice System and Beyond*, Willan, Cullompton, pp. 50–73, Ashworth, A. (2007) Sentencing in Maguire *et al.* (2007), *op. cit.*, pp. 991–1023.

[296] See Ashworth (2001), *op. cit.*, p. 72.

[297] Ashworth (1992), *op. cit.*, pp. 197–200, Kelk, C., Koffman, L. and Silvis, J. (1995) Sentencing Practice, Policy, and Discretion in Fennell, P., Harding, C., Jörg, N. and Swart, B. (eds.) *Criminal Justice in Europe: A Comparative Study,* Clarendon Press, Oxford, pp. 319–339, pp. 332–338, Cavadino and Dignan, *op. cit.*, p. 87. Brownlee, *op. cit.*, p. 9.

[298] Stern, *op. cit.*, pp. 56–57.

detailed guidelines and statutory provisions.[299] In 1989, the Magistrates' Association developed the Magistrates' Associations' Sentencing Guidelines, elaborating factors affecting the sentencing decision and providing indications of an appropriate penalty for certain types of offences.[300] In the 1990s, in statutes including very detailed sentencing provisions, e.g. the Criminal Justice Act 1991, the discretion of the judge was limited. The English legislature went further in its sentencing policy by pronouncing 'mandatory minimum sentences' in relation to such offences as drug-trafficking, possession of prohibited arms and residential burglary. The policy of regulating the sentencing process has been further translated into practice with the establishment of the Sentencing Advisory Council by the 1998 Crime and Disorder Act,[301] and the Sentencing Guidelines Council by the Criminal Justice Act 2003.[302]

Furthermore, for the first time, The Criminal Justice Act 2003, spells out the following underlying purposes which guide a sentencing decision for offenders aged 18 and over[303]: the punishment of offenders, the reduction of crime (including its reduction by deterrence), the reform and rehabilitation of offenders, the protection of public, and the making of reparation by offenders to persons affected by their offences. There is no further statement in the Act which indicates any priority of these objectives.

3.8 The Framework

Section 152(2) of the Criminal Justice Act 2003 provides a custody threshold that clearly reveals the hierarchy between different sentences. Pursuant to this section, a custodial sentence must not be imposed unless the court is of the opinion that the offence "was so serious that neither a fine alone nor a community sentence can be justified". Thus, in accordance with the seriousness of offence, a fine, community sentence or a custodial sentence might be deemed appropriate.[304] Sentencing

---

[299] For the background of this change in the official attitudes see, Morgan, R. and Clarkson, C. (1995) The Politics of Sentencing Reform in Clarkson, C. and Morgan, R. (eds.) the *Politics of Punishment and Sentencing* Oxford University Press, Oxford, pp. 4–9.

[300] Court of Appeal guideline judgements generally have limited relevance for magistrates, and for this reason the Magistrates Association has developed its own sentencing guidelines. These were first introduced in the 1970s for motoring offences, but in 1989 were extended to cover most offences dealt with by magistrates.

[301] Section 80–81.

[302] For an early review on the subject, see Hutton, N. (2003) 'Sentencing Guidelines' in Tonry, M. (ed.) *Confronting Crime*, Willan, Cullompton, pp. 112–139.

[303] Section 142(1).

[304] The Criminal Justice Act 2003 does not define the term offence seriousness, but states that (Section 143 (1)): "In considering the seriousness of any offence, the court must consider the offender's culpability in committing the offences and any harm which the offence caused, was intended to cause or might forseeably have caused". Under the Criminal Justice Act 2003, in considering the seriousness of an offence, recent and relevant previous convictions must also be

options are not limited to the respective penalties. There are also absolute and conditional discharges available for both adult and juvenile offenders, as well as sentences specifically designed for juvenile offenders. Furthermore, as is already clear from the preceding section, in England and Wales the police may issue a formal caution to a person over 18 who admits to an offence, and who consents to the application of cautioning. This is a non-statutory power of the police which has been so far governed by Home Office circulars.[305] In addition to the 'simple caution', the Criminal Justice Act 2003 adopted the conditional caution which contains conditions e.g., treatment for drug or alcohol dependency, attendance in an anger management course or a restorative justice programme with which the offender must comply.[306] With regard to juvenile offenders, the police are vested with the power (through Crime and Disorder Act 1998)[307] to issue either a reprimand or final warning. A reprimand may be issued where the offence is admitted and the juvenile offender has not previously been convicted, reprimanded or 'warned'. A final warning is a more onerous option available to the police, on the other hand, and may be given where the juvenile offender has not received a warning within the previous 2 years and involves a referral of the juvenile offender to the local youth offending team.

The following outline of sentencing options in England and Wales begins with discharge. It then deals with fine and compensation orders. Having examined the community order, this section continues to deal with the suspended sentence. Finally, there will be an outline of penalties designed for juvenile offenders.

3.8.1 Discharge

It is generally agreed that the mildest form of non-custodial penalty is a discharge.[308] A discharge is imposable when, having regard to the circumstances, including the nature of the offence and the character of the offender, the court takes the view that it is "inexpedient to inflict punishment".[309] There are two forms of discharge in English law. An absolute discharge is a 'nominal' penalty which contains no obligation or requirement for the offender. The conditional discharge

taken into account as an aggravating factor. As such, by making previous offences as a factor determining the severity of the sentence, the Criminal Justice Act 2003 reversed effectively the approach brought by the 1991.

[305] See e.g., Home Office Circular 30/2005 and 016/2008.

[306] Section 22 of the Criminal Justice Act 2003, On the conditions which can be attached to a conditional caution, see the Code of Practice of the Crown Prosecution Service in the following link: http://www.cps.gov.uk/Publications/others/conditionalcautioning04.html (Access Date: March 2010).

[307] Section 65 of the Crime and Disorder Act 1998.

[308] Ashworth (2005), *op. cit.*, pp. 295–296.

[309] Criminal Justice Act 1948, Section 7(2).

contains an explicit prohibition of future criminal conduct during the specified period, which may be up to 3 years. If a further offence is committed during a specified period, the court may sentence the offender not only for this new offence but also for the original offence for which the conditional discharge was imposed. The use of the conditional discharge with regard to juvenile offenders was limited by the Crime and Disorder Act 1998. Under Section 66 of this Act, courts cannot impose a conditional discharge upon juvenile offenders who have received a final warning within the previous 2 years, unless the court is of the opinion that there are exceptional circumstances relating to either the offender or the offence.

3.8.2 Compensation Order

Above, it was noted that the compensation order was enacted as an *ancillary* order with the Criminal Justice Act 1972.[310] Since the 1982 Criminal Justice Act, compensation as a sentence in its own right can be imposed either as an ancillary or as a sole order in cases involving death, injury of physical and/or mental nature, loss or damage.[311] The Criminal Justice Act 1988 required courts to give reasons for not ordering compensation where there is an identifiable victim. Under the present law (Powers of Criminal Courts 2000),[312] courts are required to give priority to a compensation order over a fine if the offender has limited means.

3.8.3 The Fine

In English law, theoretically a fine can be imposed in respect of any offence other than offences for which the mandatory penalty is prescribed by the statute.[313] A fine can be given to a corporate body. Notably, in English law parents may be required to pay the fine for their children when crimes were committed by their children. The Children and Young Persons Act 1933 was the first Act to empower the courts to require parents to pay the fines of a juvenile offender.[314] This provision has been retained since then.

---

[310]For an early account see, Newburn, T. and De Peyrecave, H. (1988) *The Use and Enforcement of Compensation Orders in Magistrates Courts*, Home Office Research Study 102, HMSO, London. For early legislation containing provisions of victim compensation see, for example the Forfeiture Act, see on the theme, also Softley, *op. cit.*, pp. 1–5.

[311]Gibson, B. and Cavadino, P. (2002) *Introduction to the Criminal Justice Process*, Waterside Press, Winchester, p. 180.

[312]Section 130 of Powers of Criminal Courts Act.

[313]Hungerford-Welch, P. (2004) *Criminal Litigation and Sentencing*, Routledge, London p. 681.

[314]Children and Young Persons Act 1933, Section 55(1).

There exist distinctions with respect to the regulation of the use of fines in both kinds of criminal courts. In the Crown Court, there is no statutory limit on the amount of a fine. In the magistrates' court, on the other hand, fines must generally be calculated in accordance with a standard scale consisting of five bands that was first introduced by the Criminal Justice Act 1982, depending on the seriousness of the offence. The current figures, adjusted by the Powers of Criminal Courts (Sentencing) Act 2000 are as follows:

Level

1. £200
2. £500
3. £1,000
4. £2,500
5. £5,000

Only exceptionally can the amount of a fine exceed this amount.[315]

It has been an issue of constant contention to what extent the court ought to take the means of the offender into account in calculating the amount of the fine. The issue was discussed for the first time in 1970 in the Report of the Advisory Council on Non-Custodial and Semi-Custodial Penalties, and a means-related fine system, which would make an "*equal impact*" on offenders, was proposed.[316] Nonetheless, this recommendation found little support, in so far as at this very time the prevailing approach of the academic literature was that:

> "The ability of the offender to pay is relevant only as a mitigating factor, reducing the amount which might be fixed by reference to the gravity of the offence alone; it would be inconsistent with basic tariff principles to impose a heavier fine than can be justified on the basis of the offence, on the grounds of the offender's wealth".[317]

In course of the mid-1980s, this view was subject to change. The idea that the court should take the financial circumstances of the offender into account received increasing support on the grounds of the decline in the use of a fine, in particular the decline in the imposition of a fine on low-income offenders, and the continuing presence of fine defaulters in prisons. The unit fine system was an attempt to address such problematic aspects of the existing system of the fine, as was discussed above. However, having being defined as an essential element, which must be taken into account in the first instance in fixing the amount of the fine, the financial circumstances of the offender again became a subsidiary requirement through Criminal Justice Act 1993. The Act provided that the amount of the fine should reflect the gravity of the offence and that when calculating the value of the fine, courts, both the magistrates' and Crown Courts, should take, among other things, the financial

[315] Smith, K. and Keenan, D., J. (2004) *Smith & Keenan's English Law*, Pearson, Harlow, p. 27. The general maximum fine for any offence is £5,000, although higher fines, e.g. £20,000, are available for businesses in cases involving health and safety and pollution.

[316] Advisory Council on Non-Custodial and Semi-Custodial Penalties, *op. cit.*, para. 85.

[317] Thomas, D. (1979) *Principles of Sentencing*, Heinemann, London, p. 221.

circumstances of the offender into account, "so far as they are known, or appear to the court".[318] Furthermore, the Act stipulated expressly that a decrease or increase is possible on the grounds of the offenders' means. Hence, contrary to the conventional view, which ruled out the imposition of a heavier fine on the grounds of the offender's wealth, the Act empowered the sentencers to increase the amount of fine. The framework which the 1993 Act created, has since remained unchanged; the Criminal Justice Act 2003 re-enacted the respective provisions.[319] Section 164 of the Act provides that the amount of the fine must reflect the seriousness of the offence, and that the court must consider the circumstances of the individual case and the financial circumstances of the offender.

3.8.4 Deferment of Sentence

Until the Criminal Justice Act 2003, no change was made in relation to deferment of sentence. Prior to the latter Act, both Crown Court and magistrates' courts were empowered to postpone the sentencing decision when they considered the nature of the offence and character and circumstances of the defendant to justify withholding passing a sentence. The maximum periods for which the sentence can be deferred was (and still is) 6 months, and the defendant must give her/his consent to deferment of sentence. Above, it was noted that originally deferment of sentence was recommended by the Advisory Council with some formal obligations which were to be imposed by the deferring court. The recommendation of the Council was rejected on the grounds that it was neither necessary nor practically achievable to know whether the convict complied with the requirements without supervision.

Over time, the deferred sentence has been used only very modestly,[320] owing to the fact that the position of deferment of sentence, given the existence of other similar measures, could not be precisely located. The Criminal Justice Act 2003 in this sense aimed to alter the redundant position of this measure, by adding the requirement to impose certain conditions. The 2003 Act retained the basic structure of the previous regulation of the deferred sentence. However, it authorised courts to impose requirements, without listing these requirements exhaustively.[321] Notably, in Schedule 23 of the Act, it is indicated that in deferring passing a sentence, a drug treatment and testing orders may be imposed.[322] After the period of deferment, in passing the sentence courts are obliged to consider not only whether or not the offender complies with the requirements imposed by the court, but also any change in circumstances of the offender. Examples given are as voluntary desistence from

---

[318] Section 18(3) of the Criminal Justice Act 1993.

[319] Criminal Justice Act 2003, Section 164(4).

[320] Wasik (2004), *op. cit.*, p. 307, Ashworth (2005), *op. cit.*, p. 326.

[321] Section 278 of the Criminal Justice Act 2003, Schedule 23.

[322] *Ibid.*

drugs or alcohol, the commencement of employment, and changes in personal relationships.[323]

3.8.5 *Community Order*

As was demonstrated above, the Criminal Justice Act 1991 was an attempt to provide a coherent and consistent framework for non-custodial sanctions. Under the Act, the term 'community sentence' applied to the probation order, the community service order, the combination order, curfew order, the attendance centre order and the supervision order.[324] The Crime and Disorder Act 1998 added to this catalogue the drug testing and treatment order. Furthermore, the Powers of Criminal Courts Act 2000 extended the scope of the curfew order and, without changing their content, renamed the probation order, community service and the combination order as community rehabilitation, community punishment and community rehabilitation and punishment order respectively.

The structure of 'community sentences' formed over the years was, in many accounts, found to be far from satisfactory. In the above-mentioned Halliday Report, the case was strongly made that the existence of various community penalties with their own requirements complicated the sentencing process; and that despite such a detailed outline of these sanctions, the purposes and "the punitive weight" ascribed to each penalty was not clear.[325] The corollary of the latter was, it was believed, the difficulty of the application of the proportionality principle. Moreover, the existing community threshold was seen as being partly responsible for the decline in the use of fines, as it was considered that the 'graduation' of sanctions with reference to seriousness might have possibly caused the reservation of fines for least serious cases.[326] In addition to these objections concerning the substance, from a legal technical point of view, the Halliday Report pointed out the numerous repetitions which occurred in the conditions and breach procedures of community sentences. The recommendation of the report was the creation of a single generic community order.

These ideas are largely embodied in the Criminal Justice Act 2003. The Act subsumed everything previously known as community penalties under a single generic community order, and enabled sentencers to determine the exact content of the order out of twelve requirements.[327] Under the Act, courts are empowered to

[323]Wasik (2004), *op. cit.*, p. 307.

[324]Subsequently re-named as community rehabilitation order and community punishment order, respectively.

[325]Home Office (2001) *op. cit.*, pp. 38–39.

[326]Home Office (2001), *op. cit.*, p. 39.

[327]See Taylor, R., Wasik, M. and Leng, R. (2004) *Blackstone's Guide to the Criminal Justice Act 2003*, Oxford University Press, Oxford, Ashworth (2005), *op. cit.*, pp. 312–325.

impose one or more requirements[328] which are suitable for the offender in a given case. Before outlining these requirements, it must be noted that the 2003 Act retains a seriousness threshold.

Section 148 (1) of the Act provides that the court should not impose any community sentence unless satisfied that the offence is serious enough to warrant such a sentence.[329] The exception to this criterion is provided in relation to persistent offenders: Section 151 of the Act enables courts to impose a community sentence in cases where a person aged 16 or over has been fined on three or more previous occasions, despite the fact the current offence is not serious enough to warrant a community sentence.

The new generic community sentence can be up to 3 years in length, although shorter terms can be specified. To this order can be attached any of the following twelve different requirements:

The unpaid work requirement[330] obliges the offender to perform unpaid work. The working hours range from between 40 and 300 h and must be performed within 12 months.

The activity requirement[331] (previously attendance at a probation day centre) requires the offender to present herself/himself in a community rehabilitation centre or the premises approved by the Home Office and to participate in activities specified by the court order. The maximum length of the activity requirement is 60 days. The activities contain training in social skills, communication, and so forth.

The programme requirement[332] obliges the offender to participate in an 'accredited programme' for a number of days specified by the court; there is no statutory maximum length. The examples of such programmes are those of dealing with the treatment of sex offenders, anger management and drink-impaired drivers.

The prohibited activity requirement[333] requires the offender to refrain from participating in certain activities e.g. prohibiting from using a firearm on a specified day or days, or else during a specified period.

The exclusion requirement[334] obliges the offender to refrain from entering a specified place for a specified period. This prohibition must not exceed 2 years. An exclusion requirement may consist of a prohibition from entering different places for different periods and days.

The residence requirement[335] requires the offender to reside for a specified period at a certain place such as a probation hostel, the offender's own home or a relative's home.

---

[328] Section 177 of the Criminal Justice Act 2003.

[329] *Ibid.*, Section 148(1).

[330] *Ibid.*, Section 199.

[331] *Ibid.*, Section 201.

[332] *Ibid.*, Section 202.

[333] *Ibid.*, Section 203.

[334] *Ibid.*, Section 205.

[335] *Ibid.*, Section 206.

The mental health requirement[336] obliges the offender to undergo a treatment by or under the direction of a medical practitioner or a psychologist (or both, for different periods) in order to improve her/his mental condition. In course of the treatment, the offender may be a resident or non-resident patient.

The drug rehabilitation requirement[337] obliges the offender to submit to drug treatment and regular testing for use of illicit drugs during a period specified by the court. The offender's consent is necessary for the imposition of this order. Under the Criminal Justice Act 2003, courts are empowered to review periodically the enforcement of the order.

The alcohol treatment requirement[338] requires the offender to undergo alcohol treatment. In order to impose the order, the court must ensure that the offender is dependent on alcohol and that a treatment of such dependency is necessary. A court may not impose an alcohol treatment requirement unless the offender expresses her/his consent.

The supervision requirement[339] is the current version of the probation order, and is basically the placement of an offender under the supervision of a probation officer for a specified period, which would involve regular meetings with the probation officer at a specified time and a specified place.

The attendance centre requirement[340] requires an offender who is under 25 years of age to attend an attendance centre specified in the court order for a specified number of hours. The maximum number of hours cannot be less then 12 or more than 36. In an attendance centre, typically, physical exercise or instruction for occupation is provided in a group environment.

The curfew requirement[341] obliges the offender to remain for a specified period at a specified place. The minimum and maximum periods are stipulated by Section 204 (2) of the Act as 2 and 12 h, respectively. In conjunction with the curfew requirement, the court must impose an electronic monitoring requirement, although there are exceptions to this rule.[342] Where the enforcement of electronic monitoring depending on the consent of another person is necessary and the required consent is not secured, where electronic monitoring in the area in question has not as yet been established, or finally where the court, having regard to particular circumstances of the case, comes to the conclusion that it is inappropriate to impose an electronic monitoring requirement, an electronic monitoring requirement cannot be imposed.

The scope of the application of electronic monitoring is not limited to the curfew requirement. The exclusion requirement must likewise be imposed in conjunction with an electronic monitoring requirement. The imposition of electronic monitoring

[336] *Ibid.*, Section 207–208.

[337] *Ibid.*, Section 209–211.

[338] *Ibid.* Section 212.

[339] *Ibid.*, Section 213.

[340] *Ibid.*, Section 214.

[341] *Ibid.*, Section 204.

[342] *Ibid.*, Section 190(3).

is facultative in relation to the rest of 'community orders', subject to the above-mentioned restrictions.

Under the Act, when deciding the requirements in the particular case, the court must take the view that the restriction on liberty is commensurate with the seriousness of the offence and that the requirement(s) are the most suitable for the offender. Hence, the legislature addresses both retributive and rehabilitative considerations without making any of one of these as a principal objective.[343]

Going one step further, the Sentencing Guidelines set three ranges of sentence within community orders, graduated according to seriousness of offence: low, medium and high. The guidelines propose that for less serious offences such as petty persistent offences (shoplifting and minor public order offences), the community order should include 40–80 h of unpaid work, a curfew requirement (of up to 12 h a day for a few weeks), an exclusion requirement (without electronic requirement) of a few months, a prohibited activity requirement or an attendance centre requirement. For more serious offences such as the handling of stolen goods exceeding a certain value, burglaries of commercial premises and some cases of taking vehicles without consent, the penalty involves an increased number of hours of unpaid work, 80–150, an activity requirement of 20–30 days, a prohibited activity requirement, a curfew requirement lasting 2–3 months; or an exclusion requirement of around 6 months. For the most serious offences falling under scope of the community order, such as first-time domestic burglary, the guidelines propose the use of 150–300 h of unpaid work, activity requirements up to the 60-day maximum; or curfew orders lasting 4 to 6 months.

3.8.6 The Non-custodial Sanctions Specific to the Juvenile Justice

3.8.7 Youth Rehabilitation Order

The introduction of the Criminal Justice and Immigration Act 2008 appears to have changed the landscape of juvenile justice substantially. Prior to this Act, two main statutes administered the sentencing of juveniles. The first of these statutes was the Criminal Justice Act 2003, which was dealt with in some detail above. Under the latter Act, juveniles aged 16 and over could be given a community order. The second piece of legislation was the Powers of Criminal Courts Act 2000, which,

[343] In this sense, the Act retained the basic structure provided by the 1991 Act. The 1991 Act also contained 'desert' and 'suitability' criteria. This formulation was then criticised by Wasik that the Act should "indicate the proper priority between these objectives in cases where they conflict". Since, "there are sure to be cases where an onerous community sentence (such as combination order together with a curfew enforced by electronic monitoring) seems to the court to be "suitable" (given perhaps a history of the offender's untrustworthiness under supervision), but where that sentence is not commensurate with the offence committed". See, Wasik, M. (1991) Non-Incarcerative Sanctions in England, *Federal Sentencing Reporter*, July/August 1991, pp. 42–44, p. 43.

despite the provisions of the Criminal Justice Act 2003 and in concurrence with this Act, continued to be in force for *juveniles aged 16 or 17*.

With the title 'youth rehabilitation order' which is somewhat at odds with the *Zeitgeist*, the Criminal Justice and Immigration Act 2008 contains, akin to the community order, a single generic non-custodial sentence for offenders aged under 18 – up to 3 years in length. A youth rehabilitation order is composed of one or more of the requirements which will be briefly outlined below. In each case, the Act requires the sentencers to take particular account of circumstances of the offender and her/his social and educational needs. Generally, the imposition of one of these requirements requires that the courts consult with a probation officer or a local authority social worker. In appropriate cases, the juvenile offender's parents or her/his guardian must be consulted. Certain requirements are similar to those which are provided in the Criminal Justice Act 2003, which has been dealt with above, but due to their different length and their partly different content, it is deemed necessary to mention them here again.

The activity requirement[344] requires the juvenile offender to participate in activities or present herself/himself at specified places. The activities such as basic skills assessment and training may take place in residential places and the offender may be obliged to participate in more than one activity. The duration of the activity requirement cannot exceed 90 days.

The supervision requirement[345] places the juvenile offender under the supervision of a 'responsible officer' for a specified period. The supervision contains regular meeting with the responsible officer.

The unpaid work requirement[346] is available for offenders of 16 and 17 years of age. It consists of unpaid work ranging from 40 to 240 h, and must be performed within 12 months.

The programme requirement[347] requires the offender to participate in "a systematic set of activities" specified by the court, and thereby comply with instructions given. A programme requirement may oblige the offender to reside at a specified place.

The attendance centre requirement[348] requires the offender to attend an attendance centre in order to engage in an occupational activity specified in the court order. The maximum number of attendance centre orders varies in accordance with the age of the offender. If the offender's age is between 14 and 16, the attendance centre order must be not less than 12 and no more than 24 h, and if the offender's age 16 and over, while the minimum length of hours is again 12 h, the maximum is 36 h.

---

[344]Schedule 1, Part 2 of the Criminal Justice and Immigration Act.

[345]*Ibid.*, Section 9.

[346]*Ibid.*, Section 10.

[347]*Ibid.*, Section 11.

[348]*Ibid.*, Section 12.

The prohibited activity requirement[349] requires the offender to refrain from certain activities specified by the court order at specified times. The court may, for example, order that the juvenile offender does not possess and use firearms.

The curfew requirement[350] obliges the offender to remain in a specified place at a specified time. The curfew requirement may contain different places, periods and days, but the number of hours it encompasses cannot be less than 2 h or more than 12 h in any day. Furthermore, the length of the duration of the curfew requirement cannot exceed 6 months.

The exclusion requirement[351] obliges the offender to refrain from entering a specified place for a specified period. The specified period cannot exceed 3 months.

The residence requirement[352] is available for offenders aged 16 and over, and it requires the offender to reside for a specified period at a certain place or reside with an individual specified in the court order.

The local authority residence requirement[353] requires the offender to reside in accommodation provided by or on behalf of a local authority specified in the court order. The consultation with the parents or guardian is obligatory before deciding to impose a local authority residence requirement on its own or along with other requirements. The length of this requirement cannot be longer than 6 months and will expire when the offender has reached the age of 18.

The mental health treatment requirement[354] obliges the offender to undergo treatment by or under the direction of medical personal or a (chartered) psychologist. This requirement can only be imposed when the court is satisfied that the offender is susceptible to treatment. In cases where a hospital order appears to be more appropriate, taking the circumstances of the offender into account, the court should impose the latter order.

The drug treatment requirement[355] is available for offenders aged 14 years or over. This requirement obliges the offender to submit to drug treatment in order to eliminate and reduce the drug dependency. Furthermore, the Criminal Justice and Immigration Act 2008 provides a drug testing requirement,[356] according to which drug testing is to be conducted regularly during a period specified by the court.

The intoxicating substance requirement[357] requires the offender to undergo treatment in order to reduce or eliminate of the offender's dependency on and abuse of intoxicating substances, i.e. alcohol or any other substance other than drugs which causes intoxication.

---

349 *Ibid.*, Section 13.
350 *Ibid.*, Section 14.
351 *Ibid.*, Section 15.
352 *Ibid.*, Section 16.
353 *Ibid.*, Section 17.
354 *Ibid.*, Section 20.
355 *Ibid.*, Section 22.
356 *Ibid.*, Section 23.
357 *Ibid.*, Section 24.

The education requirement[358] requires the offender to comply with 'approved education requirements' during a period specified in the court order. The related provision explains 'approved education requirements' as the arrangements for the offender's education which may be made either by parents or guardian or the local education authority.

Furthermore, a youth rehabilitation order can be imposed with *intensive supervision and surveillance* or in appropriate cases with *a fostering* requirement in cases where in absence of these requirements a custodial sanction would have been meted out, or, for offenders aged under 15, where the offender is deemed 'persistent'. Where the court imposes an intensive supervision and surveillance requirement, the length of it cannot be shorter than 90 days or longer than 180 days.

In order to secure the compliance of the specified requirement(s) in the order, the Act envisages the use of electronic monitoring,[359] unless the particular circumstances of the case do not justify the use of electronic monitoring.

3.8.8 Referral Order

The referral order was introduced by the Youth Justice and Criminal Evidence Act 1999. It is available for 10–17-year-olds pleading guilty and convicted for the first time by the courts, unless the crime is so serious as to justify the use of imprisonment or else an absolute discharge or a hospital order.[360] With the Criminal Justice and Immigration Act 2008, the scope of the referral order has been further extended. The latter Act makes it possible to give a second referral order on the recommendation of the 'youth offending team' in exceptional circumstances.

Where the court decides to impose a referral order, it refers the juvenile offender to a youth offender panel. The youth offender panel composes of professional and lay members. The panel, with the juvenile offender, her/his parents and the victim, if s/he so desires, determine the nature of the penalty to be imposed and the type of programme a juvenile offender should pursue. Under the Youth Justice and Criminal Evidence Act 1999, the referral order may be made for a minimum of three and maximum of 12 months depending on the seriousness of the case, as determined by the court. The Criminal Justice and Immigration Act 2008 empowers courts to reduce the term specified for a referral order or alternatively extend upon the recommendation of the youth offender panel.

---

[358] *Ibid.*, Section 25.

[359] *Ibid.*, Section 26.

[360] See, Newburn, T., Crawford, A., Earle, R., Goldie, S., Hale, C., Masters, G., Netten, A., Saunders, R., Hallam, A., Sharpe, K. and Uglow, S. (2002) *The Introduction of Referral Orders into Youth Justice System*: *Final Report*, Home Office, London, Earle, R. and Newburn, T. (2002) Creative Tensions? Young Offenders, Restorative Justice and the Introduction of Referral Orders, *Youth Justice*, vol. 1, no 3, pp. 3–13, Crawford, A. and Burden, T. (2005) *Integrating Victims in Restorative Youth Justice*, Policy Press, Bristol, pp. 5–12.

Theoretically, the referral order has been predicated upon the notion of restorative justice.[361] Central to the notion of restorative justice is the involvement of all the stakeholders in the decision-making process.[362] By providing a forum where the juvenile offender, her/his family, and where appropriate the victim, consider the circumstances surrounding the offence and the effect on the victim, in many accounts it is viewed a radical translation of the idea of restorative justice into practice.[363] The outcome of the process is also closely associated with the idea of restorative justice. The youth offender panel draws up and agrees a contract, which when signed activates the order made by the court. Courts may make an order of between three and 12 months. The contract may involve a letter of apology, a direct meeting with the victim, putting right the damage caused by the offence, or financial compensation. Where these are deemed inappropriate, reparation could also be made to the community at large, for instance by unpaid community work. In addition to this, the contract may include counselling, drug rehabilitation or educational programmes. A contract may also specify that the juvenile should not participate in certain activities, or attend particular places.

3.8.9 Reparation Order

The reparation order is also a part of new juvenile justice policy which legitimises itself by reference to restorative justice. By making reference to crime victims explicitly, the order is arguably the most radical in terms of its wider implications, but effectively less significant in comparison to referral orders. This is because, unlike referral orders, the reparation order has no mandatory nature.[364]

This order requires juvenile offenders to do some good to repay for the offence to the victim (provided that the victim of the offence consents to this), to another person otherwise affected by crime, or to the community at large by writing a letter of apology, apologising in person, repairing harm done, or doing other work for up to 24 h. The statute explicitly pronounces the principle of proportionality by noting that the reparation order must be commensurate with the seriousness of the offence.

Before making a reparation order, the court is required to obtain and consider a written report by a probation officer, a social worker of a local authority social services department or a member of a youth offending team, indicating the type of work that is suitable for the offender and the attitude of the victim or victims to the requirements proposed to be included in the order. A reparation order is carried out under the supervision of the responsible officer, and is made within a period of 3 months from the date of the making of the order.

---

[361] Smith, R. (2007), *op. cit.*, pp. 65–66.

[362] See Chapter 2.

[363] See Earle and Newburn, *op. cit.*, p. 11.

[364] Cavadino and Dignan (2007), *op. cit.*, p. 332.

3.8.10 *Suspended Sentence Orders (Custody Minus)*

Before explaining the present place of the suspended sentence in the sentencing framework, it is necessary to note two important developments, both of which have a significant impact upon the current version of the suspended sentence.[365] The first is the abolition of the suspended sentence for offenders aged 17–21 by the Criminal Justice Act 1982, which reportedly had no noticeable effect on the use of custodial sentences –for this age group the number of immediate custodial sentences remained stable to a large extent.[366] Another development which is noteworthy is the abolition of the partly-suspended sentence and the drastic restriction of the application of the suspended sentence with the 1991 Act. Under the 1991 Act, courts could impose a suspended sentence only in cases in which an immediate custodial sentence would have otherwise passed and the "exceptional circumstances" of the case could justify the use of the suspended sentence. The phrase 'exceptional circumstances' appears to have affected the use of suspended sentence dramatically. Before the 1991 Act came into effect, the use of suspended sentences was about 10% for adult males and 8% for females, whereas in 1994, these percentages were 1 and 2% respectively.[367] Nonetheless, here too, as it is convincingly argued, there was no conspicuous change in the use of immediate custody.

In view of discouraging evidence that the suspended sentence has only a modest impact upon the application of custody, with the Criminal Justice Act 2003, the aim was to revive it through extending its use and toughening its content. Under the Act, a suspended sentence may be given to persons aged *18 and above*, and may be imposed only where it is felt that an immediate custodial sanction is appropriate. The court must therefore reach the conclusion that an immediate term of imprisonment is warranted, fix the sentence and only then consider whether or not to postpone the imposition of that sentence. According to Section 189 of the 2003 Act, the term of imprisonment to be suspended must be between 28 and 51 weeks for a period of up to 2 years. The court may order the offender to comply with one or more requirements, each of which can also form a part of community sentence during the supervision period, and furthermore, the court may monitor the offender's progress on the suspended sentence. If the offender breaches the suspended sentence by being convicted of another offence committed within the operational period, the court is obliged to activate the suspended sentence in addition to the sentence for the new offence. However, the court may decide not to activate it if, in view of all the circumstances, if it is of the opinion that it would be "unjust" to do so. The new suspended

---

[365]Stone, N. (1994) The Suspended Sentence Since the Criminal Justice Act 1991, *Criminal Law Review*, pp. 399–408.

[366]Bottoms, A. (2004) Empirical Research Relevant to Sentencing Frameworks, in Bottoms, Rex and Robinson, *op. cit.*, pp. 59–82.

[367]*Ibid.*

sentence thus has two triggers for breach: the commission of a further offence and the failure to comply with a requirement in the order.

With such a regulation, the suspended sentence became almost identical with community sentences, with there being a solely terminological difference in that a suspended sentence is technically a custodial sentence. This fact led to considerations such as those which occurred earlier in its history that the suspended sentence may cause a certain degree of 'net-widening', more than was previously the case.[368] Formulated in another way, it is feared that courts may be tempted to impose suspended sentences in cases which would have previously been dealt with using other non-custodial sentences such as probation, community service and so forth. In order to prevent this, the Criminal Justice and Immigration Act 2008 notably abolished the use of suspended sentence for summary offences.

3.9 Investigating the Impact of Non-custodial Sanctions

As the discussion above suggests, in recent years the English legislature has attempted to provide a more coherent and consistent sentencing framework for community sentences. It might be expected that greater structuring of community sentences would lead to an increasing use of these sentences, and as a consequence of this, a marked decline in the use of custodial sentences could be achieved. As will be seen below, confirming expectations, with some fluctuations, community sentences have continued to show an upward trend. In considering the years between 1998 and 2008, statistics show that there is a steady increase in the total number of community sentences. In 2008, community sentences accounted for 190,000 sentences in 2008, which equated to 14% of all sentences, compared with 10% in 1998. Notably, in the same period, the total number of offenders sentenced to immediate custody displayed fluctuations.[369] Following an increase, the use of custody declined from 101,000 in 1998 to 99,525 in 2008. These changes in the use of both custody and community sentences may in part be attributed to the changing number of offenders. The total number of offenders sentenced in 2008 was 1,362,000; a figure which has reduced by 7% from 1998. In order to understand the broader meaning of the rise of community sentences and its implications in relation to other main sentencing options, however, a closer look of sentencing figures is of crucial importance (Fig. 3.4).

First, it must be noted that despite the fact that immediate custody was given for all offenders declined between 1998 and 2008, its percentage among other options stood at 7% in 2008, according with the figure in 1998. Again, the immediate custody rate for indictable offences has risen over the past decade from 23% in

---

[368] *Ibid.*

[369] See, Ministry of Justice (2010) Sentencing Statistics in England and Wales 2008 in the following link http://www.justice.gov.uk/publications/docs/sentencing-stats-2008.pdf (Access Date: March 2010).

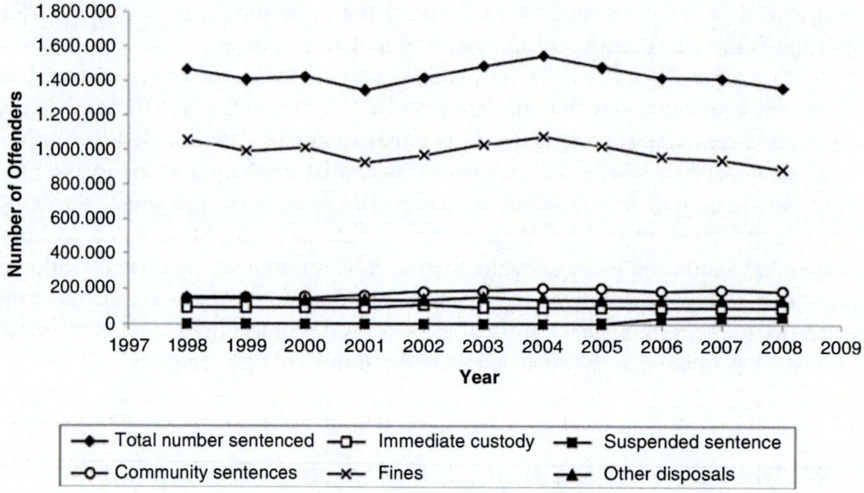

Fig. 3.4 Total offenders sentenced and disposals used for all offences at all courts 1998–2008[370]

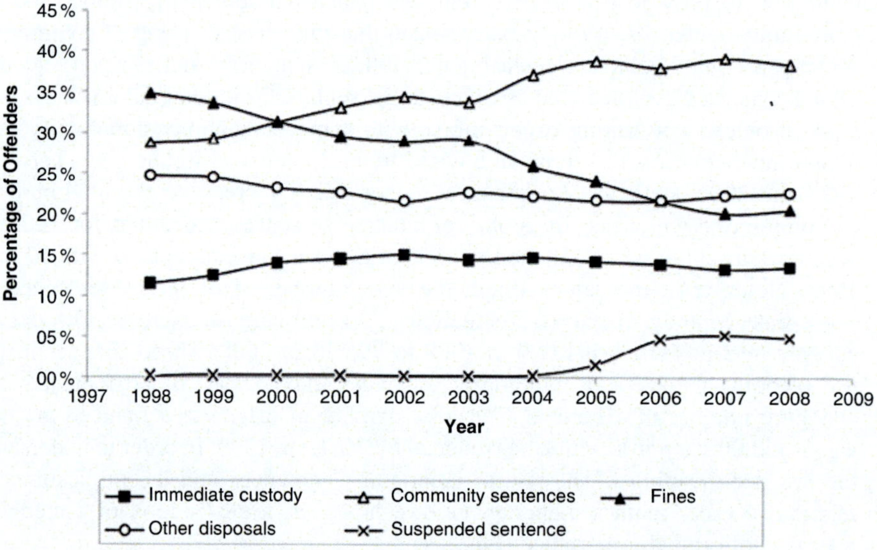

Fig. 3.5 Disposal rates for indictable offences at magistrates' courts 1998–2008[371]

1998 to 25% in 2008.[372] As can be seen from Fig. 3.5, at magistrates' courts, the proportionate use of custody was 11% in 1998 which then reached a peak in 2002, and thereafter has declined modestly. The immediate custody rate was

[370]Data compiled from Ministry of Justice (2010), *op. cit*, p.18.

[371]*ibid.*, p. 19.

[372]*ibid.*, p. 18.

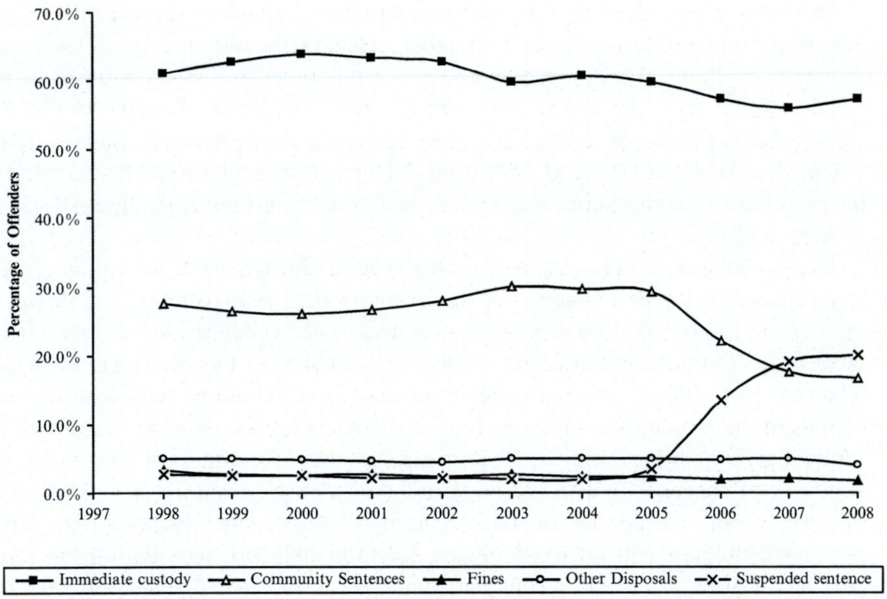

Fig. 3.6 Disposal rates for indictable offences at the crown court 1998–2008[373]

13% in 2008.[374] At the Crown Court (Fig. 3.6), immediate custody stood at over 60% of all sentencing options from 1998 to 2002 but since then has reduced to 57% of all disposals in 2008.

The decline in the use of immediate custody was attributed in part to the introduction of the suspended sentence order. With its new form applicable to offenders aged 18 and above, a marked increase in the use of the suspended sentence has been taking place. It rose from 0.2% (3,400) of all sentences in 1998 to 3% (41,200) of sentences in 2008.[375] The use of suspended sentences for indictable offenders has increased, from 0.7% of the sentences in 2004 to 9% of the sentences in 2008.[376] In the Crown Court, there was also a steady increase. The use of the suspended sentence for indictable offenders increased from 4% in 2005, to 20% in 2008.[377] However, as has recently been demonstrated, rather than being used for more serious offences, the new suspended sentences appear to substitute community orders, or are otherwise used for summary offences. The estimation is that "just over 40% of sentences orders are being used for the less serious, summary only offences".[378]

---

[373]Data compiled from Ministry of Justice (2010) *op. cit.*

[374]*Ibid.*, p. 20.

[375]Home Office (2010), p. 17.

[376]*Ibid.*, p. 18.

[377]*Ibid.*, p. 20.

[378]Ministry of Justice (2007) Penal Policy: A Background Paper, accessible from the following link, p. 9: http://www.justice.gov.uk/docs/Penal-Policy-Final.pdf.

In the same period, the overall use of community sentences grew, as they were the most common disposal for indictable offences (accounting for 33% of all sentences in 2008). Attention must be paid at this point to distinct patterns in the use of community sentences at magistrates' courts and Crown Courts. As Fig. 3.5 shows, the proportion of community sentences given at magistrates' courts were on the increase between 1998 and 2008, from 29% in 1998 to 38% in 2008. In contrast, the proportion of community sentences at the Crown Court fell from 29% in 2005 to 17% in 2008.

These differences between magistrates' courts and Crown Courts may appear self-explanatory at first glance, as these courts deal with offences of different gravity and as juveniles are predominantly dealt with at magistrates' courts. Nonetheless, the bourgeoning difference is precisely what Mair views as an evidence of what he terms 'down-tariffing': the imposition of community sentences for less serious offences than was previously the case. Mair substantiates his argument on 'down-tariffing' by pointing to the increasing use of community sentences for summary offences.[379] In a similar vein in a recent study, Bottoms *et al.* highlights that the use of community orders for summary offences has increased by 170% between 1992 and 2002 while their use for indictable offences during the same period was 50%.[380] Indeed, recent statistics show that between 1998 and 2008, the use of community sentences for summary non-motoring offences increased both in absolute and proportionate numbers. Intriguingly, as can be seen from Fig. 3.7 during the same period, summary non-motoring offenders, after an initial increase

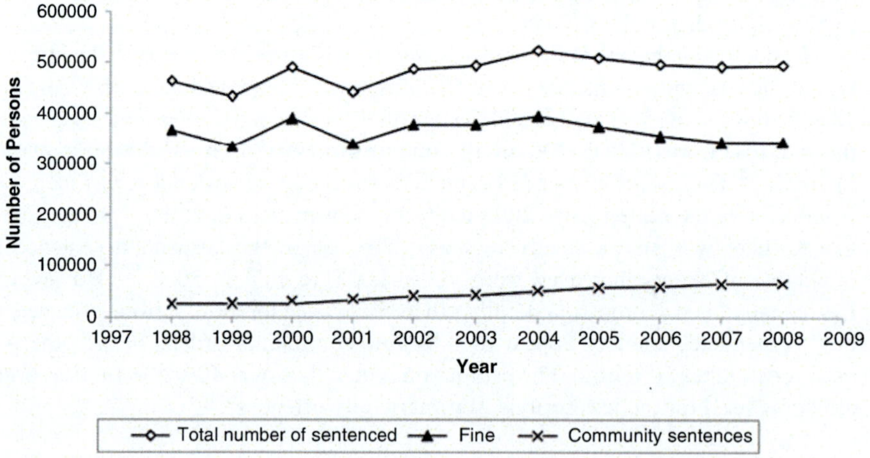

Fig. 3.7 Sentencing disposals for summary non-motoring offences 1998–2008[381]

[379]Mair (2007) *op. cit.*, pp. 261–262.

[380]Bottoms *et al.* (2004), *op. cit.*, p. 11.

[381]Data compiled from Ministry of Justice (2010) *op. cit.*

until 2004, considerably declined while the proportionate use of community sentences for summary non-motoring offences increased from an average 5% in 1998 to 13% in 2008.[382]

Bottoms *et al.*'s findings in relation to offender types are also pertinent for the present discussion. Examining both the sentencing and probation statistics they have underlined that the proportions of community sentences imposed on offenders with no prior convictions increased between 1992 and 2002.[383] This was most unequivocal with regard to the use of community service: over half of the offenders who receive a 'community service' order were convicted for the first time. Their conclusion therefore was that the increases in the use of community sentences took place at the expense of fines particularly.

In this context, the overall position of these sentences may be better appreciated if the declining use of fines is also considered. It was noted above that since the late 1970s there has been a decline in the use of fines. In 1981, magistrates' courts imposed a fine on over half of offenders sentenced for indictable offences, on 99% of those sentenced for summary motoring offences and 88% of those sentenced for other summary offences.[384] In 2008, the use of fines for summary non-motoring offences was 79%, and other summary offences accounted for 89%.[385] Crucially, the use of fines for indictable offences has continuingly declined from 28% in 1998 to 16% in 2008.[386] At magistrate's courts, fines were the most common disposal in 1998, accounting for 35% of sentences given for indictable offences. Fines have since fallen to the third most common disposal, accounting for 21% of all sentences in 2008. In the Crown Court, fines accounted for 1.8% of all sentences in 2008, compared with 3.3 in 1998.[387] In view of the decline in the fine and the increase in community sentences together, the assumption is warranted that some of those offenders who received a community order might have previously been given a fine.[388]

In the light of these figures, the English experience with non-custodial sanctions suggests that there is no straightforward relationship between the number of available sentencing options involving no term of custody and the use of custody. Most of the time, disposals intended to be alternatives to custody are used as alternatives to other non-custodial disposals rather than in place of imprisonment.

[382]Data compiled from Home Office (2010) http://www.justice.gov.uk/publications/docs/sentencing-statistics-2008-chapter1-tables.xls. (Access Date: March 2010).

[383]In this respect see also, Morgan, R. (2003) Thinking About the Demand for Probation Service, *Probation Journal*, vol. 50, no 1, pp. 7–19.

[384]Home Office (1982) *Criminal Statistics, England and Wales, 1981*, p. 124.

[385]Home Office (2010) Table 1.2 Offenders sentenced by offence group and outcome, all courts, 1998–2008.

[386]Home Office (2008) p. 18.

[387]Home Office Statistics (1998) Tables 77, 120 and (2008) Table 83645.

[388]Millie, A, Jacobson, J. and Hough, M. (2005) Understanding the Growth in the Prison Population in England and Wales, in Emsley, C. (ed.) *The Persistent Prison*, Francis Boutle, London, pp. 97–98, see also Ashworth (2007), *op. cit.*, p. 1015.

It is therefore not surprising that the prison population rate in England has been increasing constantly; from 88 per 100,000 population in 1992 to 152 in the early days of 2010 and that with a national prison population of 83,378, the capacity of prisons has been well exceed.[389] The comparative lesson which can be drawn from the English experience is that the extension of the catalogue of sanctions does not necessarily bring a reduction in the use of custody with it. It is indeed true that "offering sentencers a wider and more attractive menu of community penalties will not be, in itself, an effective way to discourage them from using custody".[390]

[389]Data compiled from the wep page of the Centre for International Prison Studies http://www.kcl.ac.uk/depsta/law/research/icps/worldbrief/wpb_country.php?country=169 (Acces Date: March 2010).

[390]Hough *et al.*, *op. cit.*, p. 61.

Chapter 4
Alternatives to Imprisonment in Germany: Less Is More?

4.1 The Foundation: Individualised Punishment

Tracing the roots of the concept of alternatives to imprisonment in Germany requires a reflection on the conceptual history of punishment and the purposes assigned to it. Chapter 2, in this context, aimed to identify the background of the shifting perceptions in respect to alternatives to imprisonment. It attempted to highlight the genealogy of ideas in the European context, within which particular attention is devoted to the debate between 'classical' and 'modern' schools. The first section takes this debate as a background and goes on to study its implications in practice, thereby highlighting the affinity between the legislative developments and the jurisprudence of the 'modern' school, in particular in the writings of von Liszt.

As a starting point it must be noted that as early as the turn of the nineteenth century, confidence in the use of short-term imprisonment and even in imprisonment in general began to decline in Germany.[1] It was at this time that a consensus began to emerge that the existing form and enforcement of short-term imprisonment could

[1]Famously, von Liszt stated that a short prison sentence is "worthless, indeed harmful. It does not deter, it does not improve, it contaminates." von Liszt, *op. cit.,* vol. 1, Kriminalpolitische Aufgaben, p. 382; Rosenfeld, E. (1890) *Welche Strafmittel können an die Stelle der kurzzeitigen Freiheitsstrafe gesetzt werden?*, Guttentag, Berlin, p. 74, Fuld, L. (1890) Die kurzzeitige Freiheitsstrafe und ihr Ersatz, *Der Gerichtsaal*, vol. 43, pp. 446–479, Appelius, H. (1891) *op. cit.*, Aschrott, P., F. (1899) *Ersatz kurzzeitiger Freiheitsstrafen – eine kriminalpolitische Studie*, Richter, Hamburg, Finger, A. (1904) Lehrbuch des deutschen Strafrechts, Heymann, Berlin, p. 459, Gennat (1905) *Das Strafensystem und seine Ref*orm, Mauke, Hamburg, pp. 24–25, Hoberg, J. (1910) *Ist die sachgemäße Ausgestaltung der Geldstrafe als Ersatz anderer Strafarten und zur Vermeidung kurzzeitiger Freiheitsstrafen für ein neues Strafgesetz zu Empfehlen?*, Noske, Leipzig, particularly, pp. 58–73, von Lilienthal, K. (1912) Der Streit um die Strafrechtsreform (Akademische Rede zur Erinnerung an den zweiten Gründer der Universität), Hörning, Heidelberg, Bamberger, G. (1917) *Geldstrafe statt Gefängnis*, Enke, Stuttgart.

Agreeing with von Liszt, Wach acknowledged that short-term imprisonment in its current form was useless. However, Wach directed his criticism against the existing enforcement method of short-term imprisonment, rather than the notion of short-term imprisonment in general, see Wach, A. (1890) *Die Reform der Freiheitsstrafe: Ein Beitrag zur Kritik der bedingten und unbestimmten Verurteilung*, Duncker & Humblot, Leipzig, p. 17. In the same direction, see e.g., Heilborn, P. (1908) *Die kurze Freiheitsstrafe*, reprinted in 1978, Scientia, Darmstadt, Krohne (1908), Welche

Ö. Sevdiren, *Alternatives to Imprisonment in England and Wales, Germany and Turkey*, 115
DOI 10.1007/978-3-642-17351-6_4, © Springer-Verlag Berlin Heidelberg 2011

hardly do any good and might even be responsible for some harm. One of the essential premises of criticism of short-term imprisonment[2]; which at the time received general support, was that prison sentences of short duration failed to 'correct', a notion which is in modern parlance referred to as resocialisation.[3] By assigning such a role to the prison beside its 'containment' function, it was taken for granted that 'correction' was a process which must be facilitated by the prison regime. Regardless of what kind of system was envisaged, liberal or vindictive, the expected 'success' of prisons could only be feasible with an appropriate duration of imprisonment. Hence, it was believed that a term of imprisonment made up of a few days, weeks or even months would be too short to exert a 'positive' influence on an offender's behaviour in preventing future criminal conduct.[4] On the contrary, it was acknowledged that a short-term prison stay could have adverse effects on first-time, petty and juvenile offenders by bringing them into contact with habitual offenders.[5] At the time, the description of prisons as 'schools of crime' shows a deep disbelief in the ability of prisons to turn inmates into law abiding citizens.[6]

Strafmittelsystem empfiehlt sich für das künftige Strafgesetzbuch?' in *Verhandlungen des 29. Juristentag*, vol. 4, Guttentag, Berlin, pp. 199–245.

See also, Exner, F. (1931) Studien über die Strafzumessungspraxis der Deutschen Gerichte, Wiegandt, Leipzig , p. 26, Lösener, M., L. (1958) *Beitrag zum Problem der kurzen Freiheitsstrafen*, unpublished PhD Thesis, University of Cologne, Stenner, D. (1968) *Die kurzfristige Freiheitsstrafe und die Möglichkeiten zu ihrem Ersatz durch andere Sanktionen*, Kriminalistik-Verlag, Hamburg, Kürzinger, J. (1984) Die Freiheitsstrafe und ihre Surrogate in der Bundesrepublik Deutschland, at p. 1834 in Jescheck, H.-H. (ed.) *Die Freiheitsstrafe und ihre Surrogate im deutschen und ausländischen Rech*t, pp. 1737–1938, pp. 1832–1835. See also, Galassi, S. (2004) Kriminologie im deutschen Reich, Steiner, Stuttgart.

For a detailed account on the intellectual foundations of alternatives to imprisonment, see Kubink, M. (2002) *Strafen und ihre Alternativen im zeitlichen Wandel*, Duncker & Humblot, Berlin, pp. 46–199, for the discussion on short-term imprisonment, pp. 107–111.

[2]The fiscal arguments against the use of short-term imprisonment were even then not absent. See Fuld, *op. cit.*, p. 446, Hoberg, *op. cit.*, p. 66.

[3]Unlike the state of affairs in the contemporaneous French literature, at this period the term rehabilitation did not belong to the academic and legal vocabulary in Germany. However, all the connotations of this term were carried by the German word, *Besserung*, which can literally be translated into English as betterment or improvement. Within the discussion concerning *early historical developments,* 'correction', as the semantically closest translation of '*Besserung*', will be used. In the forthcoming discussion, 'rehabilitation' will be employed as the generic term denoting the notion of prevention of reoffending by virtue of addressing the individual circumstances of an offender in relation to adult criminal law. Finally, the 'term' resocialisation will also be used where reference is made directly to the conceptualisation of German legal scholarship i.e. when an 'insider's' perspective is meant to be emphasised.

On the themse, see Delaquis, E. (1906) *Die Rehabilitation im Strafrecht*, Guttentag, Berlin, Peters, K. (1960) *Grundprobleme der Kriminalpädagogik*, de Gruyter, Berlin, pp. 336–341.

[4]Aschrott, *op. cit.*, pp. 1–8, Rosenfeld, *op. cit.*, p. 155, Heilborn, *op. cit.*, p. 50, Wach, *op. cit*, p. 19, Hoberg, *op. cit.*, p. 60.

[5]Particularly, von Liszt (1905), *op. cit.*, Rosenfeld, *op. cit.*, p. 173, Fuld, *op. cit.*, p. 447, Wach, *op. cit.*, p. 19.

[6]See von Liszt, Kriminalpolitische Aufgaben, p. 347. Also, Hoberg, *op. cit.,* pp. 62–63, Wach, *op. cit.,* p. 350, Rosenfeld, *op. cit.*, pp. 151–161.

The over-representation of short prison sentences in sentencing statistics and its implications for the penal justice system as a whole attracted widespread attention. Between 1882 (the first year of the publication of (imperial) statistics) and 1887, prison sentences constituted 70% of all sentences. Prison sentences of less than 3 months constituted 53% of these sentences.[7] Even more alarmingly, statistics demonstrated that a significant part of the prison population was composed of offenders sentenced to 1–8 days. In 1890, prison sentences under 4 days constituted 11.5% of all prison sentences, while those of 4–8 days constituted 10.5% of all prison sentences.[8] The documentation of the abundance of short-term prison sentences evoked the demand to raise the minimum term of imprisonment. There were a number of suggestions for the minimum length of imprisonment ranging from 2 weeks to 2 months.[9] The most disseminated and discussed suggestion was the proposal of von Liszt, who was described as "the recognised leader of German criminologists in the fight against short-term imprisonment".[10] Von Liszt proposed that the minimum sentence of imprisonment should be set at 6 weeks.[11] Ultimately, however, no solution could be reached.[12]

Notably, another direction driven by scepticism of the usefulness of short-term imprisonment was the advocacy of a more rigorous and demanding short-term imprisonment making use of corporal punishment, solitary confinement and punishment peculiar to military prisons, insofar as the use of it was deemed indispensable.[13] The central tenet of this perspective was that if short-term imprisonment could be

---

[7] Rosenfeld, *op. cit.*, p. 119.

[8] Stapenhorst, H. (1993) *Die Entwicklung des Verhältnisses von Geldstrafe zu Freiheitsstrafe*, Duncker & Humblot, Berlin, *op. cit.*, p. 37, see also, von Liszt, Kriminalpolitische Aufgaben, pp. 342–344.

[9] See Wach, *op. cit.*, p. 64, six weeks, Fuld, *op. cit.*, p. 448, two months, in Ebermayer, L. (1908) Welches Strafmittel empfiehlt sich für das künftige Strafgesetzbuch in Verhandlungen des 29. Deutschen Juristentag, vol. 1, pp. 259–312 six weeks, Krohne, *op. cit.*, 30 days, Gennat, *op. cit.*, p. 7, Heilborn, *op. cit.*, pp. 4–6. For an overview of various proposals see, Goldschmidt, J. (1908) Strafen (Haupt- und Nebenstrafen) und verwandte Maßregeln in Vergleichende Darstellung des deutschen und ausländischen Strafrechts, Allgemeiner Teil, vol. 4, in Birkmeyer, K. (ed.) Vergleichende Darstellung des deutschen und ausländischen Strafrechts, Allgemeiner Teil, vol. 4, Liebmann, Berlin, pp. 81–506, pp. 370–375.

[10] Bamberger, *op. cit.*, p. 11. See also Jescheck, H-H. (1983) Die Freiheitsstrafe bei Franz von Liszt im Lichte der modernen Kriminalpolitik in Kohlmann, G. (ed.) *Festschrift für Ulrich Klug zum 70. Geburtstag*, Deubner, Köln, p. 264.

[11] von Liszt (1905), Kriminalpolitische Aufgaben, pp. 290–467, p. 382.

[12] von Liszt, F. (1905) Kriminalpolitische Aufgaben, Aufsätze und Vorträge, vol. 1, p. 382, see also Die Reform der Freiheitstrafe, p. 515.

[13] Most provocatively by Wach, *op. cit.*, pp. 16–20, Fuld, *op. cit.*, pp. 449–453, Heilborn, *op. cit.*, pp. 31–45, Felisch (1893) 'Empfiehlt sich die Einführung von Verschärfungen der Freiheitsstrafen im Sinne des österreichischen Entwurfs, *Verhandlungen des 22. Deutschen Juristentag*, vol.3, pp. 1–42 and Kronecker (1893) Empfiehlt sich die Einführung von Verschärfungen der Freiheitsstrafen im Sinne des österreichischen Entwurfs, *ibid*, pp. 43–92.

See also Sichart (1904) *Die Freiheitsstrafe im Anklagestande und ihre Verteidigung*, Winter, Heidelberg, p. 7, Offner, J. (1896) Auf welche Weise kann der Vollzug der Freiheitsstrafen, designed as a serious hardship, the painful experience would provide an 'unforgettable lesson', and it would exert a lasting deterrent impact. In 1890, in the German Section of the *Internationale Kriminalistische Vereinigung* in Halle, this idea was further developed by spelling out the potential components of such an enforcement regime.[14] The proposed regime included hard beds, restricted diets, confinement in darkness, corporal penalties, stricter forms of compulsory work, fewer privileges and less association between inmates.[15]

Another manifestation of the quest to reduce recourse to short-term imprisonment was to expand the scope of the fine and to create alternative sentencing options. The alternatives were seen as suitable for juvenile offenders, but also for first-time and petty adult offenders.[16] Von Liszt's classification of offenders, as occasional offenders, persistent but corrigible offenders, and incorrigible offenders and their corresponding punishments, as discussed earlier, was very much reflective of the spirit of this period.[17] Notably, the alternative catalogue of sanctions under discussion was as broad as in contemporary discussions, including conditional suspension of the execution of the sentence, probation, the extension of fines, beneficial public work (*opus publicum*), particularly in lieu of imprisonment for fine default, corporal punishment, home detention and warnings. Of those options, being affected by the work of international organisations as outlined earlier in this study, the conditional conviction and the fine were attached with particular importance. Both of these sentencing measures proved to be highly 'popular' in academic writing and significantly inspired subsequent law-making.

Before going on to identify the developments concerning these sanctions, this section can be concluded with the observation that this period witnessed the formation of three approaches towards (short-term) imprisonment which were to dominate subsequent legislative initiatives and scholarly argument: legislative restriction of the reliance on custody, the creation of substitutes, and a less agreed upon but still surviving strand, particularly significant in the 1950s, known in the English terminology as the 'short-sharp-shock' approach.

---

insbesondere derjenigen von der kurzer Dauer, wirksamer gestallt werden? In *Mitteilungen der Internationale Kriminalistische Vereinigung*, vol. 5, pp.195–203.

Von Liszt was not against this perspective on principle, see e.g. ‚Die Reform der Freiheitsstrafe', *op. cit.*, vol. 1, p. 516 and 520. In this respect see also, Goldschmidt, *op. cit.*, pp. 362–370.

[14]See *die Zeitschrift für die gesamte Strafrechtswissenschaft*, vol. 11, Addendum, Zweite Landesversammlung der Gruppe Deutsches Reich (1891), the contributions of Simonson and Kronecker, pp. 21–34 and pp. 34–38, respectively.

[15]*Ibid.*, p. 50.

[16]See e.g, von Liszt, Kriminalpolitische Aufgaben, *op. cit.*, Wach, *op. cit.*, pp. 9–10, Heilborn, *op. cit.*, p. 38, Fuld, *op. cit.*, pp. 453–469, Schmölder, R. (1894) Die verwahrlosten Kinder und die jugendlichen Verbrecher, *Der Gerichtsaal*, vol. 49, pp. 157–201.

[17]See above Chapter 2.

4.1.1 *Conditional Pardon (Bedingte Begandigung)*

Virtually nowhere had the reception of the notion of suspension of the imposition and/or execution of punishment generated such prolonged and zealous controversy as in Germany.[18] Given the magnitude of *Schulenstreit* and the subsequent dramatic historical developments, it was not surprising that in contradistinction to many other European countries as outlined in Chap. 2, the reform here took a rather tedious and slow course. Hence, in retrospect, von Liszt's description of the reception of the conditional sentence, which in his account was a most suitable means of limiting the use of short-term imprisonment, as "victory without struggle" at the *fin de siècle* appears to be an overly optimistic prophecy, when the rather belated and *sui generis* evolution of the latter in Germany is considered.[19]

To begin with, reference should be made to the German Jurists' Assembly in 1891. At this meeting, concurrent with the 'trends' both in the civil and common law jurisdictions[20] and upon the resolution adopted by the general assembly of the *Internationale Kriminalistische Vereinigung*,[21] the desirability of the introduction of the conditional sentence (*bedingte Verurteilung*) into law was considered. Notwithstanding strong opposition from an influential group of German scholars, the majority voted in favour of its incorporation into German penal law.[22] It was in this period that the conditional sentence, as predominantly the subject of academic debate, entered also into the domain of penal policy discussions in the parliament.[23]

[18]Among numereous studies see Lammasch, H. (1889) Empfiehlt sich die Einführung der bedingten Verurteilung (belgisches Gesetz vom 31 Mai 1888) in die Strafgesetzgebung der übrigen Länder und unter welchen Voraussetzungen? in *Mitteilungen der Internationale Kriminalistische Vereinigung*, pp. 34–43, Appelius, H. (1891) *Die Bedingte Verurteilung und die Anderen Ersatzmittel für Kurzzeitige Freiheitsstrafen:eine Kritik der neusten Reformbestrebungen auf dem Gebiet des Strafrechts*, 4th edition, Keßler, Cassel, von Liszt, F. Bedingte Verurteilung und Bedingte Begnadigung in Vergleichende Darstellung des deutschen und ausländischen Strafrechts, Allgemeiner Teil vol III, pp. 1–91, Kirchenheim (1890) *op. cit.*, pp. 51–69, Zucker (1892) Noch ein Wort zur Frage der sogenannte bedingte Verurteilung, *Gerichtssaal*, 47, pp. 255–263, Ebermayer (1908) *op. cit.*, pp. 283–286, Hoegner, H., W. (1911) Die bedingte Strafaussetzung nach dem Vorentwurf (verglichen mit der bedingten Begnadigung), Schreiber, München. For a detailed historical account on the theme see, Timasheff, *op. cit.*, Peters, J. (2000) *Die Entwicklung von Sanktionspraxis und Strafrechtsreform 1871 bis 1933 – eine Rechtshistorische Untersuchung unter besonderer Berücksichtigung der Reformmodelle zur Freiheitsstrafensubstitution,* Shaker, Aachen, Meyer-Reil, A. (2006) *Strafaussetzung zur Bewährung – Reformdiskussion und Gesetzgebung seit dem Ausgang des 19. Jahrhundert*, LIT, Berlin, pp. 13–159.

[19]"Sieg ohne Kampf", cited in Wach, *op. cit.*, p. 22.

[20]See Chapter 2.

[21]Internationale Kriminalistische Vereinigung (1889) *Mitteilungen der Internationalen Kriminalistischen Vereinigung*, Berlin, Guttentag, vol. 1, pp. 177–184.

[22]See Mener, H. (1892), Ist die bedingte Verurteilung im Strafrecht einzuführen?', *Verhandlungen des 21. Deutschen Juristentages*, vol. 1, pp. 206–226 and Seuffert, H. (1892), Ist die bedingte Verurteilung im Strafrecht einzuführen?', *ibid.*, pp. 227–258.

[23]The subject also appeared in the daily press. See, Kirchenheim, *op. cit.*, p.53.

On various occasions, the German *Reichstag* witnessed the presentation of different arguments for and against the conditional sentence.[24]

The ongoing discussion on the suitability of the conditional sentence in innumerable articles, books and congress reports, eventually led to the adoption of a measure, which was called the conditional pardon (*bedingte Begnadigung*) – what von Liszt viewed as "the first concession to the new direction of penal law" and hence "a precursor to the conditional sentence".[25] Originating from the earlier decrees on the power of mercy of the Crown,[26] and 'early release',[27] the conditional pardon differed from conditional conviction in so far that it was laid at the disposal of administrative bodies (ultimately at the ministry of justice), rather than letting the courts decide on postponing the execution of a prison sentence or a part of it, having regard to the nature of the offence and the character of the offender.[28] For, it was recognised in official circles that pardoning was a Crown prerogative and its award could therefore only be delegated to administrative bodies on its behalf. A measure in the service of courts enabling them to grant the postponement of the execution of a sentence would have been regarded as a violation of the principle of the separation of powers.[29]

After its introduction in Saxony in 1895, all but two *Länder*[30] adopted this measure.[31] From the very beginning, however, the administration of the conditional pardon varied significantly.[32] In 1903, in order to secure uniformity throughout Germany on the principles of this measure, the *Länder*, with the mediation of the Imperial Justice Ministry (*Reichjustizamt*), agreed upon a number of *generales clausulae*.[33] According to these principles, offenders who had not yet attained the age of 18 were to be given priority, although the measure could also be applied to adults. Furthermore, conditional pardon could be granted only to offenders who had not previously served a prison sentence. This did not rule out granting more than

---

[24]Wach, A. (1900) Die bedingte Verurteilung vor dem Reichstag, pp. 81–84, *Deutsche Juristen-Zeitung*, vol. 5, no. 4, von Liszt (1908), *op. cit.*, p. 44, Hoegner, *op. cit.*, pp. 15–16. For the report, Meyers-Dunkel, *op. cit.*, p. 7.

[25]Kirchenheim, *op. cit.*, pp. 63–64, von Liszt (1908) *op. cit.*, p. 56, Lilienthal, *op. cit.*, p. 20.

[26]For these origins see Appelius, H. (1892) *Die Behandlung jugendlicher Verbrecher und verwahrloster Kinder*, Guttentag, Berlin, von Liszt (1908) *op. cit.*, p. 7, See Lissner. P., H. (1935) *Historische Entwicklung der Begnadigung und ihrer Grenzen*, Zentraldruckerei, Berlin.

[27]Vorläufige Entlastung, Section 23–26 of the Imperial Penal Code.

[28]For the individual characteristics of the conditional pardon in various Länder see von Liszt (1908) *op. cit.*, p. 46.

[29]*Ibid.*

[30]Mecklenburg-Strelitz and Reuß, see von Liszt (1908), *op. cit.*, p. 45.

[31]See von Liszt (1908), *op. cit.*, pp. 42–47.

[32]See von Liszt (1908) *op. cit.*, p. 46, Roeder, J. (1913) *Bedingte Strafaussetzung und Strafaussetzung für Fürsorge- und Anstaltszöglinge*, Halle/Saale.

[33]Reprinted in von Liszt (1908), Drucks. d. Reichstages 1903/04, No. 230, p. 995, see also, Klee, P. (1904) Die bedingte Begnadigung in den deutschen Bundesstaaten unter rechtsvergleichender Berücksichtigung der bedingten Verurteilung des Auslands, *Zeitschrift für die gesamte Strafrechtswissenschaft*, vol. 24, pp. 69–87, pp. 70–80.

one conditional pardon, since only the execution of a prison sentence would make an offender ineligible for the conditional pardon. Even when the offender had already served a term of imprisonment, the postponement of the execution of the sentence was still possible if extenuating circumstances existed. The rules did not set a maximum term of imprisonment for pardoning. However, in practice the conditional pardon was used primarily in relation to juveniles convicted for the first time, whose penalty would not exceed 6 months imprisonment.[34] Finally, the minimum probation period for conditional pardon, with respect to prison sentences not exceeding 2 years, was set at 1 year, and for prison sentences of more than 2 years, at 2 years.

The adoption of the conditional pardon by no means ended the discussion; it merely led to a shift in the debate from the compatibility of the conditional sentence with German penal law towards a contrasting of the conditional pardon with its 'functional equivalents' in the Anglo-American and European jurisdictions.[35] For those who held the view that pardoning was a privilege of the Crown, the institution of conditional pardon fulfilled the goals which conditional sentencing were expected to achieve, hence a uniform imperial regulation would suffice to deal with such problems as an uneven application in the various *Länder* associated with the use of this measure.[36] For others, the term conditional pardon, describing the widespread practice of suspension of the execution of the sentence, was essentially a misnomer, as the quality of the act required that it be imposed as a judicial decision rather than as an administrative pronouncement.[37] The latter body of opinion, thus, deemed a mere improvement in the regulation and procedure of the conditional pardon to be unsatisfactory. Rather than an imperial regulation of the competence of the pardon, a re-regulation of what was hitherto known as the conditional pardon was contemplated as the urgent task of legislation.[38]

Without ending the discussion conclusively on principle, the preliminary draft (*Vorentwurf*) of 1909 contained a section which empowered courts to suspend prison sentences of a term up to 6 months for offenders who had not previously received a sentence of imprisonment (*Gefängnissstrafe*) or detention (*Haft*).[39] The discretion of courts in this respect was considerably fettered by a section on assessment criteria. According to the preliminary draft, the measure could only be

[34]For a statistical analysis, see Klee, K. (1906) Die bedingte Begnadigung innerhalb der letzten sechs Jahre, *Zeitschrift für die gesamte Strafrechtswissenschaft*, vol. 26, pp. 458–487, see also Fritsch, M. (1999) *Die jugendstrafrechtliche Reformbewegung (1871–1923)*, ed. iuscrim, Freiburg, pp. 50–54, Hoegner, *op. cit.*, pp. 17–19.

[35]Liszt (1908) *op. cit.*, p. 54, Pistorius, E. (1934) *Die bedingte Strafaussetzung im Jugendgerichtgesetz*, Nolte, Düsseldorf p. 10, Fischer, *op. cit.*, pp. 18–19.

[36]See references in von Liszt (1908), *op. cit.*, pp. 58–59.

[37]*Ibid*, pp. 61–63.

[38]*Ibid.*

[39]Reichjustizsamt (1909) *Vorentwurf zu einem deutschen Strafgesetzbuch*, Guttentag, Berlin and Reichjustizsamt (1909) *Vorentwurf zu einem deutschen Strafgesetzbuch Begründung (Allgemeiner Teil)*, Guttentag, Berlin

used in cases where the assessment of the offence and the previous history of the offender warranted a special regard and it was to be expected that the offender would behave well in the future even without execution of the custody.[40] The suspension of custody on 'good conduct' was regarded as an exceptional measure to be used only when extenuating circumstances existed.[41] Another clause indicated that in the application of this measure, priority was to be given to juvenile offenders.[42]

Kahl, Liszt, Lilienthal and Goldschmidt's 'counter-draft' of 1910,[43] while being largely in agreement with the conditions and procedures of the preliminary draft, conceived of this measure in such a way[44] that it bore marked resemblance to the Anglo-American system of probation. The measure was called 'conditional execution of punishment', which meant that in line with the preliminary draft,[45] postponement rather than imposition was at issue. In contrast to the preliminary draft, however, the counter-draft proposed protective supervision (*Schutzaufsicht*), which was to be imposed in conjunction with the postponement of punishment and would continue during the probationary period specified by the court,[46] unless special circumstances justified an exception. Protective supervision was in essence conceived of as a measure of 'patronage'. It was meant to prevent the offender from associating with certain persons and from drinking alcohol. The supervisor also had the function of giving the offender advice and assistance in finding a suitable job.[47] After the expiration of the probationary period, the court was to consider whether the convict had followed the requirements of the probationary period. Notably, postponement of punishment also applied to fines.[48]

Subsequent draft penal codes of 1913[49] and 1919 replaced executive conditional pardon by a judicially imposed measure of analogous effect.[50] The statement of reasons attached to the draft of 1919 recognised that conditional pardon, theoretically to be granted only in exceptional cases, had over time become a standard device and an integral part of penal justice.[51] Conditional pardon, as an administrative

[40]Section 39/1 of the Preliminary Draft.

[41]Reichjustizsamt, *op. cit.*, p. 141.

[42]Section 39/2 of the Preliminary Draft.

[43]Kahl, W., von Lilienthal, K., von Liszt, F., and Goldschmidt, J. (1911) *Gegenentwurf zum Vorentwurf eines Deutschen Strafgesetzbuchs*, Guttentag, Berlin.

[44]Sections 92–94 *'Bedingte Strafvollstreckung'*.

[45]The counter-draft did not contain any priority clause in relation to juvenile offenders, as its authors were of the belief it would be unjust and inexpedient. For the justificatory reasons, see Kriegsmann, N., H. (1911) *Begründung Denkschrift*, Guttentag, Berlin, p. 123.

[46]The probationary period was, according to the counter-draft, from 2 to 5 years. (Section 92 paragraph 2).

[47]Section 60 of the Counter Draft.

[48]Section 92 of *ibid.* (justificatory reason, p. 123).

[49]See, Reichsjustizministerium (1921) *Entwürfe zu einem deutschen Strafgesetzbuch*, vol. 1: Entwurf der Strafrechtskommission (1913), Berlin, de Gruyter, Section 74.

[50]The 1919 Draft in Reichjustizministerium (1921) *op. cit.*, vol 2., Section 63.

[51]Denkschrift zu dem Entwurf von 1919 in Reichjustizministerium (1921), *op. cit.*, pp. 64–66.

disposal, *praeter legem*, achieved its mission for the authors of the draft, which was to experiment with the idea of conditional suspension in Germany, and gather experience in this regard.[52] Based on these premises, the draft of 1919 put special emphasis on the need for a uniform legislative regulation following the Franco-Belgian model of 'sursis', the conditional suspension of the execution of the sentence.[53] Nonetheless, the respective draft still held resemblance to the Anglo-American conception of probation supervision in so far as the Counter-Draft's proposal on protective supervision was incorporated as a facultative measure applicable in combination with the suspension of the execution of the sentence.[54]

Informed by the legislative initiatives, during the same period of time a significant shift in the conception and practice of conditional pardon was taking place in a number of *Länder*. In 1919 and 1920, Bavaria, Baden, Hamburg and Prussia transferred the power to grant conditional pardon from the executive to courts for offences punishable by imprisonment less than 6 months.[55] Yet, under the new system, courts were still not empowered to act with independence, they acted as an organ of judicial administration bound by the directives of the ministry of justice. It was not until the enactment of the Juvenile Court Law that suspension of the sentence as a 'truly' judicial measure was recognised for the first time.

4.1.2 Alternatives to Imprisonment in Juvenile Justice Legislation

The reform described in the previous section cannot be adequately appreciated without reference to the role of the 'juvenile court movement'. Conditional pardon was conceived principally for juvenile offenders. It was certainly with regard to juvenile offenders that reform demands acquired greater support or otherwise met 'weaker resistance'.[56]

In Germany, as in many other western countries, the development of the juvenile court and its legislation was backed by growing concern for juvenile criminality and calls for prevention of juvenile re-offending.[57] In a broader sense, the demands of separate bodies and mechanisms dealing with juvenile offenders were marked by the recognition of the need for greater care, protection, and even more importantly,

---

[52] *Ibid.*

[53] *Ibid.*

[54] For a comparison, see Timasheff (1943), *op. cit.*

[55] For details see, see See Hellwig, A. (1921) *Die bedingte Strafaussetzung der Strafvollstreckung in Preußen, in Preußen und im Reich*, Müller, Berlin, Müller, Meyer-Reil, *op. cit.*, pp. 145–150.

[56] Schaffstein, F. and Beulke, W. (2002) *Jugendstrafrecht*, Kohlhammer, 14th edition, Stuttgart, pp. 36–37, Voß, M. (1986) *Jugend ohne Rechte*: die Entwicklung des Jugendstrafrechts, Campus-Verl, Frankfurt, Fritsch, M. (1999), *op. cit.*

[57] See e.g., Appelius, *op. cit.*, p. 8, Aschrott (1892) *Die Behandlung der verwahrlosten und verbrecherischen Jugend und Vorschläge zur Reform*, Liebmann, Berlin, von Liszt, Die Kriminalität der Jugendlichen, *op. cit.*, vol 2 and Kriminalpolitische Aufgaben, pp. 447–467, Liepmann, M. (1909) *Die Kriminalität der Jugendlichen und ihre Bekämpfung*, Mohr, Tübingen.

control and monitoring of juveniles as a fundamental task of the emerging welfare state.[58] One expression of this new more interventionist and, in Foucauldian terms, 'disciplinary' approach were several initiatives to expand state powers and institutions to protect juveniles who were judged to be at risk. Chief among these was the enactment of the Juvenile Welfare Law of 1922.[59] Another manifestation of the changing approach towards juvenile offenders was a critical appraisal of the existing penal system, which was generally found to fail to live up to 'the crime prevention agenda' of the time.[60] The critical view of the ability of the existing system to cope with juvenile criminality appears to have eventually paved the way for the emergence of a specialised court for juvenile offenders.[61]

Undoubtedly, the development of juvenile justice in foreign jurisdictions, in particular in the Anglo-Saxon jurisdictions provided a further stimulus for the institution of a separate system of juvenile justice.[62] In the early years of the last century, the first juvenile courts were established in Cologne, Frankfurt, and Berlin. The inauguration of these courts was followed by a rapid spread to other cities. It was also in this period that the first juvenile prisons opened.[63] These institutional developments were accompanied by legislative initiatives to provide a distinctive set of rules regulating the adjudication and sentencing of juveniles. The principles of juvenile legislation were established as a basis of juvenile court legislation, under the influence of the notion of individual prevention, most particularly through the inspiration and guidance of von Liszt.[64] A radical shift of focus took place from an orientation towards retribution and general deterrence to individual deterrence. A growing body of opinion viewed crime as a symptom of educational and material deficiencies. The slogan 'education instead of punishment' expressed the agenda of individual prevention, which ultimately found its legislative expression in the enactment of the Juvenile Court Law in 1923.

---

[58]Two historical studies are in this respect highly relevant, Peukert, D., J., K. (1986) *Grenzen der Sozialdisziplinerung (Aufstige und Krise der deutschen Jugendfürsorge von 1878 bis 1932)*, Bund-Verlag, Köln, pp. 37–139 and Dickinson, E., R (1996) *The Politics of German Child Welfare from the Empire to the Federal Republic*, Harvard University Press, Cambridge.

[59]Voß (1986), *op. cit.*, pp. 175, Dickinson, *op. cit.*

[60]Appelius in IKV Halle (1891), pp. 67–55. See also Ruscheweyh, H. (1918) *Die Entwicklung des deutschen Jugendgerichts*, Dietsch & Rückner, Weimar, pp. 49–74.

[61]For recent studies on the theme, see Miehe, O. (1968) Anfänge der Diskussion über eine strafrechtliche Sonderbehandlung in Schaffstein, F. and Miehe, O. (eds) *Weg und Aufgabe des Jugendstrafrechts, Wissenschaftliche Buchgesellschaft,* Darmstadt, Fritsch, pp. 22–27.

[62]See in particular, Freudenthal, B. (1907) *Amerikanische Kriminalpolitik, Das Jugendgericht in Frankfurt*, Ruscheweyh, *op. cit.*, 36–48, also, Cornel, H. (1984) *Geschichte des Jugendstrafvollzugs*, Beltz, Weinheim.

[63]The first juvenile prison was opened in Wittlich (in Rhineland) in 1911.

[64]Cornel, *op. cit.*, pp. 77–85, Oberwittler, D. (2000) *Von der Strafe zur Erziehung (Jugendkriminalpolitik in England und Deutschland 1850–1920)*, Campus, Frankfurt, *op. cit.*, pp. 92–101, see also Wolf, J. (1986) Die Entwicklung der Gesetzgebung im Jugendstrafrecht, *Zeitschrift für Rechtssoziologie*, vol. 7, pp. 123–142, p. 126.127.

Central to this law was the idea that imprisonment should be a last resort, only to be used when educational measures (*Erziehungsmaßregeln*) were deemed to be insufficient as a deterrent. Educational measures included warnings, referral to the custody of legal guardian or school, the imposition of conditions, placement under protective supervision and corrective training (*Fürsorgeerziehung*).[65] An appropriate measure was to be imposed, taking into account the personality of the offender and the circumstances of the offence. Only when educational measures were insufficient was recourse to 'punishment' permitted in the sense of adult criminal law, i.e., imprisonment. The Juvenile Court Law also contained the possibility of dispensing with punishment when sufficient educational measures had already been applied on the juvenile.[66]

Together with the abolishment of penal servitude for juvenile offenders and the limitation of the principle of mandatory prosecution,[67] the enactment of educational measures was a significant attempt to replace the traditional system, which had limited itself to mitigating sentences for young offenders.[68] The break with the past was probably most discernible in the adoption of the suspended sentence probationary assistance that was conceived as a genuine alternative to juvenile confinement. The Juvenile Court Law empowered courts to suspend the execution of an imprisonment term for a period from 2 to 5 years.[69] Suspension of a prison term was particularly advised when the immediate execution of the sentence would endanger the feasibility of an educational scheme. Suspension was not limited to first-time offenders.[70] The court was authorised to prescribe certain rules of conduct for the juvenile offender,[71] or place her/him under protective supervision,[72] which could be modified during the probation period. The probationary period could extend up to 5 years.

The 'conditional sentence', as stipulated in the Juvenile Court Law, inspired various later draft laws. But none of these draft penal laws were enacted. It was not until 1953 that a form of conditional sentence was introduced into the Penal Code.

---

[65] Section 7 of the Juvenile Court Law.

[66] Section 9 (3).

[67] Section 32 of the Juvenile Court Law vested the public prosecutor with the power to waive prosecution with the consent of the juvenile court judge, where the offence was of a petty nature and the guilt of the offender was minor and where adequate 'educational' measures had been undertaken either by an institution or by individuals including teachers, parents or other relatives.

[68] All sentences of imprisonment were required to be mitigated by one half. The minimum age for the imposition of an imprisonment term, in accordance with the minimum age of criminal responsibility, was 14, which was considerably higher in many other countries in Europe. Section 9 (2) of the Juvenile Court Law.

[69] Section 10 and Section 12 (1) of the Juvenile Court Law.

[70] Explanatory note of Section 10.

[71] Sections 34, 36.

[72] Section 12 of the Juvenile Court Law.

4.1.3 The Fine

In the Imperial Penal Code, the fine, as a sole sanction or alongside a custodial sentence, was conceived for a relatively small number of offences compared to certain other jurisdictions in Europe.[73] Under Section 28 of the Code, fine defaulters were liable to a prison sentence (*Gefängnisstrafe*) or a detention (*Haft*) sentence, depending on the classification of the offence. The maximum amount of the fine in relation to each offence was statutorily provided and in any case could not be less than three marks for *Vergehen* (misdemeanours) and one mark for *Übertretungen* (infractions).[74] The initial version of the Code made no mention of the consideration of the financial circumstances of the offender, which fit well with the strictly offence-based orientation of the Code. Against the backdrop of the intellectual movement searching for alternatives to custodial sentences,[75] there was widespread agreement that the range of offences punishable by fine should be extended.[76] By increasing the scope of the fine, it was hoped that its "effectively meaningless" position could be reversed in court practice.[77]

During the early years of the Weimar Republic, demands were made to extend the use of the fine. The preliminary draft of 1909 contained a number of significant changes to that effect.[78] The draft proposed that the financial resources of the offender be taken into account in determining the amount of the fine, and that offenders be permitted to pay the fine in instalments, and to do public work in the case of fine defaults.

In the aftermath of the First World War, under the conditions of sharply increased national debt, inflated currency and reparations payments due to the

[73]See, Schmölder, R. (1902) *Die Geldstrafe (Vortrag gehalten auf der 74. Jahresversammlung der Rheinisch-Westfälischen Gefängnisgesellschaft in Düsseldorf am 15 Oktober 1902)*, Griebsch, Hamm for the exact figures p. 8, for the comparison see Hoberg, *op. cit.*, p. 14, von Liszt, F. (1908) *Lehrbuch des deutschen Strafrechts*, 16/17th edition, Guttentag, Berlin, p. 262, Goldschmidt, *op. cit.*, pp. 398–411. See also a detailed study of the fine in the Imperial Code, Gutmann, H. (1909) *Die Natur der Geldstrafe und ihre Verwendung im heutigen Reichsstrafrecht*, Hirschfeld, Leipzig, See IKV Halle, pp. 51–67, see also Häger, J. (2006) from Section 40 to 43 in Laufhütte, H. W, Rissing-van Saan, R. and Tidemann, K. (eds.) *Leipziger Kommentar*, vol. 2, pp. 836–952, pp. 841–842.

[74]Section 27 of the (Imperial) Penal Code.

[75]Von Liszt, Kriminalpolitische Aufgaben, pp. 406–410, Bamberger, *op. cit.*

[76]Hoberg, *op. cit.*, p. 49, Schmölder, *op. cit.*, p. 8 and 22, Trager, L. (1911) Die Geldstrafe als Hauptstrafe, *Gerichtssaal,* vol. 78, pp. 241–330.

[77]Hoberg, *op. cit.*, pp. 68–73, Aschrott, *op. cit.*, p. 59.

[78]Georgi, P., G. (1914) *Die Reform der Geldstrafe im Vorentwurf zu einem Deutschen Strafgesetzbuch und im Gegenentwurf zu Diesem Vorentwurf unter Berücksichtigung der veröffentlichen Beschlüsse der Strafrechtskommission*, Schulze, Meerane, Büddemann, H.(1912) *Die Geldstrafe nach dem Vorentwurf zu einem Deutschen Strafgesetzbuch und dem Gegenentwurf* von Kahl, Lilienthal, Liszt, Goldschmidt, Erlangen, Fuld, *op. cit.*, pp. 456–458.

Versailles Treaty, these proposals found a particularly favourable setting.[79] Rebuilding the German economy required the parsimonious use of public expenditure, and at this juncture the fine was deemed a cost-efficient measure of raising revenue for the state treasury without consuming additional resources in its implementation.[80] Under these circumstances the arguments of the sceptics on the limitations of the fine, i.e. its unequal impact upon individual offenders and the transferability of the financial burden to third persons,[81] appear to have lost their former strength. On the other hand, a dramatic depletion in monetary value made an adjustment of the provisions on the fine particularly urgent, a necessity which, for many, could not be deferred to a complete reform of the penal code.[82] Against this background, the draft of 1919 broadened the scope of the fine by making a greater number of *Vergehen* punishable by fine.[83] Furthermore, this draft required courts to ensure whether 'the purpose of the punishment' could be fulfilled by an imposition of a fine in cases where the law provided for the fine and imprisonment alternatively.[84] In the latter case, courts were to empower to convert a custodial sentence of up to 1 month into a fine.[85]

In 1921, the 'Law on the Extension of the Application Field of the Fine and the Restriction of Short-Term Imprisonment' was enacted.[86] This law multiplied the maximum amount of the fine by ten, whereas the minimum sum of money was set at 100,000 Marks.[87] The law authorised courts to grant the offender leave to pay the fine in instalments within a specified period of time if immediate payment of the total amount could not reasonably be expected.[88] Section 4 of the Law obliged courts to take financial circumstances into account in determining the amount of the fine. Section 7 of the Law provided for work to be used as a way of dealing with fine defaulters; the implementation of this provision was conferred upon *Länder* administrations. More significantly, this law *required* the courts to convert prison

[79]Meyer, K. (1919) Strafensystem und Geldstrafe, *Deutsche Strafrechtszeitung*, vol. 6, no 7/8, pp. 242–243, Lösener, *op. cit.*, p. 11, Grebing, *op. cit.*, p. 34.

[80]Hellwig, A. (1922) *Das Geldstrafegesetz vom 21 Dezember 1922*, Müller, München, Meyer, K. (1919) Strafensystem und Geldstrafe, Peters, J, *op. cit.*, p. 59. Kubink, *op. cit.*, pp. 183–185, Bookbinder. P. (1996) *The Weimar Germany: the Republic of the Reasonable*, Manchester University Press, Manchester, p. 165.

[81]Peters, J., *op. cit.*, p. 36.

[82]Meyer, *op. cit.*, Peters, J., *op. cit.*, p. 61, Grebing, *op. cit.*, pp. 33–34, Häger, *op. cit.*, p. 842.

[83]Oetker, F. (1922) Die Geldstrafe nach dem Strafgesetzbuch von 1919, *Gerichtssaal,* vol. 88, pp. 161–268.

[84]Section 108 of the Draft 1919; see also Reichjustizministerium (1921), *op. cit.*, p. 97.

[85]*Ibid.*, Section 115 paragraph 2.

[86]RGBI, Nr. 118, p. 1604, "Gesetz zur Erweiterung des Anwendungsgebietes der Geldstrafe und zur Einschränkung der kurzen Freiheitsstrafe". 21.12.1921, see Hellwig, A. (1922) *Das Geldstrafengesetz*, Müller, München, pp. 1–16. See, Erwig, J. (1927) *Die Strafrechtliche und Strafprozessuale Bedeutung des § 27b des Reichsstrafgesetzbuches*, Janssen & Beine, Hüls, Kleber, H. (1933) *Die Ersatzgeldstrafe nach § 27b Strafgesetzbuch*, Tageblatt-Haus, Coburg.

[87]Section 1 of the respective law.

[88]*Ibid.*, Section 5.

sentences under 3 months imposed for *Vergehen* into fines whenever 'the purpose of punishment' could be achieved just as well by a fine.[89] In the case of non-payment of a fine without the offender's fault, the execution of a prison sentence could be avoided.[90] A second reform law of 1923 endeavoured to adjust fines to the level of precipitately increasing inflation.[91] Furthermore, this law incorporated the provisions of the law of 1921 (Sections 27b commutation to the fine, 27c consideration of financial circumstances of the offender, 28b performance of work instead of imprisonment in case of fine default) into the Penal Code, and also made it possible to convert *Haft* for *Übertretungen* (infractions) into a fine.[92]

The ideas underpinning the legislation from 1921 and 1923 were even more ambitiously espoused in the draft of the Penal Code prepared by Professor Gustav Radbruch, whose draft was viewed as "by and large the zenith of the legislative reform work" beginning in the nineteenth Century.[93] Gustav Radbruch, a disciple of von Liszt, served as Minister of Justice in the early 1920s; in this capacity he gave full support to the legislation regarding the fine. In Radbruch's Draft, the fine was conceived as a primary reaction against *Vergehen.* As long as the purpose of punishment could be achieved by a fine, this sanction could be imposed *regardless* of the maximum prison sentence prescribed for the offence.[94] As Baumann observed, the intention of Radbruch was to place the fine at the centre of the penal system.[95] This radical conception of the place of the fine in penal justice was also retained in the amended form of Radbruch's draft, which was adopted as the official draft in 1925, but it was abandoned in the draft penal codes of 1927 and 1930,[96] both of which maintained the 3 month maximum in the commutation of prison sentences to fines.

---

[89]*Ibid.*, Section 3.

[90]*Ibid.*, Section 8.

[91]See Alsberg, M. (1924) Geldentwertung und Strafrechtspflege, *Juristische Wochenschrift*, vol. 10, no 5, pp. 276–277.

[92]Verordnungen 23.11.1923 (RGBI I p. 1117) and 6.2.1924 (RGBI, I p. 44).

[93]Jescheck, H.-H. cited in Kubink, *op. cit.*, p. 173, see also pp. 174–175.

[94]Section 72/2 of the Radbruchs' draft. See Radbruch, G. (1952) Entwurf *eines Allgemeinen Deutschen Strafgesetzbuches*, Mohr, Tübingen. See Baumann, J. (1968) *Konsequenzen aus einer Reformarbeit –Nicht Aufgenommene Vorschläge Für die Strafrechtsreform in* Kaufmann, A. (ed.) *Gedächtnisschrift für Radbruch*, Vandenhoeck & Ruprecht, pp. 337–343.

[95]Baumann, J. (1969) Besteht heute die Möglichkeit die Freiheitsstrafe bis zum 6 Monaten zu beseitigen? In *Weitere Streitschriften*, Gieseking, Bielefeld, pp. 54–75, Zipf, H (1966) *Die Geldstrafe*, Luchterland, Berlin, p. 102, a critical consideration, see Peters, J., *op. cit.*, pp. 79–81. Nevertheless, his draft also had some intrinsic limitations. For example, the conversion of imprisonment to the fine in Radbruch's draft was provided as a special way of mitigating punishment laid at the discretion of the court. Hence, the commutation from custody to the fine in the framework of the respective draft was only possible where extenuating circumstances warranted it.

[96]See Kubink, *op. cit.*, p. 179.

The amendments with regard to fines proved to have had a significant impact upon practice.[97] In 1882, the proportionate use of fine constituted 25% of all the convictions concerning adults, while after the enactment of the legislation concerning fines in 1924 this proportion was more than twofold; 52.5%.[98] By 1928, fines were applied at a rate of 70%.[99] This significant change in the sanctioning practice has rightly been called a "turning point of German penal policy".[100]

4.2 Alternatives to Imprisonment and the Third Reich

As far as the conceptualisation of alternatives to imprisonment is concerned, prima facie it may appear that in the Third Reich era, there was continuity rather than discontinuity. On the surface, there was no rejection on principle[101] of prison substitutes insofar as they were compatible with the National Socialist conception of the (primary) purpose of punishment: the protection of the *Volksgemeinschaft* (folk community).[102] The National Socialist regime made use of amnesty laws, as had also been passed during the Weimar period. Considering these developments, Rusche and Kirchheimer talked of 'dualism'; a policy which deeply embodied the distinction between minor and 'dangerous' offenders.[103] However, a close look into this period reveals clearly that, even disregarding the discriminatory practice of the application of such disposals on various grounds, the draconian changes introduced in juvenile justice, the drastic restriction of the scope of alternatives to imprisonment,

---

[97] Even before this legislation, a significant increase in the use of the fine was occurring, which was explained by the influence of the academic discussions on the adverse effects of short-term imprisonment, see Bamberger, *op. cit.*, p. 20, also Kubink, *op. cit.*, p. 183.

[98] Stapenhorst, *op. cit.*, p. 42.

[99] Exner, *op. cit.*, p. 9.

[100] Heinz, W. (1981) Entwicklung, Stand und Struktur der Strafzumessungspraxis (Ein Übersicht über die nach allgemeinem Strafrecht verhängten Hauptstrafen von 1882 bis 1999), *Monatsschrift für Kriminologie und Strafrechtsreform*, vol. 64, pp. 148–173, p. 159, Stapenhorst, *op. cit.*, p. 45.

[101] See, Gürtner, F. and Freisler, R. (1936) *Das neue Strafrecht - Grundsätzliche Gedanken zum Geleit*, 2nd edition, Decker's Verlag, Berlin.

[102] Denkschrift des Preußischen Justizministers (1933) *Nationalsozialistisches Strafrecht*, Decker, Berlin, p. 138, see also Rietsch (1934) Strafensystem in Gürtner, F. (ed.) *Das kommende deutsche Strafrecht*, Vahlen, Berlin, p. 85.

[103] It is worthwhile to cite the paragraph in its entirety. "An interesting dualism is revealed in (the other fields of) criminal law. The great mass of minor offences against the existing social order is growing steadily with the growing economic difficulties and the increase in bureaucratic regulations, but it is not followed by a corresponding intensification of the repressive programme. The system of fines, the epitome of rationalised capitalist penal law, is at its height, despite the ideological attacks against it. Periodic amnesty laws discharge a mass of petty offenders in unprecedented numbers. It is noteworthy, however, that many minor offences (whole categories or merely individual cases) are singled out as injurious to the welfare of the nation and classed with the more serious crimes. They are treated with greater severity than before." Rusche and Kirchheimer, *op. cit.*, p. 206.

and the emphasis on deeply intrusive supervision measures severely limited the scope of such a 'dualist/bifurcatory' approach by limiting the number of eligible candidates for more lenient sentencing options.

The National Socialist government installed a Criminal Law Commission, with the mission of a wholesale renewal of the penal law.[104] The report of the Criminal Law Commission recognised that in exceptional cases the *Volksgemeinschaft* can waive its right to punish; that is the case when the nature of the offence and the personality of the offender justify a waiver and the protection of the *Volksgemeinschaft* does not make punishment necessary. In such a case, a departure from retribution was regarded as tolerable.[105] This was true especially where the offender, despite her/his wrongdoing, could still be regarded as a valuable member of society. In order to justify the desistance from 'punishment' in such cases, reference was made to such adverse effects of short-term imprisonment as criminal infection as well as uprooting the offender from her/his family and social milieu. The conclusion was that the avoidance of short-term prison sentences was an essential requirement for penal policy. In this sense, giving up the state's right to punish was regarded as the application of a utilitarian approach as expressed in the German proverb "*einmal ist keinmal*" (once does not count).[106] It was believed that a measure with special obligations, lasting several years, would be more conducive to individual deterrence than short-term imprisonment.[107]

Justified in this way, the conditional sentence, in a form similar to the Anglo-Saxon system of probation, did not seem to conflict with the premises of Nazi penal policy.[108] The Commission proposed a system of supervision accompanying the suspended sentence entitled 'warning with suspension of punishment' (*Verwarnung mit Strafvorbehalt*),[109] which was claimed to be capable of preventing stigmatisation of the offender as well as exerting greater 'educative impact' upon the offender without having the perceived disadvantages of the Anglo-American system.[110] According to the proposal, the court could suspend a sentence of a fine or of imprisonment up to 6 months, if the interest of protecting the *Volksgemeinschaft* did not require an immediate execution of the sentence and if it expected the offender to lead a law-abiding life. The court was to set a probationary period between 1 and 3 years and could order the offender to comply with certain

[104]On the codification attempts of the Nazi legislature, see Schmidt, E. (1965) *Einführung in die Geschichte der deutschen Strafrechtspflege*, 3rd edition, Vandenhoeck & Ruprecht, Göttingen, pp. 449–452.

[105]Grau (1934) Verwarnung mit Strafvorbehalt, in Gürtner and Freisler, *op. cit.*, pp. 117–127, p. 117.

[106]Freisler, R. (1934) Strafensystem in Grundzüge eines Allgemeinen Deutschen Strafrechts in Freisler, R. and Luetgebrune, W. (eds.) *Denkschrift des Zentralausschusses der Strafrechtabteilung der Akademie für deutsches Recht,* Decker, Berlin, pp.114–115.

[107]*Ibid.*

[108]See Grau (1934) *op. cit.*

[109]*Ibid.*

[110]Ibid, pp. 122–123, see also Gürtner and Freisler, *op. cit.*, p. 146.

conditions, e.g., to repair the damage, to make a payment or to submit to protective supervision. The draft of 1936 limited the use of this measure to prison sentences (*Gefängnissstrafe* and *Haft*) of up to 1 month and to 30 unit fines.[111]

Furthermore, the Criminal Law Commission questioned the significance the fine had acquired during the Weimar Republic.[112] The rise in the use of the fine and its move towards the centre of the penal system was seen as an unfortunate development which was to be halted. The fine was viewed, in the words of a member of the Commission, as "an unpleasant and unworthy means of punishment, a stopgap", and its more parsimonious use was demanded.[113] Only three areas for the application of fines were identified: petty offences, such as libels and minor bodily injuries, avoidance of short custodial sentences for "offences whose punishment does not deserve an aggravation in their execution", and as an ancillary penalty in cases of crimes of profit-making. The Commission also wished to eliminate the "plutocratic" nature of the fine. That purpose was to be achieved by using the offender's daily income as a basis for determining the amount of the fine.[114] In the case of fine default, the Commission favoured public work instead of a prison sentence. The draft of 1936, following the lines of the Commission's recommendations, permitted the court to impose up to 90 unit-fines instead of a term of *Haft* not exceeding 3 months, unless the attitude of the offender justified the imposition of a custodial sentence.[115] Imprisonment for non-payment of a fine could be imposed only if the offender did not perform the specified work, appeared to be unworthy of the imposition of this measure, did not make an application, or if it was not possible to find a work place.[116]

Since the draft law of 1936 was not adopted, the recommended changes remained mere proposals.[117] However, a number of laws were passed which significantly altered the sanctioning framework and practice. Some of these laws remained in force even after the end of the National Socialist regime.

The most dramatic developments occurred in the realm of juvenile justice, whose basic foundations were seriously undermined by a number of decrees and later with the enactment of the Juvenile Court Law of 1943.[118] According to

---

[111]Section 60 of the Draft reprinted in Vormbaum, T. and Rentrop, K. (2008) *Reform des Strafgesetzbuches Sammlungen der Reformentwürfe*, vol. 2, pp. 357–358.

[112]Rietsch, *op. cit.*, pp. 100–101.

[113]*Ibid.* In 1933, the proportionate use of the prison sentence was 44.3, while for the fine it was 52.3 percent; in 1939 the ratio was 40.4 to 54.8 percent. During the war years, from 1939 to 1943, the proportionate use of prison sentences remained largely steady, on average 41.3 percent, whereas the use of the fine declined by 17 percent, reflecting the impact of the official disapproval of upon fines, Stapenhorst, *op. cit.*, p. 66.

[114]*Ibid.* Gürtner and Freisler, *op. cit.*, pp. 121–134.

[115]Section 43.

[116]Section 44.

[117]For the reasons, see Schmidt, *op. cit.*, p. 450.

[118]Cornel, *op. cit.*, pp. 106–108, Wolf, J. (1992) *Jugendliche vor Gericht im Dritten Reich – Nationalsozialistische Jugendstrafrechtspolitik und Justizalltag*, Beck, München, pp. 118–167, Kubink, *op. cit.*, pp. 285–287. For a rather biased view, see Schaffstein and Beulke, *op. cit.*, p. 39.

Section 20/1 of the Juvenile Court Law of 1943, the juvenile offender could be sentenced under general criminal law if "in view of her/his mental and moral development", s/he could justifiably be regarded like a person over 18 and, if due to the offender's "particularly degraded criminal character" and the seriousness of her/his act, "the sound sentiment of the people" required such a punishment.[119] The same applied if the overall assessment of the offence and of the personality of the offender showed that s/he was a major criminal of a degenerate character and the protection of the *Volksgemeinschaft* required application of adult criminal law.[120] In this way, it was made possible to expose juvenile offenders to such penalties as the death penalty, penal servitude or prison sentences exceeding 10 years available under general criminal law. Another drastic change was the reduction of the age of criminal responsibility to 12 years in cases involving 'serious wrongdoings'.[121] All these measures were targeted at offenders who were deemed to have committed 'serious crimes'. For offenders guilty of less grave crimes, so-called 'disciplinary measures' were introduced. Their seriousness was halfway between educational measures and imprisonment.[122] Disciplinary measures included juvenile detention (*Jugendarrest*)[123] of up to 4 weeks, a new form of short-term custody in juvenile justice. In harmony with the newly introduced short-term imprisonment, the minimum length of prison sentences was set at 3 months.[124] Furthermore, the new Juvenile Court Law provided the generic name 'juvenile imprisonment' (*Jugendstrafe*) for prison sentences imposed pursuant to this law. 'Juvenile imprisonment' could be imposed for a period of up to 10 years or indeterminately,[125] and it had its own enforcement regime. The National Socialist legislature repealed the institution of the suspension of imprisonment on probation.

Through the introduction of 'measures (Maßregeln) of security and rehabilitation', the Nazi legislature turned one of the significant reform demands of the preceding decades into law.[126] *Maßregeln* were not an invention of National

---

[119]Section 20 (1) This regulation went back to a provision in an ordinance enacted in 1939. See, RGBI (1939), 1, p. 2000, Section 1.

[120]Section 20 (2).

[121]Section 3.

[122]Section 7, see Kümmerlein, H. (1944) Reichsjugendgerichtsgesetz vom 6 November 1943, Beck, München.

[123]Section 8.

[124]Section 5 (1) of the Juvenile Court Law.

[125]*Ibid.*, Section 6.

[126]Von Liszt, Kriminalpolitische Aufgaben, pp. 290 Kern, E. (1927) *Zur Strafrechtsreform (1. Der Alkoholsverbrecher, 2. Der Gewohnheitsverbrecher und 3. Der Strafrichter im Dienst der Spezialprävention)* Bensheimer, Mannheim. In his book, Schmidt provided inter alia a detailed account on the foundations of measures of rehabilitaton and security and legislative proposals concerning them, see Schmidt, E. (1965), *op. cit.*, pp.379–399, further on the respective law, see pp. 430–432.

Eser, A. (2001) Zur Entwicklung von Maßregeln der Besserung und Sicherung als zweite Spur im Strafrecht in Britz, G. (ed.) *Grundfragen des staatlichen Strafens*, Beck, München, pp. 213–236, pp. 216–217.

Socialist policy-makers. Long before had it been pointed out that there were three groups of offenders for which the penal system had no adequate response: offenders with a mental disorder unable to form a guilty state of mind, offenders deemed at risk of committing new offences such as vagabonds and beggars, and habitual offenders whose long-term segregation from society was considered essential.[127] The perceived 'gap' in the system in this regard had inspired various draft laws. Not surprisingly, the prevention-based National Socialist penal policy provided a particularly fertile ground for these ideas.[128] In 1933, the Law against 'Dangerous Habitual Offenders and Measures of Rehabilitation and Security' addressed the reform demands in relation to these offender groups by establishing a 'double-track system of sanctions'.[129] The measures of security and rehabilitation included committal to a mental hospital and to an asylum for alcoholics, committal to a workhouse, preventive detention, protective supervision, deportation of foreigners, castration of dangerous sexual offenders and exclusion from a specific trade or profession.

4.3 The Extension of Alternatives

The existence of various drafts since the beginning of the twentieth century demonstrates that a thorough reform of the penal code was always on the agenda of penal policy.[130] In the post-war years, reform ideas drew further stimulus from 'restoration' and 'denazification' initiatives.[131] Proposals related to the system of punishments and *measures* lay at the forefront of reform discussions. This state of affairs could be explained on the one hand by the continued debate between different conceptions of the purpose(s) of punishment, though the debate was of lower intensity than before,[132] and on the other hand by the reality of penal justice,

[127]A theoretical reflection on the theme, see Frommel, M. (1991) Verbrechensbekämpfung im Nationalsozialismus, pp. 47–64 in Stolleis, M. with Frommel, M., Rückert, J., Schröder, R., Seelmann, K., Wiegand, W. (eds.) *Die Bedeutung der Wörter – Studien zur europäischen Rechtsgeschichte, Festschrift für den Sten Gagner zum 70. Geburtstag*, Beck, München,

[128]See Gürtner and Freisler, *op. cit.*, p. 147, Denkschrift des Preußischen Justizministers (1933) *op. cit.*, pp. 138.

[129]Müller, C. (1997) *Das Gewohnheitsverbrechergesetz: Kriminalpolitik als Rassenpolitik*, Nomos, Baden-Baden.

[130]Schmidt, E., *op. cit.*, pp. 449, Stammberger, W. (1963) Die Geschichte der Strafrechtsreform bis zum Strafgesetzbuchentwurf 1962 in *Probleme der Strafrechtsreform*, Schriftreihe der Friedrich Naumann-Stiftung zur Politik und Zeitgeschichte, Stuttgart, pp. 11–29, Jescheck and Weigend, *op. cit.*, pp. 99–100.

[131]E.g., in an article about the reform of the sanction system, Bockelmann, P. (1951) Zur Reform des Strafensystems, *Juristische Zeitung*, pp. 494–498. For a detailed examination see, Kubink, *op. cit.*, pp. 315–382.

[132]Bockelmann, *op. cit.*, Roxin, C. (2006) *Strafrecht Allgemeiner Teil*, vol. 1, 4th edition, Beck, Münchem, p. 109.

the contours of which remained in some ways akin to those at the turn of the century. Indeed, after a short-lived decrease in the use of short-term imprisonment and a corresponding increase in the overall use of the fine, reliance upon short-term imprisonment increased. Short prison sentences still constituted a significant proportion of all prison sentences. From the 1950s onwards, the use of prison sentences of up to 3 months increased by 7% annually.[133] From 1959 to 1965, the number of sentences of 1 month imprisonment rose from 41,672 to 62,824.[134] Imprisonment of 3 months increased less dramatically from 39,150 to 40,833.[135]

The increase in the number of short-term prison sentences was subject to critical evaluation, with frequent reference to the criticism of the modern school of the ineffectiveness of short-term imprisonment for rehabilitative purposes.[136] For some writers, this assumption had become an undesirable axiom of German penal law.[137] Whether, and to what extent, such a broad consensus existed and had solid foundations is questionable in the face of the obstinate resistance to the idea of abolishing short-term imprisonment which took place in the early years of the criminal law reform movement. Before coming to a broader analysis regarding the reform of the penal system, it is necessary to note the enactment of the suspended sentence.[138]

Clearly, as one of the long-standing demands of the reform movement in Germany, in which great hope and support was invested,[139] the enactment of the suspension of the execution of imprisonment on probation (*Strafaussetzung zur Bewährung*)[140] represented an unequivocal challenge to the 'orthodox' conception of the objectives of punishment as manifested in the penal code. In 1953, the suspended sentence with probationary assistance became available for courts with respect to adult offenders despite objections raised on the grounds that it would weaken the general preventive effect of criminal law and that the corresponding infrastructure to cope with the demands of such a legislative provision was largely absent.[141] In its initial version, it was applicable for prison sentences of up to

[133]Nüßlein, A. (1969) *Freiheitsstrafen in Hessen 1969*, Verl. Kriminalistik, Hamburg, p. 21.

[134]*Ibid*, p. 22.

[135]*Ibid.*

[136]Hall, K. (1954) Die Freiheitsstrafe als kriminalpolitisches Problem, *Zeitschrift für die gesamte Strafrechtswissenschaft,* vol. 66, pp.77–110, Schmidt, E. (1952) Eröffnungsansprache auf der Tagung der Arbeitsgemeinschaft zur Reform des Strafvollzuges, *Zeitschrift für gesamte Strafrechtswissenschaft*, vol. 64, pp. 1–16.

[137]Welzel in *Niederschriften über die Sitzungen der Großen Strafrechtkommission* (1956), vol. 1, (Grundsatzfragen 1 bis 13. Sitzung), Bonn, p. 101, also, Peters, K. (1960) *Grundprobleme der Kriminalpädagogik*, de Gruyter, Berlin, pp. 310–311.

[138]For a brief account, see Stammberger, *op. cit.*, pp. 11–29.

[139]Welzel in Niederschriften über die Sitzungen der Großen Strafrechtkommission, *op. cit.*, p. 103, see also, Lange, H. (1990) Geschichtliche Entwicklung, Nachkriegssituation und Aufbauphase der Gerichtshilfe, pp. 107–136, Kerner, H.-J. (ed.) *Straffälligenhilfe in Geschichte und Gegenwart*, Verlag Godesberg, Bonn.

[140]StÄG v. 4.8.1953 (BGBI. I, 735).

[141]For a detailed analysis, see Meyer-Reil, *op. cit.*, pp. 192–223.

9 months imprisonment (*Gefägnisstrafe*, *Einssclißungstrafe* or *Haft*) for offenders who had not previously received a prison sentence longer than 6 months within the last 5 years, provided that it could be expected that the offender would lead an 'orderly life', without the use of imprisonment, unless a sentence of imprisonment was deemed necessary for general preventive purposes.[142]

Concurrently, in 1953, with an amendment to the Juvenile Court Law, the suspension of juvenile imprisonment was re-introduced with probationary assistance. Accordingly, juvenile imprisonment not exceeding 1 year was to be suspended, "where the consideration of the juvenile's personality and her/his previous history gives rise to the expectation that the conviction would serve as a warning and without a prison sentence, under the educational influence of the probationary period ranging from 2 to 5 years, the juvenile would conduct a law-abiding and orderly life."[143] The amendment to Juvenile Court Law furthermore incorporated the suspension of the *imposition* of juvenile imprisonment.[144] The related provision empowered courts to pronounce the guilt of the offender, but defer passing sentence on her/him for a specified period, where "the inquiry into the case does not unequivocally demonstrate that the harmful tendencies of the juvenile justify an imposition of a term of juvenile imprisonment." The length of the probationary period in the latter case can range from 1 to 2 years, which could subsequently be extended or reduced by the court.

4.3.1 The Reform

4.3.1.1 Discussions: Two Generations and Two Distinct Routes

One year later, in 1954, following the adoption of the suspended sentence, a complete reform of criminal law was finally officially resumed.[145] In this year, the Ministry of Justice commissioned the Grand Commission of Criminal Law, which was composed of academics, politicians, members of the judiciary and officers from the ranks of the judicial administration. A great deal of work in the Grand Criminal Law Commission was devoted to the place of short-term imprisonment in the penal justice.[146] Despite the dissenting opinions within the Commission, most vocally represented by Eberhard Schmidt, a disciple of von Liszt,[147] it

142 Previously, Section 23 of the Penal Code.

143 Sections 20 and 21 of the Juvenile Court Law.

144 *Ibid.*, Section 27.

145 Lange, R. (1954) Neuaufnahme der Strafrechtsreform, *Zeitschrift für gesamte Strafrechtswissenschaft*, vol. 66, pp. 167–170.

146 For a summary see Dreher, E. (1955) Die zweite Arbeitstagung der Großen Strafrechtskommission (12. bis 15. Oktober 1954), *Zeitschrift für die gesamte Strafrechtswissenschaft*, vol. 67, pp. 77–107.

147 See Niederschriften über die Sitzungen der Großen Strafrechtkommission, *op. cit.*, p. 107.

appears that the Commission's meetings were dominated by the view that there are always certain cases where neither the suspended sentence nor the fine do not represent a sufficiently adequate response and therefore the imposition of a prison sentence of short length is indispensable.[148] The latter category was exemplified by negligence offences, e.g. traffic crimes.[149] In dealing with these types of offences the adoption of a distinctive method was deemed as a penological necessity.[150]

One proposal, which received vigorous support during the proceedings of the Commission,[151] envisaged a new kind of short-term custodial sentence available to courts which ought to be meted out with respect to minor offences and offences of medium gravity. The primary target group of the proposed type of short-custody, according to the aforementioned proposal, was to be offences committed through negligence, the offenders of which supposedly required no rehabilitative intervention but the 'shocking effect of custody'.[152] Predicated upon this presumption it was proposed that such a new custodial sentence was not necessarily required to have rehabilitative content. In order to prevent 'contamination', it was to be executed in special types of penal establishments. It was acknowledged, however, that the intricacy of this solution had the potential to cause the overlap between the ordinary term of imprisonment (*Gefängnissstrafe*) and the proposed short sentence. Having agreed on the retention of short-term imprisonment without prescribing any minimum length,[153] the Commission's work was mainly concerned with the nature, scope, enforcement type (the recommendation was solitary confinement),[154] place and legal consequences relating to the registration of the proposed new sentence, and hence the extent to which this sentence might be qualitatively and quantitatively differentiated from the *Gefängnissstrafe*. Consequently, the majority of the members of the Commission did not only regard the retention of short-term imprisonment as indispensable, but they also supported the proposal for the adoption of a new short-term sentence which was called 'Strafhaft' (penal detention).[155] The duration of the penal detention was set at between 1 and 6 weeks.[156]

---

[148]*Ibid.*, pp. 105–108 and 140–155.

[149]*Ibid.*, p. 141.

[150]*Ibid.*

[151]See, *ibid*, Vorschläge und Bemerkungen der Sachbearbeiter des Bundesjustizministeriums zu Grundsatzfrage 5b,Wie kann der kriminalpolitisch unerwünschten kurzfristigen Freiheitsstrafe entgegenwirkt werden', pp. 361–363 (Anhang B no 19).

[152]*Ibid.*, p. 145.

[153]See *ibid.*, pp. 140–155.

[154]See *ibid.*, pp. 104, 106 and 107.

[155]*Ibid.*, pp. 210–211.

[156]This rather conservative inclination with respect to short-term imprisonment is even more evident, given the fact that at this time the struggle with it once again had a strong international accent. As early as in the Twelfth International Penal and Penitentiary Congress held at The Hague, Mannheim most authoritatively concluded that "in conformity with the prevailing tendency in modern penology we take it for granted that sentences which do not provide that undisturbed period of at least 6 months (for education and treatment) are harmful." Cited in

Somewhat contradictorily, having assigned short-term imprisonment with such a significant place in the penal justice system for comparatively *minor offences*, the Grand Commission considered the ways in which to reduce its use. Not surprisingly, the inconsistency inherent in the Commission's approach left it with the enormously difficult task of qualifying suitable 'candidates' for the sanction modalities which it deemed to have a substitute function. This was even more problematic as the potential overlaps between actual and proposed modalities of sanctions and measures, for example, between the suspended execution of the prison sentences, the warning with suspension of punishment,[157] and the procedural alternative, Section 153 of the German Criminal Procedure Code, remained largely unaddressed.

With regard to fines, the Commission considered an adoption of the day-fine system such as was applied in the Scandinavian countries. There was agreement for the most part that the existing general clause (Section 27c) of the Penal Code, requiring courts to take the income and resources of the offender into account, was too general and vague, and thus an insufficient obligation for courts.[158] Lacking any clear guidance on the extent to which guilt and financial circumstances determined the amount of the fine, courts were left to intuitively assess rather than rationally judge on this issue. The frequency of fine defaults was, in this sense, seen as a consequence of this shortcoming, which imperilled the position of the fine as an alternative to imprisonment. It was believed that a day fine system would overcome many difficulties of the existing system by relating the amount of the fine systematically to the offender's ability to pay. The Commission, with a clear majority, came to the conclusion that the day-fine system offered an adequate solution.[159]

The Commission also considered the feasibility of the introduction of a new form of sentencing disposal: 'warning with suspension of punishment'.[160] According to its proponents in the Commission, the 'warning with suspension of punishment' was capable of serving as an alternative sentence without stigmatising the offender with the pronouncement of a prison sentence.[161] Furthermore, it would be more conducive to the rehabilitation of the offender, in that the imposition of the sentence was to be dependent on the offender complying with the conditions. Several members of the Commission supported the integration of 'warning with suspension of punishment' into the sanctioning system, as a measure less onerous than conditional postponement of the execution of the sentence, applicable for a term of imprisonment from 1 to 3 months. Others asserted that there was no need for the creation of another measure alongside the suspended sentence, provided that the

European Committee on Crime Problems (1967) *The Effectiveness of Punishment and Other Measures of Treatment*, Council of Europe, p. 207.

[157]See below.

[158]For the discussion, see Niederschriften über die Sitzungen der Großen Strafrechtskommission, *op. cit.*, pp. 155–184, and for the proposals, see pp. 375–385, see also Grebing, *op. cit.*, p. 37.

[159]*Ibid.*, see the reports of the subcomission, pp. 382–385.

[160]Welzel, *ibid.*, p. 361, Annex 18.

[161]*Ibid.*, p. 189.

conditions imposed on the offender were broadly conceived in order to make greater individualisation in the application of the suspended sentence possible.[162] The fear of the cynics in the Commission was that the introduction of the respective measure would mean a considerable impairment of the general preventive effects of the sanctioning system and that its application would reduce the scope of the fine. Such criticism was fruitful in hindering a favourable resolution on this measure.[163]

After 5 years of discussion, the Great Commission of Criminal Law produced a draft of the general part of the penal code in 1958 and a draft of the law of particular offences in 1959.[164] These drafts were embodied in the official draft code of 1960, and finally this draft, with a small number of changes, was adopted as an official draft in 1962 (hereafter the 1962 draft). The 1962 draft was characterised by its heavy reliance upon retribution as the primary purpose of punishment, as illustrated most clearly by the restatement of the degree of individual guilt as a sole basis for sentencing,[165] and the retention of penal servitude (*Zuchthaus*).[166] Three points deserve particular attention in relation to the draft.

Firstly, in line with the Commission's approach, 'penal detention' was adopted as a new form of short-custody ranging from 1 week to 6 months.[167] The draft provided that penal detention could only be applicable in cases "where with respect to intentional acts, if the perpetrator has acted with minor guilt and with respect to negligent acts, and if the perpetrator has not acted recklessly or with grave guilt."[168] This type of confinement was to be used for offenders whose previous history does not show that they are prone to reoffending. Secondly, the fine as a substitute for imprisonment of up to 3 months, as conceived by the hitherto law in force, constituted a part of the punishment catalogue of the 1962 draft. It provided that where the offence in question is a *Vergehen* and neither the guilt of the offender nor 'the purpose of punishment' (to deter crimes) warrants the use of imprisonment a fine in lieu of up to 3 months imprisonment was to be imposed if there is reason to expect that the fine would suffice to serve as a warning.[169] Thirdly, the 1962 draft retained the existing provision of the suspended sentence. It provided that the suspension of the sentence could only be granted if the offender's guilt or 'the purpose of punishment' (to prevent commission of offences) did not require

---

[162]See *ibid.*, pp. 197–200.

[163]*Ibid.*, p. 311.

[164]Rentrop, pp. XXXII–XXXVI in Vormbaum, T. and Rentrop, K. (2008) *Reform des Strafgesetzbuches*, Wissenschaft's Verlag, Berlin, vol. 1, Roxin (2006) *op. cit.*, pp. 115–116.

[165]Section 60 (1) of the 1962 Draft, *Entwurf einen Strafgesetzbuch (mit Begründung)*, Drucksache 200/62.

[166]*Ibid.*, Section 44–45.

[167]*Ibid.*, Section 46. Begründung p. 165.

[168]*Ibid.*, Section 48.

[169]Grebing, *op. cit.*, p. 37, see also Kiwull, H. (1979) *Kurzfristige Freiheitsstrafen und Geldstrafen vor und nach der Strafrechtsreform, einschließlich der Entziehung der Fahrerlaubnis und des Fahrvebots als Mittel der Spezialprävention* (unpublished PhD Thesis of the University of Freiburg), p. 27.

the execution of a prison sentence.[170] Suspension was only possible for offenders who had not previously served more than 3 months of imprisonment.

4.3.2 The Sanction Catalogue of the Alternative Draft

The 1962 draft was subject to severe criticism for its failure to inaugurate a new era in penal reform.[171] This criticism was made most vocally and systematically by several young German and Swiss scholars who submitted another draft entitled the 'Alternative Draft' in 1966.[172] The authors of the Alternative Draft maintained that the 1962 draft lacked a modern criminal political conception,[173] in that there was no break with the Kantian and Hegelian conceptions of punishment of the 18th and 19th centuries.[174] The 1962 Draft, according to them, confined its mission to removing doctrinal inconsistencies within the Penal Code[175] and incorporating case law into the Penal Code. It was effectively described as a codified commentary on the existing penal code.[176]

---

170 Section 72 of the 1962 Draft.

171 Schmidt, E. (1957) Kriminalpolitische und Strafrechtsdogmatische Probleme in der deutschen Strafrechtsreform, *Zeitschrift für die gesamte Strafrechtswissenschaft*, vol. 69, pp. 359–396, Heinitz, E. (1958) Der Entwurf des Allgemeinen Teils des Strafgesetzbuches vom kriminalpolitischen Standpunkt aus, die *Zeitschrift für die gesamte Strafrechtswissenschaft*, vol. 70 pp. 1–24, Würtenberger, T. (1965) Kriminologie und Strafrechtsreform in Gedanken zur Strafrechtsreform in Heinitz, E., Würtenberger, T. and Peters, K. (eds.) *Gedanken zur Strafrechtsreform*, Schöningh, Paderborn, pp. 21–38, Mayer, H. (1962) *Strafrechtsreform für Heute und Morgen*, Duncker & Humblot, Berlin, Mergen, A. (1967) Die Antwort der Gesellschaf auf das Verbrechen – Strafe oder Maßnahme, pp. 40–55 in Reinisch, L. (ed.) *Die deutsche Strafrechtsreform*, Beck, München.

172 The General Part of the Alternative Draft was prepared by Jürgen Baumann, Anne-Eva Brauneck, Ernst-Walter Hanack, Arthur Kaufmann, Ulrich Klug, Ernst-Joachim Lampe, Theodor Lenckner, Werner Maihofer, Peter Noll, Claus Roxin, Rudolf Schmitt, Hans Schultz, Günter Stratenwerth, Walter Stree. Baumann *et al.* (1966) *Alternativ-Entwurf eines Strafgesetzbuches Allgemeiner Teil*, Mohr, Tübingen.

173 Baumann, J. (1965a) Zum Entwurf Eines StGB in *Kleine Streitschriften zur Strafrechtsreform*, Verlag Ernst & Werner Gieseking, Bielefeld, pp. 42–60, (1967) Die reform des Allgemeinen Teils Eines Strafgesetzbuches in Reinisch, *op. cit.*, pp. 56–71 and (1969) Was erwarten wir von der Strafrechtsreform, in *Weitere Streitschriften zur Strafrechtsreform*, Gieseking, Bielefeld, pp. 9–39.

Also, Roxin, C. (1969) Franz von Liszt und die kriminalpolitische Konzeption des Alternativentwurfs, *Zeitschrift für die gesamte Strafrechtswissenschaft*, vol. 81, pp. 613–649 and (1991) Zur neueren Entwicklung der Kriminalpolitik in Stolleis, M. with Frommel, M., Rückert, J., Schröder, R., Seelmann, K., Wiegand, W. (eds.) *Die Bedeutung der Wörter: Studien zur europäischen Rechtsgeschichte (Festschrift für Sten Gagner zum 70. Geburtstag)*, Beck, München, pp. 341–356, p. 342.

174 Bauer, F. (1967) Das Strafrecht und das heutige Bild vom Menschen in Reinisch, *op. cit.*, pp. 11–23.

175 Baumann (1965a) *op. cit.*, p. 42, Kaufmann, A. (1968) Die Dogmatik im Alternativ Entwurf, *Zeitschrift für die gesamte Strafrechtswissenschaft,* vol. 80, pp. 34–53, p. 35.

176 Baumann, J. (1965) Grundprobleme der Strafrechtsreform, *op. cit.*, pp. 198–221. See also, Bauer, F (1967) Die Reformbedürftigkeit der Strafrechtsreform, Gestern & Heute, München.

In contrast to the 1962 Draft, the authors of the Alternative Draft intended to restructure the Penal Code on the basis of the notions of individual and general prevention.[177] Under the title 'the purpose and limits of penalties and measures of rehabilitation and security', Section 2 of the Alternative Draft stipulated the purpose of punishment as "the defence of legally protected interests and reintegration of the offender into law-abiding society (re-socialisation)". In this way, the draft sought to achieve some form of reconciliation between general and special preventive considerations. Section 59 of the Alternative Draft furthermore confirmed this principle in relation to fixing the punishment by stipulating that "punishment proportionate to the offender's guilt should be imposed only as required for her/his readjustment to society or for the defence of legally protected interests". The authors of the draft, however, did not call for an absolute elimination of guilt-oriented punishment in determining punishment,[178] and hence "a purely preventive penal law".[179] According to the Alternative Draft, guilt as manifested by the offence (*Tatschuld*) set the upper limit of punishment.[180] The exact content of the punishment was to be determined in accordance with the criteria specified in Section 2, i.e. deterrence and rehabilitation.[181]

Ascribing rehabilitation as a primary position, the Alternative Draft defined the minimum term of imprisonment as 6 months, underlining that short-term prison sentences are damaging in that they disrupt the offender's employment and training as well as personal and social relationships without allowing rehabilitative intervention to take place.[182] The authors of the Alternative Draft were opposed to the penal detention (*Strafhaft*) conceived by the 1962 Draft on the grounds that a custodial sentence characterised by its 'shocking' effect does not belong to the notions of modern penology, and that short-term imprisonment would be made redundant with the existence of adequate alternatives.

According to the Alternative Draft a prison sentence of up to 2 years can be substituted for a fine if to do so would assist the offender to lead a law abiding life.[183] Notably, the Draft created a system of 'running fines',[184] which would effectively replace prison sentences of that term. Going a step further, the authors of the Alternative Draft sought to override the presumed flaws of the day fine.[185]

---

[177] For an overview, see Roxin (1969), *op. cit.*, pp. 613–649.

[178] Baumann (1969) *op. cit.*, p. 21.

[179] *Ibid*, p. 23.

[180] See the explanatory notes on Section 2 and 59, Baumann *et al.* (1966), *op. cit.*, pp. 29–30 and p. 109, respectively.

[181] Section 59, Baumann *et al.* (1966), *op. cit.*, p. 109.

[182] See Baumann *et al.* (1966), *op. cit.*, p. 71.

[183] Section 50 (1), see Baumann, J. (1965), *op. cit*, pp. 61–81, and (1968) *Beschränkung des Lebensstandards anstatt kurzfristiger Freiheitsstrafe*, Luchterland, Berlin, see also Grebing, *op. cit.*, p. 82.

[184] Section 49 of the Alternative Draft.

[185] See the explanatory note on Section 49, Baumann *et al.* (1966), *op. cit.*, p. 45. For a detailed analysis of the Alternative Draft's conception of the fine, see e.g., Stenner, *op. cit.*, pp. 102–110.

In order to achieve this, the framework proposed the deduction of the amount specified by the court 'in obligatory instalments' from the weekly wages or salary of the offender, in accordance with her/his financial circumstances. In this way, it was thought that the fine would exert a continuing influence on the living standard of the offender over a period of time. In conjunction with the fine, the court could impose the condition of reparation, submittal to probation assistance or otherwise impose instructions.[186]

In the cases where the offender lacked the financial ability to pay the imposed fine, the Alternative Draft provided for 'community service' ('kommunale Arbeit') in charities, particularly in hospitals, educational institutions, homes for senior citizens and similar organisations. Community service could be ordered upon the application of the offender, in lieu of the whole or part of the fine.[187] One day of work was to be calculated to be equivalent to one unit day fine. It was also possible that in cases of hardship the court responsible for the execution of punishment subsequently modified the content of work, or even revoked it. As this description already reveals, the Alternative Draft did not conceive this measure in its own right, an independent sanction, but rather as a substitute for a fine where a danger of default exists. The authors of the Alternative Draft reflected the view that an introduction of work as a punishment in its own right was not politically and penologically desirable. Yet, despite discarding public work as a main penalty on the grounds that its practice might be in a certain way reminiscent of the Concentration Camps of the National Socialist regime,[188] this rejection was, as is clear from Baumann's writings (one of the pioneers of the Alternative Draft), not made on principle. It was thought that time was not yet ripe for disregarding potential undesirable historical connotations,[189] but the path to this sort of punishment should not be closed.

Under the Alternative Draft, another type of main punishment was the revocation of the driver's licence, which was to be applicable for offences committed by or in connection with the operation of a motor vehicle or in violation of the duties of the driver of a motor vehicle.[190] It was to last between 1 month and 1 year. As distinct from the existing law, the Alternative Draft promoted revocation of drivers' licences not merely as a *measure* of security and rehabilitation and as an ancillary penalty, but it envisaged the imposition of it in place of or in addition to a fine in lieu of imprisonment,[191] if to do so would "better serve the purpose of punishment and not unreasonably interfere with the way in which the offender leads her/his life".[192]

[186]Section 56 of the Alternative Draft.

[187]Section 52, *ibid*, see Baumann *et al.* (1966), *op. cit.*, pp. 98–100.

[188]See, Baumann *et al.* (1966), *op. cit.*, p. 99.

[189]Baumann (1969) *op. cit.*, p. 33.

[190]Section 55 (4), see Baumann *et al.* (1966), the explanatory note on Section 55, Baumann *et al.* (1966), *op. cit.*, p. 105.

[191]*Ibid.*

[192]Section 55 (4).

A revocation of a driver's licence for up to 6 months could also be combined with the condition of reparation, submittal to probation assistance and imposition of instructions by court order.[193]

The Alternative Draft viewed the suspended sentence as a "genuine sentence of custody in freedom", which was to be governed primarily by rehabilitative considerations.[194] The Draft provided that a prison sentence of up to 2 years could be suspended if the personality, attitude and social circumstances of the offender gives rise to the hope that without imprisonment the offender can be expected to make amends for her/his offence and not reoffend just by instructions and obligations or custody by a probation officer.[195] Notably, no reference was made to the guilt of the offender or general prevention. The suspension of sentence was only applicable for offenders who had not previously served a prison sentence of more than a year.[196] Notably, after the successful completion of this period, the conviction was to be regarded as non-existent in the record of the offender.[197]

The Alternative Draft was conceived of a warning with punishment as a reaction against first-time offenders (of petty forms of mass criminality).[198] This provision was based on the proposition that first-time offenders should be dealt with as leniently as possible. It was to be applicable for offenders incurring imprisonment for not more than 1 year or a revocation of the driver's licence, and for offenders who are deemed to have a positive prognosis that this sanction would suffice to hinder the commission of future crimes.[199] In the latter case, the court was to suspend the sentence on probation lasting up to 1 year.[200] In conjunction with this measure, no other conditions and instructions could be imposed. Moreover, after the expiry of the probationary period without commission of further offences, the offender was to be deemed not convicted, and only in case of reoffending during this period was the determined punishment to be imposed.

Finally, the Alternative Draft contained a more restrictive repertoire of *measures* of security and rehabilitation than the law at the time in force allowed. These included the committal to care institutions, institutions of withdrawal treatment, social therapy institutions and preventive detention.[201] It envisaged the abolishment of the workhouse and police supervision (*Polizeiaufsicht* Section 38 and 39 of the Penal Code). Not only the scope, but also the use of measures of security and

---

[193] Section 56.

[194] See Baumann *et al.* (1966), the explanatory notes on Sections 40–48, p. 79.

[195] Section 40 (1) of the Alternative Draft.

[196] *Ibid.*, Section 40 (2).

[197] Section 47 (2).

[198] See Baumann *et al.* (1966), the explanatory note on Section 57, p. 107, also Baumann, J. (1980) Über die Denaturierung eines Rechtsinstituts (§59 StGB), *Juristische Zeitung*, pp. 464–469.

[199] Section 57 (1) of the Alternative Draft.

[200] *Ibid*, Section 57 (2).

[201] Section 66 of the Alternative Draft. For an overview, see Baumann, *et al.* (1966), *op. cit.*, p. 121.

rehabilitation were restricted to those of 'grave public interest'.[202] What subsequently proved to be of significance to the discussions for the overall orientation of penal justice was the institution of social therapy based on the Danish example.[203] The social therapy institution was to be applicable to all offenders who had three prior convictions and who had served a prison term of at least 2 years. It was intended to provide therapy, which would develop the offender's will and capability to lead a lawful life through special psychiatric, psychological and pedagogical methods.

4.3.3 The Legislation

The political climate of the second half of the 1960s was particularly favourable for the realisation of reform ideas. In 1966 the liberal Free Democratic Party (FDP) adopted the Alternative Draft as its draft proposal. The then incumbent government composed of the coalition of Conservatives (CDU/CSU) and Social Democratic Party (SPD) espoused the endeavours to re-codify the penal code.[204] Backed by strong political will, the Alternative Draft inspired the work of the Parliamentary Special Committee for Criminal Law Reform, which was appointed in 1963 to advise the government on the reform of the Penal Code. The Special Committee sought to reconcile the demands of the Alternative Draft with the 1962 Draft. The view formed during the course of the meetings of the Special Committee was that short-term imprisonment, as an indispensible instrument of penal policy, cannot be abolished, but the frequency of its use ought to be restricted for the purpose of relieving the overcrowding in prisons among other reasons.[205] Hence, contrary to the radical step, as conceived in the Alternative Draft, of proposing the abolishment of prison sentences up to 6 months, the Special Committee advised the retention of short-term imprisonment but agreed to reduce the recourse to short-term imprisonment in numerous ways, which in turn constituted the spirit of the incoming legislation.

Ultimately, the First Law on Criminal Law Reform was passed in 1969; the Second Law on Criminal Law Reform was promulgated in the same year. It was not until 1975 that the Second Law on Reform came into force, as it was thought that the necessary introductory and correction laws would take a longer time and that the entire second part of the reform ought to be adopted as a whole.[206] Below, for the

---

[202] *Ibid.*

[203] Section 69, Baumann *et al.* (1966), *op. cit.*, p. 127–129.

[204] Eser, A. (1988) Hundert Jahre deutscher Strafgesetzgebung – Rückblick und Tendenzen in Dijk, J., J., M. and Stolwijk, S. (eds.) *Criminal Law in Action: An Overview of Current Issues in Western Societies*, Kluwer, Deventer, p. 54, Vormbaum, T. (2009) *Einführung in die moderne Strafrechtsgeschichte*, Springer, Berlin, p. 235.

[205] See, Erster Bericht der Sonderausschuss, Bundestagsdrucksache, V/4094.

[206] Eser (1988) *op. cit.*, p. 55, Vormbaum, *op. cit.*, p. 236.

sake of clarity, the changes introduced by the aforementioned laws will be analysed together.

One of the significant changes was the reformulation of the provision regarding the determination of punishment. Section 46 of the Penal Code states that guilt is the basis for fixing the sentence, but that the effects of punishment on the offender's future life are also to be taken into account. With regard to the imposition of measures of security and rehabilitation, the proportionality principle found explicit recognition. The new provision reads that a *measure of security and rehabilitation* should not be imposed where it would be disproportionate to the seriousness of the unlawful conducts or those expected to be committed by the offender as well as to the danger s/he would cause. Furthermore, within the reform legislation, the committal to the work house was abolished.

As a compromise, the minimum duration of short-term imprisonment was set at 1 month, and in another provision, Section 47 of the Penal Code, it is stipulated that the recourse to it should be made only as a last resort (which is sometimes referred to as the 'ultima ratio' clause). As a compromise, both general and special preventive considerations found their expression in the wording of the respective provision. Paragraph 1 of this section reads that, "a court may impose imprisonment for less than 6 months only when special circumstances relating to the offence and offender exist, which make the imposition of a prison sentence indispensable to the purpose of exerting influence on the offender or to defend the legal order." Highly germane here was the redefinition of the scope of the fine as a substitute for short-term imprisonment. Accordingly, in cases, where a confinement term of 6 months or more is not justified (pursuant to the first paragraph), a fine must be imposed, unless the defence of legal order demands an imposition of a prison term.[207] Significantly, the system of fines was remodelled on the basis of the Scandinavian day fine system, according to which the court assesses the seriousness of the offence in terms of a number of day-fines (within upper and lower limits) and separately assesses the offender's means in order to determine the amount of each day fine.[208] Furthermore, Section 293 of the Introductory Law, also currently in force, empowered *Länder* to regulate (by means of ordinances) the possibility of performing work in lieu of imprisonment in cases of fine default.[209]

With regard to the suspended sentence, while not going as far as the authors of the Alternative Draft which made rehabilitative considerations the sole criterion, the legislature chose to develop a graduated system encompassing both special and general prevention considerations. Accordingly, as will be outlined in some detail below, prison sentences of less than 6 months must always be suspended if it could be expected that the convict would not commit further offences. Under this condition, prison sentences between 6 and 12 months must also be suspended unless the 'defence of the legal order' requires otherwise. Finally, prison sentences between

[207]Section 47 (1) of the Penal Code.

[208]*Ibid*, Section 40.

[209]See below.

1 and 2 years can only be suspended on the basis of special circumstances relating to the offence *and* personality of the offender in addition to the aforementioned criteria.

Another proposition of the Alternative Draft, 'warning with punishment', was also incorporated into law, but rather as an alternative to imprisonment instead of as a primary reaction against first time offenders. As it was conceived in the Alternative Draft, its application was reserved only for exceptional cases (there is no requirement that it be applicable for 'first-time' offence), where it is positively assessed that the offender would not commit further offences, and that there are special circumstances relating to the offender and offences, and the imposition of this measure would not conflict with general prevention expressed as the phrase 'defence of the legal order'. As distinct from the Alternative Draft, the court can only suspend the imposition of fines of up to 180 daily units.

Also noteworthy in the reform agenda was the introduction of the social therapy institution. Distinct from the Alternative Draft, its purview was restricted to dangerous habitual offenders with major personality dysfunctions, dangerous sexual offenders, adolescents with a record of serious offences who have shown a disposition to become habitual offenders, and persons with mental problems who could be committed to a psychiatric hospital, but a submittal to the social therapy institution is deemed more appropriate.[210] An offender should be committed only if it can be expected that s/he will respond to treatment. Confinement in the institution should not exceed 5 years.

4.3.4 The Zenith of Reform: Rehabilitation and Diversion

Besides the fundamental alterations in the substantive penal law two other developments were highly germane in the reformation of the sanctioning practice and philosophy in the years to come: the beginning of what is sometimes referred to as the 'informal sanctioning' practice by means of diversion measures, and the enactment of the Penal Enforcement Code[211] regulating the execution of prison sentences and *measures* involving institutional confinement.[212]

The pertinence of the Penal Enforcement Code can be traced to its placement of rehabilitation as the primary goal of imprisonment. Section 2 of the Code states that, the purpose of imprisonment is to "enable convicts to lead a socially responsible life without recourse to further offending". "The protection of the public from the commission of further crimes", as the next clause reads, is also stipulated as the goal of confinement, but as is generally agreed, public protection is subordinated to

---

[210]Section 65 of the Penal Code, repealed. See below.

[211]It came into force on 1st January 1977.

[212]Section 1 of the Penal Enforcement Code.

the aim of resocialisation.[213] Notably, even before the enactment of the Code, the idea received a major boost from a ruling of the Constitutional Court holding that resocialisation is the overarching goal of imprisonment and that rendering this principle in practice is the task of the *Sozialstaat*.[214] At this juncture such internal developments in Germany could not be understood without emphasising the significance attached to the systems of the Scandinavian countries, the United States and the Netherlands, which had been viewed as a beacon of hope to the idea that appropriate treatment methods could prevent a relapse into crime, as has been discussed earlier.[215] With the inspiration drawn from the experiences of these countries, it was precisely in this period that the concept of 'treatment' (*Behandlung*) in prisons and in social therapy institutions that had been slowly established, became a significant component of the penological discourse and mobilised research activities in the field. Nevertheless, from the very beginning, the preeminence which the rehabilitative approach had acquired through the Penal Enforcement Code, and, as such, the subordinate position of the purpose of public protection was for many far from satisfactory.[216] Curiously, the empirical and ideological crises which the rehabilitative approach encountered in other countries, in particular in the United States, and to a lesser extent on the domestic front, engendered a questioning of the *raison d'etre* of the proviso on the supremacy of resocialisation. This occurred despite the fact that the notion of rehabilitation had a modest presence compared to the afore-mentioned countries, even in the newly reformulated law. Nonetheless, such ready acceptance of the 'nothing works' philosophy[217] exerted far-reaching influence for both law and practice afterwards, as will be seen.

On the other hand, the extension of the 'diversionary' power of public prosecutors, through the enactment of Section 153a in the Criminal Procedure Code was

---

[213]Feest, J. and Bammann, K. (2000) *Kommentar zum Strafvollzugsgesetz*, 4th edition, Luchterland, Neuwied, pp. 15–20, Kaiser, G. and Schöch, H. (2002) *Straffvollzug*, 5th edition, p. 232 (by Schöch), Müller, Heidelberg, Callies, R.-P. and Müller-Dietz, H. (2005) *Strafvollzugsgesetz*, 10th edition, Beck, München, pp. 39–59. Laubenthal, K. (2008) *Strafvollzug*, 5th edition, Springer, Berlin, p. 63. See also Müller-Dietz, H. (1979) *Grundfragen des strafrechtlichen Sanktionensystems*, v. Decker, Heidelberg, pp. 107–130.

[214]Examined in Kurry, H. (1986) *Die Behandlung Straffälliger*, vol.1, Duncker & Humblot, p. 19.

[215]Blau, G. (1988) Die Entwicklung des Strafvollzugs seit 1945 – Tendenzen und Gegentendenzen, in Schwind, H.-D. and Blau, G. (eds.) *Strafvollzug im Praxis*, 12th edition, de Gruyter, Berlin, pp. 17–29, at pp. 17–26, Kaiser, G. and Schöch, H. (2002) *Strafvollzug*, Müller, Heildelberg, pp. 52. For a summary see, Kury, H. (1999) Zum Stand der Behandlungsforschung oder vom nothing works zum something works in Feuerhelm, W., Schwind, H.-D., Bock, M. (eds.), *op. cit.*, pp.251–274. See also, Jescheck (1979) *op. cit.*, pp. 1037–1064.

[216]Walter, M. (2001) Strafvollzug – Ende der Resozialisierung? in Bieschke, V. (ed.) *Strafvollzug im Wandel*, Wiesbaden, Kriminologische Zentralstelle, pp. 25–38. See also Baumann, J. (1988) Vollzugsgestaltung unter Schuldgesichtspunkten in Schwind, H.-D., Steinhilper, G. and Böhm, A. (eds.) *10 Jahre Strafvollzugsgesetz, Resozialisierung als alleiniges Vollzugsziel?*, Kriminalistik-Verlag, Heidelberg, pp. 69–78, p. 69, Kury (1999) *op. cit.*, p 251

[217]Kaiser (1977) *op. cit.*, pp. 359–372, Weigend (1982) *op. cit.*, pp. 801–814.

also a crucial turning point in German penal policy. Alongside Section 153, Section 153a empowered the public prosecutor with the approval of the court[218] to waive prosecution of *Vergehen* conditional upon the satisfactory completion of a specific task such as reparation or the payment of compensation to the victim, "when the guilt of the offender was minor and the public interest did not require prosecution." Under the same conditions the court could also terminate a continued proceeding. The legislator heralded its aim as being to accelerate the pace of the criminal process in order to cope with the steadily growing workload of the prosecutors.[219] Minor criminality was the key element in the justification of the new provision.[220] Given the strictly formal nature of German criminal law, it was not surprising that this regulation, already in its draft form, was sharply criticised by legal scholars on various accounts.[221] Pointing to the absence of public trial and due process rights, the provision was found to be inconsistent with the presumption of innocence.[222] In a similar vein, it was argued that defendants may be pressurised into admitting offences of which they are not guilty.[223] Some suspects may prefer to admit offences and be diverted rather than face court proceedings, regardless of their guilt or innocence. Further, the extension of the power of the public prosecutor was seen as seriously affecting the constitutional balance of powers, even a return to the merging

---

[218]Aside from those cases involving property crimes, with regard to them, no approval of the court was necessary.

[219]For the objectives of this law see, Ahrens, W. (1978) Die Einstellung in der Hauptverhandlung gem. § § 153 II, 153 a II StPO – Eine Empirische Analyse über neue Formen der Bekämpfung der Bagatellkriminalität, Schwartz, Göttingen, p. 11–13, *op. cit.*, pp. 13–18, Kausch, E. (1980) *Der Staatsanwalt, ein Richter vor dem Richter? Untersuchungen zu § 153a StPO*, Duncker & Humblot, Berlin p. 16, Kunz, K.-L. (1980) *Die Einstellung wegen Geringfügigkeit durch die Staatsanwaltschaft (§§ 153 Abs. 1. 153a Abs. 1 StP0): Eine Empirische Untersuchung in kriminalpolitischer Absicht,* Athenäum, Königstein, pp. 11–23, Hertwig, V. (1982) *Die Einstellung des Strafverfahrens wegen Geringfügigkeit – Eine empirische Analyse der Handhabung der § 153, 153a StPO in der staatsanwaltlichen und gerichtlichen Praxis*, Schwartz, Göttingen, p. 1. See Beulke, W. (2008) on Section 153 and 153a in Ebb, V., Esser, R., Franke, U., Graalmann-Scheerer, K, Hilger, H. and Ignor, A. (eds.) *Löwe-Rosenberg, Die Strafprozeßordnung und das Gerichtsverfassungsgesetz*, 26. Auflage, pp. 61–181, 66–67.

[220]Hünerfeld, P. (1978) Kleinkriminalität und Strafverfahren, *Zeitschrift für die gesamte Strafrechtswissenschaft*, vol. 90, pp. 905–926, see also Hirsch, H., J. (1978) Zur Behandlung der Bagatellkriminalität in der Bundesrepublik Deutschland, *Zeitschrift für die gesamte Strafrechtswissenschaft*, vol. 90, pp. 218–254, Kausch *op. cit.*, pp. 17–31.

[221]Dencker, F. (1973) Die Bagatelldelikte im Entwurf eines EGStGB, *Juristenzeitung*, vol. 28, no 5, pp. 144–151, Hanack, E.-W. (1973) Das Legalitätsprinzip und die Strafrechtsreform, Bemerkungen zu § 153a des Entwurfs für ein Erstes Gesetz zur Reform des Strafverfahrenrechts vom 13.04.1972 in Lackner, K., Leferenz, H., Schmidt, E., Welp, J. and Wolf, E., A. (eds.) *Festschrift für Wilhelm Gallas*, Walter de Gruyter, Berlin, pp. 339–364.

[222]Dencker *op. cit.*, p. 150, Schmidhäuser, E. (1973) Freiverkaufen mit Strafcharakter im Strafprozess, *Juristenzeitung*, vol. 28, no 17, p. 531.

[223]Dencker, *op. cit.*, pp. 149–150, Schmidhäuser, *op. cit.*, p. 534, Hermann, J. (1984) Diversion und Schlichtung in der Bundesrepublik Deutschland, *Zeitschrift für die gesamte Strafrechtswissenschaft*, vol. 96, no 2, pp. 455–484.

of roles of the inquisition process,[224] for, with this legislation the role of the trial judge was marginalised as the public prosecutor was given authority to impose certain conditions which are in essence of nature of the punishment.[225] The payment of a sum of money may breach the equality of treatment, by which the rich may buy their way out of the court (*Freikauf von Strafe*).[226] While scepticism about the dramatic legislative change was continuously expressed, the practice swiftly adapted to the new regulation. In 1980, it is estimated that about 151,000 cases were dealt with means of Section 153a.[227]

4.4 Impact of Reform

The reform legislation had brought about a considerable shift in sentencing practices, although the extent to which 'epochal' changes occurred due to the latter is a matter of certain controversy.[228] Whilst earlier accounts draw a much more positive picture,[229] in particular by means of longer time span analysis, a more cautious and differentiated analysis of the achievements of the reform legislation in practice is noticeable since the 1980s, particularly that of Heinz.[230] The data provided and discussed here was compiled from Heinz's time trend analyses.

Figure 4.1 illustrates the major trends in sentencing practice between 1950 and 1980. The total number of offenders sentenced increased during this period from 275,182 to 599,832, reaching a peak of 614,252 in 1978. As Figs. 4.1 and 4.2 show, despite the overall upward trend, with some fluctuations, in the number of convictions, at two points the number of prison sentences decreased sharply. The first occurred soon after the introduction of the unsuspended prison sentence into

---

224 Hirsch, *op. cit.*, p. 230.

225 See above.

226 Hanack, *op. cit.*, p. 349, Schmidhäuser *op. cit.*, p. 535, Hirsch, p. 251, see also Müller, R. (1975) Begünstigung der Steuer- und Wirtschaftstraftäter durch den Staat?, *Zeitschrift für Rechtspolitik*, vol. 8, no. 3, pp. 49–56, p. 55.

227 Heinz, W. (1982) Strafrechtsreform und Sanktionsentwicklung – Auswirkungen der sanktionenrechtlichen Regelungen des 1. und 2. StrRG 1969 sowie des EGStGB 1974 auf die Sanktionspraxis, *Zeitschrift für die gesamte Strafrechtswissenschaft*, vol. 94, no 3, pp. 632–668, p. 644.

228 Kiwull, *op. cit.*, p. 4, Stapenhorst, *op. cit.*, p. 92.

229 Kaiser, *op. cit.*, p. 29.

230 But as Heinz has noted, time trend analysis have serious limitations due to the data sources, changing the category of, in particular, the kind of custodial penalties and their duration, see, Heinz (1981), *op. cit.* See also, Voß, M. (1987) Verwahrvollzug – Behandlungsvollzug. Der strafrechtliche Gebrauch der Freiheitsstrafe im Zuge ihrer Veränderten Ansprüche. Zugleich eine Kritik der Kurzstrafenkritik in Sievering, U., O. (ed.) *Problem Strafhaft- Alternative Sanktionen*, Frankfurt, Haag & Herchen, pp. 224–253, pp. 224–253.

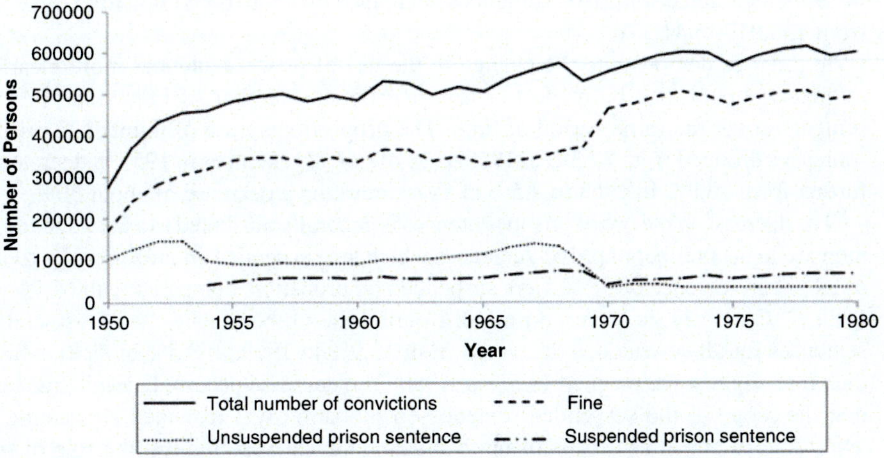

Fig. 4.1 Sentencing practice in the former Länder of Germany 1950–1980[231]

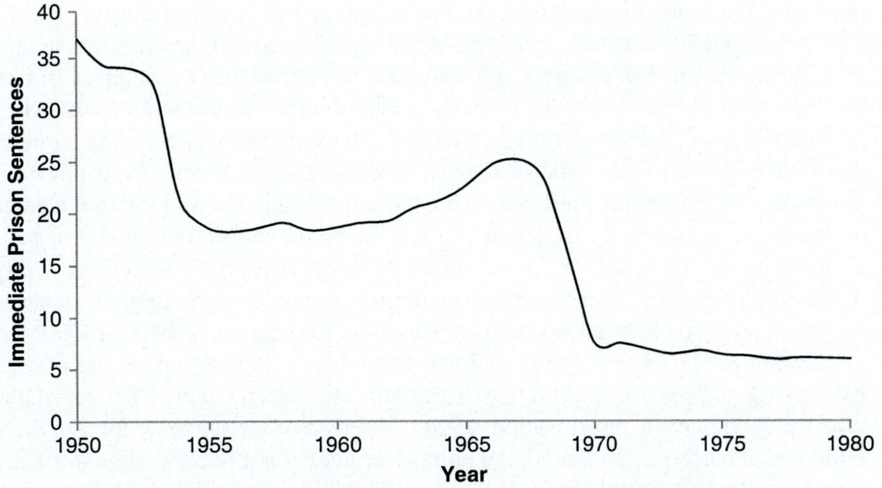

Fig. 4.2 Immediate prison sentences in the former Länder of Germany 1950–1980[232]

general criminal law in 1953.[233] The number of immediate prison sentences in this year was 148,743. In 1954, this number decreased by 66% to 98,172. An even sharper decrease took place in 1969, after the First Law on Reform came into force.

[231]Data compiled from Heinz (1982), *op. cit.*

[232]Data compiled from Heinz (1982) *op. cit.*

[233]Kaiser described this shift as 'one of the most significant changes in sanctioning practice'. Kaiser, G. (1980) *Kriminologie*, Müller, Heidelberg, p. 297.

In 1970, the number of prison sentences decreased by about 69% compared to 1968, from 136,017 to 41,276.

In order to demonstrate the change in the use of prison sentences more clearly, reference should also be made to the proportionate number of immediate prison sentences over the same period of time. The proportionate use of immediate prison sentences dropped from 37.3% in 1950 to 28.4% of all sentences in 1955. It decreased further from 23.8% in 1968 to 7.5% in 1970, marking a decrease of about 30%.

The decrease in the use of prison sentences is generally attributed to a corresponding increase in the number of prison sentences which are suspended on probation. In 1968, of all prison sentences, 35.6% were suspended on probation, compared with 65.7% in 1980.[234] Curiously, however, during this period the proportionate use of suspended sentences for all convictions decreased from 13.9% in 1969, to 8.5% in 1970, which then rose slightly and reached 11.5% in 1980. The decrease occurred, despite the fact that the scope of the suspended sentence on probation was extended by making it applicable to prison sentences of up to 2 years. Given these figures, the role of the '*ultima* ratio' clause provided for in Section 47 in reducing the number of incarcerated persons could be better appreciated.

Indeed, the strict criteria that the respective provision entailed appear to have persuaded the courts to use short-term imprisonment more parsimoniously. In 1967/1968, of all prison sentences imposed, 86% were short-term imprisonments of up to 6 months. Within this category, the duration of half of these sentences did not exceed a term of 1 month.[235] In 1973, this proportion decreased to 63%. In 1980, it further decreased; the proportionate use of prison sentences *not exceeding* 6 months constituted 60.9% of all prison sentences. Nonetheless, the reservation is made that the respective clause fell short of making the imposition of short term confinement an exception provided for by law and aimed at by the legislature, though it had a stronger impact upon the actual execution of short-term prison sentences.[236] Significantly, short-term imprisonment including sentences of 6 months made up 19.8% of all immediate prison sentences in 1968 dropping to 1.7% in 1980.[237]

Another implication of Section 47 was that with the increase in the use of fines, by making imprisonment of up to 6 months an 'ultima ratio', the legislature effectively created a prioritisation of the fine over imprisonment for a term of 6 months of custody.[238] In 1950, the number of fines was 172,575, while this figure increased almost threefold in 1978. During this period, the proportionate use of the fine for all convictions rose from 62.7 to 82.4%. However, a caution must be issued that the fine appears to have, for the most part, replaced the least short terms of

---

[234]Heinz (1982) *op. cit.*, p. 651.

[235]Heinz (1982) *op. cit.*, p. 651.

[236]See, Heinz (1981) *op. cit.*, pp. 162–163.

[237]Heinz (1982) *op. cit.*, p. 652.

[238]See also Albrecht, H.-J. (1978) Statistische Angaben über die Geldstrafe in der Bundesrepublik Deutschland in Jescheck and Grebing, *op. cit.*, pp. 165–191, Kaiser (1980) *op. cit.*, pp. 289–290 and 303–305.

custody. Between 1975 and 1980 of all sentences of the fine, 98.5% did not exceed 90 daily unit fines; only 1.3% were over 90 and finally, only 0.16% contained more than 180.[239] The conclusion, therefore, was that the fine was primarily used with regard to relatively less serious offenders, for up to a 3 months prison sentence.[240] Its use for more serious offenders was by and large of negligible significance, which as will be seen below continues to be the case so far.

These changes in sentencing practice had an immediate impact on the prison population. The number of prisoners in a marked decrease of 27% dropped from 41,744 in 1968 to 30,450 in 1970.[241] However, by 1980, the decrease had already turned into an increase of 14% to reach 35,537. This state of affairs has generally been explained by the increase in long-term prison sentences for drug offences, serious violent offences and sexual offences.[242] Confirming the overall pattern in the western world, drug related offences were growing, and so did the use of longer prison sentences for these offences.[243] The statistical assessment of the impact of the reform in the light of the most recent figures will be continued, but before that an account of current legislative framework and proposals for change is crucial.

4.5 Current Legislative Framework

It was noted above that since the 'Law against Dangerous Habitual Offenders and on the Measures of Security and Rehabilitation' was enacted in 1933, the German penal system has been characterised by, in the German terminology, the two-track system (*Zweispurigkeit*). This system is made up of punishments: imprisonment and the fine that are meted out in accordance with individual guilt (*Strafen*), and *measures* (*Maßregeln*), which are rehabilitative (curative), protective and incapacitative, and are applied with a view to the degree of dangerousness as revealed by the offence and the previous criminal record of the offender.[244] When the offender lacks the mental capacity to do so, entirely or partly, no, or diminished liability to punishment arises. In the latter case, under German law, placement in a mental

[239]Heinz (1982) *op. cit.*, p. 639.

[240]*Ibid.*

[241]*Ibid.*, p. 659.

[242]Homann, C. (1984) Freiheitsentziehende Sanktionen und Haftplatzbedarf, dargestellt an der Entwicklung von Verurteiltenzahlen und Belegungszahlen der Gefangenen in den Justizvollzugsanstalten 1971 bis 1982, *Monatschrift für Kriminologie*, vol. 67, no. 5, pp. 332–338, Voß (1987), *op. cit.*, pp. 236–253.

[243]In this context, see Dünkel, F. (2002) Der deutsche Strafvollzug im internationalen Vergleich, p. 3, in the following link accessible
http://www.erato.fh-erfurt.de/so/homepages/janssen/scripte/strafvollzug/Strafvollzug_BRD.pdf (Access Date March 2009).

[244]On *Zweispurigkeit*, Jescheck and Weigend, *op. cit.*, p. 83, Streng, F. (2002) *Strafrechtliche Sanktionen*, 2nd edition, Kohlhammer, Stuttgart, p. 150, Schöch, H. (2008) On Section 61 in Leipziger Kommentar, *op. cit.*, pp. 215–402, pp. 215–229, Eser, *op. cit.*, pp. 213–216.

hospital is to be imposed as a *measure*.[245] In a similar vein, where, due to excessive alcohol intake or use of other intoxicating substances, an offender lacks penal responsibility or her/his responsibility is diminished, a committal to a detoxification centre can be imposed. Furthermore, predicated upon the notion of the dangerousness of the offender, there are such *measures* as supervision (*Führungsaufsicht*),[246] driving ban[247] and prohibition to exercise a certain profession or trade.[248] These measures are imposed alongside her/his penal responsibility arising from the unlawful conduct. Section 62 stipulates that a *measure* of rehabilitation and security ought not to be imposed if it is incommensurate to the significance of the offences the offender has committed or the future crimes that s/he may commit and the danger s/he poses. As this short description shows, the measures of security and rehabilitation can be imposed collaterally with imprisonment and fine. Therefore, a *measure* does not substitute for imprisonment in all cases except where, on the grounds of mental incapacity, no punishment can be imposed.

The Penal Code makes distinction between main and ancillary penalties and the ancillary consequences. Imprisonment and the fine are the primary punishments, which are thought to make up a dual system.[249] The duration of a prison sentence can range from 1 month to 15 years. A sentence containing an imprisonment term of 6 months can be imposed only as *ultima ratio* where the defence of the legal order renders its imposition essential. On the other hand, German law retains life imprisonment, which is mandatory for murder and genocide. Along with these offences, the Penal Code provides the possibility of the imposition of a life sentence with regard to a number of offences such as high treason, aggravated manslaughter, and robbery having fatal consequences. The only ancillary punishment laid down in the Penal Code is withdrawal of driver's licence, which has been discussed in the preceding section. Under German law, forfeiture and confiscation are designed as 'ancillary consequences'.[250]

Although outside of the system of the German Penal Code, it would be incorrect to overlook the place of 'informal sentencing' practice in Germany. In 2006, the proportion of persons receiving sanctions pursuant to the penal law was 47.5% while the 'rest', 52.5% were dealt with by means of diversion procedures.[251] The diversion practices of public prosecutors and courts are not merely quantitatively important. It will be clearly evident from the forthcoming overview of sentencing

[245] Section 63 of the German Penal Code.

[246] *Ibid.*, Section 68.

[247] *Ibid.*, Section 69.

[248] *Ibid.*, Section 70.

[249] Jescheck and Weigend, *op. cit.*, p. 755

[250] Sections 74 and 73 of the Penal Code.

[251] Heinz, W. (2008) Sanktionierungpraxis in Deutschland, Internet Publication, p. 48. Accessible from the following link
http://www.uni-konstanz.de/rtf/kis/Sanktionierungspraxis-in-Deutschland-Stand-2006.pdf.

disposals that the content of diversion measures and sentencing disposals display substantial similarities. A recapitulation of the provisions related to diversion under the general criminal law is therefore necessary at this point.

There are various forms of diversion laid down in the German Criminal Procedure Code. The first possibility is dismissal of prosecution or proceeding pursuant to Article 153 of the respective Code. Based on the distinction of offences as *Vergehen* and *Verbrechen*,[252] this provision empowers public prosecutors to dismiss a case with the approval of the court in respect to a *Vergehen*, provided that the "the guilt of the offender is considered of a minor nature" and "there is no public interest in the prosecution". The approval of the court is not required if the offence in question is not subject to a punishment beyond the statutory minimum of five unit day fines or 1 months' imprisonment, pursuant to Articles 38 and 40 of the German Criminal Code, and where the consequences ensuing from the offence are minimal.[253] According to Paragraph 2 of this provision, the court, with the consent of the public prosecutor and the indicted accused, may terminate the proceedings at any stage. A second possibility is laid down in Article 153a of the German Criminal Procedure Code. In order to drop a case which involves a *Vergehen* on the grounds of 153a, where the public prosecutor imposes a number of specified conditions and instructions with the view that they are "of such nature as to eliminate the public interest in prosecution" and that the offender's "culpability does not present an obstacle" in this respect. These conditions or instructions can include the offender's payment of compensation to the victim, payment of a sum of money to a charity or to the treasury, performance of community service, fulfilment of family maintenance obligations, participation in victim offender mediation, or attendance at a traffic course. The public prosecutor is required to have the approval of the court to which the case would have otherwise been brought (competent court) and the consent of the accused. Under the same conditions, pursuant to Section 153a (2), courts can also provisionally terminate a proceeding after a formal accusation has been filed. What was not mentioned above is another possibility, which is provided under the purview of the Drug Law *(Betäubungsmittelgesetz)*.[254] Accordingly, the public prosecutor or subsequently the court can refrain from prosecution where the drug consumer committed an offence subject to a maximum punishment of less than 2 years imprisonment on the condition that s/he submits to a course of therapy of at least 3 months duration.

[252]According to Section 12 of the German Penal Code, Verbrechen are crimes which are punishable by imprisonment for one or more years, while Vergehen are crimes the minimum punishment of which is less than one year's imprisonment or a fine.

[253]Volk, K. (2002) *Strafprozessrecht*, Beck, München, p. 113.

[254]Section 31.

4.5.1 Sentencing Measures Under the German Penal Code

As distinct from English law, the Penal Code and other relevant laws prescribe the minimum and maximum penalties (generally a prison sentence). In this way the discretion of judges is considerably constrained, albeit the difference between the minimum and maximum limits is comparatively broad in general, which effectively gives a large amount of discretion.[255] In fixing a penalty in the individual case, the statement in Section 46 (1) of the Penal Code that the guilt of the offender is the basis for determination of the sentence. Owing to reform efforts in the 1960s, the next clause reads that in fixing the penalty in the individual case, the effects of the punishment on the offender's future life must also be taken into consideration. In so doing, according to Section 46 (2) the court is required to take various circumstances of the offender into account which are listed therein, and which in turn reflect the rationales of the sentencing as specified in Paragraph 1 with the addition of an explicit reference to reparation. These include the motives and aims of the offender, the state of mind and the wilfulness of the offender as revealed in the commission of the act, the extent of the breach of any duties, the manner of execution and liable effects of the act, the perpetrator's prior history, her/his personal and financial circumstances and her/his conduct after the commission of the offence, among which particular consideration is to be given to the offender's reparative efforts. In the next section, various sentencing options which courts may resort to will be discussed.

4.5.2 Dispensing with Punishment

Section 60 of the Penal Code empowers courts to dispense with the imposition of punishment if the consequences of the act to the offender were so grave that an imposition of punishment would be inexpedient and the punishment which otherwise would be imposed would not exceed 1 year of imprisonment. The classical example given in this context is a drunk-driving accident that has serious consequences for the offender or a close relative.[256] Furthermore, pursuant to Section 46a, courts can refrain from the imposition of punishment on the offender's reparative efforts. Accordingly, where by means of victim-offender mediation, the offender made amends for her/his act entirely or to a large extent, made a genuine effort to reach a settlement, or otherwise compensated the damage caused to the victim in a

[255] Weigend highlights that „Overall statutory sentence ranges in Germany give only a broad indication of the legislature's estimation of the relative seriousness of an offence and fail to offer significant guidance to the sentencing court for the resolution of individual cases. Weigend, T. (2001) Sentencing and Punishment in Germany in Tonry, M. and Frase, R. (ed.) *Sentencing Sanctions in Western Countries,* Oxford University Press, pp. 189–221.

[256] Jescheck and Weigend, *op. cit.*, p. 862.

way which required substantial personal achievement or sacrifice on the part of the offender, the court can mitigate the sentence or dispense with punishment, provided that the maximum punishment which the offender would have otherwise received would not exceed a prison sentence of 1 year or a comparable amount of fine (360 unit fines).

4.5.3 Warning with Suspension of Punishment

In the German system, fines cannot be suspended; however, the 'warning with suspension of punishment' serves a similar purpose. Under Section 59 of the German Penal Code, the court, having pronounced the guilt of the offender may postpone the imposition of a punishment made up of up to 180 day fines. This measure is imposable only where the court is satisfied that a warning instead of the actual imposition of a fine of up to 180 day fines may suffice to prevent the commission of further crimes by the offender and that the overall assessment of the offence and personality of the offender reveals *special circumstances*, which justify a waiver of punishment. In Subsection 3, it is stated that its use can be limited with general preventive considerations by using the formulation of the provision: 'the defence of the legal order'. Furthermore, the respective section bars the use of this measure for offenders who had previously been warned through this measure or received a punishment during the 3 years preceding the commission of the offence.

Having decided to impose this measure, the court determines a probationary period, the length of which ranges between 1 and 3 years. In doing so, the court may attach a number of instructions to be undertaken during the probationary period. These include mediation with the victim, compensation, payment of a sum of money to a charity or the treasury, committal to treatment in a care institution or a detoxification centre, participation in traffic courses and the fulfilment of family maintenance obligations.

4.5.3.1 The Fine

In German penal law, fines can only be imposed with respect to adult offenders, and hence cannot be meted out with regard to juvenile offenders or corporate bodies. Yet, the payment of a sum of money can be imposed as a disciplinary measure according to the Juvenile Criminal Law or as a condition of termination of a proceeding pursuant to Section 153a of the Criminal Procedure Code. Notably, the German Penal Code does not provide for any offence which is punishable solely by the fine. It does, however, provide for the fine as an alternative to imprisonment for all types of *Vergehen* punishable by a term of imprisonment not exceeding 1 year of imprisonment, e.g. for minor forms of bodily injuries, petty forms of property crimes and fraud. Beside this, Section 47 (2) establishes the priority of the fine for prison sentences of up to of 6 months, in so far as the offence of the defence of the legal order does not preclude it. Fines and prison sentences cannot to be imposed in conjunction, the only exception to this rule is provided in Section 41, where the offender acted with the intention of pecuniary benefit. In the latter case, having regard to personal and financial circumstances of the offender, the court may deem an imposition of the fine in addition to a prison sentence expedient.

The German system of day-fines is justified by the principle of equal impact of fines on offenders with different income levels (*Opfergleichheit*).[257] Under this system, fines are fixed in two steps. In the first step, the number of day fines is determined pursuant to the above-mentioned Section 46, commensurate with the culpability of the offender. The daily units range from 5 to 360. The maximum limit of the fine, which an offender cumulatively receives under Section 54, cannot exceed 720 daily units. In the second step, taking the personal and financial circumstances of the offender into account, the amount of a single day unit is fixed. Thereby the average daily income of the offender (*Nettoeinkommen*) is assessed.[258] The minimum amount of the fine cannot be less than 1 Euro. Courts are *ex offico* required to give consideration as to whether there is a need for payment in instalments or deferment of payment.[259]

The ultimate sanction for offenders who default on payment, as discussed in detail, is imprisonment. The minimum length of imprisonment for fine default is 1 day, while the outstanding amount determines the maximum length. In case of the fine default, under the auspices of Section 293 of the Introductory Law, all *Länder* adopted the possibility of performing community service instead of serving a prison term, if the convict consents to it. At present, the rate of equivalency between fine and community service is laid down generally as 6 h of work for one daily unit fine.[260]

4.5.3.2 Suspended Sentence

Various opinions exist on the exact legal nature of the suspended sentence. It is viewed as a ‘third track of legal reaction’, as ‘the modification of the execution of the prison sentence’, and as ‘a *sui generis* sanction’ under German penal law, technically the suspended sentence is a custodial sentence.[261]

---

[257]Jescheck and Weigend, *op. cit.*, p. 770, Streng, *op. cit.*, 61–62, Meier, B. (2006) *Strafrechtliche Sanktionen*, 2nd edition, Springer, Berlin, pp. 67–68. An overview in Häger, *op. cit.*, pp. 868–912.

[258]Section 40 (2) of the Penal Code.

[259]Stree, W. (2006) on Section 42 in *Schönke/Schröder Strafgesetzbuch Kommentar*, 27th edition, Beck, München, p. 743, Häger, *op. cit.*, p. 927.

[260]Häger, *op. cit.*, p. 947.

[261]Meier (2006), *op. cit.*, pp. 109–110, Streng (2002) *op. cit.*, pp. 79–86.

According to Section 56, the suspension of a prison term is only granted where it is expected that the conviction would serve as a warning and in the future, without the influence of a prison stay, the offender would not reoffend. Requiring a positive prognosis in this way, the law makes no explicit mention by which means it could be ascertained.[262] However, it provides a general set of criteria by virtue of which a probability of further offending behaviour could be assessed. These are the following: the personality of the offender, her/his life conduct, previous life history, the circumstances of the offence in question, her/his behaviours after the commission of the office and the expected effects of the suspension.

Depending on the length of the prison sentence, the Penal Code provides three different arrangements.[263] With regard to prison sentences up to 6 months, it is generally agreed that the only requirement is positive prognosis.[264] Prison sentences between 6 months and 1 year can be suspended unless the 'defence of the legal order' necessitates the execution of the sentence.[265] Finally, prison sentences between a term of 1 and 2 years can be suspended, where the overall assessment of the personality of the offender and the offence reveal special circumstances which justify the suspension of the imprisonment term.

In granting a suspension of the prison term, the court specifies a probationary period. It cannot exceed 5 years and cannot be less than 2 years. The period of probation can be lengthened or shortened afterwards.[266] By suspending the prison sentence, the court *can* impose a number of conditions and instructions. Section 56b of the Penal Code lists the 'conditions'. These include making amends for the offence to the victim, payment of an amount of money to a charitable institution, performing community service, and making a donation to the treasury. On the other hand 'instructions' can be imposed with a view to preventing the offender from reoffending[267] which may be concerned with compliance with the orders regarding abode, education, work, free time and financial affairs, report of the whereabouts to the court or any other specified place, fulfilment of family maintenance obligations, prohibition from possessing certain objects or intercourse with certain persons which may offer the opportunity or incitement to commit further criminal acts or otherwise submittal to therapeutic programmes. The latter, however, can only be imposed, where the offender consents to it.[268] Furthermore, the court *may* place the defendant under the supervision of a probation officer. The supervision in the probationary period is mandatory whenever the suspended sentence exceeds

[262]Streng (2002), *op. cit.*, p. 78, Stree in Schönke/Schröder, p. 868, see also Hubrach, J. (2008) on Section 56, Laufhütte, H. W, Rissing-van Saan, R. and Tidemann, K. (eds.) *Leipziger Kommentar StGB*, 12th edition, vol. 4, pp. 1–106, p. 13.

[263]Section 56.

[264]Jescheck and Weigend, *op. cit.*, p. 834, Meier (2006), *op. cit.*, p. 100.

[265]Jescheck and Weigend, *op. cit.*, p. 834.

[266]Section 56a.

[267]Paragraph 1 of Section 56(c).

[268]Section 56 of the Penal Code.

9 months or the defendant is younger than 27 years. During the course of the probationary period, the court may modify the specified conditions and instructions. Within this time interval the commission of another offence automatically leads to a revocation of the suspended sentence. After the expiration of the probationary period the sentence is cancelled, but conviction and sentence are registered in the criminal record of the defendant.

4.5.3.3 Juvenile Justice

The German juvenile justice system has its own systemic adjudication procedures and sentencing disposals. The primary purpose of the juvenile justice system is to be found in the notion of 'education'; theoretically the presumed educational needs of the juvenile offender determine the kind and content of sanctions or measures, whereas the 'guilt' of the juvenile or adolescent offender, where applicable,[269] has a 'limiting' function in sentencing decision.[270] Despite the central importance attached to the notion of education, the Juvenile Court Law does not explicitly define the term 'education'. Not surprisingly, the meaning given to it has varied greatly from time to time.[271] Faced with the crisis of the effectiveness of treatment programmes but also with a powerful theoretical questioning of the implications of the principle of 'education' from a rights rhetoric perspective, 'education' as an overarching objective of juvenile justice has been the subject of a heated debate for quite some time.[272] It exceeds the scope of this section to deal with the theme as such, suffice it at this point to reemphasise that the empirical, ideological and theoretical crisis of the orthodox conceptions of 'education' facilitated a diversionary approach towards juvenile criminality.[273] Notably, in 2006, the proportion of persons dealt with by diversionary measures amounts to 68.1%, in comparison with

---

[269]The first is that under certain circumstances, adolescent offenders (18–20 twenty years old) can be adjudicated and sentenced under the Juvenile Court Law, when it is deemed that the overall assessment of the personality of the adolescent offender indicates that at the time of the commission of the offence in question the moral and mental development of the juvenile offender was equal to a juvenile and that given the type, circumstances and the motives of the offence in question, concerns "a typical juvenile wrongdoing".

[270]Brunner, R. and Dölling, D. (2002) *Jugendgerichtsgesetz*, de Gruyter, Berlin, pp. 50–51, Loos, F. (1990) Der Schuldgrundsatz als Sanktionslimitierung im Jugendstrafrecht, Wolff, J. and Marek, A. (eds.) *Erziehung und Strafe*, Forum, Bonn, pp. 83–91.

[271]Walter, M. (1990) Der Erziehungsgedanke im Jugendstrafrecht – Abschied oder Reformulierung, pp. 51–61 and Heinz, W. (1990) Die Bedeutung des Erziehungsgedankens für Normsetzung und Normanwendung im Jugendstrafrecht der Bundesrepublik Deutschland in Wolff and Marek, *op. cit.*, pp. 28–49.

[272]For summary, see Ostendorf, H. (2007) *Jugendstrafrecht*, 4th edition, Nomos, Baden-Baden, pp. 15–21, Brunner and Dölling, *op. cit.*, pp. 40–49.

[273]But see Walter (1990), *op. cit.*, Heinz (1990), *op. cit.*, pp. 37–39.

43.8 in 1981.[274] Thus, it would not be an overstatement to portray these measures as constituting the first tier of the sentencing framework.

The Juvenile Court Law provides for various diversion options. Section 45 (1) empowers the juvenile prosecutor to dismiss a case in accordance with Section 153 of the Criminal Procedure Code if the offence was a minor one and the guilt of the offender is negligible, resulting in there being little purpose in pursuing prosecution. This can be done without referring the case to the juvenile judge for an approval. In the application of this measure, unlike other diversion possibilities stipulated by the Juvenile Law Court, it is generally agreed that only *Vergehen* fall under the scope of this measure.[275] Furthermore, the juvenile court prosecutor according to Section 45 2 (1) can dismiss a case if an educational measure has already been applied. The term 'educational measure' encompasses a wide variety of activities of public institutions and parents, teachers, social workers. The juvenile court prosecutor according to Section 45 3 (1) can recommend that the judge impose a number of obligations or instructions such as a warning, performing some activity in the public interest, mediation, participation at a training course, provided that the juvenile admits her/his guilt. The dismissal of the prosecution in this case is only possible after the juvenile has fulfilled these obligations or instructions. According to Section 47, after the prosecutor has filed the indictment, the judge may, if the offender admits her/his guilt, also conditionally dismiss a case with the agreement of the prosecutor. Conditions of the dismissal can include participation in victim-offender mediation, participation in social training courses or participation in a traffic education scheme.

The German Juvenile Court Law divides 'formal' sentencing disposals into three categories: educational measures, disciplinary measures and juvenile imprisonment. Disciplinary measures and juvenile imprisonment may only be resorted to where educational measures are deemed inadequate to deal with the individual juvenile offender. This provision has to be read together with Section 17 (2) which states that juvenile offenders can be exposed to juvenile imprisonment in cases in which educational or disciplinary measures are judged to be insufficient for the 'education' of the offender or not an adequate response given the gravity of the juvenile's guilt.[276] Hence, prima facie a hierarchy exists among different types of measures. Yet, as various sanction modalities are provided for both as educational and disciplinary measures, a mere change in the nomenclature makes a graduation between different measures hardly possible.

Section 10 (1) of the Juvenile Court Law provides for educational measures, which according to this section are imposed with a view to regulating the conduct of the juvenile, while enhancing the conditions of socialisation and securing her/his education. These are the following:

---

[274] Heinz (2008), *op. cit.*, p. 90.

[275] Albrecht, P.-A. (2000) *Jugendstrafrecht*, Beck, 3rd edition, München, p. 121, Laubenthal, K. and Baier, H. (2006) *Jugendstrafrecht*, Springer, Berlin, p. 109.

[276] Section 17 (2) of the Juvenile Court Law.

1. Compliance with instructions relating to residence
2. Residence with a foster family or hostel
3. Commencement of an apprenticeship training programme or employment
4. Performance of work
5. Placement under the supervision of a probation officer
6. Participation in a social training course
7. Efforts to reach a mediation with the victim
8. Prohibition concerning the intercourse with particular persons or being in certain places
9. Attendance at a traffic course, and finally, with regard to offenders in need of drug or alcohol treatment, a submittal to therapeutic programmes can be ordered[277]

According to Section 13 of the Juvenile Court Law, disciplinary measures are warnings by the juvenile judge, fulfilment of certain conditions and the juvenile detention. The conditions which may be imposed by the juvenile court judge include[278]:

1. Compensation of the victim
2. A formal apology
3. Performance of work
4. Payment of a sum of money for the benefit of a charitable organisation, where it can be ensured that the juvenile offender can undertake this payment from her/his own resources or otherwise s/he had earnings or rewards from the commission of the offence[279]

Since its enactment in 1943 during the National Socialist regime, the most severe disciplinary measure is short-term detention, which is meted out either as intermittent custody during the spare time, which in this case contains 1 or 2 weekends,[280] or as an uninterrupted duration of time, which may last up to 4 weeks.[281]

The minimum imprisonment term provided in the respective law is 6 months. The maximum duration of juvenile imprisonment is 5 years, unless for a specific offence, more than 5 years of imprisonment is provided for.[282] In the latter case, the maximum juvenile imprisonment cannot exceed a term of 10 years. In the determination of juvenile imprisonment, the Juvenile Court Law stipulates that, the 'educational needs' of the juvenile are to be taken into account.[283] The execution of a sentence of juvenile imprisonment up to 1 year can be suspended where it is expected that the suspension would serve as a sufficient warning for her/his future

[277] Section 10 (2).
[278] Section 15.
[279] Section 15 (1).
[280] Section 16 (2).
[281] Section 16 (3) and (4).
[282] Section 18 (1).
[283] Section 18 (2).

life and that without 'educative influence' the offender would lead a law-abiding life.[284] A term of imprisonment of up to 2 years could also be suspended where it is judged that the execution of the sentence for the development of the juvenile offender is not necessary.[285]

4.6 The Initiatives of 'Reforming' Reform

The penal reform legislation in Germany, which was once introduced to foreign audiences as a "truly revolutionary change",[286] realised various demands of progressive penology, but as argued above, it was soon vulnerable to 'nothing works' pessimism. Against this background the social therapy institution, in which great hope was initially invested, did not get a chance for full realisation.[287] In 1985, the provision concerning the social therapy institution (Section 65) was repealed.[288] This rather symbolic setback for the treatment of serious offenders was accompanied by a general retreat of the belief in the corrective function of institutional treatment, as German evaluative research's findings were generally confirming the conclusion that the institutional setting does not represent an appropriate milieu for 'treatment'.[289] Likewise, in the realm of juvenile justice, the 'pedagogical impact' of custody as the principle justification of juvenile imprisonment was being severely undermined by a body of research.[290] Undoubtedly, such local or 'localised' empirical challenges to the rehabilitative approach constituted a powerful stimulus to further reforms in sentencing.[291] The interest in developing new approaches to criminality was particularly heightened by the impulse to reduce

---

[284] Section 21 (1).

[285] Section 21 (2).

[286] Eser, A. (1973) Germany, *American Journal of Comparative Law*, vol. 21, no 2, pp. 245–262. For an overall analysis of penal reform, see also Hirsch, H.-J. (1986) Bilanz der Strafrechtsreform in, H.-J., Kaiser, G. and Marquardt, H. (eds.) *Gedächtnisschrift für Hilde Kaufmann*, de Gruyter, Berlin, pp. 133–165.

[287] See Müller-Dietz, *op. cit.*, pp. 205–229.

[288] Blau, *op. cit.*, p. 25.

[289] For the summary of the research studies see, Kurry (1986) *op. cit.*, Feest, *op. cit.*, pp. 20–24 and 44–51, also Kury (1999) *op. cit.*, pp. 28–56. See also, Feltes (1982) *op. cit.*, pp. 223–227.

[290] Heinz. W. (1997) Entwicklungstendenzen des Jugendstrafrechts in der Bundesrepublik Deutschland in Dünkel, F. and Kalmthout, A. (eds.) *Entwicklungstendenzen und Reformstrategien in Jugendstrafrecht im europäischen Vergleich*, Forum, Mönchengladbach, pp. 3–65, pp. 29–30 and 62.

[291] Ortner, H. (1986) Ambulante Alternativen – Die Begleitmusik des Strafvollzugssystems? Anmerkungen zu einer neuen Doppelstrategie, in Ortner, *op. cit.*, pp. 187–195, Pilgram, A. and Steinert, H. (1986) Plädoyer für bessere Gründe für die Abschaffung der Gefängnisse und für Besseres als die Abschaffung der Gefängnisse, pp. 196–217, *ibid.*

overcrowding in prisons.[292] In the beginning of the 1980s, due to an increase in middle and long term prison sentences and remand prisoners the number of prisoners reached 65,000, (about 30% higher than its level in 1971) making the prisoner rate 106 per 100,000.[293] Ultimately, the empirical, evidence, theoretical arguments and the prison numbers crises together provided a context from which the recent search for new non-custodial penalties has stemmed. Before going on to discuss concrete proposals, it is worthwhile to highlight two eminent features of recent penal policy which appear to have partially filled the 'void' in the discourse caused by the decline of the rehabilitative approach.

The earliest and most crucial indication in Germany of the changing intellectual climate was the rise of the ideas underlying a diversionary approach in academic discussion. In the German context, the debate over diversion was particularly fruitful, in that the law already facilitated diversionary mechanisms; the discussion here concentrated on how to operationalise the existing provisions. The 18th German Juvenile Court Day in this context may be regarded as the initiator of diversion debate.[294] One year later in Göttingen, on the German Juvenile Court Day, significant attention was devoted to the experience of other countries (in particular the experience of diversion in the United States)[295] and the diversion possibilities in the German Juvenile Court Law. The concept was then rapidly absorbed by a number of existing projects such as the Brücke Project in Cologne and Munich,[296] and the STOP-Programme and Shoplifting Project in Mönchengladbach[297] and Lübeck[298] which made use of the related provisions in the Juvenile Court Law that provide the opportunity to waive prosecution under certain circumstances.[299]

---

[292]For a detailed study on the overcrowding in German prisons see, Oberheim, R. (1985) *Gefängnisüberfüllung, Ursachen, Folgen und Lösungsmöglichkeiten in der Bundesrepublik Deutschland mit einem International Vergleich*, Lang, Frankfurt am Main.

[293]Dünkel, F. (1986) Alternativen zur Freiheitsstrafe im europäischen Vergleich in Ortner, H. (ed.) *Freiheit statt Strafe (Plädoyers für die Abschaffung der Gefängnisse Anstöße machbarer Alternativen)*, AS-Verlag, Reutlingen, p. 148.

[294]Deutsche Vereinigung für Jugendgerichte und Jugendgerichtshilfen (1981) *Die Jugendrichterlichen Entscheidungen- Anspruch und Wirklichkeit,* Schriftenreihe der Deutschen Vereinigung für Jugendgerichte und Jugendgerichtshilfen, Heft 12, Arbeitskreis III Diversion: Wege zur Vermeidung des Förmlichen, Verfahrens, München, pp. 176- 2004.

[295]Deutsche Vereinigung für Jugendgerichte und Jugendgerichtshilfen (1984) *Jugendgerichtsverfahren und Kriminalprävention*, Schriftenreihe der Deutschen Vereinigung für Jugendgerichte und Jugendgerichtshilfen, Heft 13.

[296]Pfeiffer, C. (1983) *Kriminalprävention im Jugendgerichtsverfahren – Jugendrichterlichen Handeln vor dem Hintergrund des Brücke-Projeckts*, Heymann, Köln.

[297]Kirchoff, G., F. (1985) *Diversion im Jugenstrafrecht: Das STOP-Programm der INTEG nach zwei* Jahren, in Kury, H. (ed.) *Kriminologische Forschung in der Diskussion*, Heymann, Köln, pp. 341–369.

[298]Sessar, K. and Hering, E. (1985) Bedeutung und Reichweite Pädagogisch Gemeinter Verfahreneinstellungen durch den Jugendstaatsanwalt: Das Beispiel des "Lübecker Modells" in Kury (1985), *op. cit.*, pp. 371–415.

[299]Jannsen, H. (1985) Diversion im Jugendstrafrecht als kriminalpolitische Alternative, *Kriminalistik*, vol. 39, no 4, pp. 208–212, pp. 209–211.

As the idea of diversion, which once was described as a "North-American import article"[300] began to gain ground in Germany, in general two main arguments and/or research findings underpinned the diversionary approach: that crime is a deviation in the process of growing up, which disappears as individuals mature, and that involvement with the criminal justice system has negative consequences for the future lives of juveniles.[301] In this way, diversion programmes marked a clear shift from the education conception, which is formally embodied in the Juvenile Court Law that juvenile criminality comes out as a result of individual educational deficiency or pathology.[302] Challenging the orthodox conception of education along these lines, diversion programmes were theoretically expected to prevent the creation of deviant labels, thereby reducing "unnecessary social control"[303] while preventing repeated contact with criminal justice agencies.[304] They were rarely seen as direct 'alternatives to custody'.[305]

From the beginning of the 1990s, largely with the impulse of administrative/managerial and fiscal considerations, the scope of diversion was further extended.[306] For example, in 1990, with the amendment of the Juvenile Court Law, diversion was endorsed as a "swifter, more cost-effective and more humane" means of dealing with petty and non-serious juvenile criminality.[307] The scope of diversion

---

[300]Walter, M. (1985) Wandlungen in der Reaktion auf Kriminalität. Zur kriminologischen und insbesondere dogmatischen Bedeutung von Diversion, *Zeitschrift für die gesamte Strafrechtswissenschaft*, vol. 93, no. 1, pp. 32–68, p. 32.

[301]Hermann, J. (1984) Diversion und Schlichtung in der Bundesrepublik Deutschland, *Zeitschrift für die gesamte Strafrechtswissenschaft*, vol. 96, no 2, pp. 455–484, Kerner, H., J. (1984) Jugendgerichtsverfahren und Kriminalprävention, Opening Speech, in *Deutsche Vereinigung für Jugendgerichte und Jugendgerichtshilfe*, *op. cit.*, pp. 14–45, pp. 29–30, Kuhlen, L. (1988) *Diversion im Jugendstrafverfahren: rechtliche Probleme von Alternativen im Jugendstrafverfahren*, Müller Juristischer Verlag, Heidelberg, pp. 4–6, Heinz (1997), *op. cit.*, pp. 37–39.

[302]Heinz (1997) *op. cit.*, pp. 29–31.

[303]Sonnen, B.-R. (1981) Die §§ 45 und 47 JGG- Eine Betrachtung der Anwendungspraxis und der Möglichkeiten, Deutsche Vereinigung für Jugendgerichte und Jugendgerichtshilfen (ed.) *Die Jugendrichterlichen Entscheidungen – Anspruch und Wirklichkeit*, München, pp. 177–190, pp. 177–180.

[304]Dölling, D. (1998) Diversion in Elster, A., Lingemann, H., Sieverts, R. (eds.) *Handwörterbuch der Kriminologie*, de Gruyter, Berlin, pp. 275–287, p. 275.

[305]Lerchenmüller, H. (1981) Bedeutung der Diversion zur Vermeidung von Prisonisierungsschäden in Kury and Lerchenmüller, *op. cit.*, pp. 127–161.

[306]See for example, Weigend, T. (1997) Das Opportunitätsprinzip zwischen Einzelfallgerechtigkeit und Systemeffizienz, *Zeitschrift für die gesamte Strafrechtswissenschaft*, vol. 109, no. 4, pp. 103–121, Walther, S. (2004) Communication over Confrontation: Modern Criminal Procedure in Transformation in Eser, A. and Rabenstein, C. (eds.) *Strafjustiz im Spannungsfeld von Effizienz und Fairness*, Duncker & Humblot, Berlin, pp. 367–379, Meier, B.-D. (2000) Wiedergutmachung im Strafrecht? Empirische Befunde und kriminalpolitische Perspektiven in Bender, D. and Jehle, J.-M. (eds.) *Täterbehandlung und neue Sanktionsformen: Kriminalpolitische Konzepte in Europa*, Forum Verlag, Bonn, pp. 255–276, p. 257.

[307]See Government Bill for the *Erstes Gesetz zur Änderung des Jugendgerichtsgesetzes* (BT-Drucksache 11/5829).

was significantly broadened in 1993 in an amendment to Section 153a.[308] The new form of respective provision is indicative of the extension of diversion from minor criminality to the domain of offences of medium gravity.[309] By this amendment, the formulation of "if the guilt of the offender is minor" was changed to the following: "if the degree of the guilt of the offender does not present an obstacle" for the dismissal of the case through article 153a of the German Procedure Code. This law was essentially justified by economic problems due to the re-unification of Germany.[310]

Prompted by, *inter alia*, the waning of rehabilitative optimism, another perspective which gained significant attention was the (re)emergence of 'Wiedergutmachung', known as 'restorative' or 'reparative' justice' in Anglo–American countries.[311] The German criminal justice system has always contained some elements of reparation. The so-called adhesion procedure,[312] the pursuance of civil claims during criminal litigation, and the participation of the victim in the trial as an accessory prosecutor in offences specified by the Penal Code (*Nebenklage*, *action civile*[313]) have long been established. The reparative activity of the offender has long been recognised as criterion of measurement for the sentencing decision. A requirement upon the offender to repair the harm done by the offence could be imposed with regard to the conditional dismissal of prosecution and proceedings, the warning with suspension of punishment, the suspended prison sentence and conditional release, and, thus, in a broader sense, the notion of 'restorative justice' even prior to the proliferation of victim-oriented initiatives had legal foundations. However, until the beginning of the 1980s these provisions, remained in the Penal Code without any appreciable practical importance.[314] In this sense, the interest in

[308]Gesetzt zur Entlastung der Rechtspflege 11.11.1993, Bundesgesetzblatt, p. 50.

[309]Böttcher, R. and Mayer, E. (1993) Änderungen des Strafverfahrensrechts durch den Entlastungsgesetz, *Neue Zeitschrift für Strafrecht*, vol. 13, no. 4, pp. 153–158, at p. 154, Ranft, O. (2005) Strafprozessrecht, 3rd edition, Richard Boorberg Verlag, Stuttgart, pp. 390–391.

[310]Böttcher, *op. cit.,* p. 153.

[311]Kerner, H.J. (1986) Die Wiedereinsetzung des Opfers als Subjekt des (Straf-)Rechts in Janssen, H. and Kerner, H.-J. (eds.) *Verbrechensopfer, Sozialarbeit und Justiz: Das Opfer im Spannungsfeld der Handlungs- und Interessenkonflikte*, Deutschen Bewähhrungshilfe, Bonn, pp. 495–521, Feltes, T. (1985) Konfliktbereinigung zwischen Täter und Opfer: Institutionalisierung oder Reprivatisierung? in Jannsen and Kerner, op, cit., pp. 407–435, Frehsee, D. (1987) *Schadenswiedergutmachung als Instrument strafrechtlicher Sozialkontrolle: ein kriminalpolitischer Beitrag zur Suche nach alternativen Sanktionsformen*, Duncker & Humblot, Berlin, pp. 3–4, Weigend, T. (1989) *Deliktsopfer und Strafverfahren*, Duncker & Humblot, Berlin, p. 527, Hartmann, A. (1995) *Schlichten und Richten der Täter Opfer Ausgleich und das (Jugend-) Strafrecht*, Fink Verlag, München, pp. 99–107.

[312]Section 403 of the Criminal Procedure Code.

[313]*Nebenklage*, Section 395 of the Criminal Procedure Code.

[314]See e.g, Meier (2000) *op. cit.*, p. 427, Kaiser, G. (1979) Viktimologie an der schwelle der 80er Jahre –ein kritisches Resümee in Kirchoff, G., F. and Sessar, K. (eds.) *Das Verbrechensopfer*, Brockmeyer, Bochum, pp. 481–496, Sessar, K. (1985) Über das Opfer: Eine viktimologische Zwischenbilanz in Vogler, T. with Herrmann, J., Krümpelman, J., Moos, R., Triffterer, O.,

the "forgotten" crime victim was truly a phenomenon of the recent times.[315] From as early as the mid 1980s onwards the first mediation schemes in juvenile justice were established.[316] These projects were followed by the establishment of mediation schemes dealing with adult offenders.[317]

It was within this setting that the Alternative Draft 'Wiedergutmachung' was promulgated by a number of German, Austrian and Swiss scholars in 1992.[318] The authors of the draft endeavoured to provide a normative justification for the integration of the notion of 'Wiedergutmachung' into both substantive and procedural criminal law. Therein, 'Wiedergutmachung' is defined as the compensation of the consequences of the criminal conduct by the perpetrator to the victim or to the community at large.[319] Identifying the purpose of criminal law as the (controlled) restoration of the disturbed peace and order and its maintenance in the future,[320] the authors of the draft deemed 'Wiedergutmachung' as potentially an autonomous means of achieving this purpose. Hence, they advocated alongside the existing penal disposals, i.e. punishments and *measures*, the recognition and establishment

Leibinger, R., Schaffmeister, D., Meyer, J., Hünerfeld, P. and Behrendt, H.-J. (eds.) *Festschrift für Hans-Heinrich Jescheck*, vol. 2, pp. 1137–1157, de Gruyter, Berlin.

[315]Weigend, T. (1984) Viktimologische und kriminalpolitische Überlegungen zur Stellung des Verletzten im Strafverfahren, *Zeitschrift für die gesamte Strafrechtswissenschaft*, vol. 96, pp. 761–793, p. 761.

[316]On the early victim-offender mediation schemes see among others, Marks, E. and Rössner, D. (ed.) (1989) *Täter-Opfer-Ausgleich: vom zwischenmenschlichen Weg zur Wiederherstellung des Rechtsfriedens*, Forum, Bonn, Kuhn, A., Rudolph, M., Wandrey, M. and Will, H.-D. (1989) *"Tat-Sachen" als Konflikt. Täter-Opfer-Ausgleich in der Jugendstrafrechtspflege, Forschungsbericht zum Modelprojekt "Handschlag"*, Forum, Bonn, Schreckling, J. (1991) *Täter-Opfer-Ausgleich nach Jugendstraftaten in Köln – Bericht über Aufbau, Verlauf und Ergebnisse des Modellprojekts "Waage"*, Bundesministerium der Justiz, Bonn.

[317]Marks, S., Hering, R.-D., and Rössner, D. (1993) *Täter-Opfer-Ausgleich im Allgemeinen Strafrecht – Theorie und Praxis konstruktiver Tatverarbeitung*, Forum, Bonn, Marks, E., Meyer, K., Schreckling, J. and Wandrey, M. (1993) Wiedergutmachung und Strafrechtspraxis, Forum, Bonn, Bannenberg, B. (1993) *Wiedergutmachung in der Strafrechtspraxis: Eine empirisch-kriminologische Untersuchung von Täter-Opfer-Ausgleichsprojekten in der Bundesrepublik Deutschland*, Forum, Bonn.

[318]Jürgen Baumann, Anne-Eva Brauneck, Manfred Burgstaller, Albin Eser, Barbara Huber, Heike Jung, Ulrich Klug, Horst Luther, Werner Maihofer, Bern-Dieter Meier, Peter Rieß, Franz Riklin, Dieter Rössner, Klaus Rolinski, Claus Roxin, Heinz Schöch, Horst-Schüler Springorum and Thomas Weigend, Baumann *et al.* (1992) Alternativ-Entwurf Wiedergutmachung, Beck, München.

Roxin, C. (1987) Die Wiedergutmachung im System der Strafzwecke in Schöch, H. (ed.) *Wiedergutmachung und Strafrecht,* Symposion aus Anlass des 80. Geburtstages von Friedrich Schaffstein, Fink, München, pp. 37–55, in Roxin, C. (1992) Zur Wiedergutmachung als einer „Dritten Spur im Sanktionensystem in Arzt, G., Fezer, G., Weber, U., Schlüchter, E. und Rössner, D. (eds.) *Festschrift für Jürgen Baumann (70. Geburtstag 22 Juni 1992)*, Gieseking Verlag, Bielefeld, pp. 243–254.

[319]Baumann *et al.*, *op. cit.*, p. 39.

[320]*Ibid*, p. 23.

of *Wiedergutmachung* as a third type of reaction, in this sense, the third track (*dritte Spur*) of criminal law instruments.[321]

Justifying 'Wiedergutmachung' in this way, in order to facilitate an independent and meaningful implementation of 'Wiedergutmachung', the Draft envisaged a *re*-formation or rather re-orientation of the penological responses to crime in accordance with the notion of reparation. Under the scheme developed by the Alternative Draft *Wiedergutmachung*, depending upon the severity of the crime, in the individual case, the reparative efforts of the offender, e.g. compensation, an apology or 'community service', would determine the appropriate penal instrument.[322] Accordingly, at the first level for petty forms of criminality, the Draft favoured a diversionary approach (both formally and informally). For more serious offences, refraining from punishment was deemed to be the appropriate method, where the offender had made amends for her/his act and such waiver of punishment was expedient for preventive purposes. For offenders punishable by imprisonment, the reparative activity of the offender still ought to be taken into account as a mitigating factor or as grounds for the suspension of punishment or its execution. There were numerous corresponding *lex ferenda* recommendations in the Draft which were reflective of endeavours to translate a reparation-oriented perspective into legislation and practice.

The Alternative Draft was met with some fierce opposition for its emphasis on the shift from the guilt oriented punishment approach to the reparative approach[323]; on some accounts it was even accused of being in accordance with the 'abolitionist' perspective. Viewing the draft as incompatible with German law, some claimed that any *such large scale* substitution of the guilt oriented system of sanctions is wrong in principle. Eventually, the polarisation of the arguments, once again, resulted in a compromise solution in legislation insofar as the recognition of the reparative efforts of the offender in legislation gradually found greater recognition.

The 1990s witnessed a series of legislative initiatives which strengthened the position of the victim in criminal justice.[324] The First Amendment to the Juvenile

---

[321]Roxin (1987) *op. cit.*, pp. 37–55, Roxin (1992) *op. cit.*, pp. 243–254.

[322]Section 2 of the Alternative Draft Wiedergutmachung, see Baumann *et al.* (1992), *op. cit.*, pp. 43–48.

[323]Hirsch, H., J. (1990) Wiedergutmachung des Schadens im Rahmen des materiallen Strafrechts, *Zeitschrift für die gesamte Strafrechtswissenschaft*, vol. 102, pp. 534–562, Lampe, E.-J. (1993) Wiedergutmachung als "dritte Spur" des Strafrechts?, *Goltdammer's Archiv für Strafrecht*, vol. 140, pp. 485–494, Loos, F. (1993) Zur Kritik des Alternativentwurfs Wiedergutmachung, *Zeitschrift für Rechtspolitik*, vol. 26, no 2, pp. 51–56, see also Dölling, D. (1992b) Der Täter-Opfer-Ausgleich – Möglichkeiten und Grenzen einer neuen Kriminalpolitischen Reaktionsform, *Juristen Zeitung*, pp. 493–499. See also discussion on Wiedergutmachung in the 59th German Jurists' Assembly, Teil O Sitzzungsbericht: Über die *Verhandlungen Der Abteilung Strafrecht ,Empfehlen sich Änderungen und Ergänzungen bei den strafrechtlichen Sanktionen ohne Freiheitsentzug?* (16–17 September 1992) pp. 85–114.

[324]For an overview, see Meier, B.-D. (2004) Restorative Justice – Bericht über Deutschland in Schöch, H., Jehle, J.-M. and Aebersold, P. (eds.) *Angewandte Kriminologie zwischen Freiheit und Sicherheit*, Kriminalistik-Verlag, Heidelberg, pp. 415–428.

Court Law in 1990 explicitly stipulated that efforts towards reconciliation should be a reason for refraining from prosecution (Section 45 (2)).[325] In 1999, the legislature added two more provisions to the Criminal Procedure Code: Sections 155a and 155b. Accordingly, prosecutors and judges are required to assess (at every stage of the criminal process) whether or not victim-offender-mediation is attainable, if necessary they are required to initiate attempts and foster all reconciliation attempts by the parties. For that purpose, the Criminal Procedure Code allows for the referral of a case to a victim-offender mediation programme run by a criminal justice agency or a dispute resolution programme run by an association outside the criminal justice system.

With regard to substantive law, in the 1990s the place of reparation was further strengthened. In 1990, victim offender mediation was incorporated into the juvenile justice system as an educational measure (Section 10).[326] In 1994 the Crime Prevention Law brought about a number of changes. Most notably, the law, with an explicit stipulation, empowered courts, having regard to the offender's reparative efforts (trying to reach a settlement, making amends for her/his acts in part or in whole or a serious attempt to make amends) to mitigate a sentence or to refrain from imposing a sentence in cases where there is a maximum of 1 year imprisonment or a comparable fine.[327] In this law, the scope of reparation with regard to the suspended sentence and warning with punishment was further extended.[328] Consequently, with these enactments, 'victim-offender mediation' became an established legislative element of the German sanction system.[329]

---

[325] Heinz, W. (1993) Neues zur Diversion im Jugendstrafverfahren- Kooperation, Rolle und Rechtsstellung der Beteiligten, *Monatsschrift für Kriminologie und Strafrechtsreform*, vol. 76, no 6, pp. 355–375, p. 356, Frehsee, D. (1999) Restitution and Offender-Victim Arrangement within Criminal Law in Germany, *Buffalo Criminal Law Review*, vol. 3., no 1, pp. 235–259, p. 240, Kilchling, M. (2005) Victim-Offender Mediation with Juvenile Offenders in Germany in Mestitz, A. and Ghetti, S. (eds.) *Victim-Offender Mediation with Youth Offenders in Europe*, Springer, Dordrecht, pp. 229–257, pp. 232–233, Rössner, D. (2000) Ergebnisse und Defizite der aktuellen TAO-Begleitforschung. rechtliche und empirische Aspekte in Gutsche, G. and Rössner, D. (eds.) *Täter-Opfer-Ausgleich*, Forum Verlag, Godesberg pp. 7–40, pp. 7–9.

[326] Section 10 paragraph 1 of the Juvenile Court Law.

[327] Verbrechensbekämpfungsgesetz (BGBI, p. 386), 28.10.1994.

[328] See below.

[329] Other methods of restorative justice, such as family conferencing in England and Wales, are still not regarded as compatible with the objectives of the German juvenile justice policy. By rejecting the use of family conferencing in the German system, Hartmann and Kilchling argue that "mediation according to our system *does not* and *cannot* work on the basis of the conception of 'reintegrative shaming' which is the theoretical basis for the work of so-called family group conferencing. . .It is with regard to this stigmatising element that the shaming approach –at least in its pure form- is opposed to one of the leading principles of the Juvenile Justice System in Germany which demands to avoid all kind of stigmatising effects or side effects that can result from prosecution." "A conferencing model which includes participation of a 'community public' or parts of the social vicinity –which are important preconditions for initiating shaming process- cannot be realised within our system." Hartmann and Kilchling (1998) *op. cit.*, pp-261–282, pp. 262–263.

4.6.1 New Non-custodial Penalties: In Between or at Back?

Somewhat at odds with international trends, unlike countries where the decline in the rehabilitative approach was followed by the rise of short-sharp-shock agenda[330] and despite political demands for making greater use of juvenile custodial disposals,[331] in Germany in the last decade the thematic importance of non-custodial penalties was mounting in penal policy-making. In juvenile criminal law, the beginning of the 1990s witnessed the consolidation of the practice of diversion as noted in the preceding section, but also the introduction of a set of non-custodial disciplinary measures which were conceived of as alternatives to 'short-term detention' (*Jugendarrest*)[332]: supervision, participation in social training courses and community service, and the extension of the suspension of juvenile imprisonment up to 2 years.[333] With these revisions, the already diversified sanction catalogue in the Juvenile Court Law has been further enlarged.

In comparison to the wide variety of sanctions in juvenile law, adult criminal law in Germany, strictly speaking, is characterised by two main forms of punishment: fine and imprisonment. Since the beginning of the 1980s, most vocally during the proceedings of the 59th German Jurist Assembly in 1992, there have been calls for an extension of the range of the existing measures by devising new sentencing measures and enlargement of the remit of the existing provisions.[334] These demands have been predicated upon the belief that the sanction system applicable to adult offenders falls short, it lacks sufficient diversity and flexibility in that it is based on two primary methods of punishment: either deprivation of the liberty or the financial means of the offender.[335] There must be other sanctions in the middle range which bridge the gap between fines and prison. The sentences must be more individualised, where possible, they ought to suit to the needs of different offender

---

[330]See Rutherford, *op. cit.*, pp. 57–59.

[331]See e.g. Heinz (1997), *op. cit.*, pp. 62–63, Koepsel, K. (1999), Jugendarrest – eine zeitgemäße Sanktionsform des Jugendstrafrechts?' in Feuerhelm, Schwind and Bock, *op. cit.*, pp. 619–634.

[332]Bundesministerium der Justiz (1986) *Neue ambulante Maßnahmen nach dem JGG, Bielfelder Symposium,* and *(1989) Jugendstrafrechtsreform durch die Praxis*, Konstanzer Symposium, Bonn, Heinz (1997) *op. cit.*, pp. 46–49 and 53.

[333]BT-Drs. 11/5829.

[334]See e.g, Verhandlungen des 59. Deutschen Juristentag (1992), *op. cit.*, Schöch, H. (1992) Empfehlen sich Änderungen und Ergänzungen bei den strafrechtlichen Sanktionen ohne Freiheitsentzug?, (Gutachten C für 59. Deutschen Juristen Tag), Beck, München, Weigend, T. (1992) Sanktionen ohne Freiheitsentzug, *Goltdammer's Archiv für Strafrecht*, vol. 139, pp. 345–367, Müller-Dietz, H. (1999) Der Ort des Strafvollzuges in einem künftigen Sanktionensystem, Feuerhelm, Schwind and Bock, *op. cit.*, pp. 3–23, see also Stöckel, H. (2002) Strafen mit Fantasie: Zur Frage neuer Sanktionen im Strafrecht in Dölling, D. and Ebb, V. (eds.) *Festschrift für Karl Heinz Gössel zum 70. Geburtstag am 16 Oktober 2002*, Müller, Heidelberg. Stöckel, (2007) Gedanken zur Reform des Sanktionenrechts in Helgerth, R., Konig, P. and Schöch, H. (eds.) *Recht gestalten- dem Recht dienen*, de Gruyter, Berlin, pp. 329 -344. See also, Julius, K.-P. (1999) Tagungsbericht, *Zeitschrift für die gesamte Strafrechtswissenschaft*, vol. 111, pp. 889–915.

[335]'Zwischen Sanktionen', Meir, *op. cit.*, p. 364.

categories, as an extended catalogue of sanctions would better serve to prevent further offending.[336] In summary, in contrast with England, where "a moratorium on new initiatives,"[337] and a simplification of the sentencing law has been demanded, in Germany a more sophisticated and broad spectrum of sentencing options has been the demand of those scholars who place special emphasis on greater diversity and flexibility in sentencing.

These calls acquired support in broader circles, particularly as regards areas where there is thought to be a certain deficiency of the existing system, and hence, a need for 'modification and addition' is pressing.[338] Legislative initiatives in this regard have concentrated particularly on the area of imprisonment for fine default, the extent of which, due to comparatively loose regulation in German penal justice, [339] has been relatively high.[340] Since the 1980s, with the deteriorating economic situation and high rates of unemployment, an aggravation of this problem has been widely documented.[341] In 1976, the number of persons on whom a fine was imposed in the old German *Länder* was 492,561, in the same year 5.6% of this number, 27,469, defaulted. In 2000, the number of persons who received a fine was 513,336, while 9% of them, 46,250, defaulted on the payment of a fine.[342] The increase in numbers is reportedly particularly dramatic in the former *Länder* of East Germany. Here, the numbers soared from almost zero to 10,000 in the year 2000.[343] Although viewed as an "indispensable structural element" of the penal system,[344] the incompatibility of imprisonment for non-payment of a fine with the German system, characterised by its heavy reliance on individual guilt and on such

---

336 Weigend (1992) *op. cit.*, p. 348.

337 See e.g., Wasik (2004) *op. cit.*, p. 305.

338 Frommel, M. (1999) Alternative Strafen und Alternativen zum Freiheitsentzug, *Neue Kriminalpolitik*, no 3, pp. 9–13, Weßlau, (1999), *op. cit.*, pp. 278–287, see also Helgerth, R. and Krauß, F. (2001) Der Gesetzentwurf zur Reform des Sanktionenrechts, *Zeitschrift für Rechtspolitik*, vol. 34, no 7, pp. 281–283, p. 283.

339 See, Albrecht, H.-J. (1985) Ansätze und Perspektiven für die gemeinnützige Arbeit in der Strafrechtspflege, *Bewährungshilfe*, vol. 32, no 2, pp.121–134, p. 121. The Criminal Procedure Code provides for the remission of the fine in case of hardship (Section 459f), but its use was found to be insignificant. Feuerhelm, *op. cit.*, p. 70.

340 For a statistical analysis between 1971 and 1988, see Stapenhorst, *op. cit.*, pp. 103–105.

341 Schädler, W. (1983) Das Projekt "Gemeinnützige Arbeit" die nicht nur theoretische Chance des Art. 293 EGStGB, *Zeitschrift für Rechtspolitik*, vol. 16, no 1, pp. 5–10 and (1985) "Der weiße Fleck" im Sanktionensystem: Ein Beitrag zur Diskussion um Geldstrafe, freie Arbeit und Ersatzfreiheitsstrafe, *Zeitschrift für Rechtspolitik*, vol. 18, no 7, pp. 186–192, Dolde, G. (1999) Vollzug von Ersatzfreiheitsstrafen –ein wesentlicher Anteil im Kurzstrafenvollzug, *Zeitschrift für Strafvollzug und Straffälligenhilfe*, no. 6, pp. 330–335, p. 330, Seebode, M. (1999) Problematische Ersatzfreiheitsstrafe in Feuerhelm, Schwind and Bock, *op. cit.*, pp. 519–552.

342 Heinz, W. (2008) Internet Publication, p. 56.

343 Dünkel, F. (2004) Reducing the population of fine defaulters in prisons: experiences with community service in Mecklenburg-Western Pomerania (Germany) in *Criminal Policy in Europe*, Council of Europe, Strasbourg, pp. 127–138, p. 128.

344 Schädler, W. (1985) *op. cit.*, p. 191, for a critical view see Köhne, M. (2004) Abschaffung der Ersatzfreiheitsstrafe, *Juristische Zeitung*, no. 11, pp. 453–456.

constitutional principles as human dignity and equal treatment,[345] have represented such an anomaly that imprisonment for fine default understandably holds particular weight in the reform proposals of the sanction system as will be demonstrated below.

In the 1990s, a series of legislative initiatives for reforming the sanction system took place.[346] Here particular attention will be given to the most recently launched reform work on the penal system under the Commission on the Reform of Sanctions (hereinafter the Commission). This Commission was set up to review reform proposals regarding the penal system in 1998. Its mission was defined as adjusting the existing system to the requirements of the changing societal, technical and criminal political conditions.[347] In formulating a "sustainable reform policy", the principle task of the Commission was identified as an appraisal of the demands for the extension of the sanction catalogue with regard to minor offences and offences in the middle range of severity. In due course, the Commission produced a final report in 2000 which constituted the basis for the Experts' Draft (*Referentenentwurf*), and with some small but significant changes, the official draft law.[348]

The central premise of the proposals embodied in the respective drafts may be rephrased with the statement that the range of non-custodial penalties available to courts is not sufficiently diversified to make an effective prevention policy with regard to minor and middle severity criminality possible.[349] An extension of non-custodial options would enable courts to 'individualise' sentencing decisions to a greater degree, thereby enhancing the contribution of sentencing to crime reduction. The desire to further reduce the use of short-term imprisonment and avoid custody for fine default also finds specific emphasis in the memorandum to the draft law.[350] The key aspects of the draft law, preceding the Commission proceedings, and appearing to be particularly controversial and of relevance to the subject matter of this study will be outlined below. Before going on to consider these proposals against the backdrop of previous discussions, it must be noted that soon after its promulgation, the draft law was subject to opposition, in particular from the representatives of the *Länder* on the grounds that it goes too far, in that some proposals the draft law contains represent "a threat of collapse of penal justice and

---

[345]Human dignity (*Menschenwürde*, Section 1 of the Basic Law), equal treatment (*Gleichheitsgebot*, Section 3 of the Basic Law).

[346]See summary of the Justification of the Referentenentwurf: Referentenentwurf eines Gesetzes zur Reform des Sanktionenrechts (8.12.2000). Accessible from the following address: http://www.bib.uni-mannheim.de/fileadmin/pdf/fachinfo/jura/refentw-ref-des-sanktr.pdf (Access Date: March 2009).

[347]Kommission zur Reform des strafrechtlichen Sanktionensystems (2000)Abschlußbericht, p. 12, accessible from the following link: http://www.bmj.bund.de/media/archive/137.pdf (Access Date: March 2009).

[348]BT-Drs. 15/2725 (17.03.2004).

[349]In the Experts' Draft, see p.1, in the official draft law (BT-Drs. 15/2725) see p. 1 and p.15.

[350]BT-Drs. 15/2725, p.15.

considerable impairment of the security interests of citizens".[351] In spite of the critics, in 2003 the Federal Cabinet endorsed it and in 2004 brought it before the *Bundestag*, but due to the dissolution of the *Bundestag* further progress ceased. The draft has as yet not been brought before the new *Bundestag*, and at the time of writing no further movement is apparent.[352]

4.6.1.1 Community Service

Despite scattered provisions in the both the juvenile and adult sanction systems, containing an element of work in various guises,[353] the practical significance of *community service* in Germany has been comparatively limited.[354] As has been pointed out in outlining the Alternative Draft (1966), the formidable policy of forced labour under the Nazi regime, long constituted a mental barrier to the assessment of the merits of work as a punishment in its own right. Along with the historical disrepute that this form of penalty enjoys in Germany,[355] which explains the reserved attitude towards this form of penalty, it may be argued that the German case delivers a confirmation of Pease's thesis that "community service owes its popularity to the inefficiencies of fining".[356] More clearly, the fact that the fine is quantitatively the most important penalty and a standard response to offences of a certain gravity, appears to have made 'community service', effectively redundant as a primary form of penalty. Looking from this perspective, it is not surprising that it has acquired broader appeal as a substitute for imprisonment for fine default.

Indeed, the notion of community service as a penalty received greater recognition in relation to Section 293 of the Introductory Law, which empowered the governments of the *Länder* to pass ordinances to regulate the execution of 'substitute imprisonment' for fine default by means of community service.[357] Before 1977

[351]Cited in Wilkitzki, P. (2006) Vom Beruf unserer Zeit zur Sanktionenreform, *Goltdammer's Archiv für Strafrecht*, vol. 153, pp. 399–402, p. 401.

[352]See, Morgenstern, C. (2007) Alternativen zur Freiheitsstrafe – Ursprung, Bedarf und Probleme, *Zeitschrift für Strafvollzug und Straffälligenhilfe*, vol. 56, pp. 248–252, p. 251.

[353]See below.

[354]Feuerhelm, W. (1997) *Stellung und Ausgestaltung der Gemeinnützigen Arbeit im Strafrecht*, Kriminologische Zentralstelle, Wiesbaden. See also, Pfohl, M. (1983) *Gemeinnützige Arbeit als strafrechtliche Sanktion eine Untersuchung unter Berücksichtigung der britischen Community Service Order*, Duncker & Humblot, Berlin. Speis, F. (2008) *Gemeinnützige Arbeit als selbstständige Hauptsstrafe im Erwachsenenstrafrecht*, Kovac, Hamburg.

[355]The historical disrepute of the community sentence is clearly discernible in the objection of the Criminal Law Commission of the German Bar Association on its introduction as a primary option of sentencing, Strafrechtsausschuss des Deutschen Antwaltvereins (2000) *Reform des strafrechtlichen Sanktionensystem*, Deutscher Anwaltverlag, München.

[356]Pease (1985), *op. cit.*, p. 53.

[357]E.g., Rolinski, K. (1981) Ersatzfreiheitsstrafe oder Gemeinnützige Arbeit, *Monatsschrift für Kriminologie*, vol. 63, no 1/2, pp. 52–62, Schädler (1983), *op. cit.*, Gerken, U. and Henningsen, J. (1987) Ersetzung der Ersatzfreiheitsstrafe durch freie Arbeit – Ein Betrag zur Diskussion um die Geldstrafe und ihre Surrogate, *Zeitschrift für Rechtspolitik*, vol. 20, pp. 386–390, Feurhelm, W.

Hamburg was the only federal state which made use of the aforementioned provision, which was followed by other *Länder*.[358] There was initially a considerable disparity between various *Länder*; one of the major problematic issues has been to establish a uniform rate of equivalency between the fine and community service. Over time, the differences in this respect have largely been removed and community service has been applied to a greater degree.[359] However, the enforcement frequency and the practice of community service have still been portrayed as far from satisfactory; it is even argued to cause some "bitter disillusionment".[360] Numerous reasons are given to explain the failure of the practice of community service. Research studies have found that in many cases fine defaulters are prone to not coping with the demands of work. A significant percentage of fine defaulters are composed of persons having alcohol and drug abuse problems, suffering from physical or mental illness, being socially isolated, being without a fixed abode or otherwise people with comprehension problems.[361]

The fact of the under-achievement of 'community service' and its well disseminated net-widening effects[362] in foreign jurisdictions where 'community service' operates as a primary penalty have not deterred those academics who attach significant value to this penalty.[363] Optimistic accounts have asserted that community service has proven to be a viable alternative, and demanded the conception of working in the public interest as a primary option in sentencing. Such academic praise of the merits of public work, however, appears so far to have relatively restricted resonance in the domain of penal policy discussions.[364]

(1991) *Gemeinnützige Arbeit als Alternative in der Geldstrafenvollstreckung*, Kriminologische Zentralstelle, Wiesbaden.

358 See e.g., Schall, H. (1985) Die Sanktionsalternative der gemeinnützigen Arbeit als Surrogat der Geldstrafe, *Neue Zeitschrift für Strafrecht*, no. 3, pp. 104–111, pp. 105–106, Streng, F. (2000) Entwicklung neuer Sanktionsformen in Deutschland in Bender and Jehle, *op. cit.*, pp. 207–233, p. 218.

359 Häger, *op. cit.*, pp. 947–948.

360 Stöckel (2002) *op. cit.*, p. 334.

361 Kawamura, G. (1998) *Gemeinnützige Arbeit in Bayern am Schnittpunkt von sozialer Arbeit und Justiz*, Schriftenreihe der Georg-Simon-Ohm Fachochschule, Nürnberg, pp. 25–33, Dolde, G. (1999) Zum Vollzug von Ersatzfreiheitsstrafen: Eindrücke aus einer empirischen Erhebung in Feuerhelm, Schwind and Bock (ed.), *op. cit.*, pp. 581–596, see also Kommission zur Reform des Strafrechtlichen Sanktionensystems (2000), *op. cit.*, the contributions of Boll, O. and Meyer, J., pp. 48–56.

362 See also general remarks, van Kalmthout, A. and Dünkel, A. (2000) Ambulante Sanktionen und Maßnahmen in Europe, *Neue Kriminal Politik*, pp. 26–27.

363 Schöch (1992), *op. cit.*, Schneider, U. (2001) Gemeinnützige Arbeit als „Zwischensanktion", *Monatschrift für Kriminologie und Strafrecht*, vol. 84, no. 4, pp. 273–287. See also, Rössner, D. (1985) Eine konstruktive Alternative zu Geld- und Freiheitsstrafe, *Bewährungshilfe*, vol. 32, no 2, pp. 105–110, Albrecht, H.-J. (1985) Ansätze und Perspektiven für die gemeinnützige Arbeit in der Strafrechtspflege, *Bewährungshilfe*, vol. 32, no 2, Schädler (1985), *op. cit.*, Feuerhelm (1997) *op. cit.*, more cautiously, Weigend (1992) *op. cit.*, pp. 359–360.

364 See BT-Druck 13/10485, Böhm, *op. cit.*, Feuerhelm, W. (1999) Die gemeinnützige Arbeit im Strafrecht, *Neue Kriminalpolitik,* no 1, pp. 22–27.

During the course of the above-mentioned Commission on the Reform of Punishments, the feasibility and desirability of community service was a particular focus. Although differing on their conceptions of community service, in two (expert) papers submitted to the Commission, the extension of its scope was supported.[365] However, the prevailing view formed in the Commission meetings rejected the adoption of community service in its own right, citing a number of reasons. First of all, it was believed that the introduction of community service into the sentencing framework in this manner would fill no gap; the existing measures provide a sufficiently broad spectrum of sanctions, and its adoption would effectively mean a systematic break with the premises of the German sanction system. The place of public work as a largely preventive measure in a guilt-oriented system would not be easily reconcilable.[366] The latter opinion was based, dubiously, on the assumption that working in the public interest is not a punishment, and could only act as a substitute form of sanction, or at best a prevention measure prior to sentencing decision by means of the procedural alternative according to Section 153a of the Criminal Procedure Code, but it itself lacks a penal character. Hence, as a primary means of punishment, it is alien to German penal law tradition.[367] From a practical angle, it was argued that the experience of other countries could not be transferable, since in these countries financial penalties are not imposed to the same extent as in Germany.[368] Furthermore, the role of community service as an 'alternative to short-term imprisonment' would also be very limited in that the German system strongly discourages the use of short-term imprisonment. Finally, doubts were expressed on the feasibility of community service with reference to the high costs of the necessary infrastructure for the adoption of a work penalty, including the costs of supervision and monitoring.[369]

On these grounds in the draft law of 2004 community service was not conceived of as a sanction in its own right, but as substitute for fines and imprisonment of up to 6 months, the use of which required the consent of the offender.[370] Accordingly, as

---

[365]Kommission zur Reform des Strafrechtlichen Sanktionensystems (2000) *op. cit.*, Bendel, E. and Riehe, B., pp.104–111.

[366]*Ibid.*, p. 112.

[367]This opinion was in some way reflective of the Constitutional Court's approach. In discussing the compatibility of the instruction to perform work under the Juvenile Court Law with the Basic Law (Section 12 II, III), the Court ruled that community service can be seen neither as compulsory work, nor as a measure in its own right. The Court emphasised that it is subordinated to the aim of exerting a pedagogical influence on the offender, and therefore, lacks a punitive nature. Likewise, in discussing the attachment of work to a suspended order, the court held that the condition of performing community service is merely a method of the execution of the suspended sentence. On constitutional considerations see, Hönicke, F. (1999) *Arbeitszwang als Kriminalrechtsreaktion, Gemeinnützige Arbeit in der Strafrechtspflege unter Art. 12 Abs. 2, 3 GG*, Florentz, München, Streng (2000), *op. cit.*, pp. 207–233, pp. 216–217.

[368]On this point, see also Dünkel, F. (2003) Reform des Sanktionenrechts – neuer Anlauf, *Neue Kriminalpolitik*, vol. 15, no. 4, pp. 123–124.

[369]Kommission zur Reform des Strafrechtlichen Sanktionensystems (2000) *op. cit.*, pp. 116–117.

[370]See p. 18 BT-Drucks, 15/2725.

a direct substitute for the fine, the option of performing community service is to be offered at the sentencing stage. Three hours of work sentence would be considered equivalent to one day unit fine. It is believed that the procedure as laid down in the draft law would shorten the bureaucratic procedure in comparison to the present regulation, according to which the prosecutor first collects the fine, then imposes substitute detention and only after that informs the offender that in lieu of imprisonment, a performance of community service can come to consideration. Regrettably, the threat of imprisonment for fine defaulters is not wholly abandoned by the draft; substitute imprisonment is retained for cases where the offender does not consent to the performance of work, or has not performed the work in the specified time or appropriately enough. In the latter case, two unit fines are considered to equate to a 1 day prison sentence.[371] As regards prison sentences, the draft places community service before imprisonment as a "last chance".[372] It would be applicable to offenders who have not previously received a prison sentence and for whom the suspension of imprisonment on probation, due to failing to meet the criteria, it is deemed inappropriate, *or* otherwise where it is considered that the imposition of the prison sentence would likely considerably endanger the reparation of the damage caused by the offence. In both cases, community service would be imposed, unless it appears that the work is unlikely to be done. In the conversion of a prison sentence to a work penalty, the draft provides for an equation of 6 h of work with a 1 day prison sentence.

Consequently, however, even the draft's greatly moderated proposal of the extension of 'community service' failed to achieve consensus. The *Bundesrat*'s statement on the proposed forms of community service was severely critical to the extent that the extension of this sanction was deemed inadvisable.[373] In the statement of the *Bundesrat*, the view was reflected that the existing legislation, as it stands, provides for a flexible and fair way to deal with fine defaulters by means of community service, according to the different resources of each *Länd*. Furthermore, a uniform regulation was deemed unacceptable as it is thought to create enormous additional costs. Finally, 'softening' the law with respect to conversion rates between the fine, imprisonment and community service was regarded as having the potential to severely reduce the general and special preventive effects of the penal system overall. Such a change in law is found to be incongruent with the guilt-oriented strands of German penal philosophy. Discredited on these premises, it appears that without unequivocal political support, community service as a direct substitute for imprisonment would have little chance of gaining a place in the Penal Code in the near future.

---

[371] *Ibid.*

[372] In the Statement of Reasons, p. 23. Critical commentaries on this modality see, Wolters, G. (2002) Der Entwurf eines "Gesetzes zur Reform des Sanktionenrechts", *Zeitschrift für die gesamte Strafrechtswissenschaft*, vol. 114, pp. 63–87, p. 74, Stöckel, *op. cit.*, p. 624.

[373] See pp. 5–8 and pp. 11–14 of Stellungnahme des Bundesrates, 13.02.2004.

4.6.1.2 Electronic Monitoring

The discussion of electronic monitoring in Germany began in the late 1980s.[374] The idea was initially met with a vigorous rejection by the academic and professional community. In an annual meeting of the Probation Assistance Service (*Bewährungshilfe*), electronic monitoring was interpreted as an expression of the rise of the surveillance society, and as such as a "dangerous experiment" having broader implications for social control.[375] Besides these 'Orwellian anxieties' about the surveillance society, from a more practice oriented perspective, no need was seen for the adoption of such a penalty in German penal law, even if its supposed aim of the reduction of imprisonment was, without objection, taken-for-granted.[376] Since then three main areas of concern have been continually highlighted. The first set of considerations are concerned with constitutional objections, among them, inviolability of the home, privacy of correspondence, post and telecommunications, freedom of movement, personal freedoms, and dignity and privacy of offenders.[377] The second area of concern involves the nature and implementation of this measure in terms of the adverse effects of frequent control, the danger of public opprobrium or social stigmatisation and the inevitable mechanics of the 'selection' of socially stable offenders, and thereby exclusions of such groups as the homeless, asylum seekers and foreigners.[378]

---

[374]Feltes, T. (1988) Kriminalität und soziale Kontrolle im 21. Jahrhundert – Ein futuristisches Szenario vor dem Hintergrund aktueller Entwicklungen, *Bewährungshilfe*, vol. 35, no. 1, pp. 90–102, Schall, H. (1988) Auf der Suche nach strafrechtlichen Modifikationen und Alternativen, *Bewährungshilfe*, vol. 35, no 4, pp. 433–447, Weigend, T. (1989) Privatgefängnisse, Hausarrest und andere Neuheiten, *Bewährungshilfe*, vol. 36, pp. 289–301.

For a detailed account see, Wittsam, K. (1998) *Elektronischer Hausarrest? Zur Anwendbarkeit eines amerikanischen Sanktionsmodells in Deutschland*, Nomos, Baden-Baden, Hudy, M. (1998) *Elektronisch überwachter Hausarrest – Befunde zur Zielgruppenplanung und Probleme einer Implementation in das deutsche Sanktionensystem*, Nomos, Baden-Baden, Walter, M. (1999) Elektronisch überwachter Hausarrest als neue Vollzugsform, *Zeitschrift für Strafvollzug*, pp.287–295, Haverkamp, R. (2002) *Elektronischer überwachter Hausarrest*, edition iuscrim, Freiburg.

[375]Deutsche Bewährungshilfe, Dokumentation der 13. Bundestagung der Deutschen Bewährungshilfe, Forum, Bonn, reprinted in Schall (1988), *op. cit.*, p. 446, See also, Feltes (1988), *op. cit.*, Kaiser (1996), *op. cit.*, p. 1040.

[376]Bundesarbeitgemeinschaft für Straffälligenhilfe (1997) *Elektronisch überwachter Hausarrest – Alternativen zum Strafvollzug*, Bonn, p. 23.

[377]Vosgrau, R. (1990) Elektronische Überwachung: Auf dem Weg zur Abschaffung von Freiheitsstrafen oder on die totale Kontrolle, *Bewährungshilfe*, vol. 37, no 2, pp.166–168, Deleuze, G. (1992) Das elektronische Halsband, *Kriminologisches Journal*, vol. 24, pp. 181–186, Ostendorf, H. (1997) Die elektronische Fußfessel – Wunderwaffe im Kampf gegen die Kriminalität, Zeitschrift für Rechtspolitik, vol. 30, no 12, pp. 473–476, p. 465, Haverkamp *op. cit.*, pp. 182–193, Walter, *op. cit.*, pp. 291–292.

[378]Streng, F. (2000) Entwicklung neuer Sanktionsformen in Deutschland in Jehle and Bender, D. (eds.), *op. cit.*, pp.207–233, p. 214, Stöckel (2002) *op. cit.*, p. 333.

Informed by the experience abroad, the third area has been the potential net-widening effects of this measure. Many commentators appear to have not been convinced of its potential to act as a genuine alternative, and rather shared the fear that the adoption of this penalty intrinsically runs the risk of the danger of net-widening.[379] The dangers that its adoption would pose in the German penal system have been considered particularly threatening, in that the candidates for electronic monitoring in other jurisdictions are generally composed of drunk-driving offences, which are not generally dealt with by means of (short-term) imprisonment in Germany.[380] Hence it was believed that given the *ultima ratio* clause (Section 47), the use of fines in lieu of short-term imprisonment and the suspended sentence, electronic monitoring would not serve as an alternative to short term imprisonment. With these arguments, the German Jurists' Assembly rejected electronic monitoring as a primary or an ancillary penalty in 1992. At the same time, however, somewhat paradoxically in the resolution of the Assembly, its experimental use as a condition of bail (*Haftverschonung*) and as a method of the execution of a prison sentence was recommended.[381]

In 1997, the *Land* of Berlin brought a law proposal regarding electronic monitoring before the *Bundesrat* which envisaged electronic monitoring as a substitute for prison terms of up to 6 months (as an alternative to the execution of imprisonment) and as a measure of penal enforcement applicable within the last portion of the sentence in the context of preparation for release.[382] Due to implementation issues, an experimental phase was envisaged that was to be guided provisionally through ordinances. Around the same time, with the promulgation of this proposal, in a meeting, the *Länder's* ministries of justice came to the agreement that the German law permits the use of electronic monitoring *de lege lata* (as an instruction of the suspended sentence on probation under Section 56c, as a condition of conditional release under Section 57a and as an alternative to remand detention) and, that electronic monitoring should be experimented with.[383] In the parliamentary discussions the aforementioned law proposal met with strong opposition from the Greens.[384]

However, in spite of the libertarian political opposition and warnings issued by academics, the Hessian project on electronic monitoring began in 2000 in Frankfurt

---

379Weigend (1992), *op. cit.*, p. 363, Schöch, *op. cit.*, pp. 100–102, Kaiser (1996), *op. cit.*, pp. 1040–1041, Walter (1999), *op. cit.*, p. 292, Streng (2000), *op. cit.*, p. 214.

380See, Weigend (1992), *op. cit.*, p. 363, Walter (1999), *op. cit.*, p. 23, Streng (2000), *op. cit.*, p. 214, Stöckel (2002), *op. cit.*, pp.333–334, Heghmanns *op. cit.*, pp. 301–302.

For an opposing argument see, Albrecht, A. (2003) Elektronischer Hausarrest Das Konzept des hessischen Experiments in Schöch, H., Jehle, J.-M. and Aebersold, P. (eds.) *Angewandte Kriminologie zwischen Freiheit und Sicherheit*, Forum, Bonn, p. 116–117.

381Sitzungsbericht, O173.

382Bundesratdrucksache 698/97, "Entwurf eines Gesetzes zur Änderung des Strafvollzugsgesetztes".

383Reported in Ostendorf (1997), *op. cit.*, p. 473.

384Bündnis 90/Die Grünen 1998 reported in Haverkamp, *op. cit.*, p. 163.

am Main. Under the scheme, electronic monitoring has been piloted in several contexts; it has been applied as an 'instruction' of the suspended sentence[385] with regard to the revocation of the suspended sentence, conditional release[386] protective supervision,[387] suspension of remand detention and finally as a measure of pardon under the auspices of the Hessian *Landsrecht*. Whether and to what extent such a pilot project is admissible under German penal law remains open to discussions. So far it seems that no cogent explanation has been made, if it can be made at all, why such a form of penalty whose greater intensity and intrusiveness could hardly be comparable with the 'ordinary' forms of, for instance suspended prison sentence on probation and conditional release, does not require a separate legislative regulation. At best, the deviation from the principle of 'nulla poena sine lege' might be justified by the nature of the experimental phase; a process which is also espoused by the Commission on Reform of Sanctions. Some, arguably, overly optimistic accounts on the Hessian pilot project are already available[388]; despite these positive evaluations, however, it is still difficult to predict the further development of electronic monitoring in Germany at this stage.

4.6.1.3 Driving Ban

Under the German Penal Code, there currently exist two types of sanctions peculiar to offences that are committed in the course of or in connection with driving a motor vehicle or in violation of the duties of a driver of a motor vehicle.[389] The first, the driving ban, prescribed under Section 44 of is an *ancillary penalty* which cannot be imposable on its own but in conjunction with a sentence of prison *or* a fine for a period of 1–3 months. The second is withdrawal of driver licence provided for by

---

[385] Section 56 of the Penal Code.

[386] *Ibid.*, Section 57.

[387] *Ibid.*, Section 68.

[388] Albrecht, H.-J., Arnold, H. and Schädler, W. (2000) Das hessische Modelversuch zur Anwendung der „elektronischen Fußfessel", vol. 33, no. 11, *Zeitschrift für Rechtspolitik*, vol. 33, pp. 466–469, Albrecht (2003), *op. cit.*, Mayer, M. (2003) The German Pilot Project: Potentials and Risks in Mayer, M., Haverkamp, R. and Levy. R. (eds.) *Will Electronic Monitoring have a Future in Europe?*, Freiburg, pp. 168–176, Mayer, M. (2004) *Modellprojekt elektronisch Fußfessel – Studien zur Erprobung einer umstrittenen Maßnahme*, Freiburg, Edition Iuscrim, particularly pp.153–195. See also Schädler, W. and Wulf, R. (1999) Thesen zur Erprobung der elektronischen Überwachung als Weisung und elektronischer Hausarrest, *Bewährungshilfe*, vol. 46, no 1, pp. 3–10, Schlömer, U. (1999) Die Anwendbarkeit des elektronisch überwachten Hausarrests als Bewährungsweisung nach geltendem Recht, *Bewährungshilfe*, vol. 46, no 1, pp. 31–43. Also in this issue critically Lindenberg, M. (1999) Elektronisch überwachter Hausarrest auch in Deutschland? *Bewährungshilfe*, vol. 46, no 1, pp. 11–22.

[389] The Juvenile Court Law also contains this measure, see Section 8 (3) (2). For a detailed analysis of the driving ban in general criminal law, see Gronemeyer, D. (2001) *Zur Reformbedürftigkeit der strafrechtlichen Fahrerlaubnisentziehung und des strafrechtlichen Fahrverbots*, Lang, Frankfurt, pp. 15–52.

Section 69 as a *measure* whenever the court is of the opinion that the offender, regardless of her/his penal responsibility, is unfit to drive. As a *measure* the driving ban can be imposed temporarily for a period of 6 months to 5 years or permanently when the court is of the opinion that the danger that the offender poses justifies so doing.[390]

Encouraged by the positive experience in this area, a proposal by Schöch, who submitted an expert paper, forwarded by the German Jurists' Assembly in 1992 conceived of the incorporation of the driving ban as a sanction in its own right regardless of the offence type, i.e. whether or not the offence in question was committed in connection with driving a motor vehicle, for instance with regard to property crimes, for a period ranging from 1 month to 1 year.[391] The proposal was justified by the value attached to mobility in modern societies, and, in this context, to the motor vehicle as its significant means as well as with reference to such advantages as cost-effectiveness and non-transferability to third persons. Subsequently, a number of legislative proposals contained the driving ban, varying from its mere extension from 3 to 6 months, to its adoption as a sanction in its own right.[392]

Academic opinion on the driving ban as a penalty in its own right is characterised by competing claims. Opponents argue that without bearing a (meaningful) connection with the committed offence, such a form of punishment, which serves as no more than a symbolic warning, would fail to convey the 'sense of justice' both in the eyes of the individual offender and for the public at large. Hence, on its potential for 'positive general prevention' doubts must be cast.[393] The response to this is that such a 'taken-for-granted' relationship between the given offence and the penalties of the fine or imprisonment is not readily traceable, and further, the demand for a talion punishment is an archaic approach in modern times.[394] During the meetings of the Commission on the Reform of Sanctions, Schöch's proposal appears to have been 'sophisticated' in this respect by restricting the scope of the prospective provision to the cases where a "temporal and causal relationship" between the offence and driving a motor vehicle could be discerned from the commission of the offence, even though the offence itself is not strictly related to driving a motor vehicle.[395]

---

[390] Section 69a of the Penal Code.

[391] Compare with the related provision in the Alternative Draft of 1966.

[392] See Stöckel (2002), *op. cit.*

[393] Streng (2000), *op. cit.*, see also the report of Riehe, B. in Kommission zur Reform des Strafrechtlichen Sanktionensystems (2000), *op. cit.*, pp. 28–30.

[394] Schöch, *op. cit.*, p. C120, Frommel, M. (1999) Fahrverbot statt Freiheitsstrafe, *Neue Justiz* 1999, p. 5, Wilkiztki, P. (2000) Neue kriminalpolitische Akzente in Deutschland in Jehle and Bender, *op. cit.*, pp. 447–454, p. 451, Stöckel (2007), *op. cit.*, p. 627.

[395] Meyer, J. in Kommission zur Reform des Strafrechtlichen Sanktionensystems (2000), *op. cit.*, pp. 30–31.

More potently, it is recognised that punishment in that form would only be applicable to offenders who possesses a driver's licence. This would make it a 'special punishment', whose legitimacy is seriously undermined by equal treatment considerations.[396] Against this objection, somewhat tautologically, it was claimed that the introduction of the driving ban as a primary means of punishment would not change the usual criteria and procedures for the determination of the punishment; the latter would be imposed only when it is appropriate and corresponds with the individual guilt of the offender.[397]

Another, and here more pertinent, controversy concerns the relation of the proposed kind of punishment with imprisonment and the fine. Many considered the driving ban as an alternative to the fine rather than imprisonment, based on the grounds that between the driving ban and imprisonment a correlation would be a mismatch.[398] These sanctions, imprisonment and the driving ban, have incomparable grades of intrusiveness and thus they would accord with the varying degree of individual guilt. Thus, rather than as an alternative to imprisonment it could serve as an alternative to the fine.[399]

While rejecting the extension of it, the draft law of 2004 envisaged the driving ban as a primary penalty for a 6 month period, applicable only for crimes committed in connection with the driving of a motor vehicle or in violation of the duties of a driver of a motor vehicle.[400] Accordingly, if an offender is found guilty of an offence involving a motor vehicle, the court may oblige the offender to refrain from driving or otherwise restricting the use of a motor vehicle in a specified way for a period from 1 month to 1 year. This punishment may be meted out in addition to or in lieu of a prison sentence or fine. Notably, in its statement on the draft law, the *Bundesrat* considered it unfortunate that no extension was conceived of in the remit of the driving ban in respect of offence categories. By combining it, particularly with the fine, it is believed that, the prospective punishment of the driving ban could be instrumental in reducing the frequency of short-term imprisonment.[401] Whether the driving ban could be a genuine alternative to imprisonment, or would solely increase the instensity of ordinary forms of punishment (in this case most probably the fine), at this stage could only be speculated, but surely such fundamental considerations as 'equal treatment' deserve more attention than has so far been the case.

---

[396]Particularly, Weßlau, E. (1999) In welche Richtung geht die Reform des Sanktionensystems, *Strafverteidiger* vol. 19 no 5, pp. 278–287, pp. 285–286.

[397]Stöckel (2007) *op. cit.*, p. 625.

[398]Heghmanns, *op. cit.*, p. 297, Wolters, *op. cit.*, p. 71.

[399]Heghmanns, *op. cit.*, p. 299.

[400]See p. 18 of the Bundestag-Drucksache 15/2725.

[401]*Ibid.*, p. 1 and pp. 15–16.

4.6.1.4 Warning with Suspension of Punishment

In sentencing practice, the role of warning with suspension of punishment, despite the gradual increase in its use since its introduction, has always been rather insignificant.[402] This has generally been explained by the "concurrence" between the scope of this measure and the conditional termination of prosecution (and court proceedings) pursuant to the above-mentioned Section 153a of the Criminal Procedure Code,[403] effectively giving some form of sanctioning power to prosecutors for offences ranging from minor to those of middle range severity. As a consequence, currently, one of the major application fields of this measure is made up of cases in which prosecutors fail to waive prosecution or otherwise no consent of the offender to waive the prosecution is secured. Furthermore, it has reportedly been used for cases "where awareness of wrongdoing is low, e.g. demonstration offences", or the defendant displayed amenability to therapeutic measures, but has also been applied when a default in the payment of a fine would likely occur.[404]

In the reform proposals, particular importance has been attached to the extension of this measure.[405] For, it is believed that its potential function of suspending fines could be better exploited, and that crimes up to the middle range of severity, without being liable to the objections which the application of 153a, on the grounds of transparency, equality and fair trial are subjected to, could be more adequately dealt with by means of this measure. In the meantime, it is believed that a purposeful extension of conditions and instructions attached to this measure could correspondingly extend its individual deterrent effects.[406] Central to the reform proposals was the rephrasing of the wording of the related provision in order to enable sentencers to have a broader latitude of discretion in deciding 'suitable cases'. The Commission was in favour of loosening the criteria of the existing provision in the following manner: firstly, repealing the existing condition on the previous criminal record, so that a previous warning or sentence would no longer be an exclusion ground, and secondly, by making its use a *requirement* in cases

[402] Schöch, H. (1992) Zum Aufblühen der Verwarnung mit Strafvorbehalt nach § 59 StGB in Arzt *et al. op. cit.*, pp. 255–268, Kropp, C. (2004) Ist die Verwarnung mit Strafvorbehalt noch zeitgemäß?, *Zeitschrift für Rechtspolitik*, No.7, pp. 241–242, Heinz (2008), *op. cit.*, p. 43 and pp. 74–75.

[403] Weigend (1992), *op. cit.*, p. 353, Hirsch (1986), *op. cit.*, p. 138, Schöch, H. (1992) Verwarnung statt Strafe zum Aufblühen der Verwarnung mit Strafvorbehalt nach 59 StGB, in Arzt, *op. cit.*, pp. 255–268, Dölling, D. (1992a) Die weiteren Entwicklung der Sanktionen ohne Freiheitsentzug im deutschen Strafrecht, *Zeitschrift für die gesamte Strafrechtswissenschaft*, vol. 104, pp. 259–289, pp. 269–271. See also Müller, E. and König, P. in Kommission zur Reform des Strafrechtlichen Sanktionensystems (2000), *op. cit.*, pp. 39–43. Doganay, G. (2002) *Zur Reform der Verwarnung mit Strafvorbehalt – Eine Darstellung und Kritik aktueller Änderungsvorschläge*, Mainz, Shaker Verlag, pp. 69–74.

[404] Pursuant to Section 59a paragraph 2 (2), see Müller in Kommission zur Reform des Strafrechtlichen Sanktionensystems (2000), *op. cit.*, pp. 39–41.

[405] Schöch (1992), Gutachten, p. 90.

[406] Schöch (1992), *op. cit.*, p. 90, Dölling (1992a), *op. cit.*, p. 270.

where the overall assessment of the offence and the personality of the offender justifies so doing.[407]

Following these lines, the draft law of 2004 ardently envisaged the extension of the use of this measure.[408] A similar enthusiastic approach on its merits, however, was absent in the statement of the *Bundesrat*.[409] Therein, without restricting the scope of Section 153a of the Criminal Procedure Code, it was not found advisable to create a further measure, through which too many repeated offenders would be 'let off'. For, it would mean the creation of another filter of impunity from punishment. Another, and related, consequence of such an extension, according to the *Bundesrat's* statement, would be the *de facto* concurrence of it with the fine. If enacted, it is inevitable that some offenders who are punished currently by the fine would be subjected to conviction with suspension of punishment, and for run-of-the mill offenders the latter would surely have more onerous consequences, e.g. 2 years of probation, rather than a fine of a limited number of units would. All in all, in comparison with the diversionary measures laid down in Section 153a and the fine, it is argued, a potential upgrading of this sanction would be exceedingly uneconomical in terms of resources which would be devoted to its enforcement. As this brief description already reveals, even an extended form of 'warning with suspension of punishment' is virtually nowhere seen as a 'rival' of the short-term prison sentence.

4.6.2 Interim Appraisal

The analysis of the reform initiatives demonstrates that the notion that the present sentencing framework requires some form of adjustment is widely agreed upon, but depending on the penal philosophies which are primarily adhered to, retribution, general and special deterrence or reparation, opinions differ to the extent to which it ought to take place. Not surprisingly at a preliminary level there are divergent assessments of the abilities of the dual system of punishments i.e. imprisonment and the fine. In this context, the question as to whether or not the present significance of the fine in sentencing ought to be preserved has proven to be controversial. Objections have been raised against an extension of sentencing options that such a development is undesired not solely because it would be a systemic break from the established nature of the German system, but also rather than serve as alternatives to imprisonment, new options would replace the fine. In response to discussion, by disfavouring an enactment of new non-custodial penalties as primary dispositions in the sentencing framework, the recent official draft represents modest rather than radical changes. Its significance, on the other hand, lies in its clear

[407] Kommission zur Reform des Strafrechtlichen Sanktionensystems (2000), *op. cit.*, pp. 43–46.

[408] See p.1 and pp.15-16 15/575 Bundestag-Drucksache.

[409] Stellungnahme des Bundesrates, pp. 14–16.

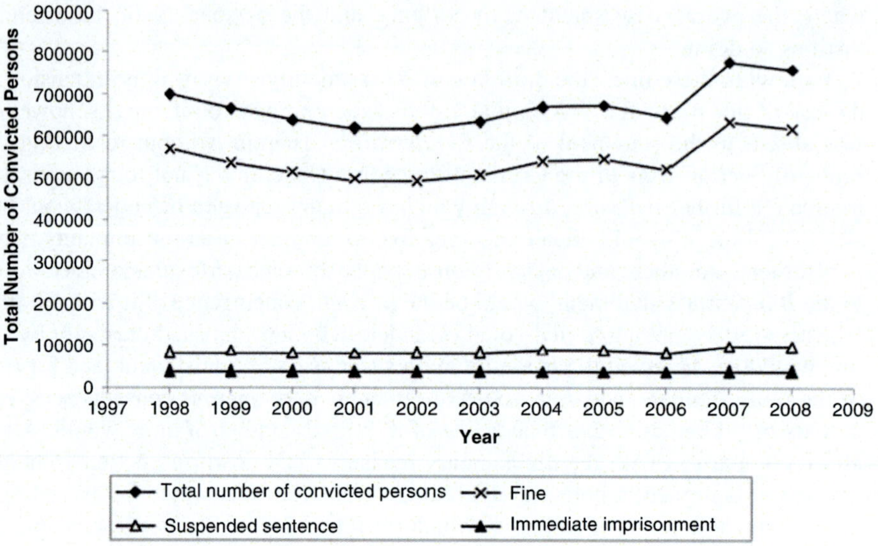

Fig. 4.3 Sentencing practice in the former Länder of Germany 1998–2008[410]

commitment to resolve such issues as fine default and further reduction of the frequency of short-term imprisonment. These issues will be discussed in due course following the outline of the current sentencing framework and practice.

4.7 A Statistical Review

As is clear from Fig. 4.3, between 1998 and 2008, there are fluctuations in the number of convictions. The total annual number of convicted persons (according to general criminal law) in 1998 was 699,548. This number dropped to 618,279 by 11% in 2002, it then increased until 2006. Thereafter the number of convictions increased by 18% and stood at 758,413 in 2008. These fluctuations are most apparent in the use of the fine. The number of fines dropped from 561,238 to 493,083 in 2002, thereafter, this figure grew steadily to reach 634,529 in 2007, the peak figure in the last 10 years. The number of immediate prison sentences in the period 1998–2006 decreased from 41,751 to 37,605, nearly by 10%, but then it increased to 41,239 in 2008. Between 1998 and 2008, the number of prison sentences suspended on probation also showed fluctuations, from 83,015 in 20001, it increased by 19% to 99,040 in 2008.

[410]Data compiled from, Statistisches Bundesamt, Fachserie 10, Reihe 3, Strafverfolgung, 1998, 1999, 2000, 2001 and 2002, Metzler Poeschel, Stuttgart. 2003; Statisticsches Bundesamt, Fachserie 10, Reihe 3 (2003), (2004), (2005), (2006), (2007) and (2008) is available in electronic format in the following address http://www.destatis.de (Access Date March 2010).

Table 4.1 The proportionate use of sentencing disposals in the former Länder of Germany 1998–2008[411]

Year	Immediate imprisonment	Suspended imprisonment	Fine
1998	5.9	12.6	81.3
1999	6.1	13.3	80.3
2000	6.3	13.2	80.3
2001	6.4	13.3	80.1
2002	6.3	13.8	79.7
2003	6.2	13.8	79.8
2004	5.7	13.6	80.5
2005	5.6	13.3	81.0
2006	5.3	12.8	80.6
2007	5.3	12.8	81.7
2008	5.4	13.0	81.5

Significantly, as Table 4.1 shows, despite a small 1% increase and decrease, in proportionate numbers, both the use of fine and imprisonment remained stable over the same period of time. The fine continued to be by far the most commonly imposed punishment, constituting on average just over 80% in the last 10 years, while suspended and unsuspended prison sentences constituted 5 and 13% of all convictions.

One point here must be given particular emphasis. As noted above, Section 47 of the Penal Code provides for a replacement of prison sentences of up to 6 months, unless general and special preventive considerations justify the use of imprisonment. Since the introduction of day fines, however, courts appear to have been much less keen to impose fines beyond the 30 day unit-fines, hence 30 days imprisonment.[412] In 2006, the average number of day fines imposed amounted to 47. Only 7% of all sentences of fine include more than 90 day fines.[413] In 2006, almost half of the imposed fines did not exceed 30 daily units. Hence, the fact that in about half of all cases, fines did not replace short-term imprisonment, particularly given that the minimum term of short term imprisonment is set at 1 month according to Section 38 of the Penal Code.

During the same period, the number of convictions which were processed under the Juvenile Court Law increased by 20% from 92,001 in 1998 to 116,278 in 2008. As is seen in the Fig. 4.4, educational measures as the sole imposed sanction by juvenile courts remained stable, while the number of disciplinary measures witnessed an increase of 24% from their level in 1998. The increase in disciplinary measures is partly explained by the adoption of supervision instruction and community service.[414] Nonetheless, a closer consideration of disciplinary measures

[411] Data compiled from, Statistisches Bundesamt, Fachserie 10, Reihe 3, Strafverfolgung, 1996, 1997, 1998, 1999, 2000, 2001, 2002, 2003, 2004, 2005 and 2006, 2007 and 2008.

[412] Section 40.

[413] See Heinz (2008), *op. cit.*, pp. 53–54.

[414] Ostendorf (2007), *op. cit.*, pp. 115–118, on Section 13–16.

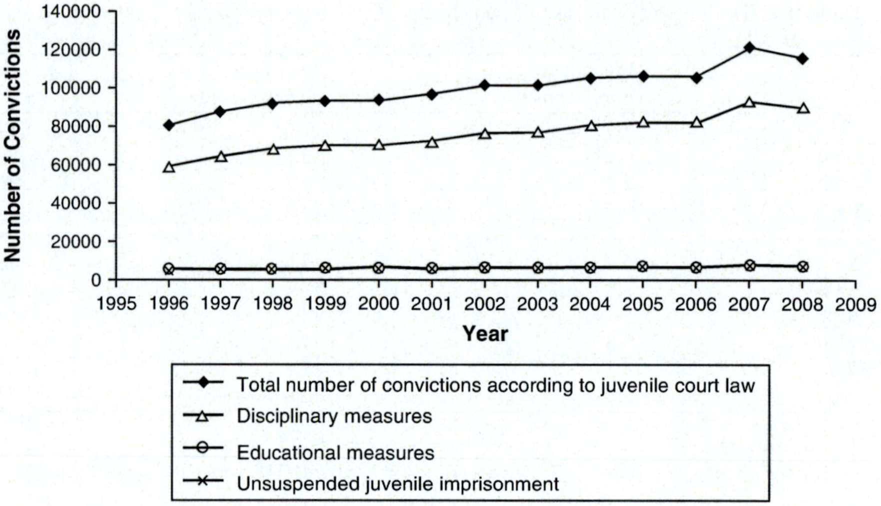

Fig. 4.4 Sentencing under juvenile penal law in the former Länder of Germany 1996–2008[415] (According to most grave sanction)

shows that that there is also an increase in the absolute as well as the proportionate numbers of the 'juvenile detention'. Furthermore, despite the increase in the use of disciplinary measures, during this period, the number of immediate juvenile prison sentences steadily increased. The number of unsuspended imprisonment sentences went up from 6,243 in 1996 to 7,265 in 2008, recording a 16% increase.

Table 4.2 shows that a higher proportion of disciplinary measures were imposed as the sole sanction in juvenile court proceedings. In 1996, the proportionate use of disciplinary measures made up of 73% of all the convictions, and in 2006 this percentage grew to 77%. Over the same period, the use of immediate juvenile imprisonment decreased only marginally, whereas educational measures witnessed a small decrease of just over 1%. These figures suggest that the growth of disciplinary measures occurred to a large extent at the expense of educational measures.

The statistical review suggests that in the last 10 years, both with regards adult and juvenile offenders, there is only a small percentage change in the proportionate use of imprisonment and its suspension and available non-custodial sanctions (fines, educational and disciplinary measures). Despite the stable figures in sentencing, the size of the prison population is growing. In 1992, the number of prisoners increased by 31% from 57,447 in 1992 to 75,719 in 2007. In the 1992,

[415] Data compiled from, Statistisches Bundesamt, Fachserie 10, Reihe 3, Strafverfolgung, 1998, 1999, 2000, 2001, 2002, 2003, 2004, 2005, 2006, 2007 and 2008.

Table 4.2 The proportionate use of sanctions under juvenile penal law in the former Länder of Germany in 1998–2008[416]

Year	Juvenile imprisonment	Disciplinary measures	Educational measures
1998	6.7	74.1	7.1
1999	6.8	74.5	6.6
2000	6.6	74.4	6.6
2001	6.7	74.6	7.0
2002	6.7	75.5	7.0
2003	6.5	76.0	6.8
2004	6.2	76.3	7.1
2005	6.1	77.3	7.0
2006	6.3	77.6	6.4
2007	6.6	76.6	6.3
2008	6.2	77.3	6.9

the imprisonment rate per 100,000 was[417] 72 while this figure was 92 in 2007.[418] Between 1996 and 2006, the number of persons serving a custodial sentence or preventive detention increased by 30% to reach 64,152. The change in the legislation on preventive detention partly accounts for this growth. On the other hand, the growing use of longer term prison sentences is also responsible for the expansion.[419] As a consequence, the imprisonment rate in Germany in 2006 was 96 per 100,000 much higher than some other jurisdictions in Europe.[420]

Conceivably, in the face of the growing prison population, avoiding the use of imprisonment as far and as much as possible occupies a perpetual place in both academic and policy discussions. Nonetheless, the veracity of the curious premise that the present framework fails to offer sufficient alternative non-custodial penalties to imprisonment seems to be quite doubtful. In fact it might be plausibly argued that the present system provides for sufficient procedural and substantive alternatives containing no prison term,[421] even though the whole potential of the fine has

[416]Data compiled from, Statistisches Bundesamt, Fachserie 10, Reihe 3, Strafverfolgung, 1996, 1997, 1998, 1999, 2000, 2001, 2002, 2003, 2004, 2005 and 2006, 2007 and 2008.

[417]Data compiled from, Statistisches Bundesamt, Fachserie 10, Reihe 3, Strafverfolgung, 1998, 1999, 2000, 2001, 2002, 2003, 2004, 2005, 2006, 2007 and 2008.

[418]For a comparison see, 'World Prison Brief' in the following link: http://www.kcl.ac.uk/depsta/law/research/icps/worldbrief/wpb_country.php?country=139 (Access Date March 2010).

[419]Impressively, there is a long tradition of confronting with the place of short-term imprisonment in Germany. It appears that, however, the avoidance of short-term imprisonment here has led to a growing use of longer terms, guided by the dubious assumption that longer term prison sentences are more suitable for rehabilitative purposes. This state of affairs has rarely been problematised as such. Critically, Weigend, T. (1986) Die kurze Freiheitsstrafe – eine Sanktion mit Zukunft, *Juristenzeitung*, pp. 260–269, Voß (1987), *op. cit.*, pp. 236–248.

[420]Heinz (2008) *op. cit.*, pp. 116–117.

[421]See, Frommel (1999), *op. cit.*, Weßlau, *op. cit.*, see also Köhler, M. (2000) Reformen des strafrechtlichen Sanktionensystems, no 2, *Neue Kriminalpolitik*, pp. 10–11, Dölling (1992a), *op. cit.*, p. 286.

not yet been entirely utilised. The objection that any further extension would reduce the scope of the fine is well-founded, particularly when taking the English experience in this regard into account.

Clearly, new options for example community service as a main penalty, would not inherently bring the obvious danger of net-widening, but reservation of imprisonment as an ultimate punishment for breach could seriously undermine the original intention of keeping a greater number of offenders out of prisons when frequent revocations occur. Instead of an extension of non-custodial options, revitalising such measures as the warning with suspension appears to be more promising, not only because an extension of the scope of this measure would allow it to play an increasing role at the first tier, but due to its potential function of suspension of fines, reducing the magnitude of the fine default and imprisonment for it. A uniform and more flexible conception of community service as a back-door option could further reduce the number of persons serving imprisonment for fine defaulting. On the other hand, given the frequent application of longer term prison sentences, an extension of the scope of the suspended prison sentence on probation, in Germany, could be an important part of a 'reductionist' agenda.

Chapter 5
Alternatives to Imprisonment in Turkey: A 'Schattendasein'?

5.1 Introduction: Historical Context

So far, the Ottoman-Turkish penal historiography has limited itself within narrow periodical and geographical boundaries, and only rarely tried to conduct a macro analysis in examining issues related to crime and punishment.[1] This gap in the literature represents a major challenge in understanding the peculiarities of the penal transformation in the territory of the Ottoman Empire. In light of this fact, only a number of tentative explanations with regard to the reasons of the apparently belated reception of the concept of alternatives to imprisonment can be made.

To begin with it must be highlighted that the development of imprisonment as a dominant form of punishment in Turkey barely coincided with that which occurred in Europe. Until the end of the eighteenth century, places of confinement, *Zindans* (fortresses in Persian) were mainly used to detain suspects and debtors, and no prisons existed in the modern sense.[2] From this period onwards the construction and rental of a number of prisons is recorded.[3] It was not, however, until the third quarter of the nineteenth century that prisons had proliferated. The assumption is then warranted that in the Hegelian sense, for the creation of the prison's 'antithesis' (alternatives to imprisonment) no such comparable 'material' and 'intellectual' dynamics in Turkey were in existence at the time at which the notion of prison was

[1]For critical approaches see, Göral, S., Ö. (2007) 19. Yüzyil Istanbul'unda Suc, Toplumsal Kontrol ve Hapishaneler Üzerine Calismak in Levy, N and Toumarkine, A.(eds.) *Osmanli'da Asayis, Suc ve Ceza, Tarih Vakfi Yayinlari*, Istanbul.

[2]Demirbas, T. (2000) Hürriyeti Baglayici Cezalarin and Cezaevlerinin Evrimi in Naskali, G., E. and Altun, O., H. (eds.) *Hapishane Kitabi*, Kitabevi, Istanbul.

[3]The first prison in the modern sense was established in 1831 with name of 'Hapishane-i Umumi'. This was followed by other prisons: Nevsehir (1849), Diyarbakir (1864), Sürüc (1852), Manavgat (1852), Vezirköprü (1870), Kozan (1875) Sirnak (1886), Sinop (1886), Kirklareli (1887), Kütahya (1889), Kastamonu (1889), Alacam (1890), Bafra (1894), Ordu (1898) Erzurum (1900), Usak (1900), Hinis (1905), Bilecik (1906), Ipsala (1906), Kinik (1907), Manyas (1910), Üsküdar (1916), Zara (1919) and Cicekdag (1922) were established. Demirbas, *op. cit.*, p. 34. See also Mengüc, A., R. (1968) *Ceza Infaz Hukuku ve Infaz Müesseseleri*, Cezaevi Matbaasi, Istanbul.

Ö. Sevdiren, *Alternatives to Imprisonment in England and Wales, Germany and Turkey*,
DOI 10.1007/978-3-642-17351-6_5,

becoming rapidly 'obsolete' in major European countries.[4] While the significance attributed to prisons was already in decline elsewhere, the institution of the prison in the late Ottoman Empire was untarnished as a brand new idea. Needless to say, the slow pace of this process was a product of a combination of complex factors.

In this context the relationship between the emergence of imprisonment as a dominant mode of punishment and that of secularisation of (criminal) law is highly germane. Until the first penal code of the Ottoman Empire (1841) the content of Ottoman criminal law was derived from *Sharia* supplemented by the *Qanun* enactments of the sultans.[5] In order to understand the place of confinement in this law, reference ought to be made to the Islamic penal law, *Uqubat*. Under this 'divinely' defined law, in accordance with crime types, punishments are divided into three categories.[6] The first type of crimes, *hudud* crimes are believed to be those committed against the rights of God. These crimes are exhaustively determined and their corresponding punishment (e.g. capital punishments, flogging, amputation and stoning) is provided by the Quran.[7] The *hudud*-crimes include stealing, highway robbery, fornication, false accusation of fornication without evidence (*kazf*), drinking alcoholic beverages, and apostasy from the religion of Islam. The second types of crimes, *qisas-crimes*, are those which are presumed to be committed against the rights of persons: murder, intentional killing, intentional physical injury and unintentional injury. The punishment of the latter crimes is principally a talion punishment, albeit such a punishment could be waived by the victim or her/his family through 'blood money' (*diya*). Finally, the third types of crimes, *tazir-crimes,* are those crimes for which either no hudud-punishment in the Quran is prescribed, or, due to evidential insufficiency, i.e. the standards of proof required for *hudud*-crimes could not be met, the crime in question cannot be considered as a *hudud-crime*. The punishment of the latter category of crimes was to be determined by the chief executive (*ulul-amr*). According to Muslim jurists, *tazir*-crimes may be punished by the death penalty, heresy and banishment, but also by deprivation of liberty. Notably, however, as studies on Islamic criminal law show that deprivation

---

[4]See Chapter 2.

[5]See Akgündüz, A. (1990) *Osmanli Kanunnameleri ve Hukuki Tahlilleri*, Fey Vakfi, Istanbul, Gerber, H. (1994) *State, Society and Law in Islam: Ottoman Law in Comparative Perspective*, State University of New York Press, Albany, pp. 32–42, Heyd, U. (1973) *Studies in Old Ottoman Criminal Law*, Oxford University Press, Oxford, see also Ücok, C. (1947) Osmanli Ceza Kanunnamelerinde Islam Ceza Hukukuna Aykiri Hükümler, *Ankara Üniversitesi Hukuk Fakültesi Dergisi*, vol. 4, no 1–4, pp. 48–73.

Non-Turkish speakers might find the following also useful: Bozkurt, G. (1992) Review of the Ottoman Legal System, *Ankara Üniversitesi Osmanli Tarihi Arastirma ve Uygulama Merkezi Dergisi*, vol. 3, pp. 115–128.

[6]See Cin, H. and Akgündüz, A. (1989) *Türk Hukuk Tarihi*, vol. 1, Kamu Hukuku, Selcuk Üniversitesi Yayinlari, Konya, pp. 264–277, Aydin, M., A. (2009) *Türk Hukuk Tarihi*, Beta, Istanbul, pp. 187–207, Sentop, M. (2004) Tanzimat Dönemi Osmanli Ceza Hukuku, Istanbul, pp. 16–20.

[7]Haleem, M., A., A. and Sharif, A., O. and Daniels, K. (2003) *Criminal Justice in Islam: Judicial Procedure in Sharia*, Tauris, London, p. 37.

of liberty was regarded and treated as a *supplementary* measure to corporal punishments, rather than recognised as being of independent nature.[8] This characteristic of Islamic jurisprudence partly explains the late appearance of prisons as places of punitive detention in the Ottoman Empire.

It was no surprise therefore that the attempts to create positive statutes based on the European penal laws, in particular that of France, challenged the major strands of the hitherto penal policy and practice. In this context, both *attempts* of codification of penal law, the acts of 1840 and 1851, incorporated various forms of imprisonment into law.[9] Noteworthy is that both acts were far from forming a criminal *code* in their form and content. They did not comprise a general section on crime and punishment and in this sense they were truly a 'digest' of the perceived most serious crimes and penalties.[10] Since both of these codes were seen as being far from meeting the demands for a penal code, soon after a quest for a penal code began again. In 1858, very closely modelling the French Penal Code of 1810,[11] the Royal Penal Code (*Ceza Kanunname-i Hümayun*) was introduced.[12] Corporal punishment was not retained in this Code, as in previous codes. In accordance with the offence types which the Code encompassed, three categories of imprisonment type were recognised[13]: prison sentence, custody in fortresses and penal

[8]For a detailed examination see, Schneider, I. (1995) Imprisonment in Pre-Classical and Classical Islamic Law, *Islamic Law and Society*, vol. 2, no. 2, pp. 157–173.

Heyd noted that under Ottoman penal law "imprisonment as a penalty is inflicted, often in addition to chastisement (tazir) and a fine, for a few sexual offences and for a man's beating his father or mother.", *op. cit.*, p. 302.

[9]Berkes, N. (1964) *The Development of Secularism* in Turkey, McGill University Press, Montreal. See, Sentop, *op. cit.*, pp. 22–105, also Taner, T. (1953) *Ceza Hukuku Umumi Kisim*, 3rd edition, Ismail Akgün Matbaasi, Istanbul, pp. 147–149, Baer, G. (1977) The Transition from Traditional to Western Criminal Law in Turkey and Egypt, *Studia Islamica*, vol. 45, pp. 139–158, Gökcen, A. (1987) *Tanzimat Dönemi Osmanli Ceza Kanunlari ve Bu Kanunlardaki Ceza Müeyyideleri*, (unpublished master thesis, University of Istanbul).

[10]Gürelli noted that "these codes were rather incomplete lists of the most serious crimes and their penalties, and for this reason, it would be more appropriate to refer them as statutes rather than codes". Gürelli, N. (1965) Introduction for *Turkish Criminal Code*, The American Series of Foreign Penal Codes, Sweet & Maxwell, London, p. 1. Baer underlines that "the Ottoman *qanuns* of 1840 and 1851 deal meanly with disturbance of public order and security and with tyranny and corruption of officials". p. 144, see also Berkes, *op. cit.*, pp. 160–164.

[11]See Ücok, C., Mumcu, A. and Bozkurt, G. (1999) *Türk Hukuk Tarihi*, Ankara, p. 283.

[12]Note that according to the Royal Penal Code, Section 1 stipulated that the Code did not repeal the penal provisions of the *Sharia*, that it was enacted merely to codify within the limits of the rights of *tazir* of the 'ulul-amr' (the chief executive) and that it would not infringe upon claims for *qisas*, *diya* or personal rights recognised by the Sharia. For a detailed examination, see Berkes, *op. cit.*, pp. 164–166.

[13]With regard to *delicts*, life imprisonment, with regard to *crimes*, imprisonment from one week to three years and finally with regard to *contraventions* twenty-four hours to one week was provided for. See Saner, Y. (2007) Osmanli'nin Yüzlerce Yil Süren Cezalandirma ve Korkutma Refleksi: Prangaya Vurma in Levy and Toumarkine, *op. cit.*, pp. 163–189.

servitude on galleys. The enactment of the penal code was followed by the promulgation of the Ordinance on Prisons.[14]

Crucially, western influence did not only lead to an almost contemporaneous codification work and as such *partial* secularisation in the field of punishment, but motivated the Ottoman penal bureaucracy to keep up with the perceived standards of the 'civilised' west in prisons.[15] It was during this period that in various official documents and journal reports the state of prisons was addressed.[16] These documents reveal that the prisons of this period suffered from an extreme shortage of food allotments, poor sanitation, heating and ventilating problems, and overcrowding.[17] Characterised by such urgent problems in prisons and faced with the enormous fiscal problems of putting such ideas as the construction of new prison buildings into practice,[18] the 'internationalised' debate on crime and punishment in the Ottoman penal justice could not be expected to exert the impact that it did across Europe. The Ottoman Empire was represented occasionally in the international congresses,[19] but scholarly consideration of those ideas took much longer than elsewhere.

5.2 Non-custodial and Custodial Penalties in the Previous Turkish Penal Code

As soon as the proclamation of the republic, the cadres of the *Kemalist Revolution* hastened to replace the old penal code, which was believed to give undue place to the protection of the Ottoman Dynasty, with a new one underlining the new values of the republic.[20] This was only another area, like the change of the capital city from

[14]With the title *'Memaliki Mahrusai Sahanede Bulunan Tevkifhane ve Hapishanelerin Idarei Dahiliyelerine Dair Nizamname'*. 21 May 1880. Kunter (1948), *op. cit.*, p. 574.

[15]Gönen, S., Y. (2000) Osmanli Imparatorlugu'nda Hapishaneleri Iyilestirme Girisimleri, 1917 Yili in Naskali and Altun, *op. cit.*, pp. 173–183, Sen, H. (2007) Osmanli'da Hapishane Mefhumu in Levy and Toumarkine, *op. cit.*, pp. 200–211, Schull, K. (2007) Tutuklu Sayimi: Jön Türklerin Sistematik Bir Sekilde Hapishane Istatistikleri Toplama Calismalari ve Bunlarin 1911–1918 Hapishane Reformu Üzerine Etkileri, *ibid.*, pp. 212–238, Demirbas (2000), *op. cit.*, pp. 30–31.

[16]Sofuoglu. E. (2000) 'Osmanli Hapishanelerinde Islah ve Firar Tesebbüsleri', pp. 163–172, Karaca, A. (2000) XIX. Yüzyilda Osmanli Devletinde Fahise Hatunlara Uygulanan Cezalar: Hapis ve Sürgün, pp. 152–162, p. 156 in Naskali and Altun, *op. cit.*, pp. 152–162.

[17]See particularly, Gazel, A., A. (2000) Tanin Muhabiri Ahmet Serif Bey'in Notlarinda Osmanli Hapishaneleri in Naskali and Altun, *op. cit.*, pp. 143–151, Sofuoglu (2000) *op. cit.*, pp. 165–168.

[18]Also from the archive documents, briefly, Yildiztas, M. (1991) *Mütareke Döneminde Suc Unsurlari ve Istanbul Hapishaneleri* (unpublished master thesis, Istanbul University), pp. 43–44.

[19]Demirel, F. (2001) 1890 Petersburg Hapishaneler Kongresi, *Toplumsal Tarih*, no. 89, pp. 11–14.

[20]Kunter (1948), *op. cit.*, pp. 548–549, Artuk, M., E. (1998) 1926 Tarihli Türk Ceza Kanunu'nun Degistirilmesi Yönündeki Calismalar Hakkinda Düsünceler, *Istanbul Barosu Dergisi*, vol. 72, pp. 830–847, pp. 834–835. See also, Sözüer, A. (2008) Das neue türkische Strafgesetzbuch in Tellenbach S. (ed.) *Das neue türkische Straf- und Strafprozessrech*t, Berliner Wissenschaftsverlag, Berlin, pp. 11–40, p. 11.

Istanbul to Ankara, where a need for a break from the 'old' was felt to be essential.[21] From this perspective, the penal administration of this period was in search of a new law that would provide appropriate means to protect the Revolution and Republic.[22] In searching for a penal code that was suitable and agreeable to the social conditions of the country, preference was given to the Italian Code of 1889 (known as the Zanardelli Code), which for some time enjoyed a high reputation worldwide as well as in Ottoman legislation.[23] It was, for example, the major source of inspiration in the amendments to the Ottoman Penal Code in 1911 and 1914.[24] In 1926, the penal code was adopted from the Zanardelli Code, with a small number of important changes, by retaining some provisions of the Royal Penal Code (e.g. death penalty) or otherwise making new rules.[25]

Drawing upon the jurisprudence of the (neo)classical school in Italy, the Zanardelli Code facilitated modest measures for the individualisation of punishment.[26] Suspension of the execution of imprisonment was, for example, supplemented to the Code in 1904.[27] Interestingly, as the original version, which constituted the basis for the previous Turkish Penal Code, did not provide for such a measure, the

[21]In a speech at the opening of the Law Faculty of the University of Ankara, in 1925, Atatürk exposed this perspective with the statement that:

"The Turkish revolution signifies a transformation far broader than the word revolution suggest. . .It means replacing an age-old political unity based on religion with one based on another tie, that of nationality. This nation has now accepted the principle that the only means of survival for nations in the international struggle for existence lies in the acceptance of contemporary Western civilisation. . .This nation has also accepted the principle that all of its laws should be based on secular grounds only, on a secular mentality that accepts the rule of continuous change in accordance with the change and development of life's conditions as its law. The time has come to lay the legal foundations and educate new men of law satisfying the mentality and needs of our revolution". Cited in Berkes, *op. cit.*, p. 470.

[22]Artuk, M. E. and Cinar, A., R. (2004) Yeni Bir Ceza Kanunu Arayislari ve Adalet Alt Komisyonu Tasarisi Üzerine Düsünceler in Ergül, T. (ed.) *Türk Ceza Kanunu Reformu*, Ikinci Kitap, TBB Yayinlari, pp. 43–45.

[23]The code of criminal procedure was also intended to be adopted from the Italian code of penal procedure, but after a while the commission empowered to prepare the draft, proposed to the Ministry of Justice to switch from Italian to German code of criminal procedure for the reasons that the German code was not as complicated as the Italian code and was more expedient. See, Gürelli, N. (1983) The Recent Development of Turkish Criminal Procedure and the Practice of the Turkish Judiciary, pp. 147–163, *Annales de la Facultés de Droit d'Istanbul,* vol.29, no 45, p. 6. See also, Dönmezer, S. (1981) Mukayeseli Hukukta Yasalastirma Egilimi ve Ilkeleri in *Atatürk'ün 100. Dogum Yildönümü Kutlama Calismalari, Kolokyumlar ve Tartismalar* (14 Ocak 1981), pp. 15–16.

[24]Kunter (1948), *op. cit.*, p. 541.

[25]Law no 765, 1.3.1926, Official Gazette 13.3.1926.

[26]See for general remarks, Ancel, M. (1958) The Collection of European Codes and the Study of Comparative Law, *University of Pennsylvania Law Review*, vol. 106, no 3, pp. 329–384. Wise, E., M. and Maitlin, A. (1978) *The Italian Penal Code*, Rothman, Colorado, pp. xxvi–xxviii.

[27]Kleve (1906) Das italienische Gesetz über die bedingte Verurteilung (Lex Ronchetti), *Deutsche Juristen-Zeitung*, vol. XI, no 4, pp. 237–241. Dolcini, E. and Paliero, E. (1990) Alternativen zur kurzen Freiheitsstrafen in Italien und im Ausland, *Zeitschrift für die gesamte Strafrechtswissenschaft*, vol. 102, no 1, pp. 223–246, p. 226.

provisions in the Turkish legislation displayed a degree of difference from the Italian regulation in this regard. From this fact, it can be concluded that the Turkish legislature tried to reconcile different systems.[28] Under the Turkish version of 'sursis' heavy and light fines (without specifying an amount), banishment and custodial sentences (except for heavy imprisonment), i.e. imprisonment and light imprisonment of up to 6 months could be suspended if the offender had not previously received a sentence other than a fine and having regard to her/his previous history and attitudes, the court was of the opinion that s/he would not reoffend.[29] The maximum limit that could be suspended for was set at 1 year for persons up to age of 18 and over 70. Originally, when the probationary period (1 year for contraventions, five years for 'crimes')[30] had passed without conviction, the conviction was required to be considered as 'null and void'. With a law in 1937, it was altered in the following manner: after the successful completion of the probationary period, the sentence that was suspended was deemed to be executed.[31] Finally in 1941, in an amendment to the related provision, once again it was provided that after the completion of the *probationary* period without revocation, the suspended sentence would be deemed as not having been imposed.[32]

The Italian scholars Dolcini and Paliero note that from the very beginning that the fine in *Italy* was never treated as an alternative to imprisonment.[33] Correspondingly, in the Turkish Penal Code, the fine was conceived of only a punishment dealing with minor criminality; in this sense no concurrence between fine and imprisonment was envisaged. The fine in the Penal Code was classified as light and heavy.[34] In the first version, the minimum limits of the heavy fine were determined as one Turkish Lira and no maximum limit was specified. The maximum and minimum limits of the light fine ranged from one half to 200 Turkish Liras. In the determination of the fine, there was no mention of taking into account the individual offender's financial circumstances. Due to the depreciation of the currency, the first change in these limits was made as early as 1936.[35]

The Penal Code contained relatively lenient provisions relating to fine default. Accordingly, after the imposition of the fine, the convict needed to be invited to pay the imposed fine within 2 months.[36] In cases in which the fine was not paid within this period, it was to be converted to imprisonment, on a basis of one day's

[28] Taner (1953) *op. cit.*, p. 458.

[29] Section 89 of the previous Penal Code.

[30] *Ibid.*, Section 95.

[31] Law no 3112, 3.2.1937, Official Gazette, 11.2.1937.

[32] Law no 4055, 2.6.1941, Official Gazette, 6.6.1941.

[33] Dolcini and Paliero, *op. cit.*, p. 226.

[34] Section 19 of the previous Penal Code was concerned with heavy fines and Section 24 with light fines.

[35] Law no 3, 11.6.1936, Official Gazette, 23.6.1936.

[36] Section 29/2.

imprisonment for one Lira.[37] In any case, however, the duration of the converted imprisonment could not exceed 1 year.[38] Significantly, the Code provided the possibility for fine defaulters to work in the service of the state, provincial administrations and municipalities.[39] This regulation was subject to amendments in 1936 and 1941. In 1933, it was provided that prior to the conversion of the unpaid fine to imprisonment, a referral to the process peculiar to the collection of public debts was to be resorted to. Accordingly, only where it was ascertained that this process remained unsuccessful, imprisonment for fine default was to be imposed. The law in 1941 also constituted a 'volte-face' in this regard. The effectively automatic conversion of the fine to imprisonment as foreseen in the former system was incorporated into the Code, yet with a crucial modification that if the convict paid one third of the specified fine, the rest of the payment could be made in two instalments.[40]

Under this code, judicial warning was another alternative to imprisonment.[41] It could be meted out for offences punishable by up to 1 month of imprisonment or light imprisonment or 30 Liras or (without specifying any limit) a light fine, provided that there were extenuating circumstances and that the offender had not previously been sentenced for a 'crime' or had not received a prison sentence longer than 1 month for contraventions.

With regard to juvenile offenders, the Penal Code did not provide separate sentencing measures; they were subject to the same type of penalties that were prescribed with minimum and maximum limits in the Turkish Penal Code with a statutory mitigation of the sentence.[42] Setting the age of criminal responsibility at eleven, the Penal Code provided that those juveniles who had not attained the age of 12 at the commission of an offence were not to be prosecuted and punished, unless the offence in question is a *crime* punishable by more than 1 year or more severe punishment. In the latter case, upon the request of the public prosecutor the court, were required to place the juvenile in an institution under government administration or supervision, or place the juvenile into the custody of her/his parents or guardian.[43] This provision was also applicable for juveniles aged between 11 and 15, when at the commission of the offence the juvenile was incapable to realise that her/his act was an offence. Where the juvenile was incapable of knowing that her/his conduct was an offence, the given punishment in the concrete case was to be reduced in the following manner: instead of death sentence, heavy imprisonment for not less than 15 years and instead of heavy imprisonment for life, 10–15 years

[37] Section 29/3.

[38] Section 29/7.

[39] *Ibid.* After the change in 1941, it was explicitly stipulated that one-day imprisonment was deemed equal to two working days.

[40] Section 29/5.

[41] Section 26 and 27 of the previous Penal Code.

[42] *Ibid.*, Section 54 and 55.

[43] *Ibid.*, Section 53 (With a warning to the effect that they will be charged with a fine not more than 200 liras if juveniles commit a crime through their carelessness and negligence.).

were to be imposed. Other punishments were to be reduced by one half. Finally, with regard to juveniles aged between 15 and 18, in lieu of the death penalty, heavy imprisonment for not less than 20 years and instead of heavy imprisonment for life, heavy imprisonment for 15–20 years was to be given. Other punishments for this age category were required to be reduced up to one third. In any case, the punishment of 'disqualification to hold public office'[44] could not be applied as an ancillary penalty.[45] Notably, the Penal Code also made provision that juveniles who have not attained the age of 18 before s/he began to serve her/his sentence must be placed in special custodial institutions called reformatories (*islahevi*).[46]

Another pertinent aspect of the penal code was the measure on police supervision. Under the first version of the Penal Code, it was possible to place the offender under the supervision of the police in addition to the given punishment, whenever the law specifies so.[47] This measure could not be applied on juvenile offenders. The duration of police supervision could not be less than one and more than 3 years. During this period, the convict was required to comply with directions and warnings by the police including the whereabouts of the offender. As is clear from this description, police supervision was provided as what in modern parlance may be called 'security measure',[48] unless the court deemed it appropriate to impose it as an "additional" penalty to heavy imprisonment.[49]

Within the realm of custodial sentences, three types of imprisonment were distinguished: heavy imprisonment, imprisonment and light imprisonment.

1. Heavy imprisonment could be temporary or for life.[50] The temporary form of heavy imprisonment consisted of a term of imprisonment ranging from 1 to 24 years. Originally, heavy imprisonment was to be enforced through solitary confinement[51] in conjunction with hard labour. However, this system, due to shortage of prisons and absence of appropriate single cells,[52] could not be

---

[44]Disqualification to hold public office comprised prohibition from being elected to office, voting, loss of political rights, exclusion from the Grand National Assembly or any other elective public agency, or holding public office or service assigned by the government, province, municipality, grant of rank, government title or by any scientific board, services regarding guardianship, except parental rights. It might be for life or temporary. Section 20 of the previous Penal Code.

[45]Section 54/3 of the previous Penal Code.

[46]*Ibid.*, Section 54/4.

[47]Section 28 of the previous Penal Code.

[48]The law did not use the term 'security measure', but regarding its nature, it was named as such. Erem F. (1943) Türk Ceza Kanunu'nda Emniyet Tedbirleri, *Ankara Üniversitesi Hukuk Fakültesi Dergisi*, vol. 1, no. 3, pp. 351–378.

[49]Section 28/5 of the previous Penal Code.

[50]*Ibid.*, Section 13.

[51]During the day- and night-time in the first period.

[52]Gölcüklü, F. (1956) Acik Müesesseler, *Ankara Üniversitesi Hukuk Fakültesi Dergisi*, vol. 11, no 2, pp. 91–106, pp. 96–97.

implemented and was repealed in 1933.[53] Subsequently in 1937, another system for the administration of heavy imprisonment was adopted that comprised the progressive and gradual administration of heavy imprisonment.[54] Under this system, the first period entailed solitary confinement ranging between 1 and 6 months. This period would follow the isolation of the convict only during the night-time. Subject to good behaviour in the third and fourth period the convict could contact other inmates and her/his punishment could be remitted as specified in the Penal Code.

2. The sentence of imprisonment ranged from 3 days to 20 years.[55] Those facing prison sentences exceeding 6 months (after the remand period was subtracted), while not to be subject to solitary confinement, were to have their sentences administered in accordance with provisions designed for heavy imprisonment.
3. Finally, light imprisonment ranged from one day to 2 years.[56] Significantly, for juveniles and women who were not previously sentenced, the court might decide that the execution of the sentence could take place at the domicile or in a specified place or could be served by working in factories or for the municipality.[57]

Not only did such alternative execution methods of short-term imprisonment remain unimplemented, overall the state of prisons was far from able to cope with the demands of the system that was envisaged by policy-makers.[58] The prison system was largely composed of old buildings. In many prisons, problems such as epidemics threatened the health of inmates, where living arrangements were clearly below the basic minimum. In such circumstances, both the maintenance of prison inmates and idleness in prisons was increasingly the focus of penal administration.[59] A development that met the needs of the early republican era was the establishment of work-based prisons.[60] These prisons were to make prisoners engage in useful activities, while contributing to the accumulation of the capital necessary to establish open prisons.[61] The work in these prisons consisted mainly of industrial and agricultural labour. This rather pragmatic move of the penal administration was justified by the perceived value of prison labour to inmate

---

[53]Law no. 2275, 8.6.1933, Official Gazette, 20.6.1933.

[54]Law no 3112, 3.2.1937, Official Gazette, 11.2.1937.

[55]Section 15 of the previous Turkish Penal Code, if a maximum limit was not prescribed by law, it was to be five years.

[56]Section 21, *ibid.*

[57]Section 21/2, *ibid.*

[58]Kunter (1948), *op. cit.*, pp. 576–584, Gölcüklü, F. (1966) *Türk Ceza Sistemi (Hürriyeti Baglayici Cezalar),* Sevinc Matbaasi, Ankara, pp. 46–60, Demirbas, T. (2003) *Infaz Hukuku*, Seckin, Ankara, pp. 144–145.

[59]Sipahi, A. (2006) The Labour-Based Prisons in Turkey (1933–1953) (unpublished master study, University of Bogazici).

[60]See Taner (1953), *op. cit.*, pp. 618–622, Gölcüklü (1956) *op. cit.*, pp. 96–99. For a detailed account of labour-based prisons, see Sipahi, *op. cit.*

[61]Gölcüklü (1956), *op. cit.*, pp. 96–99.

rehabilitation (*islah*). Yet, it would be wrong to assume that the concept of rehabilitation at the time in question received more than passing attention among official circles.[62] This 'neglect' was most apparent in the approach towards juvenile offenders. With regret, Tahir Taner, one of the prominent criminal scholars of this period, noted that only in two prisons (Eskisehir and Izmir) was separation of adult and juvenile inmates, aged between 15 and 18, as required by the Penal Code, possible.[63] Due to the lack of suitable institutions, juvenile offenders did not serve their punishment before attaining the age of 18. It was not until 1937 that the first reformatory for juveniles aged between 11 and 15 was established in Edirne.[64]

5.3 A Need for Change and Change Without Genuine Progress

Until the 1940s, the Penal Code was changed several times, being by and large influenced by the Italian Rocco Code that rested "on the whole political, moral, religious and social concept of fascism".[65] This influence was most unequivocally observable in the increase of the severity of punishment for certain types of offences and in the creation of a number of new offences committed against state security.[66] In the beginning of the 1940s, however, rather than fragmented changes in this form, a comprehensive adjustment of the penal code to the *Zeitgeist* was deemed a necessity.[67] For, having regard to developments in the 'civilised countries' (that is saying West Europe and North America), it was generally agreed that the Penal Code was no longer up to date, and that it lagged behind the

[62] Taner underlined that "inmates received no meaningful intervention let alone to implement a system guided by rehabilitative considerations". Taner (1953) *op. cit.*, p. 617.

[63] Taner (1953) *op. cit.*, p. 338, Kunter (1948) *op. cit.*, p. 580, Dönmezer, S. (1943) Cocuk Suclulugu Nevi Sebep ve Saikleri, *Siyasi Ilimler Mecmuasi*, vol. 1, no.1, pp. 227–244. Taner, T., Dönmezer, S., Gökay, F., K., Findikoglu, Z., F., Kunter, N., Sensoy, N., Erman, S., Karaorman, T., N. (1951) The Prevention and Treatment of Juvenile Delinquency in Turkey (a report submitted to the relevant department of the United Nations Report of the Prevention and Treatment of Juvenile Delinquency it was stated that "Although it is said that they (juvenile over 11 and under 15) will be put to the special sections of the general prisons there are not special sections in every prison). We must also add that although in almost every part of the world of the correctional centres for the children are considered as school where the employment of the children occupying a secondary importance, the correctional centre of Kalaba (the only correctional centre in Turkey) has restricted teaching and, emphasised mainly on the showing of craftsmanship to children to make them earn their livings. The handcrafts which are taught in these centres are those which do not need expensive utensils, which can be useful in every part of the country, such as shoe making, tailoring, masonary, etc". *Annales de la Facultés de Droit d'Istanbul*, no 1–4, pp. 1–42.

[64] Taner (1953) *op. cit.*, p. 580, but then was moved to Ankara.

[65] See Kunter (1948), *op. cit.*, pp. 549–558. In 1931, 1937, 1938, 1939 and 1941.

[66] Battaglini, G. (1933) The Fascist Reform of the Penal Law in Italy, *Journal of Criminal Law and Crimino*logy, vol. 24, no 1, pp. 278–289, p. 284.

[67] See, Kunter (1948), *op. cit.*, pp. 558–561, Köni, B. (1943) Ceza Hukukunda Tenkil ve Önleme Müessesesi, *Ankara Üniversitesi Siyasal Bilgiler Fakültesi Dergisi*, vol. 1, no 1, pp. 47–55.

postulates of modern penal policy.[68] A commission composed of professors, members of the Cassation Court and officials from the Ministry of Justice was set up to draft a new penal code. Nonetheless, this initiative was subsequently discontinued due to budget considerations.

Another failed attempt during this period was the reform efforts to ameliorate the position of juvenile offenders. The first draft law relating to the establishment of the separate body of juvenile courts was then put forward.[69] According to this draft, the juvenile court was to be empowered to deal with both juvenile offenders and those in need of care and protection. The jurisdiction of the juvenile court was to contain all categories of offences committed by juveniles aged between seven and 18, excluding those offences that are punishable by a sentence of light imprisonment and fines (which were to be dealt with by the courts of the Justice of Peace).[70]

It was also during this period that criminology as an academic discipline gained significant attention.[71] In 1944, a criminology institute at the University of Istanbul was established. The institute conducted a number of pioneering criminological studies.[72] As early as 1935, after the publication of official statistics, statistical data became available. The growing enthusiasm for the study of criminality and its causes was given a major boost by a lively debate on the treatment of offenders, and measures for the individualisation of punishment in the international platforms such as La Haye Congress.[73] The ideas of the positivist school and social defence

---

[68]Kunter (1948) *op. cit.*, p. 558.

[69]For the text, see Kunter, N. (1949) 'Cocuk Mahkemeleri Kanunu Nasil Olmali?', *Istanbul Üniversitesi Hukuk Fakültesi Mecmuasi*, vol. 14, pp. 55–95.

Taner *et al.*, noted that (p. 30) "a rate of juvenile delinquency has never been found in Turkey such as been found in the western world especially during the Second World War. The problem of Turkey on the subject of juvenile delinquency is the lack of application of modern conceptions achieved in legislation and in the institutions. Even if the child centres provided by law for the deserted children is established it will be impossible to put young delinquents in to these centres. The only precaution which is applied to young delinquents is their handing over their parents or guardians".

[70]Another draft on juvenile courts which became the bill of the government was prepared in 1965. This Bill re-produced largely the previous drafts, with the difference that the age of criminal responsibility was to be increased from eleven to twelve years. A second attempt to establish juvenile courts was also made in 1952, but this lost its actuality in a very short period. See, Günal, Y. (1965a) Yirmi Yildir Gerceklesmeyen Bir Tasari – Cocuk Mahkemeleri Kanunu Tasarisi, *Ankara Üniversitesi Siyasal Bilgiler Fakültesi Dergisi*, vol. 20, no 1, pp. 337–340.

[71]Köni, B. (1956) Kriminoloji, *Ankara Üniversitesi Siyasal Bilgiler Fakültesi Dergisi*, pp. 76–90. Aybar, C. (1943) Türkiye'de Mahkumlar ve Suclar, *Siyasi Ilimler Mecmuasi*, pp. 604–642.

[72]Türk Kriminoloji Enstitüsü (1948) *Türkiye'de Adam Öldürme Cürmü Mahkumlari Hakkinda Kriminolojik Istatistik*, Hüsnütabiat Matbaasi, Istanbul. For a summary on the study crime and criminality, Kunter, N. (1951) Türkiye'de Suclulugun Ictimai Amilleri, *Ankara Üniversitesi Hukuk Fakültesi Dergisi*, vol. 8, no 3–4, pp. 98–121, on the juvenile criminality see Dönmezer (1943), *op. cit.*

[73]See, Kunter, N. (1950) Ceza ve Ceza Infazi Milleterarasi Onikinci Kongresi (La Haye, 14–19 Agustos 1950), *Istanbul Üniversitesi Hukuk Fakültesi Mecmuasi*, vol. XVI, pp. 591–614, Gölcüklü (1956), *op. cit.*, pp. 91–92.

movement become known in wider circles whilst the gap between Turkey and the western world in the application of modern conceptions in legislation and institutions was frequently pointed out.[74]

Within this climate, in 1958, another penal code was drafted with the statement that due to numerous changes the existing penal code had lost its harmony and consistency and that it no longer answered the needs that emanated from economic, cultural and societal changes.[75] Ultimately, however, this draft did not gain recognition. A brief consideration of the internal political affairs during these years is at this point essential in order to understand the background against which this draft was abandoned and a thoroughgoing reform was launched in the mid 1960s.

Prior to the end of the 1940s, the political situation in Turkey was characterised by a one party system. In 1950, with the electoral victory of the Democrat Party, a multi-party system emerged.[76] The Democrat Party's rule began with promises of constitutional amendments elementary to strengthen democracy. However, in spite of the pledges made by the Democrats before coming to power, little change took place during the rule of this party. In 1960, with a *coup d'état*, the army removed the Democrat Party from power, with the justification that the secular structure of the state was being threatened by the rule of the Democrat Party.[77]

Soon after the return of power to civilians in 1961, a new constitution was enacted. Central to the mission of this constitution was the creation of various provisions in which the state was entrusted with economic, social and cultural planning, land reform, health care and housing, organisation of social security, helping to assure full employment and similar tasks.[78] Under this climate, a renewal of law regarding the nature and execution of punishment attracted growing consensus.[79] The view was widely shared that a penal law based on vengeance and retribution was outdated and modern penal policy should rather aim to achieve reintegration of criminals into society as industrious and law-abiding people, by means of education, training and work. In this regard, for some commentators,

---

[74]Kunter (1948) *op. cit.*, pp. 558–560, Köni (1956) *op. cit.*, Artuk (1998) *op. cit.*, pp. 837–838.

[75]Adalet Bakanligi (1958) *Türk Ceza Kanunu Tasarisi*, Ankara.

[76]Karpat, K., H. (1959) *Turkey's Politics: the Transition to a Multi-Party System*, Princeton University Press, Princeton, Hale, W. (1994) *Turkish Politics and the Military*, Routledge, London, pp. 88–118, Ahmad, F. (1993) *The Making of Modern Turkey*, Routledge, London, pp. 102–120, Tuncay, M. (1997) Cagdas Türkiye, 4. Cilt (1908–1980), Cem Yayinevi, Istanbul, Özbudun, E. (2000) *Contemporary Turkish Politics: Challenges to Democratic Consolidation*, Lynne Rienner Publishers, London, pp. 53–54.

[77]For a closer analysis see Hale, *op. cit.*, pp. 88–118, Ahmad, *op. cit.*, pp. 121–147.

[78]Promulgated through Law no 334, 9.7.1961, Official Gazette 20.7.1961. Section 2 of the 1961 Constitution stated that "the Turkish Republic is a nationalistic, democratic, secular and social State governed by the rule of law, based on human rights and fundamental tenets set forth in the preamble". Tanör, B. (1986) *Iki Anayasa* (1961–1982), Beta, Istanbul, Azrak, A., Ü. (1962) 'Sosyal Devlet ve 1962 Türk Anayasasinin Sistemi', *Istanbul Üniversitesi Hukuk Fakültesi Mecmuasi*, vol. 27, no 1–4, pp. 208–224. Özbudun, (2000), *op. cit.*, pp. 53–54.

[79]Günal, Y. (1965b) Ceza Infaz Kanunu Tasarisi, *Ankara Üniversitesi Siyasal Bilgiler Fakültesi Dergisi*, vol. 20, no. 2, pp. 889–901, p. 890.

a revision of the penal code would be sufficient.[80] For others, who observed an increasing tendency in foreign jurisdictions to create a special code for penal enforcement, an enactment of a code which would comprise fundamental issues about execution of sentences and the rights of prisoners was essential.[81] The latter was also because adjusting a penal enforcement code to the day's circumstances in the future would be less complicated than that of the penal code.

Several numbers of drafts were prepared. Ultimately, the draft written by Professor Manuel Lopez-Rey,[82] one of the most prominent penologists of the twentieth century, constituted the basis for the Penal Enforcement Code in 1965.[83] If the retention of the death penalty is disregarded for a moment, it would not be an exaggeration to state that the Code comprised the most innovative methods of the time and so an example of mild and elegant legislation. In numerous ways, the Penal Enforcement Code addressed the issues which had long been seen as in need of modification. At the heart of this law was the attempt to restructure custodial sentences and creation of a range of alternative sentencing options. The Penal Enforcement Law contained a distinction between long- and short-term prison sentences.[84] This effectively meant a repeal of the provisions concerning the distinction between heavy imprisonment, imprisonment and light imprisonment which had hitherto little practical meaning. The distinction was formally retained in the Penal Code, as there were several references to the type of imprisonment in relation to the suspension of imprisonment, judicial warning, alternative execution

---

[80] *Ibid.*, p. 892.

[81] *Ibid.*

[82] In his essay, Analytical Penology' written in 1964 at a time during which he was working fort he Ministry of Justice in Ankara in Turkey, Lopez-Rey summarised fundamental issues the contemporary penal regimes should address as follows:

1. The necessity of reducing to a minumum the number of persons sent to prison await trial;
2. The use of short-term imprisonment only in exceptional cases;
3. The integration of prison labout with free labour and the national economy;
4. The organisation of adequate general treatment services and programmes;
5. The reduction to a minimum of the closed cellular prison;
6. The reinforcement of the prisoner's relations with his family and facilities for the satisfaction of normal sexual needs;
7. Better pre-release preparation and better and greater use of parole;
8. The treatment of prisoners should be regarded as a part of the criminal judicial function and the present organisation and functions of the Prison Administration should be reduced to a minimum as a separate service;
9. The transformation of the prison personnel into a service in which administrative and custodial functions are reduced to a minimum and social functions increased to a maximum;
10. The organisation of adequate statistics on institutional treatment.

Lopez-Rey, M. (1964) ‚Analytical Penology' in *Studies in Penology* (dedicated to the memory of Sir Lionel Fox) Lopez-Rey, M. and Germain, C. (eds.), Martinus Nihhoff, The Hague.

[83] Law no 647, 13.7.1965, Official Gazette, 16.7.1965.

[84] *Ibid.* Section 3.

methods of imprisonment, and the application of procedural law e.g. the determination of the competency of court and so on.

One of the central innovations of this code was the pledge behind it to avoid prison sentences shorter than 6 months.[85] In 1962, 91% of the people received a custodial sentence that was less than 6 months. In the same year, 70% of the prison population was composed of prisoners who had received a custodial term of less than 6 months.[86] This required the devotion of a significant amount of the budget-allocated for short-term prisoners. In 1962, this proportion amounted 38% of the budget allocated for prisons and penal establishments.[87] The extension of the range of sentencing options was to alleviate prison overcrowding, but also to save resources.

Under this Code,[88] having regard to personal circumstances, the commission of the offence and other circumstances of the offender, the court could convert prison sentences not exceeding 6 months to the following:

1. Fine (with regard to contraventions punishable by five to ten Liras, with regard to crimes by ten to 30 Liras)
2. Performance of work in a state, municipality and public or private enterprise
3. Restitution and compensation
4. Attendance at an educational or reformatory institution
5. Refraining from going to certain places or performing certain professions and activities
6. Withdrawal of driver's licence or other licences

The Penal Enforcement Code also contained the special type of execution methods as house arrest and intermittent custody, which could be imposed upon the request of the offender. Under this Code, house arrest could be imposed on those offenders aged 65 or older, or offenders suffering from illness, whose health would be endangered by a prison stay, provided that the sentence to be executed did not exceed more than 30 days.[89] In 1967, with an ordinance,[90] it was provided that after the judgement was finalised, the public prosecutor was required to specify precisely the place in which the offender was to serve her/his punishment and inform her/him that a breach would lead to a revocation of the sentence. In order to secure the compliance with the sentence, the local police were also to be informed.

The Penal Enforcement Code contained two forms of intermittent custody to be served on the weekend, which would not exceed 30 days and 3 months respectively

[85]Günal, Y. (1965b), *op. cit.*, pp. 890–893. Dönmezer, S. (1965) Cezalarin Infazi Hakkinda Kanun, *Istanbul Üniversitesi Hukuk Fakültesi Mecmuasi*, vol. 30, no 1–4, pp. 8–35.

[86]Günal (1965b), *op. cit.*, p. 890.

[87]*Ibid.*

[88]Section 4 of the previous Penal Enforcement Code.

[89]*Ibid.*, Section 8 (1).

[90]Ordinance on the Administration of the Penal Execution Institutions and Remand Centres and Execution of Punishments, issued on 5.7.1967 and was promulgated in the Official Gazette on 1.8.1967.

or at night.[91] Significantly, prison sentences meted out for negligence offences, regardless of the duration of the prison sentence, could have the aforementioned special type of executions imposed.

The Penal Enforcement Code extended the scope of the suspension of the execution of punishment.[92] As highlighted above, previously only imprisonment and light imprisonment up to 6 months and fines could be suspended. Without altering provisions applicable for juveniles and persons aged 70 and over and the suspension of fines, the code allowed the suspension of heavy imprisonment up to 6 months and of light imprisonment and *imprisonment* up to 1 year.

On the other hand, the Code brought about principles which completed the provisions concerning fixing of the amount of the fine and payment.[93] With these changes, it was possible to pay a fine in instalments within a 2 year period. In determining the amount of the fine the court was required to take the financial circumstances, family maintenance, occupation, age, state of health, and the 'social and preventive' impact of punishment into account.[94] Imprisonment for fine default was retained only for those cases where it could be ascertained that the convict intentionally did not pay, or due to her/his neglect payment could not be secured, which could not exceed 1 year. In all other cases, the imposed fine was to be secured through the Law on the Collection of Public Debts and if this process remained unsuccessful, due to the individual convict's lack of financial means to pay the convict might require to work up to 1 year.[95]

By incorporating such elements into law, the Penal Enforcement Code made a bold attempt at reducing the numbers of prisoners. It was estimated that the Code led to a reduction of up to 50% in the convict population receiving short-term prison sentences.[96] However in the meantime, the Code was also subjected to criticism for its failure to adapt itself to peculiarities, e.g. customs and traditions, and the economic exigencies of the country, which were found to be an inevitable outcome of the fact that its principal author was a foreign scholar. [97] It was therefore believed that many institutions that the Code envisaged would remain without a practical enforcement. Soon, the practice of the Penal Enforcement Code confirmed what its sceptics believed: enforcement of such a regime under current conditions would be "utopistic".[98] Alternatives to short-term imprisonment could not be made use of to

[91] *Ibid.*, Section 8 (2) and (3).

[92] *Ibid.*, Section 6.

[93] *Ibid.*, Section 5.

[94] *Ibid* Section 5/2.

[95] *Ibid.*, Section 5/12.

[96] Yücel calculated that prior to 1965 the proportion of the prisoners who received prison sentences was 75 percent, after this year it reduced to 20–25 percent. Yücel, M., T. (1987) Hürriyeti Baglayici Cezaya Alternatifler: Dünyadaki Görünüm, *Adalet Dergisi*, vol. 78, no 1, pp. 95–100, p. 97.

[97] Günal (1965b) *op. cit.*, p. 897.

[98] Günal, Y. (1967) Avrupa Ceza Hukukunun Birlestirilmesinin Türkiye ile Ilgisi, *Ankara Üniversitesi Siyasal Bilgiler Fakültesi*, vo. 22, no 2, pp. 219–226, p. 225.

the desired extent, and overall the Penal Enforcement Code was only partially implemented.[99] Before going on and explaining the presumed deficiencies in this Code and reform initiatives, a brief look on the exceptional character of the Turkish penal justice is necessary.

5.4 At Odds with International Trends

The previous chapters of this study underlined that since the 1970s, the decline of faith in the notion of rehabilitation and 'politicisation' of crime and justice issues shaped the approach towards prisons and its alternatives in the western countries. During the same period in Turkey, it is hardly possible to identify a similar move that provided a context from which such themes as diversion and decarceration became the focus of government policy.[100] The exceptional position of Turkey compared to the countries which followed more or less a common pattern in Europe can be explained with the very dynamics of the penal justice that has been formed by a series of legal, cultural, sociological and political grounds.

In the preceding section, it has been argued that the Turkish prison policy was driven largely out of financial and pragmatic necessities rather than calculated penological approaches. Indeed, a rehabilitative approach based on therapy towards prison inmates, as elsewhere, would have been a utopian ideal to sustain in Turkey, where the most basic requirements of prisons remained unmet. Hence, as was emphasised in the first section of this chapter, first mention must be given to financial constraints.[101] Until 1961, the proportion of the money which had been allocated to the Ministry of Justice in the general budget amounted to only 3%. This proportion was reduced afterwards to 1%.[102] Hence, not surprisingly, in 1994,

---

[99]Erdem, M., R. (2000) Kisa Süreli Hürriyeti Baglayici Cezalarin Infazi ve Yeni Secenekler in Goethe Institut and Baskent Universitesi, Infaz Hukukunun Sorunlari, *Probleme des Strafvollzugsrechts*, 24/25.11.2000, Goethe Institut and Baskent Universitesi, Ankara, pp. 192–213, p. 213, Özgenc, I. (2004), Özgenc, I. (2004) Suc ve Yaptirim Teorisine Iliskin Yeni Gelismeler Isiginda Türk Ceza Kanunu Tasarisi in Ergül, T. (ed.) *Türk Ceza Kanunu Reformu*, Birinci Kitap, TBB Yayinlari, Ankara, p. 57.

[100]In this context, see Istanbul Üniversitesi (1972) Ceza Adalet Reformu Ilkeleri, Sempozyumu 24–26 Subat 1972, Sulhi Garan Matbaasi, Istanbul. Dönmezer acknowledged rather timidly that "Our country has not as yet reached the level to deal with the challenges of criminal justice reform, with its criminological and sociological methods... (therefore) a wider-reaching ambitious reform of Turkish Criminal Justice would be unrealistic. Our priority must be first of all providing a functioning mechanism of justice... " as and Bayraktar, K. (1984) Ceza Hukukunda Suc Olmaktan Cikarma Akimi, *Istanbul Üniversitesi Hukuk Fakültesi Mecmuasi*, vol. 50, no 1–4, pp. 197–212.

[101]See in this context, for example, Dönmezer, S. (1997) Sahsi Hürriyeti Baglayici Cezalarin Infazinda Milletlerarasi Standartlar in Adalet Bakanligi, Türkiye'de Infaz Rejimi, Ankara, pp. 11–29, p.28.

[102]Ertosun, A., S. (2001) Ceza Infaz Sisteminin Sorunlari ve Cözüm Önerileri in *Infaz Hukukunun Sorunlari, Probleme des Strafvollzugsrechts*, 24/25.11.2000, Goethe Institut and Baskent Universitesi, Ankara, p. 265.

according to the Fifth United Nations Crime and Justice Statistics, Turkey along with Hungary, Colombia and Madagascar was one of the lowest spenders in criminal justice.[103]

Undoubtedly, the problem was and is not solely financial; it also has to do with the absence of any particular proactive strategy in dealing with criminality. Given that large scale sociological and criminological studies have not been conducted yet, it is somewhat hypothetical to discuss the true extent and the perceptions of criminality in Turkey. A relatively lengthy citation from the late historian Professor Uriel Heyd, in studying the Ottoman criminal law appears to give many clues about the perception of criminality, which many would agree maintains its truth also in current times:

> For European observers of the first half of the nineteenth century claim that among the Ottomans the various penalties were not considered degrading, and that the convicted criminal was *the object of compassion rather than of contempt*. After the penalty of a crime had been paid, no moral blemish adhered any longer to the honour of the offender or of his family; the son of an executed criminal, it was even said, did not feel ashamed of his father. . ..This attitude was explained by the people's resignation to the will of God, *their fatalistic belief in predestination*, and their submission to an age-old despotism which struck at random, without distinguishing the innocent from the guilty. (Emphases added.)

Indeed, there is ample evidence that popular wisdom is that the Turkish criminal is 'the object of compassion rather than contempt'. The description of prisoners as 'victim of her/his own predestination', 'kader kurbani', in the popular idiom (meaning that her/his fate was predetermined and cannot in fact be changed), reflects, for example, the conception of Quranic predestination that nullifies in certain way the free will of the individual offender. Such deterministic approach based on 'predestination' appears to have constituted the primary justification for clemency towards criminality that found its expression in the public discussions preceding the enactment of various amnesty laws.[104]

Not only culture and religion, but also Turkish legal culture specifically seems to reproduce different precepts for the dealing methods of criminality. For example, such concepts as diversion would have been too foreign for a system in which the principle of legality has a particular place. In order to understand such a great placement of faith in the legality principle, one has to understand the fact that the term 'discretion' and as such 'the expediency or opportunity principle', as opposed to its understanding in Anglo–American legal systems[105] and probably, to a certain

---

[103]Newman, G. (1999) *Global Report on Crime and Justice, United Nations Office for Drug Control and Crime Prevention Centre for International Crime Prevention*, Oxford University Press, New York.

[104]In this respect see, Demirbas, T. (2001) Af Tartismalari ve 4616 Sayili 23 Nisan 1999 Tarihine Kadar Islenen Suclardan Dolayi Sartla Saliverilmeye, Dava ve Cezalarin Ertelenmesine Dair Kanun, *Anayasa Yargisi*, vol. 18, pp. 87–97.

[105]For an understanding of the notion of discretion in Anglo-American legal discourse see for Nelken, D. (1997) Understanding Criminal Justice in Maguire, Morgan and Reiner, *op. cit.*, pp. 559–573, pp. 565–571.

extent in the German literature, has generally been seen as a potential cause of 'arbitrariness' in pre-trial decisions in the Turkish doctrine.[106] Until recently, the prevailing opinion in the literature rejected a policy facilitating discretion at the pre-court level, as it was believed that this would cause bias and selective prosecution policies.[107] Erem, one of the pioneers of Turkish criminal law, for example, appears to have been convinced of such a potential of the opportunity principle, and posited that "its exercise in a democratic system is unacceptable".[108] This approach of the Turkish doctrine in this respect may be explained by historical and 'current' distrust against administrative bodies, the sources of which ought in part to be sought in constitutional and legislative developments of Turkey.[109]

Another relevant issue which explains the inertia which has traditionally characterised the Turkish approach towards criminality is the preoccupation with political crisis.[110] It must be emphasised that in Turkey, crime and justice issues have never been a part of political discourse about which the major parties have had differences, as is most typically the case in England in the 1960s and 1970s. As correctly observed by Green, such issues have been eclipsed by the more basic

[106] Öztürk, B. (2001) Ist das Legalitätsprinzip zu halten, und welche rechtstaatliche Anforderungen haben für das Opportunitätsprinzip zu gelten? Aus türkischer Sicht in Hirsch, E., J.(ed.) *Krise des Strafrechts und der Kriminalwissenschaften?* Tagungsbeiträge eines Symposiums der Alexander von Humboldt Stiftung, Bonn Bad Godesberg (1–5 October 2000), Duncker & Humblot, Berlin, p. 329.

[107] Öztürk (1999), *op. cit.*, pp. 42–43.

[108] Erem, F. (1970) *Ceza Usulü Hukuku*, Ankara Üniversitesi Hukuk Fakültesi Yayinlari, Ankara, p. 211. It is argued in Kunter-Yenisey, at p. 168, "In the view of *the great danger* inherent in exercising the opportunity principle, we are of the view that mandatory prosecution is currently more suitable for our country" (emphasis added), Kunter, N. and Yenisey, F. (2002) *Muhakeme Hukuku Dali Olarak Ceza Muhakemesi Hukuku*, 12th edition, Beta, Istanbul.

[109] For an overview of constitutional developments and the developments in public law in Turkey, see Tanör, B. (1986), *op. cit.*, Gemalmaz, S. (1989) *The Institutionalization Process of the "Turkish Type of Democracy": A Politico Juridical Analysis of Human Rights*, Amac, Istanbul, Örücü, E. (1999) Turkey: A Survey of the Public Law Framework, *European Public Law*, vol. 5, no. 1, pp. 30–41, Özay, I., H. (1998) A Republic with Double Constitution, *Annales de la Facultés de Droit d'Istanbul, vol.* 48, pp. 101–109 and (2002) Democracy without "Demos": Namely "*Cracy*", *Annales de la Facultés de Droit d'Istanbul,* vol. 51, pp. 137–146, for an historical account containing developments until the 1990s see also, Ahmad, F. (1993) *op. cit.*

For a case study on corruption in Turkey, Green; P. (2005) Disaster by Design: Corruption, Construction and Catastrophe, *British Journal of Criminology,* vol. 45, no. 4, pp. 528–546, see also Tellenbach (1997) Türkei in Eser, A., Überhofen, M. and Huber, B. (eds.) *Korruptionsbekämpfung durch Strafrecht*, Max Planck Institut für ausländisches und internationales Strafrecht, Freiburg, pp. 617–653.

[110] Osman Dogru is right when he said that "in Turkey, political crimes drive policy more than ordinary crimes. Criminal policy is focussed on the indivisibility of the state or on political crimes which are covered by the Anti-Terror law and articles from the general criminal court. . .there are many articles included in the penal code so I think they did not need to change the basic rules relating to ordinary crimes-but political crimes, yes". (Expressed in an interview with Green, *see* Green, P. (2000) Criminal Justice and Democratisation in Turkey: the Paradox of Transition in Green, P. and Rutherford, A. (eds.) *Criminal Policy in Transition*, Hart Publishing, Oxford, p. 212.

imperatives of security, economy and control of the state.[111] Indeed, if there could be any talk of a penal policy, the response to political dissidence and terrorism was and has been at the heart of it, which has caused numerous changes and amendments in law that could be legitimately classified as 'panic legislation'.[112]

In contrast to the heavy preoccupation with political deviancy, the 'ordinary' type of criminality and the methods to address it received only a modicum of attention.[113] In fact, such issues as the conditions in prisons attracted broader attention, only after a large number of political offenders were confined in prisons,[114] in particular after the *coup d' état* in 1980. Afterwards pressure for prison conditions came largely from human rights organisations and Bar associations.[115] Thus, it should not come as a surprise that outside a narrow circle of academics, ordinary forms of criminality as an area of academic research invoked little interest. It may come as surprise for many to learn that as an academic discipline criminology has been almost subordinated to forensic medicine both in an institutional and theoretical context.[116] And hence, except for a number of now outdated textbooks, the examination of characteristics of criminality in Turkey appears to have been by and large unfulfilled as a research task.

An interesting 'case study' in this respect can be the approach towards juvenile criminality. In Turkey, it was not until 1979 that a law on juvenile court was enacted.[117] If one considers the 'insiders' view' on the juvenile criminality, it can

---

[111]Green (2000) *op. cit.*, p. 212.

[112]Örücü observes rightly that "most developments in Turkish public law, including the Constitutions, have been and still are in reaction to immediate past events and problems, with structures and documents being blamed for failures and exchange for other models when facing problems which might be better described as a consequence of a failing 'human factor'." p. 35, Örücü (1999) *op. cit.*, Sokullu-Akinci (2005), *op. cit.*, p. 11.

[113]In this respect Professor Feridun Yenisey answered Green as "...policy-no there is no policy, the government does not have a word for criminal justice policy-making: 'policies' are dictated by daily needs, they just want to cover their daily needs". Green, *op. cit.*, p. 257. Green concludes that "crime control operates in Turkey without a formalised and coherent criminal policy and without the ideological framework of fear of crime". Green, *op. cit.*, p. 213.

[114]As Sarihan notes that the experience of offenders of political offences in particular in prisons and remand centres as subject of democratic opposition gave impulse in general the treatment of offenders in the wider public discussions, Sarihan, S. (2002) Türkiye'deki Cezaevleri Sorunu ve Tarihsel Gelisimi in Istanbul Barosu Cezaevleri Calisma Grubu, *Cezaevleri Sempozyumu* (29–30 Haziran 2002), pp. 28–37, p. 34. See also Demirbas, T. (2006) Ceza ve Güvenlik Tedbirlerinin Infazi Hakkinda Kanunun Genel Degerlendirmesi, *Ceza Hukuku Dergisi*, vol. 1, no 1, pp. 19–29, pp. 20–21.

[115]Özok, S. (2004) Barolarin Cocuk Hareketindeki Rolü (Bir Örnek: Kocaeli Barosu Cocuk Haklari Komisyonu'nun Calismalari), *Türkiye Barolar Birligi Dergisi*, vol. 51, pp. 208–212.

[116]For example the chapter 'Juvenile Justice in Turkey' in the following book was written by three scholars all of which worked for the Istanbul University Institute of Forensic Medicine: Atasoy, S, Baskan, M., T. and Ziyalar, N. (2006) Juvenile Justice in Turkey Friday, P. and Ren, X. (eds.) *Delinquency and Juvenile Justice in the Non-Western World*, Criminal Justice Press, Monsey.

[117]Yurtcan, E. (1980) Child in Turkish Criminal Law and Criminal Procedure Law, *Annales de la Facultés de Droit d'Istanbul, vol.* 27, no 43, pp. 237–242.

be seen that the delay of almost a century may well have been a consequence of the very perception of juvenile criminality. Indeed, Turkish legal scholars were of the view that juvenile delinquency in Turkey was not of a comparable scale to that which occurred in the western countries.[118] One of the few research studies on juvenile delinquency conducted by Dönmezer on the impact of industrialisation upon juvenile delinquency in a district called Eregli,[119] claimed that because the industrialisation process, due to "social values, Islamic customs and very strong family structures",[120] did not bring about such consequences as occurred in the West, the delinquency rate in Turkey is low. Yenisey, in his brief description of juvenile delinquency in Turkey, in a related but distinct vein argued that:

> The criminal acts of juveniles (in Turkey) are mostly of an antisocial nature, and public opinion does not view them as major crime. Thus there is a tolerant attitude and they are rarely reported to the authorities.[121]

There certainly may have been a tolerant attitude as Yenisey argues, but the tolerance appears also to mean neglect in that the methods of dealing with the rest of juvenile offenders clearly demonstrated an absence of a particular strategy with regard to juvenile criminality. Even after the enactment of a special law for juvenile offenders in 1979, this remained the case.[122] Two innovations of the Juvenile Court Law required a long time for the translation of the practice: the establishment of juvenile courts and institutions necessary for the implementation of the measures specified by the respective law. According to this law, each province and district with a population above one hundred thousand was to establish a juvenile court.[123] Yet, it was not until 1987 that the Juvenile Court Law came into effect. In this year, juvenile courts were established in four provinces: Istanbul, Ankara, Izmir and Trabzon.[124] Again, for the first time the law enacted measures the implementation of which would involve greater co-operation with social work agencies such as the placement of the juvenile in a care institution. As these institutions were rather limited, in a provisional section it was explicitly stipulated that the law would come into effect within a 1-year period in order to expand the number of social work institutions. However in 1980, the implementation of this law was suspended again

---

[118]Gölcüklü, F. (1962b) Türkiye'de Cocuk Suclulugu, *Ankara Üniversitesi Siyasal Bilgiler Fakültesi Dergisi*, vol.11, no 3, pp. 151–181. See also the scripts of the following symposiums: Adalet Bakanligi (1985) *Türkiye Teröristlerin Rehabilitasyonu Konulu Uluslararasi Sempozyum ile ilgili Rapor* (Hizmete Özel), Ankara, Cocuklari Suc ve Suclulardan Koruma Vakfi (2002) *Cocuk Istismari ve Önleme Konulu Panel*, Istanbul, pp. 27–39.

[119]Dönmezer, S. (1974) Criminality in a Small Community of Rapid Urbanisation and Industrialisation (The Eregli Project), *Annales de la Faculteś de Droit d'Istanbul,* vol. 22, no 4, pp. 55–71.

[120]Dönmezer (1974), *op. cit*., p. 56.

[121]Yenisey, F. (1992) Juvenile Delinquency in Turkey in Messmer and Otto, *op. cit*., pp. 409–415, p. 410. In this context, see also Demirbas, T. (2005) *Kriminoloji*, 2nd edition, Seckin, Ankara, pp. 151–152.

[122]Law no 2253, 7.11.1979, Official Gazette, 21.11.1979.

[123]*Ibid.*, Section 1.

[124]In 2002, two more juvenile courts were created in Kocaeli and Diyarbakir.

on the grounds that due to inadequate infrastructure, it was incapable of meeting the demands of legislation.[125] Consequently, even after the practical enforcement of the law, from 1982 onwards, such institutions have been by and large absent.

5.5 Towards the Reform

In view of significant changes in the penal codes of Italy, France and Germany, all of which were carefully followed by Turkish legal scholars, there was a widespread feeling in the beginning of 1980s that the existing penal code was by and large antiquated both in terms of its content and language. Although the code was subjected to change several times,[126] many believed that a comprehensive change was indispensable to keep up with the spirit of modern times. This was seen as particularly necessary, on the grounds that many provisions enacted following the Rocco Code in the Penal Code reflected clearly the authoritarian and repressive tendencies of the fascist regime in Italy, as mentioned above.[127]

A thoroughgoing reform of the penal code was not solely a scholarly demand. During this time, centred around such issues as freedom of expression and prevention of torture, the reform also became an issue of Turkish foreign policy. Just before the millennium, Turkey's accession process to the European Union, after long years of waiting, was gaining a significant momentum.[128] In 1999, in the Helsinki Summit the candidacy status of Turkey to accede to the European Union was officially recognised, on the basis of the same criteria as applied to other countries.[129] At this Summit, the European Union also recognised

[125]Section 18 of the Law no 2552, 6.11.1981. Official Gazette 25345. See, Akyüz, Y. (2002) Cocuk Suclulugu Konusunda Türk Egitim Tarihinde Ilk Önemli Arastirma in *I. Ulusal Cocuk ve Suc, Nedenler ve Önleme Calismalari Sempozyumu*, 29–30 Mart 2001, pp. 35–50.

[126]On this theme, see e.g. Yenisey, F. (1984) Die Entwicklungen im türkischen Strafrecht von 1960 bis 1983, *Zeitschrift für die gesamte Strafrechtswissenschaft*, vol. 96, no 1, pp. 212–240.

[127]See an interview made with Professor Adem Sözüer, *Radikal*, 25.04.2004.

[128]In 1949, Turkey participated in the foundation of the Council of Europe. In 1952, she became a member of the NATO. After Turkey's application for an associate membership to the European Economic Community in 1957, this status was granted under the Ankara agreement in 1963. After the military intervention in the 1980 Turkey and Europe relations were frozen. In 1987, an application for membership in the European Union was made. However, this application was dismissed on the ground that Turkey was as yet ready for the membership. Despite the initial rejection, in 1995, Turkey and European Union signed Customs' Union agreement, for a brief summary see, Yesilada, B. (2002) Turkey's Candidacy for EU Membership, *Middle East Journal*, vol. 56, no 1, pp. 94–111.

[129]See Baykal, S. (2002) Turkey-EU Relations in the Aftermath of the Helsinki Summit: An Analysis of Copenhagen Political Criteria in the Light of the Accession Partnership, National Programme and the Regular Reports, *Ankara Review of European Studies*, vol. 2, no 3, pp. 15–63. For a brief summary of the summit accessible from the following link: http://europa.eu/legislation_summaries/enlargement/ongoing_enlargement/e40113_en.htm.

a pre-accession strategy for the membership of Turkey.[130] In March 2001, the Council of Ministers adopted a European Union and Turkey Accession Partnership that established the short- and medium-term measures necessary to ensure Turkey's fulfilment of the membership criteria.[131] Among others, the Accession Partnership determined medium term objectives to be the strengthening of human rights, the prevention of the practices and abolishment of the death penalty and the improvement of prison conditions. In the same year, such demands of the European Union were addressed in the National Programme,[132] among which a re-codification of penal law was recognised as a medium term objective. Consequently, drawing further stimulus from the desire to be the fully-fledged member of the European Union in this way, the quest for a new penal code found its proponents in wider circles

As far as the penal system is concerned, one of the major concerns that lay at the forefront of discussions was the 'unification' of the penal regime, which was in part distinctly regulated by the Penal Code and the Penal Enforcement Code. In a more specific context, in the face of an increasing prison population, reforming the sanction system was considered particularly urgent.[133] Conventionally, the pressures of the prison system in Turkey were attempted to be solved by means of amnesty decrees.[134] Of these, the Amnesty Law (no.1803) in 1974 that was enacted after the military intervention in 1971[135] was particularly noteworthy, because it led to a sharp decline in the prison population.[136] However, as the preceding amnesty, it provided only a reduction over the short term and a temporary amelioration in

[130]Following Copenhagen criteria, which were adopted at the Copenhagen Summit of 1993, it was recognised that membership requires:

that the candidate State has achieved stability of institutions guaranteeing democracy, the rule of law, human rights and respect for and protection of minorities,

the existence of a functioning market economy, as well as the capacity to cope with competitive pressure and market forces within the Union,

the ability to take on the obligations of membership, including adherence to the aims of political, economic and monetary union. Accessible from the following link: http://europa.eu/scadplus/glossary/accession_criteria_copenhague_en.htm.

[131]See the document in the following link: http://eurlex.europa.eu/smartapi/cgi/sga_doc?smartapi!celexplus!prod!DocNumber&lg=en& type_doc=Decision&an_doc=2001&nu_doc=235.

[132]Official Gazette, 24.03.2001.

[133]Saglam, M., Y. (2000) Infaz Hukukunun Sorunlari in Izmir Barosu, *Yargi Reformu Sempozyumu* (5–8 Nisan 2000), pp. 746–754.

[134]Demirbas (2001) *op. cit.*, see also Soyaslan, D. (2001) Af, *Anayasa Yargisi*, vol. 18, pp. 412–436. Chief among them were the amnesty laws that were passed in 1933, 1938, 1950, 1960, 1963, 1966 and 1974.

[135]Law no 1803, 15.5.1974, Official Gazette, 18.5.1974.

[136]Pursuant to this law, 20,754 convicts were released from prisons. See also, Yücel, M., T. (1977) Ceza Infaz Kurumlarindaki Gerilim ve Secenek Yaptirimlar, *Adalet Dergisi*, vol. 68, no 5–6, pp. 325–335.

prison conditions.[137] In order to provide a permanent solution to the problem, the available sentencing options were deemed to require reconsideration.[138]

In this regard, it was recognised that alternative measures to imprisonment which were specified in the Penal Enforcement Code were, for the most part, without any practical meaning.[139] Numerous grounds were given for the explanation of this state of affairs. First and foremost, there were no such institutions as described in the Code or such organisations responsible for the supervision of the offender that would control the whereabouts of the offender. It is for this reason that in 1973, the provision on community service in the Penal Enforcement Code was repealed.[140] Second, the law provided no guidance as to the implementation of these measures, and lacking such guidance, courts were reluctant to impose such measures.[141] Third, there was a concurrence between alternatives to short custodial sentences, and the suspension of the execution of punishment in practice, whereby priority was given to the latter.[142]

Another field that was deemed to require change was the imposition and enforcement methods of fines. Although the amount of financial penalties was updated in 1949 and 1979,[143] due to strong changes in the inflation rate, the impact of this sanction was severely curtailed.[144] In order to alleviate this state of affairs, the Penal Code was amended in 1988[145] by the adoption of the proportion of the annually increase in the salary of public servants (determined each year by the Budget Law), as a basis. Nonetheless, under the pressure of the deprecation in the monetary value the system of fines appeared to be far from an effective system and this was observed to lead a consequent inclination of courts to mete out custodial sentences in lieu of fines.[146]

---

[137]Yücel (1977) *op. cit.*, pp. 325–335.

[138]Clearly articulated in Ertosun (2001) *op. cit.*, pp. 266–275.

[139]Erdem (2000) *op. cit.*, pp. 192–213, p. 213, Özgenc (2004) *op. cit.*, p. 57.

[140]Law no 1712, 3.5.1973, Official Gazette, 11.5.1973.

[141]Erdem (2000), *op. cit.*, p. 197. See for an early account on the confusion caused by the Penal Enforcement Code, Dönmezer, S. (1967) Cezalarin Infazi Hakkinda Kanun ve Bu Kanunla Ilgili Bazi Problemler, Yargitay Kararlari, *Istanbul Üniversitesi Hukuk Fakültesi Mecmuasi*, vol. 32, no 1–4, pp. 22–33, Mengüc, A.(1968), *op. cit.*, pp. 148–153.

[142]Bolle, P., H. and Yarsuvat, D. (2002) *Infaz Hukuku Alaninda Güncel Sorunlar ve Yeni Yaklasimlar*, Galatasaray Semineri Notlari, 4–7 Eylül 2002, Galatasaray Ünivesitesi, Istanbul, p. 38.

[143]Law no 5435, 10.06.1949, Official Gazette, 16.6.1949. Law no 2248 date 12.06.1979, Official Gazette, 22.6.1979.

[144]Bolle and Yarsuvat, *op. cit.*, Saglam, *op. cit.*, p. 749.

[145]Law no 3506 date 07.12.1988, Official Gazette 14.12.1988.

[146]Bolle and Yarsuvat, *op. cit.*, pp. 174–175.

5.6 The Reform

5.6.1 The Preparation of the New Penal Code

The recent history of the renewal of the Penal Code goes back to the beginning of the 1980s.[147] In 1985, the Ministry of Justice, constituted under the presidency of Professor Sulhi Dönmezer the first commission, composed of academics, members of the judiciary and officers from the judicial administration. Without envisaging major changes in the existing penal code this commission produced the draft of 1987, the so-called Dönmezer-draft. This draft had certain reminiscences to the French Penal Code.[148] However, on the whole, it substantially retained the provisions of the previous penal code. The draftspersons of the preliminary draft conceptualised the 'criminal and penal policy' upon which it is predicated as

> guaranteeing and protecting human rights and freedoms, reinforcing the respect for human personality without neglecting public protection and the maintenance of the balance between protection of individual rights and freedoms and public.[149]

This repetitious statement on the objective of 'criminal and penal policy' as protection of public and then with a confused terminology, human rights and freedom, and personal rights and freedoms was not incidental. The state's failure to prevent serious human rights violations, particularly with regard to ill-treatment of suspects while in police custody, after the *coup d'état* on September 12th 1980, was subjected to vigorous criticism by both domestic and international human rights authorities.[150] The prison population of Turkey was then booming across Europe.[151] In 1984, there were 76,258 persons in prisons and the imprisonment rate per 100,000 population was 171.

Hence, it was no surprise that 'reintegration' of offenders into community under the draft acquired special attention. A proposal in this direction was the abolishment of such ancillary and auxiliary punishments as continuing life time 'disqualification from public service' and 'disqualification from exercising a certain profession, art and trade'. Another innovation of the preliminary draft, which was seen as a necessary implication of a reintegrative perspective was spelling out the factors which were to guide the determination of punishment. This was also in reaction to

---

[147] Artuk and Cinar, *op. cit.*, pp. 48–54.

[148] The French Penal Code was considered the most excellent work of contemporary criminal law. Türk Ceza Kanunu Öntasarisi, 1997, Adalet Bakanligi, p. 136.

[149] Türk Ceza Kanunu Öntasarisi 1997, p.142.

[150] See e.g., Amnesty International (1984) *Amnesty International Documentation on Torture in Turkey*, University of Michigan, For a detailed account from Turkish perspective, see Gemalmaz (1989) *op. cit.*

[151] See, Council of Europe (1984) *Prison Information Bulletin* vol. 2, no.3. At this time, the prison population of England and Wales was 41,310 and that of Germany was 64,091. Imprisonment rate per 100,000 population in England and Wales was 83.3, while in Germany this figure was 104.4.

Turkish praxis, imposing penalties from the minimum level as prescribed in the code, as will be revisited below.[152] Under the preliminary draft, while 'heavy imprisonment' was to be repealed, the 'light' imprisonment and imprisonment categories were to be retained. This was explained as a logical outcome of the retention of the classification of offences as 'crimes' and 'contraventions'. In the preliminary draft, a number of security measures such as committal to therapy were provided, but detailed provisions on them was to be deferred to an ordinance.

The authors of the preliminary draft viewed the Law on Juvenile Courts as failing to reflect contemporary tendencies in juvenile justice in terms of its sanction catalogue, and to reveal the particular nature of juvenile adjudication and sentencing.[153] A reformulation of certain provisions and their incorporation to the penal code, as opposed to a separate law concerning juvenile offenders, was therefore considered essential. On these grounds, the preliminary draft envisaged a complete repeal of the existing provisions of the juvenile court law. It contained a separate section on the jurisdiction of the juvenile court and its procedures, the penal liability of juvenile offenders, and their sentencing.

Not many appear to have 'dared' to raise objections to the Dönmezer draft. Of those who did raise objections, those who directed criticism to the draft's increase in sanction severity for 'political offences'[154] and its retention of the death penalty[155] were particularly vocal. In 1989, the re-codification initiatives were officially resumed. Under the presidency of Dönmezer, with the participation of new members, another commission remained largely faithful to the preliminary draft. Consequently, the preliminary draft did not become the law, but some of its provisions were incorporated into law.[156]

A new initiative to draft a new penal code was launched in 1997.[157] The draft was similar to its precursor, but with some important modifications, e.g. abolishment of the death penalty. In 2000, the revised version of a new draft was adopted as an official draft. Noteworthy is that this draft was marked by the efforts of women's organisations to change the overall regulation of sexual offences, which were partly fruitful.[158] Three year later, in 2003, the respective draft was submitted to the Parliamentary Commission. In the Parliamentary Commission, which included young (associate) professors of criminal law the draft code was substantially altered

---

[152]See below.

[153]1997 Türk Ceza Kanunu Öntasarisi, p. 139.

[154]Toroslu, N. (1987) *Nasil bir Ceza Kanunu*, V Yayinlari, Ankara. For a summary of critics, see Artuk and Cinar, *op. cit.*, p. 51.

[155]On which a de facto moratorium since 1984 existed. See, Gemalmaz, S. (2002) The Death Penalty in Turkey (1920–2001) Facts, Truths and Illusions, *Criminal Law Forum*, vol. 13, no 1, pp. 91–122.

[156]In this context, se Yenisey, F. (1997) 'Zum türkischen Straf- und Strafprozessrecht: Entwicklungen zwischen 1983 and 1995, *Zeitschrift für die gesamte Strafrechtswissenschaft*, vol. 109, no 1, pp. 243–264.

[157]Adalet Bakanligi (1997) Türk Ceza Kanunu Öntasarisi 1997, Ankara.

[158]Artuk and Cinar, *op. cit.*, p. 64.

within a relatively short span of time,[159] such that it became another draft both in the eyes of the members of the commission and in wider circles.[160]

The authors emphasised that the new penal code should not be a mere revision of the old penal code; it ought to inaugurate a new era.[161] The basic principles that guided the draft have been heralded as the protection of the public, the principle of legality (both in application and in interpretation of law), the principle of culpability, human rights (the protection of the individual against the arbitrary power of the state) and the *ultima-ratio* (subsidiary) role of criminal law.[162] Interestingly, and despite subsequent objections of many commentators the draft code comprised a provision on the purpose of the penal code.[163] The purpose of the Penal Code therein is stated as "the protection of personal rights and freedoms, public order and security, the rule of law (*Hukuk Devleti*, *Rechtsstaat*), public health and environment and public peace and prevention of crimes".[164] By this provision, the multi-purpose character of a modern penal code is emphasised, but also the draftspersons were of the view that due to the notorious record of Turkish political history special emphasis should be placed on prevention of misuse of penal law.

In academic and professional circles, the groundbreaking draft and its authors were subjected to unusually intense criticism.[165] Admittedly, part of this criticism

---

[159]See commenting this issue the then Minister of Justice, Cemil Cicek, *Sabah*, 15/5/2005.

[160]Sözüer (2008) *op. cit.*, p. 14.

[161]Sözüer (2008) *op. cit.*, p. 37.

[162]See, Sözüer (2007) *op. cit.*, pp. 712–749, Özgenc (2004) *op. cit.*, also Sözüer, A. (2004) Toplumsal Degisim Sürecinde *Türk Ceza Kanunu Reformu* in Ergül, T. (ed.) Türk Ceza Kanunu Reformu, Birinci Kitap, TBB Yayinlari, Ankara, pp. 33–49.

[163]Artuk and Cinar (2004) *op. cit.*, p. 70, Tezcan, D. and Erdem, M., R. (2004) Dokuz Eylül Üniversitesi Hukuk Fakültesi'nin TCK Tasarisi Hakkindaki Raporu in Ergül (2004), *op. cit.*, p. 329.

[164]Critically, Tezcan and Erdem, *op. cit.*, p. 329. Sözüer responds such critics by emphasising that the commission aimed to demonstrate in the light of which principles the code must be interpreted. In so doing, the intention was the prevention of the misuse of the law against the individual rights and freedoms, Sözüer (2004) *op. cit.* See also, Mahmutoglu, F., S. (2004) TBMM Adalet Komisyonu'nda Kabul Edilen Türk Ceza Kanunu Tasarisi Hakkinda Görüs in Ergül, *op. cit.*, p. 357–378, p. 360.

[165]Toroslu, N. and Ersoy, Y. (2004) Kanunlasmamasi Gereken Bir Tasari in Ergül (2004) *op. cit.*, Ankara, pp. 1–20, in this book also the following contributions: Bayraktar, K. (2004) Türk Ceza Kanunu Tasarisina Iliskin Genel Bir Degerlendirme ve Genel Hükümler Üzereine Birkac Elestiri, pp. 21–35, Artuk and Cinar (2004), *op. cit.*, the report of the Galatasaray University with the title 'Türk Ceza Kanunu Tasarisi Hakkinda Galatasaray Üniversitesi'nin Görüs'ü in Ergül (2004) *op. cit.*, pp. 285–317, Tezcan and Erdem (2004), *op. cit.*, pp. 327–355. Kanadoglu, S. (2005) Yeni Türk Ceza Kanununun Genel Hükümlerine Iliskin Düsünceler, *Yeditepe Üniversitesi Hukuk Fakültesi Dergisi*, vol. 2, no 2, pp. 329–340, for the critical opinions of various civil society organisations, see *Radikal*, 7.5.2005. In response to the critics see, Sözüer (2004), (2007) and (2008), *op. cit.*

For a more 'neutral' approach see, Sokullu-Akinci, F. (2005) Suc Siyaseti Baglaminda Yeni Türk Ceza Kanunu'nun Genel Degerlendirilmesi, *Kazanci Hukuk Dergisi*, no 5, pp. 11–15. From a German perspective see, Roxin, C. and Isfen, O. (2005) *Goltdammer's Archiv für Strafrecht*, vol.

was politically motivated. It reflected an anxiety for an allegedly hidden agenda which the pro-Islamic incumbent party, Justice and Development Party (*Adalet ve Kalkinma Partisi*) intended to pursue. The draft article on the re-criminalisation of adultery in public discussions, which was highly sensationalised with media reports, was deemed a sign for it. Furthermore, for many, the timing of the reform, on the eve of the commencement of the formal membership negotiations with the European Union, represented a devastating pressure factor under which a historical chance of the renewal of the penal code would be very likely to be wasted.[166] It was argued that the issue of creating a new penal code was too crucial to be the subject of narrow political advantage, for nowhere in the entire legal field is more at stake for the individual.

The majority of members of academic and administration of the Bar Associations were of the view that the substantial number of differences that the draft penal code contained would mean a rejection of the hitherto established principles of Turkish dogmatic and case law. If implemented, this would have some disastrous consequences for the society and criminal justice system.[167] Such a comprehensive change in law required a more thorough scholarly examination of foreign penal codes and case law, and collection of data from criminological and sociological research. To them, the fragmented nature of the draft code, due to the selection of various provisions from German, Swiss, but also Spanish, Polish and Russian penal code, indicated that the draft code fails to offer an enduring, coherent and consistent model for legislation.[168] By abandoning in this way the long established

152, pp. 228–245. Tellenbach, S. (2005) *Zum neuen türkischen Strafgesetzbuch*, pp.76–93 in KAS-Auslandsinformationen, accessible from the following link:http://www.kas.de/wf/doc/kas_6625-544-1-30.pdf.

[166]Interestingly a research study conducted by Sancar and Atilgan found that a substantial portion of the judges and prosecutors have suspicious about the legal reforms that have been introduced as part of the EU harmonisation process. Sancar, M. and Atilgan, E., Ü. (2009) "*Adalet Biraz Es Geciliyor...*" *Demokratiklesme Sürecinde Hakimler ve Savcilar,* TESEV, Istanbul, p. 4.

[167]Demirbas, T. (2005) *Ceza Hukuku Genel Hükümler*, Seckin, Ankara, in preface.

[168]Kanadoglu argues that the new Penal Code was hastened with the aim to catch the deadline of the Progress Report of the European Union Commission and the Summit of 17 December, and hence it was prepared without due regard to the Turkish doctrine and the case law of the Cassation Court, Kanadoglu, *op. cit.*, p. 320. Toroslu and Ersoy argued that "the draft will not bring Turkey forth, rather it will bring the country back, it will destroy the fundamentals of Turkish criminal law application and doctrine, so the potential expectations of the European Union will not met, and in practice it will cause enormous difficulties, as it will lead to reconsideration of a considerable amount of cases. Furthermore, contrary to the proclamation of its authors, the draft was not made up with due regard to the opinions of Turkish scholars or knowledge derived from Turkish practice". Toroslu and Ersoy (2004) *op. cit.*, p. 3. Toroslu and Ersoy also think that "preparing a penal code that is consistent, systematic and reflecting a certain criminal law philosophy on the whole is not possible. The sole possible way is today whenever necessary to make necessary changes in the existing code or adopting a penal code from another country which having considering the basic philosophy, we find that it is suitable for us and compatible with our system". Toroslu and Ersoy, *op. cit.*, p. 1.

In the Report of the University of Galatasaray it was stated that "...new concepts and institutions are established at the expense of damaging certain concepts and institutions which are deeply conventions of the penal code, in such areas of law as attempt, participation, mistake of law and so on, a new code would cause great confusion and uncertainty. From a legal technique view, despite the proclamation of its authors, it did not contain accurate, clear and concise statements in various provisions. Due to the presence of outdated expressions it was also terminologically thus far the intentions of the penal reform since the 1980s. Consequently, many concluded that a proper advance preparation is necessary to produce a sustainable code which corresponds with the Turkish dogmatic and accumulated case law, if a wholesale change in law was deemed indispensable by the legislature.

Despite apparent displeasure with the draft code, in December 2004, with a small number of changes, it gained legislative recognition.[169] Following the Penal Code, the Child[170] Protection Law[171] brought also important changes, symbolising a significant shift in approach towards juvenile criminality. Finally, the Law on Enforcement of Custodial Sentences and Security Measures incorporated the international agreements on prison rules and the administration of custodial sentences.[172]

Before going on and discussing the innovations of the reform and its implications in numerical terms, as will be touched upon, it must be emphasised not only the swift drafting penal code overall, but specifically the new penal regime has encountered scepticism and uncertainties in some quarters. Against the penal regime, the objection has been raised that the range of sentencing options in the new Penal Code lacks sufficient diversity to address the needs of different offender categories.[173] Interestingly, this claim is supported by the perceived flexibility in the German and French systems in providing greater individualisation of punishment. In view of various options the Penal Code encompasses doubts may be cast on the reliability on this argument. From the context of 'imprisonment alternatives' this point will be discussed further later on this study. In what follows, the current sentencing framework that has been created by the recent legislation will be elaborated in details.

---

embedded in Turkish law. In other words, the concepts and institutions which through case law and doctrine have become settled down and gained general acceptance are now turned up side down, in this way a significant accumulation would be wiped away". p. 12.

169 Mahmutoglu, F., S. (2008) Das neue türkische Strafgesetzbuch, Allgemeiner Teil, *Annales de la Facultés de Droit d'Istanbul,* vol. 58, no.1–4, pp. 35–48.

170 There is an increasing sensitivity for the use of the word 'child' in Turkish legal phraseology. In harmony with this move, here the word 'child' as a literal translation of the Turkish word 'cocuk' will be used. See e.g., Güven, I. and Akco, S. (2004) Yeni Bir Dünya Icin Yeni Bir Dil Gerekir, *Türkiye Barolar Birligi Dergisi*, vol. 51, pp. 197–207.

171 Law no 5395, 3.7.2005, Official Gazette, 15.7.2005.

172 See, Sokullu-Akinci, F. (2006) No Midnight Express: Prison Reform of Turkey on the Way to Europe, *Annales de la Facultés de Droit d'Istanbul*, vol. 56, no 1–4, pp. 61–91.

173 The Report of the University of Galatasaray, *op. cit.*, p. 302, Artuk, M. (2007) Türk Ceza Hukukunda Yaptirimlar Sistemi, *Ceza Hukuku Dergisi*, vol. 2, no. 4, pp. 61–77.

5.7 Current Legal Framework

In the previous penal code, sentencing was regulated by a small number of provisions. Section 29 of the former code stated that "unless explicitly provided by law, punishments can neither be increased, nor decreased, nor changed". In the first version of this section, the rest of the following paragraph regulated the procedure to be pursued when both mitigation and aggravation factors which were specified by law occurred and the order of consideration of such factors as the age of the perpetrator, her/his state of mind, discretional mitigation (pursuant to Section 59[174]) and recidivism. In order to provide clarity, with an amendment to this section, in 1990, another paragraph was added to this provision.[175] Pursuant to this paragraph, in determining the individual punishment within the minimum and maximum limits, the following factors must be taken into account: the way of commission of offence, the means for its commission, the importance of the subject of offence, its time and scene, the gravity of damage or danger, the degree of intention or negligence, the motives and reasons for the offence, the perpetrator's aims, her/his previous history, personal and social situation, behaviours after the commission of the offence and other relevant factors. The reasons for the fixed punishment were to be given in the judgement, even if a penalty had been meted out from the minimum limit as prescribed in law.[176] Due to the latter requirement, courts tended to impose punishments from the minimum limit, since otherwise when the specified punishment exceeds the minimum limit, it has to be justified in the decision.[177] Where such a justification was not explicitly spelled out, the judgement was quashed by the Cassation Court.[178]

The new Turkish Penal Code provides detailed guidance to courts as to the determination of punishment. Section 61 of the new Turkish Penal Code, by taking the following into consideration the court determines the punishment

---

[174]Section 59, it was stated that: "Beside the mitigating grounds which are provided by law, wherever discretionary matters of extenuation in favour of the offender are accepted by the court, heavy imprisonment for life, instead of death, and heavy imprisonment for thirty years, instead of heavy imprisonment for life, shall be imposed. Other punishments shall be reduced by not more than one sixth".

[175]Law no 3679, 21.11.1990, Official Gazette 29.11.1990.

[176]Section 29/8/last clause of the previous Turkish Penal Code.

[177]See numerous decisions cited in Icel, K., Sokullu-Akinci, F., Özgenc, I., Sözüer, A., Mahmutoglu, F., S. and Ünver, Y. (2000) *Yaptirim Teorisi*, Beta, Istanbul, p. 160.

[178]An interesting point here is to emphasise, as Pavarini notes, that such a mild approach of courts were also the case in Italy, where the severity of sentences under the Rocco Code was considerably reduced by the practice of courts. Pavarini goes on and suggests that: "To some extent, the very existence of a severe legislation lacking political legitimacy (since it was the offspring of fascism) has fostered the process of leniency in sentencing". Pavarini, *op. cit.*, p. 50.

within maximum and minimum limits prescribed by law for the offence concerned[179]:

(a) Manner of commission of the offence
(b) Means employed to commit the offence
(c) Time and scene of the commission of the offence
(d) Importance and value of the subject of the offence
(e) Severity of the harm caused by the offence
(f) Gravity of culpability through intention or negligence
(g) Aims and motives of the offender

As is clear from the wording of the respective provision, it is required that sentencers are concerned more with the offence rather than the offender, hence supremacy is given to retributive and general preventive considerations. However, at the same time by requiring courts in Section 62 to take the perpetrator's previous history, personal and social circumstances, behaviour after the commission of the offence and other circumstances, behaviour in the course of her/his adjudication, the potential impact of the punishment on the future life of the offender and other relevant factors as discretionary extenuating grounds, special preventive considerations are also addressed.[180]

As opposed to the previous system, where sanctions could be classified as main, ancillary and auxiliary penalties and security measures, the new Penal Code, adopts a two track system[181]: punishments and security measures similar to the German system. Under the Turkish Penal Code, two types of punishments are provided, which are to be meted out in accordance with the individual guilt: judicial fine and custodial sentences.[182] Furthermore, the current penal code differentiates three

---

[179] The respective section also reads that:

"(2) Where the offence has been committed through indirect intent or conscious negligence a reduction or an increase shall be made after the determination of punishment pursuant to subparagraph 1 of this provision.

(3) Where the items enumerated in subparagraph 1 constitute already elements of an offence, they shall not be separately considered.

(4) Where less or more grave modes of an offence requiring an increase or a decrease in punishment concur, the main punishment shall be first increased and then reduced.

(5) The punishment, which is determined in accordance with above, shall be finalised by application of provisions of attempt, participation, offences of continuation, unlawful provocation, infancy, insanity, grounds for diminishing penal responsibility and discretionary matters of discretional extenuation respectively".

[180] The statement of reasons makes it clear that Section 62 of the Penal Code does not enumerate extenuating grounds exhaustively.

[181] Özgenc (2004), *op. cit.*, p. 56.

[182] See, Cinar, A., R. (2005) Yeni Türk Ceza Yasasi'nda Cezalar, *Kazanci Hukuk Dergisi*, pp. 40–65, Centel, N., Zafer, H. and Cakmut, Ö. (2005) *Türk Ceza Hukukuna Giris*, Beta, Istanbul, pp. 570–578.

forms of custodial sentence[183]: life imprisonment, aggravated life imprisonment and temporary imprisonment.[184] Unless otherwise prescribed by law, the minimum term of imprisonment is 1 month and the maximum is 20 years.[185]

On the other track, security measures may be imposed on an offender where, for example, due to a mental disorder the culpability element is absent or where due to the kind of repeated offending as defined in the Penal Code an additional sentencing option is justified. The imposition of security measures is governed as in German law by the principle of proportionality.[186] Under the new Penal Code, security measures involve deprivation of exercising certain rights, confiscation of property,[187] confiscation of gains[188] and measures related to mentally ill offenders and juveniles and recidivists. Of these, mentally ill offenders are to be placed in high security health institutions for the purposes of protection and treatment. As opposed to the previous system, according to which the custody and medical treatment continued until the offender was cured,[189] from now on the criterion will not be solely cure but the state of dangerousness.[190] Section 57/2 of the Code states that a release decision can be given only upon the report prepared by the health commission of the institution in question indicating that the danger that the offender posed to society has ceased or considerably diminished. Courts are also urged to ensure that those offenders who have alcohol or drug abuse problems are placed in health

---

[183]In accordance with the abandonment of the classification of offences as crimes and contraventions, the previous categories as heavy imprisonment, imprisonment and light imprisonment were repealed as well as light and heavy fine.

[184]The difference of aggravated life sentence from that of basic form of life sentence (Article 48 of the Turkish Penal Code) as stipulated in this provision lies in the execution manner of these sentences. However, the form of execution of an aggravated life sentence is not provided therein, rather reference is made to the law and regulations concerned. The regime of aggravated life sentence is stipulated by Article 25 of the Execution of Punishments and Security Measures Code (Book I, Part II, Chapter 5). The most basic features of the regime laid down in this provision can be outlined as:

(i) solitary confinement,
(ii) restriction of rights in terms of participation in sportive and educational activities (no longer than one hour per day),
(iii) carrying an execution of a profession only under the permission of the prison administration,
(iv) limitations in her/his contact with the closest relatives (ascendants, descendants, spouse, sister and brothers and her/his legal guardian) (not more than ten minutes in fortnight),
(v) limitations in admittance of visits from such persons (fortnightly and no longer than one hour).

[185]Section 49/1 of the new Penal Code.

[186]*Ibid.*, Section 3 states a measure of security may be imposed in accordance with the gravity of the offence.

[187]Section 54 of the new Penal Code.

[188]*Ibid.*, Section 55.

[189]Section 46 of the previous Penal Code.

[190]Sözüer (2004), *op. cit.*, p.45, Özgenc (2004), *op. cit.*, p. 65.

institutions.[191] The treatment of such persons will continue until the health commission of the institution where the patient is kept in custody and treatment approves that s/he has recovered. Furthermore, with regard to recidivists, the previous system envisaging the increase in the main punishment was abandoned. In lieu of this, recidivists[192] are now liable to a differentiated form of penal enforcement that is set forth mainly in the Penal Enforcement Code.[193] In Turkish law, no punishment can be imposed on corporate bodies, only two forms of security measures, withdrawal of licence and confiscation can be imposed.[194]

What is novel in the new sentencing framework is that deprivation of certain rights is not any more qualified as ancillary or where applicable auxiliary consequences as it was in the previous Penal Code. In the new Penal Code, they are given an independent character.[195] Deprivation of exercising certain rights may be imposed in addition to a prison sentence for an intentional offence, unless the imposed imprisonment involves short-term and is suspended or the offender had not attained the age of 18 at the commission of the offence.[196] This measure may include deprivation from:

(a) Temporary or permanent membership in the Grand National Assembly or any other elective public agency, or holding public office or service assigned by or under the supervision of the government, province, municipality and village
(b) Being elected to office, voting and from other political rights
(c) Services regarding guardianship, except the parental rights and guardianship which a convict enjoys over her/his descendants.(pursuant to 53/3)
(d) Membership of board of directors or inspectors in foundations, associations, trade unions, company, co-operations and political parties
(e) Performing an art or trade assigned by a public office or a professional organisation qualified as public office

Until the expiry of the term of imprisonment, the convict will be deprived from using these rights. In cases where a prison sentence has been imposed for an offence it committed through abuse of the rights specified above, this period may be extended up to two fold of the imposed term. Exceptionally, prohibition from the respective rights may be ordered, where the offence was committed through misuse of such rights in addition to the fine. With regard to offences committed through negligence in performing an art, trade, profession or the traffic safety, an offender may be prohibited from performing such art, trade, profession or her/his driver's licence may be withdrawn for a period of 3 months to 3 years.

---

[191] Section 57/7 of the new Turkish Penal Code.

[192] Section 58 of the new Penal Code.

[193] Section 108 of the new Penal Enforcement Code.

[194] *Ibid.*, Section 60.

[195] Turhan, F. (2007) Yeni Türk Ceza Kanununda Güvenlik Tedbiri Olarak Hak Yoksunlugu ve Yasakliligin Hukuki Niteligi, Kapsam ve Kosullari Üzerine Bir Degerlendirme, *Ceza Hukuku Dergisi*, vol. 2, no 4, pp. 171–196.

[196] Section 53/4 of the new Turkish Penal Code.

After having underlined the duality in the Turkish sanction system, various sentencing options to which courts may resort will be outlined, but before that for the sake of comparison with other countries that are featured in this study, it is necessary to identify diversion options and their place in Turkish criminal justice in the next section.

5.7.1 Diversion

Above, the paramount importance of the legality principle in the Turkish jurisprudence has been highlighted. The inception of diversionary mechanisms with the reform of criminal and criminal procedure code is reflective of this stance, in that the exceptions that are recognised by the Turkish legislature appear to be tightly structured. It might therefore come as no surprise that the newly created measures have not been counted by some commentators as a pattern of exercising the principle of opportunity per se.[197] The possible explanation for this position would be the fact that the related provisions in question are seen as leaving no discretion to the prosecutor, when the conditions that are specified are met. However as this brief outline will suggest the public prosecutor effectively enjoys a wide discretionary option.

Victim-offender mediation is provided by Section 253 of the Turkish Criminal Procedure Code. Initially the Child Protection Law adopted a different approach. However, with the amendment in December 2006, by recognising that the general provisions of mediation are to be applied to juveniles, the related sections of the former law were repealed.[198] The respective provision empowers the public prosecutor, or with her/his instruction the police or judge, depending on the stage of the criminal proceeding, to seek mediation between victim and offender. In order to institute a mediation process, both parties must agree on the mediation and the accused person must acknowledge her/his guilt.

According to the aforementioned Section, mediation is possible for offences that are prosecuted upon the complaint of the injured person.[199] The law furthermore

[197]Yenisey, F. and Nuhoglu, A. (2006) *Muhakeme Hukuku Dali Olarak Ceza Muhakemesi Hukuku*, Kunter-Yenisey, 15th edition, Beta, Istanbul, pp. 178–179.

[198]According to Article 24 of the Child Protection Law, with regard to intentional crimes punishable by a prison sentence not exceeding two years, or regardless of the culpability of the offender with regard to all offences punishable by judicial fine, the case was to be referred to a mediation process. In respect of children who at the commission of the crime had not reached the age of 15, the maximum limit for a custodial sentence that provided by the first paragraph of the respective provision was determined as three years.

[199]According to Sokullu-Akıncı those offences are indeed "a few unimportant crimes". Considering the previous legislation she argued that "...reconciliation should be possible also for legal prosecution commenced by the public prosecutor, and if it is either a negligent crime or is a crime against persons, property and the like". Sokullu-Akinci, F. (2005) Criticism of the Provisions of the New Turkish Criminal Code, Concerning Restorative Justice, *Annales de la Facultés de Droit d'Istanbul*, vol. 54, pp. 3–10, p. 5.

lists a number of crimes, for which there shall be an automatic presumption in favour of the referral to mediation.[200] These are:

1. Certain forms of intentional injury, Section 86/88 of the Turkish Penal Code
2. Negligent bodily injury, Section 89
3. Trespass, Section 116
4. Abduction and seizure of children, Section 234
5. The disclosure of information and documents which amount to commercial, banking or customer secrets, Section 239 with exception of 239/4 of the Turkish Penal Code

The related provision furthermore provides that without explicit stipulation, mediation is not possible for offences that are covered by other laws (*Nebenstrafrecht*) concerning for example tax offences or offences that are laid down in the bankruptcy, patent and trademark laws. Sexual crimes and those offences for which effective remorse possibility *(tätige Reue)* is statutorily provided for cannot be dismissed through mediation.

When the required conditions are met, the public prosecutor is obliged to refer the case to a mediation process. Since December 2005, the mediation meeting, according to the present law can be convened by the prosecutor herself/himself or by a lawyer who is appointed by a Bar Association or a person with legal education. Until December 2006, the mediator could only be a lawyer whom both parties agreed on or an appointed lawyer who would organise and 'direct' the mediation meetings. The mediation is also possible during court proceedings if it becomes clear in the adjudication process that the offence in question falls within the scope of victim-offender mediation.

Another diversion option, conditional dismissal of prosecution, is laid down in Section 171 of the Criminal Procedure Code. The respective provision vests the public prosecutor with the power of diverting crimes that are processed upon the

---

[200]In the initial form of the law, victim-offender mediation was recognised only for those crimes that are (were) processed on a complaint of the injured person. These include assault, negligent bodily injury, sexual assault, marital rape and domestic violence (*Milliyet*, 21 April 2006). In the explanatory notes of the draft law, it is explicitly provided that mediation might be applied only for those cases involving minor crimes the application of which would leave courts sufficient time to deal with more serious cases (explanatory note on Section 39 of the Bill on the Penal Code). Nonetheless, such crime types as domestic violence and sexual assault were not seen as 'minor' in certain quarters, in particular by certain women organisations. *Milliyet*, 21 April 2006, see also Nuhoğlu, A. (2005) Uzlaşma Bakımından Şikayete Bağlı Suçlar, in Yenisey, F. (ed.) *Ceza Muhakemesi Hukukunda Uzlasma*, Arikan, Istanbul, pp. 281–284, p. 284. It was feared that this regulation of victim-offender mediation would exacerbate the particularly vulnerable position of women in Turkish society. Providing a mediation possibility for sexual assault would, it has been argued, undermine the general preventive effect of this offence. Similarly, a number of women organisations and Bars argued that victim-offender mediation used for domestic violence brings with it dangers of intimidation and emotional pressures. This criticism has partly been fruitful in that the law has very recently, in December 2006, been amended, as can be seen from the discussion below. See for example, the comments of the Istanbul Bar, 31.10.2006, accessible from the following link: www.istanbulbarosu.org.tr.

complaint of the injured person, provided that the offence in question is punishable with a prison sentence of a year or less, and that the accused has not previously been subjected to a prison sentence exceeding 1 year for an intentional offence. The prosecutor should furthermore be of the view that the suspension of prosecution may serve the deterrence of the offender against future offending behaviour and that the suspension of prosecution should be viewed as more beneficial than prosecution for the suspect and for society. And finally, the accused must repair the harm caused by the offence by means of reparation. If these conditions are met, the public prosecutor may suspend the prosecution for a period of 5 years. Section 19 of the Child Protection Law sets the limit at 3 years. Unless the accused commits an intentional crime within this period, after the expiration of this period, in relation to the crime in question no prosecution can be filed.

Despite the absence of pre-court disposals until 2004, almost half of the cases were never brought to court. Indeed, even in such regime of legally mandated prosecution, an examination of the available statistics reveal that both in the realm of adult and juvenile justice a certain form of diversion did occur. Indeed, as Fig. 5.1 shows, between the years of 1986 and 2009, the proportion of the cases dropped by the public prosecution is on average 42%. It may then be plausibly

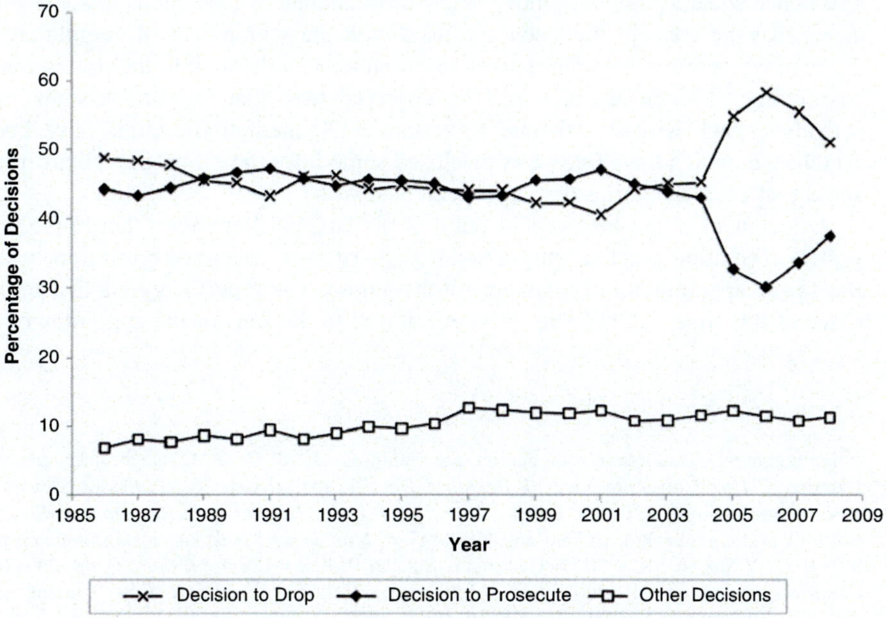

Fig. 5.1 Case ending decisions of prosecutors 1986–2009[201]
Other decisions: combination with another case, reference to another public prosecution service.

[201]Data compiled from Judicial Statistics (2008) available in the following link: http://www.adlisicil.adalet.gov.tr/istatistik_2008/cumsav/cumsav3.pdf (Acces Date: March 2010).

argued that in some cases despite the evidential sufficiency and the fulfilment of conditions of prosecution such as the complaint of the injured person or the permission of the authorised state office where applicable, the public prosecutors may to a certain extent have departed from the legality principle.

The statistics released by the Ministry of Justice reveal that in the first year of diversion measures, the cases that were dropped by the public prosecutor have increased considerably. While in 2004 the proportion of cases that were not prosecuted by the public prosecutor was 45.3 annually, in 2005, this increased to 58.4% in 2006, thereafter declined 51.2% in 2008. However, the extent to which this growth can be attributed to the new measures, in absence of relevant statistical data on crime figures, cannot be conclusively determined. It is accordingly too early to draw any conclusion as to the frequency of the use of these measures in Turkish law.

Furthermore, so far, no indication of research has existed to investigate the ways in which the legislation in question has been conceived and implemented in practice.[202] Mediation, as attracting relatively more attention and being promoted as a device of restorative justice (*onarici adalet*),[203] suffers from, for example, severe conceptual ambiguity, as it still seems to lack any normative theory or theories which could underpin its practice. As a consequence, this disposal is still not adequately known among legal professionals[204] and there is some evidence that the concept has been confused with the withdrawal of complaint.[205] There exist therefore some initiatives to introduce this theme into the professional community.[206] Once again, it can be observed here that the Bar Associations actively engage with this theme. In certain Bars, mediation centres have been established, which have *inter alia* disclosed some information on the 'client' type and the offence categories that have been deal with.

A document of the Mediation Centre of the Istanbul Bar shows that in the first year of mediation practice only a small proportion of cases were referred to the Bar for an appointment of a lawyer for mediation. The report suggests that in the space of this time only 139 cases were referred to the Bar for the appointment of

---

[202]For a general introduction of mediation, see, Sahin, C. (1998) Ceza Muhakemesi Hukukunda Uzlasma, *Selcuk Üniversitesi Hukuk Fakültesi Dergisi*, special issue for Professor Süleyman Arslan Armagani, pp. 221–297, Özbek, V. Ö. (1999) *Ceza Hukukunda Suctan Dogan Magduriyetin Giderilmesi*, Seckin, Ankara and (2006) *Ceza Muhakemesi Hukuku*, Seckin, Ankara, pp. 992–1032, Yildiz, A., K. (2005) Uzlasma – Sikayet Iliskisi in Yenisey, *op. cit.*, pp. 259–280 Centel, N. and Zafer, H. (2006) Ceza Muhakemesi Hukuku, 4th edition, Beta, Istanbul, pp. 410–425, Yenisey and Nuhoglu, *op. cit.*, pp. 1064–1068.

[203]See the explanatory note of Article 39 of the Government Bill.

[204]Istanbul Barosu Cocuk Haklari Merkezi (2006) *Cocuk Adalet Sisteminde Uzlaşma* (mediation in juvenile justice), the report of the working group in 12. 05.2006, Istanbul, p. 18.

[205]*Ibid*, p. 22.

[206]Istanbul Barosu (2006) *Cocuk ve Genc Adalet Sistemi Sempozyumu – Türk Mevzuatinin ve Özellikle Cocuklari Koruma Kanununun Degerlendirilmesi* (4–5 Haziran 2005), Istanbul.

a lawyer.[207] Of these cases, intentional and negligent injury and theft cases constituted the majority of the cases and only in 15% of these cases were the mediation meetings successful. In view of the fact that during the period concerned, it was also possible that a lawyer who both parties agreed on could convene victim-offender mediation without necessarily being approved by the Bar, the figures revealed in this study can be only limitedly representative. And given the recent extension of the scope of legislation, it still remains to be seen how the practice of mediation in Turkey will take shape.

5.7.2 Deferred Sentence

Apart from cases falling within the scope of mediation that are prosecuted upon the complaint of the injured person, the pronouncement of a term of up to 2 year imprisonment or judicial fine can be deferred where offenders have not been previously convicted of an intentional offence, the attitude of the offender during the trial phase make the court conclude that the offender would not reoffend and the damage done to the victim has been repaired through restitution or compensation.[208] Where a deferred sentence is passed, the offender is placed under probation for 5 years (3 years for juveniles). Within this period, the court *may* place the offender under supervision and may order an attendance to an educational institution, performance of work in the public interest, refraining from going to certain places, or any other obligation which the court deems appropriate.[209]

5.7.3 The Fine

One of the most innovative elements of the new penal code is its incorporation of the day fine system into law.[210] However it appears that it has not received as welcome a reception as might have been anticipated. The new system has been criticised for its potential danger of causing arbitrariness by vesting courts with such great latitude of discretion in the determination of the amount of fines. From a practical point of view, it is argued that the size of tax evasion due to informal economy, injustice in the distribution of the tax burden as such, would hinder the efficiency of the system.[211] Furthermore, it is pointed out that the determination of

---

[207] Istanbul Barosu (2006) *CMK Uygulama Servisi Faaliyet Raporu* (01.06.2005-01.06.2006), Istanbul.

[208] Section 231/5 of the Turkish Criminal Procedure Code.

[209] *Ibid.*, Section 231/8.

[210] See, Özgenc (2004), *op. cit.*, 60–61.

[211] Centel, N. (2005) Yeni Türk Ceza Kanunu'nda Cezalar ve Emniyet Tedbirleri Sistemi, *Yeditepe Üniversitesi Hukuk Fakültesi Dergisi*, vol. 2, no 2, pp. 359–368, p. 364, Öztürk, p. 322, Artuk and

the amount of the fine would increase the work load of courts and would cause delays.[212] The effects of this change in statistical terms will be discussed later, but a brief consideration of the Turkish day fine system is first necessary.

Under the Turkish regulation, the daily units range from 5 to 730 days. There are exceptions to this rule, e.g. the surveillance of phones and recording is punishable by 1,000 units or for human smuggling by 10,000 and production and trade of narcotics and psychotropic substances (in its unqualified form) 20,000.[213] A daily unit is to be fixed at a minimum of 20 and maximum of 100 of Turkish Liras. In determining the amount of the fine, first the court is required to determine the number of day fines within the minimum and maximum limits laid down for the offence in question.[214] At the second stage taking financial and other circumstances into consideration, the court determines the amount of each day fine unit within the aforesaid limits.

In so doing, the judge pronounces the deadline for payment of the fine. In this respect, a period of no more than 1 year may be granted in order to allow the convict to pay. The court may allow the convict to pay the amount in instalments of no more than four units in a period of 2 years. A partial or full non-payment shall result in the conversion of the judicial fine into imprisonment.[215] In addition to this regulation, a new law is enacted to update the amount of those fines, amount of which are prescribed by special criminal laws.[216]

5.7.4 *Alternatives to Short Term Imprisonment*

In Turkish law, there exists no *ultima ratio* rule as in the German Penal Code which envisages the priority of 'fines' over 'short-term prison sentences' (of up to 6 months). Instead of recognising an *ultima ratio* rule, since the enactment of the Penal Enforcement Code in 1965, the Turkish legislature has opted for a discretionary committal to alternative measures to imprisonment in certain cases. Notably, however, by requiring the courts to specify grounds for refraining from imposing alternative measures, the Cassation Court sought to control the use of discretion.[217]

Notwithstanding the fact that the committal to alternative measures for the most part lye in the discretionary power of the judge these measures theoretically have

Cinar (2004), *op. cit.*, p. 79, the Report of Galatasaray University, p. 286. For an opposing view, see Mahmutoglu, *op. cit.*, p. 368–369.

[212]Tezcan and Erdem (2004), *op. cit.*, p. 348.

[213]Section 188 of the new Penal Code.

[214]Justificatory reasons for Section 52, *ibid.*

[215]Section 52/4.

[216]Law no 5252 date 04.11.2004, Official Gazette 13.11.2004.

[217]See numerous decisions cited in Icel *et al.*, *op. cit.*, pp. 156–157.

a broader scope insofar as the definition of short-term imprisonment and eligible categories of offenders are concerned. Section 49 states that unless otherwise prescribed by law, the minimum limit of imprisonment is 1 month and the maximum period is 20 years. Paragraph 2 of this Section qualifies prison sentences up to one year as 'short-term' imprisonment. Accordingly, pursuant to Section 50 of the Code, in lieu of a short-term custodial sentence, having regard to the personality of the offender, social and economic circumstances and the remorse (if any) that s/he expressed during the proceedings and the way of commission of offence, courts may impose alternative measures.[218] These are:

1. Judicial fine
2. The reparation of damage to the victim or public at large restitution or compensation
3. Placement in an educational institution (which can also have residential facilities) for two years or longer
4. Refraining from going to specified places or doing specified activities
5. Withdrawal of licences and prohibition of exercising a certain profession, trade, or art, when the offence was committed through the violation of the rights or the breach of due care, and precaution requirements from one-half to two fold of term of imprisonment which would be otherwise imposed
6. Committal to *voluntary* work in the public interest up to two fold of term of imprisonment which would be otherwise imposed

In respect of persons who at the commission of the act had not attained the age of 18 or those who have attained the age of 65, and those who received no more than 30 days of prison sentences, the law envisages a mandatory committal to alternatives prescribed in the respective section. Notably, in respect of offences of negligence (unqualified as opposed to conscious negligence), the law adopts a milder approach by permitting the commutation of imprisonment to the judicial fine, irrespective of the duration of prison sentence which would be otherwise given.[219] This provision is not applicable to cases involving conscious negligence.

5.7.5 *Suspension of the Execution of Punishment*

The new Penal Code regulates 'suspension of the execution of punishment' in marked resemblance with the German system of the suspension of the execution of punishment. In the justificatory reasons, it was stated that 'suspension of the execution of punishment' was to be divorced from its hitherto position which was

[218]Colak, H. and Altun, U. (2006) Kisa Süreli Hapis Cezalari, Secenekli Yaptirimlar ve Infaz Rejimleri, *Türkiye Barolar Birligi Dergisi*, vol. 67, Kasim-Aralik, pp. 163–229.
[219]Section 50/4 of the new Penal Code.

ostensibly one of exercising mercy, to an institution of penal execution.[220] Indeed in view of the provisions that the new Penal Code provides, it appears that the scope of suspension of the execution of punishment is considerably narrowed down and its legal consequences made more onerous and, most notably, a system of supervision is provided for.[221]

First and foremost, as opposed to the old Penal Code, according to which both fines[222] and prison sentences could be suspended,[223] under the new Penal Code, only prison sentences up to two years or less may be suspended. With regard to offenders who have not attained the age of 18 and those aged 65, this duration is set at three years. A prison sentence can only be suspended, however, when the defendant has not previously received a prison sentence exceeding 3 months for an intentional offence and where having regard to the remorse that the defendant showed during the proceedings, the court is of the opinion that s/he will not reoffend. Previously, courts were required to assess the probability of the commission of a further offence by considering her/his previous history. The new penal code explicitly urges courts to assess whether the defendant shows remorse during the course of proceedings.[224]

After the suspension of the custodial sentence, the court determines a probationary period ranging from 1 to 3 years, but in any case, no less than the imposed term of imprisonment. Within this probationary period, considering the personality of the offender and her/his social situation[225] the court may order (Section 51/2 of the new Penal Code):

1. Participation in a course for a certain profession, trade or art, where the offender lacks such skills
2. Where the offender possesses necessary skills, working in a public or private institution under the supervision of a specified person, for payment
3. With regard to offenders who have not attained the age of 18, at an attendance of an educational establishment (for the purpose of ensuring that the juvenile offender is taught a trade or art) where necessary the placement in such institutions that have residential facilities

In the probationary period, courts are required to appoint a probation officer, unless considering the personality and her/his social situation, the court concludes that it is not necessary to do so.[226] The task of the probation officer is to give advice

---

[220] Özgenc (2004) *op. cit.*, p. 58, see also Turhan, F. (2006) Yeni Türk Ceza Kanununa Göre Cezalarin Ertelenmesi ve Uygulanmasinda Ortaya Cikan Bazi Sorunlar, *Erzincan Üniversitesi Hukuk Fakültesi Dergisi*, vol. 10, no 3–4, pp. 27–54.

[221] See, the report of the University of Galatasaray, *op. cit.*, p. 302, Öztürk (2004) *op. cit.*, p. 322.

[222] This has been criticised by Centel, *op. cit.*, p. 363.

[223] See above.

[224] Section 51/1(b) of the new Turkish Penal Code.

[225] *Ibid.*, Section 51/5.

[226] *Ibid.*, Section 51/6.

about dealing with bad habits, consult with other persons concerned, and to submit a report on the attitudes, social integration and feelings of responsibility of the offender. The suspended sentence is revoked when the offender commits an intentional offence or, despite a warning issued by court, does not fulfil the specified conditions.[227]

As opposed to the previous provision, under current arrangements, the successful completion of this period means that the imposed term of imprisonment has been executed.[228]

5.7.6 *Sentencing Disposals in Juvenile Justice*

In Section 4 of the Child Protection Law, under the title of fundamental principles, the fundamental purpose of the juvenile justice system are stipulated as ensuring the rights and welfare of juvenile criminals and those who are deemed in need of care and protection.[229] In this sense, a fusion of 'justice' and 'welfare' considerations constitutes the basic philosophy of the Law. On the one hand, the Law urges sentencers to take the needs and best interests of the juvenile into account in terms of the age, development, education, personality and 'social responsibility'; it requires to observe due process rights, on the other hand.[230] In this sense, courts are given a more proactive role. In determining an appropriate measure, the assistance of social workers is regarded as an essential component of the decision making process.[231]

In the new Turkish Penal Code, with regard to penal responsibility, three categories are determined.[232] Juveniles up to 12 years have no penal responsibility. With respect to this category, only measures peculiar to juvenile offenders which will be outlined below are applicable. Juveniles from 12 years to 15 do not have penal responsibility when the individual juvenile offender does not comprehend the legal meaning and consequences of her/his act, or where her/his ability to control her/his behaviours has insufficiently developed. Otherwise, instead of aggravated imprisonment a term of imprisonment from 9 to 12 years imprisonment, instead of life imprisonment a term of imprisonment from 7 to 9 years is to be imposed. Other penalties will be reduced by two thirds. With respect to juveniles from 15 to 18, instead of aggravated imprisonment, a term of imprisonment from 14 to 20 years,

---

[227] *Ibid.*, Section 51/7.

[228] *Ibid.*, Section 51/8.

[229] Section 3 defines this category as those 'children' whose physical, mental, moral, social and emotional development are in danger, those who are neglected or abused, and those victims of offences.

[230] Section 4 of the Child Protection Law.

[231] See, e.g. *ibid.*, Section 35, 38 and 39.

[232] Section 31 of the new Penal Code.

and instead of life imprisonment, a term of imprisonment from 9 years to 12 years is to be meted out. Other penalties will be reduced by one half.

The security measures peculiar to juveniles are not laid down in the Penal Code, but they are provided in detail in the Child Protection Law. Previously, in the substantial body of cases, preference was given to parental custody. This was the case despite the existence of such measures in the Juvenile Court Law as placement in a foster family or in a residential institution, performance of work, and committal to treatment for those juvenile offenders who were deemed incapable of having criminal responsibility.[233] The Child Protection Law renames measures applicable to juvenile offenders as protective and supportive measures which (security measures for juveniles)[234] include counselling, education, placement in an institution which without removing her/him from her/his family and social milieu deals with juveniles. Of these:

1. Counselling can address both the juvenile and the persons responsible for her/his upbringing. It contains training for problems relating to child education and development problem-solving methods.
2. Education measures comprise attendance at an educational institution, participation in a vocational training or performance of work in public and private enterprises.
3. Care measures involve the placement of the juvenile in a public or private institution, when the person who has custody over the child cannot care for the child adequately.
4. Health measures comprise the submittal of the juvenile for mental or physical care treatment or treatment for addictive substance abuse.
5. Accommodation measure contains the placement of juvenile (or a pregnant woman where necessary) in a residential institution.

Courts can impose more than one requirement or where necessary can modify the content of the measure subsequently.[235] Under this Law, when deciding the measures in the particular case, the court must take the view that the requirements are the most suitable for the offender and that those measures involving deprivation of liberty must be seen as a last resort of referral.[236]

In conjunction with the imposition of a security measure, dismissal of prosecution or court proceeding or deferment of sentence, the court may decide to place the juvenile under supervision. Supervision consists of counselling, guidance, examination of her/his environment, the control of the execution of the imposed measures and reporting (in 3 months). In deciding a supervision method, the following must

[233]Section 10 of the Juvenile Court Law. See, Ünver, Y. (2002) Einige strafrechtliche Probleme über Kinder und Jugendliche in der Türkei, *Annales de la Facultés de Droit d’Istanbul*, vol. 34, no 51, pp. 193–214.

[234]Section 11 of the Child Protection Law.

[235]*Ibid.*, Section 7(3).

[236]*Ibid.*, Section 4/j.

be taken into consideration: the aims, nature and duration of supervision, the needs of the juvenile, the seriousness of the (state of) dangerousness, the extent to which the potential contribution and cooperation of parents, legal custody or otherwise the person responsible for her/his care and protection, the unlawful conduct which led to the imposition of measure and the juvenile's opinion in this respect.

5.7.7 Interim Appraisal

From a dogmatic point of view, it may be concluded that the Turkish penal reform has brought a 'systemic break' in that it has formally established a double track system between penalties and measures.[237] Nonetheless, as this chapter shows, however scattered, security measures have always been a part of Turkish law.[238] It may therefore be argued that the reform retained the very basic structure of Turkish penal law which was conclusively (re)formed by the Penal Enforcement Law in 1965.

Arguably, the novelty of the penal reform must rather be sought in the institutional innovations and developments which facilitate a setting to translate the ideas and mechanisms that were embedded already in the previous legislation into practice. Indeed, a massive change appears to have been taking place.[239] With the Law on Probation and Help Services and Protection Boards, a probation system was established.[240] Beside supervision of offenders, providing help to victims, the Turkish Probation Service is also assigned to ensure the implementation of alternatives to imprisonment.[241] The work of the Probation Service, in particular in collaboration with England and Wales under 'the Twinning Project for the Development of Probation Services in Turkey' so far seems to be quite promising in establishing the necessary infrastructure and training of the personal for probation services.[242]

---

[237]See, justificatory reasons for Section 50 of the Turkish Penal Code.

[238]See, Artuk, M. (1979) *Sinn und Zweck der Strafe und die Maßnahmen zur Sicherung und Besserung im türkischen Strafrecht*, Peter Hanstein Verlag, Königstein, Nuhoglu, A. (1996) *Mukayeseli Hukukta ve Türk Ceza Hukuku'nda Özgürlügü Baglayici Emniyet Tedbirleri* (unpublished PhD thesis, Marmara University).

[239]See for example further ‚Judicial Reform Strategy' of the Ministry of Justice, accessible in English from www.cte-dsm.adaletg.gov.tr (Access Date: March 2010).

[240]Law no 5402, 3.7.2005, Official Gazette, 20.7.2005, no. 25881.

[241]The aims of the Turkish Probation Service is stated as to supervise offenders in an effective way, prevent reoffending, provide help victims, change the offending behaviours of the offenders and to rehabilitate them and ensure the widespread implementation of alternative measures to imprisonment. See the above mentioned web page of Denetimli Serbestlik ve Yardim Hizmetlerinden Sorumlu Daire Baskanligi.

[242]See Denetimli Serbestlik ve Yardim Hizmetlerinden Sorumlu Daire Baskanligi (2007) *I. Ulusal Denetimli Serbestlik Konferansi*, Ankara and (2009) *Denetimli Serbestlik ve Yardim Hizmetlerinde 2 Yil*, yayin no.14, see also Nursal, N. and Atac, S. (2006) *Denetimli Serbestlik ve Yardim Sistemi*, Yetkin, Ankara.

Equally important in this respect is the proposed improvements in the judicial machinery. It has been long recognised that the Turkish judicial system is cumbersome and ineffective. Due to the shortage of personnel, court proceedings have been notoriously long and the penal system has been inadequately resourced.[243] In response to addressing the demands of the European Union for membership,[244] a judicial reform is under way whose objectives, among others,[245] have been heralded as: enhancing efficiency and effectiveness in the judiciary (*sic*), improving the management system of the judicial organisation and improving the penitentiary system.

Nevertheless, despite a rather positive impression that would be gained considering such thorough-going reform initiatives, in the short-term 'community sanctions' would not move from the margin to the centre of the system, given the fact that the institutions which are envisaged by Section 50 of the Penal Code and the Child Protection Law have been by and large absent.[246] In this context, the prospect of community service in the form as, for instance, envisaged by the English system is even weaker. As of August 2009, the general unemployment rate was 13.4%, whereas among young population this number is some 19.7%.[247] Thus, as the present social and economic climate suggests, and as the figures which will be discussed below reveal, more realistic expectations must be made in this respect.

5.8 Post-reform

Clearly, it is still too early to assess the impact of the reform in numbers, but as will be seen from Fig. 5.2, the reform appears to have caused an abrupt change in sentencing practice, from which some tentative conclusions can be drawn. It may begin with the number of convictions. The total annual number of convictions in 2006 was 941,532 – an increase of 25% from 1994, but a decrease of 14%

---

[243] Dönmezer, S. and Yenisey, F. (2001) Ceza Adalet Sisteminin Etkinligi, TESEV, Istanbul.

[244] See e.g. Accession Partnership 2008, available in the following link (Access Date: March 2010) http://eur-lex.europa.eu/LexUriServ/LexUriServ.do?uri=OJ:L:2008:051:0004:01:EN:HTML.

[245] The aims are strengthening independence of the judiciary, promoting impartiality of the judiciary, enhancing professionalism in the judiciary, improving management system of the judicial organisation, enhancing confidence in the judiciary, facilitating access to justice, ensuring effective implementation of measures to prevent disputes and improving alternative dispute resolution mechanisms, improving penitentiary system, and harmonisation of legislation work with EU standards. See the English version of this document: http://www.sgb.adalet.gov.tr/yrs/Judicial%20Reform%20Strategy.pdf (Access Date: March 2010).

[246] See an article written by a social worker in the Canton Zürich, Cosar, Y. (2005) Kentlesen Türkiye'de Cocuk Suclulugu, *Türkiye Barolar Birligi Dergisi*, vol. 56, pp.281–325, pp. 38–39.

[247] The data compiled from the Türkiye Istatistisk Kurumu, accessible from the following link: http://www.tuik.gov.tr/PreHaberBultenleri.do?id=4146 (Access Date January 2009).

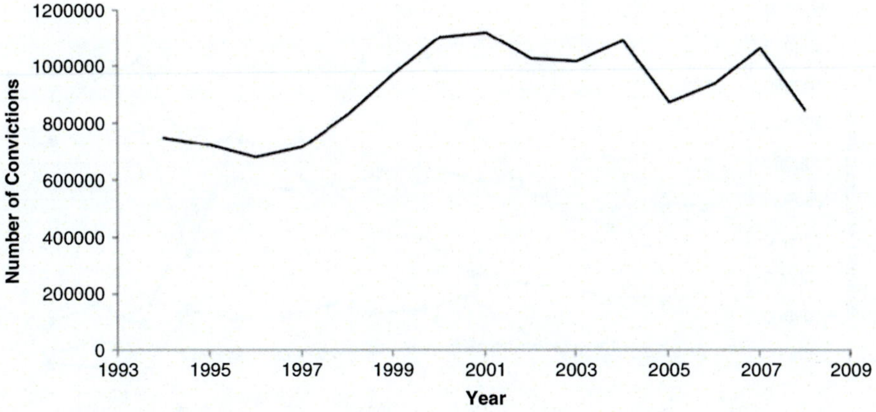

Fig. 5.2 Total number of convictions 1994–2008[248]

compared with 2000. How can the fluctuations in the total number of convictions be explained?

Generally, a factor which undoubtedly affects the total number of convictions is the increase in the police recorded crime. Regrettably, national statistics on police recorded crime, other than motoring offences (and those only since 2006), are not systematically available.[249] Currently, work is done to transfer police data to the National Statistics Institute. In view of this fact, the extent to which conviction figures reflect increasing magnitude of crime and whether or not overall in the seriousness of offences an increase occurred cannot be determined.

Yet, three major intervening factors appear to be highly germane in this respect. First, as has been discussed, with the new Criminal Procedure Code, public prosecutors have been authorised to drop prosecution or resort to mediation. This had a substantial impact upon the number of offenders brought before the courts, as was discussed above. A second factor is the enactment of the Amnesty Law (Law no 4616 on the Conditional Release and the Suspension of Trials and Sentences for Offences Committed Prior to 23 April 1999).[250] Under this Law, the investigation,

[248]Data compiled from Judicial Statistic of Turkey. Adli Sicil Istatistik Genel Müdürlügü, accessible from the following link: Judicial Statistics, http://www.adli-sicil.gov.tr/ (Access Date: March 2010).

[249]European Sourcebook of Crime and Criminal Justice Statistics does not contain therefore the corresponding Turkish figures, but according to authors will be covered in the forthcoming volume. See, Aebi, M., F., Aromaa, K., de Cavarlay, B., Barclay, G., Gruszczynska, B., von Hofer, H., Hysi, V., Jehle, J.-M., Killias, M., Smit, P. and Tavares, C. (2006) *European Sourcebook of Crime and Criminal Justice Statistics*, 3rd edition, accessible from the following link http://www.europeansourcebook.org/esb3_Full.pdf, (Access Date: March 2010), p. 92. There are however some data on, e.g. the number of homicides, available on the *Ninth United Nations Survey on Crime Trends and the Operations of Criminal Justice Systems* (2003–2004), see the following link, p. 28: http://www.unodc.org/documents/data-and-analysis/CTS9_by_country_public.pdf (Access Date: March 2010).

[250]Section 3 of the Law no 4616, 21.12.2000, Official Gazette 22.12.2000.

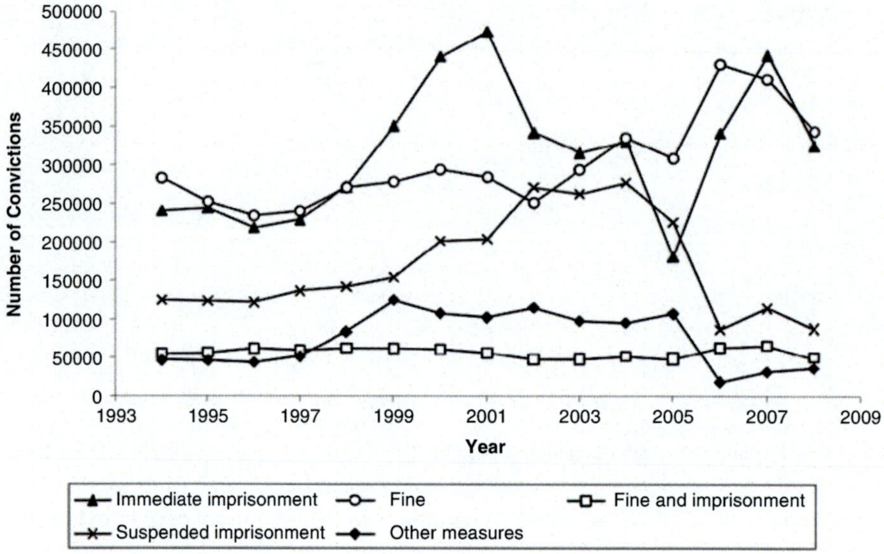

Fig. 5.3 Total offenders sentenced and disposals used 1993–2009[251]

trials and sentences of offenders who committed an offence punishable by no more than ten years imprisonment were to be suspended.[252] A third explanation of fluctuations in the number of convictions was the adoption of the deferment of sentence in the new Penal Code. Notably, the subsequent change of the provisions of the deferment of sentence through Law on Harmonising Various Laws with Basic Criminal Laws,[253] extending its scope from offences punishable by 1 year imprisonment to 2 years imprisonment according to press reports, made such a significant impact that it has been viewed as a 'mini amnesty'.[254] This was because the Court of Appeal, in one of its judgments, due to the principle of retroactivity of the milder law, recognised that the defendant must benefit from the more favourable provision on the deferment of the sentence (Fig. 5.3).[255]

Figure 5.2 shows that between 1997 and 2001, there was a sharp increase in the use of imprisonment, from 229,570 to 474,056, thereby recording a 106% growth.

---

[251]Data compiled from Judicial Statistic of Turkey. Adli Sicil Istatistik Genel Müdürlügü, accessible from the following link: Judicial Statistics, http://www.adli-sicil.gov.tr/ (Access Date: March 2010).

[252]*Ibid.* Death penalties were not to be executed for offences committed prior to 23 April 1999, a ten years reduction was to be made from prison sentences of convicted offenders (this was to be made not for each offence separately, but in total).

[253]Temel Ceza Kanununlarina Uyum Amaciyla Cesitli Kanunlarda ve Diger Bazi Kanunlarda Degisiklik Yapilmasina Dair Kanun, Law no 5728, 8.2.2008, Official Gazette, 23.1.2008.

[254]See e.g., *Milliyet*, 17 Subat 2008.

[255]Section 7 (2) of the Penal Code states that "where there is difference between the law in force at the time an offence was committed and after its commission, the law which is in favour of the defendant shall be applied and enforced".

Reaching its peak point in 2001, the number of prison sentences showed, afterwards, a downward trend. The decline in 2005 is particularly noteworthy, but as is shown in the figure, in 2007, it reached almost its level prior to the introduction of the new Penal Code. The sharp decline after 2000 until 2003 may be attributed to the above-mentioned Amnesty Law. It is difficult to ascertain the extent to which the impact of the entry of the new Criminal Procedure Code and Penal Code into effect. Between 1994 and 2008, there was an over 6 per cent increase in the proportionate use of prison sentences. In the first version of the new Penal Code, the proportionate use of imprisonment accounted for 20% of all sentences, 1 year later in 2006, the same figure equated to 36.4%.

Similar to prison sentences, the use of fines displayed some fluctuation between 1984 and 2008. The introduction of the day-fine system appears to have led to a greater use of the fine. In 2006, the number of fines imposed by courts as a single sentence reached its highest value in the decade, with a number of 431,345 – an increase from 251,902 in 2002. This growth may be attributed to the tendency of the courts to impose a fine on certain offenders who would otherwise have received a suspended or unsuspended prison sentence. Nonetheless, caution must be taken in assessing the appeal of the day fine system, since 2008, an over 20% decline in the total number of fines is recorded. In the proportionate use of the fine, there were fluctuations, reaching its peak point in 2006, 45.8% in 2006, but then dropped to 40.7% in 2008.

As is shown in Fig. 5.2, the most unequivocal development occurred in relation to the suspended sentence. After the entry of the new Penal Code into effect its use declined dramatically. The proportionate use of the suspended sentence fell from 16.7% in 1994 to 10.6% in 2007. This may be the outcome of the adoption on the deferment of sentence. Equally, due to stricter conditions attached to the suspended sentence, courts may be less inclined to use suspended sentences.

As far as the category of 'other measures' is concerned (a broad classification including alternative measures to imprisonment and security measures) rather than an increase in the use of such measures, there was a dramatic decrease. Between 1999 and 2004, other measures were imposed on average 107,000 annually. After a short-standing growth in the first year of the Penal Code in 2005, 107,264, the use of 'other measures' fell to 17,889 in 2006. These fluctuations may in part be attributed to the total number of convictions. In the same period, as Table 5.1 shows, the proportionate use of measures declined. In 2006, when a significant numbers of committal to 'other measures' took place, the use of 'other measures' accounted for 12.3% of all sentences, in the following year, yet it declined to 1.9%. Although it is reported that[256] courts are keen to rely on alternative measures pursuant to

[256]Ince, H. (2008) Kisa Süreli Hapis Cezasina Uygulanabilecek Secenek Yaptirimlardan "Kamuya Yararli Bir Iste Calistirma" Yaptirimi, (Community Service Labour Programme, *sic.*), *Adalet Dergisi*, no 30 accessible from http://www.yayin.adalet.gov.tr/30_sayi%20i%C3%A7erik/H%C3%BCseyin%20%C4%B0nce.htm.

Intriguingly, this is made in a way which accords with the perceived social reality. The use of performance of work as an alternative to imprisonment in domestic violence cases akin to 'shame sanctions' is apparently more than outcomes of merely technical judgements. Despite its potential

Table 5.1 The proportionate use of sentencing disposals 1994–2008[257]

Year	Imprisonment	Fine	Fine and imprisonment	Suspended imprisonment	Other measures
1994	32.1	37.8	7.3	16.7	6.1
1995	33.8	35.0	7.7	17.2	6.3
1996	32.2	34.5	9.0	17.9	6.3
1997	32.0	33.6	8.3	19.0	7.1
1998	32.7	32.6	8.3	17.1	10.1
1999	36.2	28.7	6.4	15.9	12.8
2000	39.9	26.6	5.4	18.3	9.7
2001	42.3	25.4	5.0	18.2	9.1
2002	33.3	24.5	4.6	26.4	11.2
2003	31.0	28.9	4.7	25.8	9.6
2004	30.3	30.8	4.7	25.4	8.8
2005	20.7	35.5	5.7	25.9	12.3
2006	36.4	45.8	6.7	9.3	1.9
2007	41.6	38.6	6.2	10.8	2.9
2008	38.5	40.7	5.9	10.6	4.2

Section 50 of the Penal Code in place of short-term imprisonment,[258] in 2007 and 2008, of all the sentences given, the proportion of other measures constituted 2.9 and 4.2%, respectively.

With regard to juvenile convictions, a remarkable development occurred. The number of convictions which were processed under the Juvenile Court Law (and subsequently under the Child Protection Law) went up dramatically in 2005 from its level in 1994; from 3,243 to 18,859. After the enforcement of the Child

positive effects, the function of punishment as a means of such kind of 'social engineering' is unquestionably highly doubtful. Among many other examples, in one case the offender was ordered to carry a small announcement paper stating that "For beating my wife, I ask apologise from my wife and people of the district". *Radikal*, 14.6. 2009. Even more in one highly publicised cases, the imposition of probation assistance on a professor probation, for insulting Atatürk, the founder of the Turkish Republic, by saying in a symposium that one-party regime was regressive in some respects and that foreign visitors would be astonished when they see the countless statutes and portraits of 'this man' (hence talking about Atatürk with demonstrative pronoun, which some including the court in question find insulting). The sentence is on appeal. After this speech, Professor Yayla made the following statement to the Guardian "After this I should maybe talk about birds and trees, but not about political ideologies or freedoms in Turkey or human rights. . .It is very sad that in Turkey we don't have academic freedom or freedom of expression. If the verdict of the court is approved, I will be really under supervision. For teaching at university that means in classes I have to be very careful because students can spy and can record what I say and complain about me to the university. It will make my life miserable and much more difficult". *Guardian*, 28.1.2008.

[257]Based on data of General Directorate of Judicial Statistics, accessible from the following link http://www.adlisicil.adalet.gov.tr/istatistik_2007/ceza%20mahkemeleri/ceza12-2007.pdf.

[258]In 2007, in some 4508 cases, an alternative measure in lieu of short-term imprisonment is imposed; this figure increased to 5448 by 20 percent in 2007. Denetimli Serbestlik ve Yardim Hizmetlerinden Sorumlu Daire Baskanligi (2008) *Uluslararasi Denetimli Serbestlik Hizmetlerinde Secenek Tedbirler Konferansi,* yayin no 17, Ankara.

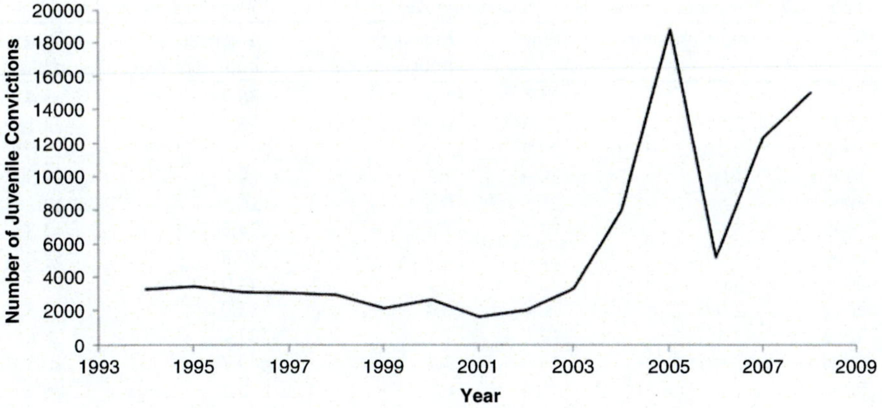

Fig. 5.4 Total number of juveniles sentenced under juvenile penal law 1994–2008[259]

Protection Law, due to the change in the above-mentioned prosecution policy a sharp decrease appears to be taking place. The total number of convictions in 2006 was 5,155 – an abrupt decrease of 266% compared with the 18,859 convictions in 2005 (Fig. 5.4).

Between 1997 and 2001, the number of custodial sentences for juvenile offenders grew sharply. The short-term decrease from 2001 onwards may be attributed both to the Amnesty Law and the decline in the number of convictions. In 2005, the number of custodial orders for juvenile offenders was 251, but afterwards it increased sharply to 2,465 in 2007, showing a nine fold increase in the total number of juvenile convictions. What is interesting is that the total number of custodial sentences in 2008 increased, while the juvenile convictions declined. In the same period, in the proportionate use of imprisonment and non-custodial sentences, dramatic changes occurred. As Table 5.2 (see below) shows, in 2005, the proportionate use of imprisonment amounted to 1.3% while this figure in 2006 was 31.3% (Fig. 5.5).

Not only the immediate form of imprisonment, but also the number of suspended prison sentences also increased. The number of suspended prison sentences increased dramatically in 2005, from 1,147 in 1994 to 16,266 in 2005, it then declined sharply 1,109 in 2007 and 2,012 in 2008. As Table 5.2 shows, in 2004 the proportionate use of suspended imprisonment accounted for almost half of all sentences, but it continued to sharply decline this year and stood at 5.5% in 2008. The decrease in the use of the suspended sentence may be explained by the reformulation of the suspended sentence, which aims at making its imposition rare and consequences more onerous.

Another remarkable change took place in relation to fines. In 1984, the number of fines that were imposed as a sole measure for juvenile offenders was 772, whilst

[259]Data compiled from Judicial Statistic of Turkey. Adli Sicil Istatistik Genel Müdürlügü, accessible from the following link: Judicial Statistics, http://www.adli-sicil.gov.tr/ (Access Date: March 2010).

Table 5.2 The Proportionate Use of Sentencing Disposals 1994–2008 under Juvenile Penal Law[260]

Year	Imprisonment	Fine	Fine and imprisonment	Suspended imprisonment	Other measures
1994	2.4	24.5	1.6	36.2	35.4
1995	3.5	27.5	0.7	35.3	33.1
1996	4.1	29.9	1.1	37.3	27.6
1997	4.0	30.3	1.5	29.8	34.5
1998	2.3	28.5	0.6	26.5	42.1
1999	3.6	27.1	1.5	24.5	43.3
2000	4.0	22.3	2.1	36.8	34.8
2001	3.0	22.5	1.1	45.9	27.5
2002	2.9	20.4	0.4	33.0	43.3
2003	3.5	19.0	1.1	37.7	38.6
2004	7.8	19.3	3.1	49.7	20.2
2005	1.3	6.4	0.8	5.2	86.3
2006	31.3	53.8	4.5	8.8	1.6
2007	19.9	60.6	5.3	5.3	9.0
2008	22.3	51.1	7.7	5.5	13.4

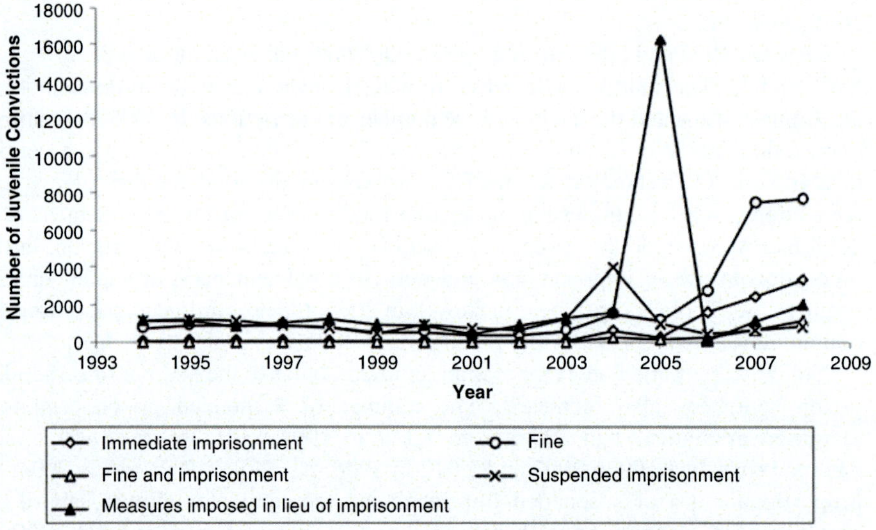

Fig. 5.5 Total number juvenile offenders sentenced and disposals used under juvenile penal law 1994–2008[261]

in 2008 this proportion reached a peak to 7,702. As is clear from Table 5.2, after the reform more than half of the cases resulted with an imposition of a fine. The fine has currently become the most imposed disposal for juvenile offenders, from 24.3% in

[260] *Ibid.*

[261] *Ibid.*

1994 to 51.1% in 2008. This may be again interpreted as an evidence for the appeal of the newly introduced day fine system. Intriguingly, the increase in the use of fines was accompanied with a decline in the suspended sentence so that the decline in the suspended sentence may be explained with the restriction of its scope only to prison sentences.

A rather exceptional development occurs with the category of 'measures'. As Table 5.2 shows, in 1994, the use of measures accounted for 35.4% of all sentences, 1,147 in absolute numbers. Recording fluctuations, in 2005 this figure stood at 86.3% in proportionate numbers, standing at 16,266. Surprisingly, a year later the use of 'measures' accounted for only 1.6% of all the sentences given to juveniles. From 2007 onwards the use of 'measures' increased steadily. The abrupt 'unpopularity' of 'measures' for courts can be explained, undoubtedly, by absence of the necessary infrastructure to cope with the demands of the legislation. In the face of the perpetual shortage of institutions envisaged by the Child Protection Law, it may well be assumed that rather than an imposition of such measures, courts tend to impose fines or immediate prison sentences. A second explanation would be the fact that many of the offenders who in 2005 received such measures may have been brought before courts for a new offence, and due to previous committal to 'measures', courts no longer deemed appropriate to order these options. This explanation is also in conformity with popular wisdom is that juvenile criminals in Turkey are generally composed of habitual offenders; for example, there have long been some legendary stories in press reports which have some undoubtedly truth in them that juveniles brought from Eastern Anatolia were continuingly forced by criminal organisations to commit offences of larceny, robbery and so forth.[262]

If these complicated figures can be summarised at all, first it might be suggested that both with regard to adult and juvenile offenders fines have become the most imposed disposal. Second, the recent change in law appears not to have any considerable impact upon the use of imprisonment. Third, the proportion of the suspended imprisonment has been in decline for both juvenile and adult offenders. And finally, alternatives to short-term imprisonment seem to be thus far from preventing the use of prison sentences. An exceptional development in this respect occurred in 2005, where over 86% of the sentences were made up of measures, but this trend was dramatically reversed in the subsequent years.

The changes in the size of the prison population reflect the fluctuating pattern of the use of imprisonment. As the Figure shows, following the three 'amnesty' laws, 1973, 1991 and 2000, after a short-term reduction, the total number convicted prisoners have been steadily growing. Concurrently, one of the factors which determines the size of prison population, namely the number of remand prisoners has also been recently increasing. In 2007, the number of remand prisoners reached the same level as during the years of military intervention. In 2009, the number of persons on remand accounted for 52.1% of the prison population.[263] In England this proportion is 16%, in Germany 15.5%. Another relevant issue is the reformulation

[262]For a recent report, see e.g, *Radikal*, 21.3.2010.

[263]ICPS (30.09.2009) http://www.kcl.ac.uk/depsta/law/research/icps/worldbrief/wpb_country.php?country=119.

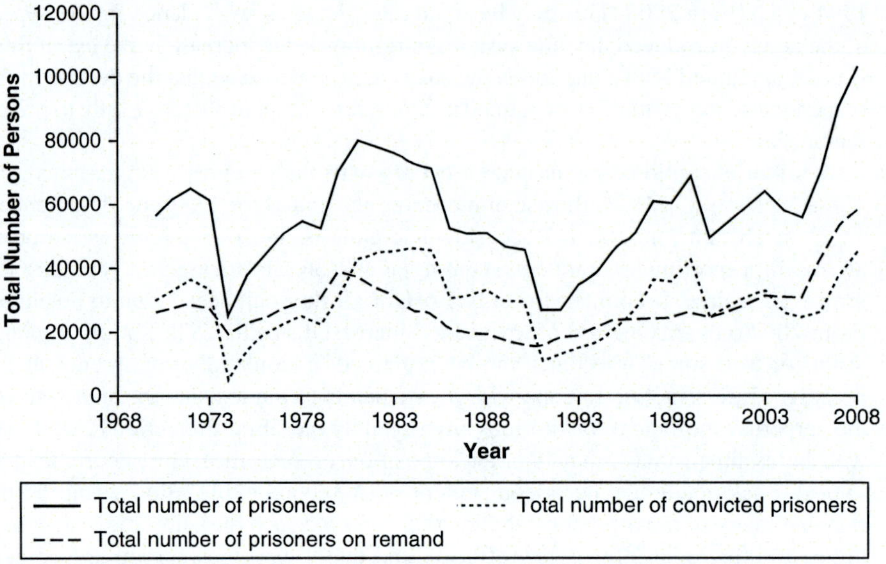

Fig. 5.6 Prison population 1970–2008[264]

of early release mechanisms.[265] According to the new Penal Enforcement Code, in order to be eligible for conditional release, the prisoner must serve two thirds of her/his sentence (Section 107/2 of the new Penal Enforcement Code). Previously this ratio was one half (Section 19 of the previous Penal Code). Furthermore, according to the new Penal Enforcement Code, with regard to offenders who have been punished by aggravated life imprisonment for offences that are specified in the Code (offences against the security of state, offences against the constitutional order, offences against national defence) and perpetrated during an 'organisational activity', conditional release is not applicable. A third explanation may also be a general increase in the length of custodial sentences (Fig. 5.6).

As both sentencing and prison statistics demonstrate, the most stable feature of the Turkish penal system is, paradoxically, its continuous instability. Needless to say that the data analysed here requires an in-depth consideration with a view of crime figures and the working mechanism of both prosecutors and courts. One aid to understanding what is actually happening would be a greater availability and dissemination of statistical data, e.g. police recorded crime. Of equal significance, a greater deal of research should be devoted for interpretation of statistics. In order to do so, academic criminology must look towards the home country. Inevitably, unless such a comprehensive and systematic approach is developed in studying crime and justice figures, the knowledge on them will remain vague.

[264]Data compiled from the web page of the Turkish General Directorate of Penal Execution Institutions and Remand Houses: http://www.cte.adalet.gov.tr (Access Date: March 2010).

[265](Section 106/16) Critically, Artuk (2007), *op. cit.*, p. 65, Centel, Zafer and Cakmut, *op. cit.*, p. 680.

5.9 Conclusion

Truly, it would have been unhistorical to consider the fate of number of de novo concepts and institutions in Turkish law and practice without considering the Eurocentric-driven reform of criminal and criminal procedure laws in 2004 and the following years which with an enormous velocity has dramatically altered the entire picture of criminal justice in Turkey. Indeed, in very short space of time, conditional suspension of prosecution has been recognised for both juvenile and adult offenders, mediation has been incorporated into Turkish law, probation assistance became the major component of various sentences and the day fine system was incorporated. Even though the criticism that the new Penal Code was hastily conceived may in part be seen as a legitimate concern stemming from the swift process of law-making, this chapter has demonstrated that the reform efforts can be traced to the 1940s, and, with some disruption, it was resumed in the 1980s.

Notably, the reform efforts were accompanied with the substantial aim and/or rhetoric to reach the stage achieved by the western nations. The major European countries including Italy, France and Germany gave inspiration to the new developments. The Penal Enforcement Code represented a pure crystallisation of this approach that was drafted be one of the leading penologists, Professor Manuel Lopez-Rey, whose liberal thoughts substantially effected Turkish legislation. However, many of the novelties of the Code such as community service, attendance centres and intermittent custody remained vastly unrealistic in the reality of the practice. Undoubtedly, financial constraints were the principal reason in obstructing the translation of ideas into practice. Coupled with Turkish 'exceptionalism' towards offending people, the heavy preoccupation with security considerations has equally overshadowed crime and justice issues.

By readopting many provisions of the Penal Code (and also Child Protection Law) and leaning considerably towards the German sanction system, the promises of the new Penal Code still stand the test of the time. Having regard for the fact that the imprisonment rate in Turkey was 161 per 100,000 (much higher than many other jurisdictions in Europe)[266] and that the problem of prison overcrowding persists, a proactive policy-making, as is often demanded for in this field, is essential. Neither the ongoing prison building programme, nor another amnesty law, which is currently under debate,[267] would offer any significant amelioration in the long-term. Despite the decline in the confidence in the ability of alternative penalties to substitute imprisonment elsewhere, their broader application still presents a more sustainable option in dealing with the growth in the size of the prison population in Turkey. In the following and final section of this study, the limits and potentials of this approach in the light of the English and German experiences will be further discussed.

[266] See the web page of the International Prison Studies at King's College, University of London. http://www.kcl.ac.uk/depsta/law/research/icps/worldbrief/wpb_country.php?country=119 (Access Date: March 2010).

[267] See, for example, *Radikal*, 8.3.2010.

Chapter 6
Summary and Conclusions

Nothing could better capture the concluding point of this study than the ancient saying "*omne ignotum pro magnificio*".[1] This study initially rested upon the assumption that if the variety of sanctions in the Turkish penal system was expanded, the use of custody would be considerably reduced. In this sense, the foreign examples of distinct forms of sanctions, particularly 'community service', appeared to offer a great deal in reducing the number of prison sentences. However, taking the experience of the other countries featured in this study into account, that assertion can no longer be considered beyond doubt. The German and English cases, which were discussed in detail in a historical and contemporary context, demonstrate in different ways the fact that the availability of a broad array of sanctions does not necessarily lead to a consequent reduction of imprisonment. The English case, as recapitulated briefly below, reveals some kind of 'net-widening' exactly during the time period when new alternatives to imprisonment entered into operation. By contrast, the German experience suggests that the use of custody can be greatly reduced, even when the catalogue of possible sentences is much less extensive than in England.

It has clearly not been the intention of this study to deliver a verdict on net-widening effects of alternatives to imprisonment. The extent to which new alternatives 'widen the net of surveillance and control', 'make the net denser', 'produce and reproduce new and different nets' clearly goes beyond the scope of this work.[2] There are valuable works, and also recent studies interpreting the wider implications of a perceived transformation of 'penality'. Both sociological debates on the new forms of social control and philosophical debates on the purposes of punishment are very relevant areas which this study, however, does not pretend to contribute to. Nor does this study pretend to fully assess the historical relevance for the sentencing reform of, for example, the National Socialist regime in Germany, and the period of martial law in Turkey, although the existence of these regimes has

[1]Translated by Nigel Walker as "anything sounds wonderful in an unknown language" cited in Hood, *op. cit.*, p. 392.

[2]Cohen, S. (1979) 'The Punitive City: Notes on the Dispersal of Social Control', *Contemporary Crises*, vol. 3, pp. 339–63, see also Cohen (1985) *op. cit.*

Ö. Sevdiren, *Alternatives to Imprisonment in England and Wales, Germany and Turkey*, DOI 10.1007/978-3-642-17351-6_6, © Springer-Verlag Berlin Heidelberg 2011 had a considerable influence on the emergence and development of alternatives to imprisonment.

Throughout this study, many similarities and differences have been determined with regard to the conceptualisation, adoption and implementation of alternative sanctions. What is essential at this point is to outline the relation between imprisonment and its alternatives against the background of reform efforts in the countries that have been studied here. But first a major difference must be highlighted. In both Germany and Turkey, alternatives to imprisonment have been incorporated into legislation primarily by means of codification. In Germany, such efforts had invariably been preceded by an impressive and extensive doctrinal debates as well as a consideration of foreign examples. The Turkish reform movements, by contrast, were carried out within a relatively short span of time amidst hectic and intense legislative and administrative activities. England has, until very recently, differed from both continental countries in that reforms tended to be sporadic and piecemeal and guided by certain degree of pragmatism.[3] This approach is perhaps responsible for the quantity and complexity of English legislation on the alternatives to imprisonment. In what follows, the outcomes of these different reform endeavours with regard to prison surrogates will be briefly reviewed.

6.1 The English Approach

In England criminal policy has attempted to reduce reliance on imprisonment through the creation of 'new' alternative non-custodial sentences. Leaving aside the distinct origin of the probation order and the broad extension of the scope of the fine through the Criminal Justice Act of 1948, the first device specifically designed to limit the use of prison sentences was the suspended sentence. As an import from continental jurisdictions, the suspended sentence was not able to fulfil the high hopes attached to it. A brief account of the turbulent history of the suspended sentence is therefore essential at this point to recapitulate the sources of pessimism that prevailed in current times about the ability of non-custodial sentencing options to substitute imprisonment.

It was the Criminal Justice Act of 1967 which introduced both mandatory and discretionary suspended sentences. Subjected to vigorous criticism that it restricts the discretionary power of the English judiciary, the life-span of the mandatory suspended sentence in England was quite short, and it was abolished by the Criminal Justice Act of 1972. It may have partly been due to such ambivalent approaches of

[3] In this sense the following argument may be shared: "it is characteristics of the English genius for practical affairs that we are suspicious of the system... the English tend rather to deal with the situation confronting them and afterwards discover on what principles they have done so, and what precedent for future action they have established". Temple, W. cited in Fox, L., W. (1952) *The English Prison and Borstal Systems*, Routledge & Kegan Paul, London, p. 3.

the judiciary towards the suspended sentence and, contrary to the intentions of the legislature, the estimations of the initial research studies highlighted that in less than half of the cases the suspended sentence was replaced by imprisonment. In the rest of the cases, rather than imprisonment, the fine was substituted. Such empirical results gave impulse to several amendments and changes in the legislative scope of the suspended sentence. Most notably, informed further by the negative research results on the use of the suspended sentence as desired by the legislature, the Criminal Justice Act 1982 abolished the suspended sentence for the age category 17–21. The Criminal Justice Act 1991 followed the policy of restricting the use of the suspended sentence by urging courts to use suspended sentences only in 'exceptional circumstances'. Lastly, the Criminal Justice Act 2003 reframed the position of the suspended sentence with the provision that courts may order an offender to comply with specified conditions such that it became similar to 'community' orders applicable for offenders aged 18 and above.

The advent of the community service order through the Criminal Justice Act 1972 shared the fate of the suspended sentence. Under this Act, community service could be given for offences punishable by imprisonment and for offenders aged 17 and over. Yet, the conception of the community service as suitable for offences punishable by imprisonment did not provide sufficient guidance as to its exact role. The English practice reflected the ambiguity on the scope of community service. Research following the national implementation of the community service order revealed that only in half of the cases, the community sentence order was imposed in lieu of imprisonment. While the overall use of community sentences grew, no appreciable reduction in the use of custody could be observed. This state of affairs was explained by the perception of judges which tend to view community service as a lenient option. The Criminal Justice Act of 1991 addressed such considerations. The Act tried to eliminate the phrase 'alternatives to custody' by labelling community service, among others, as 'community punishment' thereby underlining that the new forms of non-custodial sanctions including community service were demanding penalties in their own right which are appropriate for all but the most grave offences. However, the efforts to draw a clear line between community and prison sentences appear to have failed once again. Against this background, the Criminal Justice Act 2003 introduced new forms of sentences and combined features of both community and custodial sentences. The new forms of these unimplemented sanctions gave rise to critiques that the edges between community and custodial sentences are 'blurring'.

The recent changes of the legislative and operational framework of non-custodial sentences in England do not seem to alter the pessimistic conclusion that these disposals are, by and large, incapable of replacing the use of custody. On the contrary, these sentences have more and more been used for less serious offences, what has been termed 'down-tariffing', and the imposition of community sentences for summary offences has constantly grown. A concurrent development is the steady decline in the use of fines since the 1970s. Observing the drop in the number of fines, research has revealed that some of those offenders who received a community order might have previously been given a fine.

Recent statistical data thus cast serious doubt on the supposedly beneficial impact of non-custodial options on the use of custody. It is fair to conclude that disposals intended as alternatives to custody have supplemented rather than replaced custodial sentencing options. The proportionate use of custody by the courts has actually increased significantly while the various new alternatives have been in operation. Hence, the English experience suggests that no straightforward relationship between the number of non-custodial sentencing options and the use of custody exist.

6.2 The German Approach

German penal policy has long been characterised by its efforts to reduce short-term imprisonment. In this context, the fine was ascribed a significant role as early as in the 1920s. Not only did the number of offences punishable by fine increase dramatically, but the legislature also declared that the fine was to be the preferred sanction for minor offences whenever 'the goal of punishment' could be achieved by imposing a fine. The German version of the suspension of the execution of punishment was also the product of an endeavour to reduce the number of prisoners. In 1953, the suspension of the execution of imprisonment with probationary assistance was incorporated into both the juvenile and adult sentencing frameworks. In its initial version, the relevant section of the Penal Code provided that the execution of a prison sentence up to 9 months could be suspended if it could be expected that the offender would lead an orderly life even without being subject to imprisonment, except when the execution of the prison a sentence was deemed necessary for general preventive purposes.

The penal reform of 1975 further significantly contributed to the fight against short-term imprisonment. First, the minimum duration of short-term imprisonment was set at 1 month. Second, courts were to impose prison sentences of less than 6 months only when special circumstances relating to the offence and offender existed, making imprisonment necessary in order to impact the offender or in order to 'defend the legal order'. Third, courts were urged to impose a fine whenever there was no good reason to impose a short prison sentence below 6 months. Fourth, the adoption of the Scandinavian day fine system significantly strengthened the fairness and practicability of fines. Fifth, short-term prison sentences were suspended, whenever the offender could be expected to refrain from further offences without having had a prison experience. Sixth, even the execution of prison sentences between 1 and 2 years could be suspended if special circumstances relating to the offence and the personality of the offender existed. Seventh, the reform introduced the new option of merely cautioning an offender and suspending the imposition of a fine in cases of minor crime.

These seven ways of restricting the enforcement of short-term prison sentences seem to have contributed to a marked reduction in the number of prisoners, especially when compared with figures dating from the last quarter of the nineteenth century. The German system has remained remarkably stable since the 1970s, in spite of massive changes due to the re-unification of Germany in 1990. Despite small differences in percentages, the relative allocation of prison sentences, suspended prison sentences and fines have remained almost equal over the last 40 years, with a small shift toward suspended prison sentences. This applies to both adult and juvenile offenders.

Nonetheless, the German system has not been completely immune from criticism. It has been argued that the sanctioning system which is primarily based on imprisonment and fines lacks sufficient diversity and flexibility. The problem of fine default has been seen as an unresolved issue of German penal policy. There have been various proposals, recommending *inter alia*, the extension of community service, as well as the introduction of a longer-term driving ban and of electronic monitoring as sanctions in their own right. Defenders of the status quo have however persuasively argued that there is great danger in experimentation; it might well be that a broad diversification of criminal sanctions could make Germany follow the negative example of England, where more onerous 'intermediate' sanctions did not restrict the use of imprisonment but the use of the fine.

6.3 The Turkish Approach

What is the position of Turkish penal justice? Despite its neo-classical approach, the Penal Code of 1926 incorporated significant provisions as to alternatives to the imposition and the execution of imprisonment. The most crucial measure in this sense was the suspended execution of imprisonment (and of the fine), long before it gained a legislative base in Germany. The initial version of the provision regulating the suspended sentence permitted the postponement of the execution of imprisonment and of light imprisonment up to 6 months, of heavy and light fines as well as of banishment, provided that the offender had not previously received a sanction other than a fine and provided that the court, having regard to her/his previous history and attitudes, came to the conclusion that the suspension was appropriate. The Turkish Code of 1926 also provided for home detention as a form of executing a sentence of 'light imprisonment' – a sanctioning option which has only recently been adopted in England and is yet under discussion in Germany. The same applies to the option of work performed in the public interest in lieu of imprisonment for fine default.

These provisions and others related to the administration of prison sentences were, at the time, not implemented to a desired extent. But this fact did not discourage policy makers, in the aftermath of a *coup d'état*, to launch another significant step forward. The Penal Enforcement Code was a bold attempt to comply with the penological demands and international trends of the 1960s. According to this Code, courts were authorised to impose fines, 'community service', 'restitution and compensation', attendance at an educational or reformatory institution, a prohibition from going to certain places or from performing certain professions and activities as well as the withdrawal of a driver's licence or another licence in lieu of short-term imprisonment. Short-term imprisonment was first defined as any sentence up to 6 months and later extended to sentences up to 1 year.

The legislative and institutional innovations the Penal Enforcement Code contained were regarded by many critics as unrealistic, given the actual conditions of Turkish society at the time, and were in fact never implemented on a broad scale. 'Community service' has never been used and was eventually repealed in 1973. Other options such as attendance at an educational or reformatory institution were unable to be implemented because the requisite institutions simply did not exist. The sanction of prohibiting the offender to attend certain places or to practice certain professions failed due to the shortage of qualified personnel for its supervision. The fine was the only non-custodial option provided for in the 1965 Code that acquired any practical relevance. But its efficiency suffered greatly from the effects of inflation. Since fines could soon amount only to sums of minor value, courts tended again to resort to suspended or unsuspended prison sentences. Within a short period of time, the pessimistic forecast about the practicability of the Code proved to be true, by and large due to financial constraints. For the same reason, the implementation of juvenile courts and special measures for juvenile offenders was likewise delayed, even beyond the official introduction of juvenile courts in 1979.

The recent penal reform in Turkey has retained the basic structure provided by the Penal Enforcement Code, but introduced significant changes such as with the formal establishment of the double track system for penalties and measures, the adoption of the day-fine system, and the limitation of the scope of the suspended sentence to prison sentences. This time the legislature tried to provide a setting within which non-custodial options can actually be administered. In this context, the creation of a probation service empowered to supervise offenders and the implementation of institutional alternatives to imprisonment were important steps.

Sentencing statistics demonstrate that in the wake of the reform, the use of suspended prison sentences has been drastically reduced. This may also be attributed to the increasing use of the fine. One reason for this development may be an increased reliance of fines, which can now be adapted to the offender's income through the day-fine system. Another reason for the decrease of suspended sentences may be the fact that fines can no longer be suspended and that the suspension of prison sentences has been tied to stricter conditions and limitations. Regrettably, the newly introduced measures have not yet had any appreciable impact on adult and juvenile sentencing practice. So far they have not managed to establish themselves as viable alternatives to imprisonment. Further research into the reasons for this failure is needed, and it is to be hoped that measures may become more frequently used once they become better known to sentencing judges.

Not only due to the fact that fines can no longer be suspended, but also due to stricter conditions and consequences of the suspended execution of imprisonment, a certain reluctance of courts appears to affect the use of the suspended sentence. Again, so far non-custodial *measures* had an appreciable impact neither on the adult system, nor on the juvenile justice system. It may of course change in the long-term, but in the first years of the new Penal Code, these *measures* have been considerably far from serving as alternatives to imprisonment. Nonetheless, other than underlining the need for further research, as of yet it is difficult to come to any firm conclusion.

6.4 Conclusion: The Turkish System in Prospect

In view of the difficulty of comparing statistical developments across national borders, it is not easy to draw any lessons from this study's findings for the development of the Turkish system. But it can at least be stated that the German experience with the day fine system appears to support the view that the day-fine system may enhance the credibility of the fine as a sentencing option. There is thus reason to hope that the day-fine system may lead to a more frequent use of fines in the long-term. It might also be helpful for the law to explicitly encourage the use of fines instead of prison sentences. An increased use of fines could also lead to a more parsimonious use of the limited resources of the newly created Turkish probation service.

Another lesson from the English and German experience may be that it is more important to introduce an 'ultima ratio' clause into law, thus discouraging judges from overusing prison sentences, rather than expanding the number and variety of available non-custodial sanctions. The Turkish Child Protection Law contains a provision that imprisonment should be used as a last resort, unless the court is of the opinion that other methods of dealing with the juvenile offender appear inappropriate. The Penal Code obliges sentencers, under certain circumstances, to convert short-term imprisonment into one of several specified non-custodial options. However, it might be preferable to introduce a more general provision exhorting sentencers into the Penal Code in order to rely on custody as a last resort only.

The English experience with the expansion of non-custodial options suggests that the creation of new measures implies the risk that the new sanction replaces less intensive alternatives rather than imprisonment. Accordingly, it is not to be recommended, for example, to turn community service into a primary sentencing option. Community service can contribute to the reduction of the use of custody even when only foreseen as a substitute for short-term imprisonment, as is presently the case in Turkey as well as in Germany. Other options such as victim-offender mediation and treatment of offenders in well-organised institutions with a useful infrastructure may serve to diminish the unquestioning reliance on imprisonment still prevalent among Turkish judges. However, given the experience of other countries, one should not place too great expectations on such alternatives to imprisonment, especially in quantitative terms.

What is essential at this point is the development of a practical context within which sentencers are encouraged to use custodial sentences less extensively and to rely more on alternative disposals to imprisonment. The required sea change in judicial attitudes is mainly a matter of providing the necessary personnel and resources for making the new alternatives flourish. Without a sizeable investment into personnel training and development as well as the necessary buildings and infrastructure, it will be difficult to overcome the inertia that has haunted Turkey's criminal justice system for a long time.

Bibliography

Adalet Bakanligi (1985) *Türkiye'de Teröristlerin Rehabilitasyonu Konulu Uluslararasi Sempozyum ile ilgili Rapor*, Ankara.

Adalet Bakanligi (1997) *Türk Ceza Kanunu Öntasarisi 1997*, Ankara.

Advisory Council on the Treatment of Offenders (1957) (reprinted in 1968) *Alternatives to Short-Term Imprisonment*, HMSO, London.

Aebi, M., F. and Kuhn, A. (2000) Influences on the Prisoner Rate: Number of Entries into Prison, Length of Sentences and Crime Rate, *European Journal on Criminal Policy and Research*, vol. 8, no 1, pp. 65–75.

Ahmad, F. (1993) *The Making of Modern Turkey*, Routledge, London.

Ahrens, W. (1978) *Die Einstellung in der Hauptverhandlung gem. § § 153 II, 153 a II StPO – Eine Empirische Analyse über neue Formen der Bekämpfung der Bagatellkriminalität*, Schwartz, Göttingen.

Akgündüz, A. (1990) *Osmanli Kanunnameleri ve Hukuki Tahlilleri*, Fey Vakfi, Istanbul.

Akyüz, Y. (2002) Cocuk Suclulugu Konusunda Türk Egitim Tarihinde Ilk Önemli Arastirma in *I. Ulusal Cocuk ve Suc, Nedenler ve Önleme Calismalari Sempozyumu*, 29–30 Mart 2001, pp. 35–50.

Alacakaptan, U. (1958) *Ingiliz Ceza Hukukunda Suc ve Cezalarin Kanuniligi Prensibi*, Ankara Üniversitesi Hukuk Fakültesi Yayinlari, Ankara.

Albrecht, H.-J. (1985) Ansätze und Perspektiven für die gemeinnützige Arbeit in der Strafrechtspflege, *Bewährungshilfe*, vol. 32, no 2, pp. 121–134.

Albrecht, H.-J. (2000) Criminal Prosecutions: Developments, Trends and Open Questions in the Federal Republic of Germany, *European Journal of Crime, Criminal Law and Criminal Justice*, vol. 8, no 3, pp. 245–256.

Albrecht, P.-A. (2000) *Jugendstrafrecht*, 3rd edition, Beck, München.

Albrecht, A. (2003) Elektronischer Hausarrest Das Konzept des hessischen Experiments in Schöch, H., Jehle, J.-M. and Aebersold, P. (eds.) *Angewandte Kriminologie zwischen Freiheit und Sicherheit*, Forum, Bonn.

Albrecht, H.-J. and Kalmthout, A., M. (eds.) (2002) *Community Sanctions and Measures in Europe and North America*, Max-Planck-Institut für ausländisches und internationales Strafrecht, Freiburg.

Albrecht, A. and Kalmthout, A., M. (2002) 'Intermediate Penalties: European Developments in Conceptions and Use of Non-Custodial Criminal Sanctions' in Albrecht and Kalmthout *Community Sanctions and Measures in Europe and North America*, Max-Planck-Institut für ausländisches und internationales Strafrecht, Freiburg, pp. 1–11.

Albrecht, H.-J., Arnold, H. and Schädler, W. (2000) Das hessische Modelversuch zur Anwendung der „elektronischen Fußfessel", vol. 33, no 11, *Zeitschrift für Rechtspolitik*, pp. 466–469.

Allen, R. (1991) Out of Jail: The Reduction in the Use of Penal Custody for Male Juveniles 1981–1988, *Howard Journal*, vol. 30, no 1, pp. 30–52.

Alsberg, M. (1924) Geldentwertung und Strafrechtspflege, *Juristische Wochenschrift*, vol. 10, no 5, pp. 276–277.

DOI 10.1007/978-3-642-17351-6,

Amnesty International (1984) *Amnesty International Documentation on Torture in Turkey*, University of Michigan.

Ancel, M. (1954) Probation in Relation to European Penal Systems and Modes of Criminal Procedure in *United Nations, European Seminar on Probation*, 20–30 October 1952, United Nations Publications, London, pp. 33–48.

Ancel, M. (1958) The Collection of European Codes and the Study of Comparative Law, *University of Pennsylvania Law Review*, vol. 106, no 3, pp. 329–384.

Ancel, M. (1971) *Suspended Sentence*, Heinemann, London.

Anderson, J., F. and Dyson, L. (2002) *Criminological Theories: Understanding Crime in America*, University Press of America, Lanham.

Appelius, H. (1891) *Die Bedingte Verurteilung und die Anderen Ersatzmittel für Kurzzeitige Freiheitsstrafen: eine Kritik der neusten Reformbestrebungen auf dem Gebiet des Strafrechts*, 4th edition, Keßler, Cassel.

Appelius, H. (1892) *Die Behandlung jugendlicher Verbrecher und verwahrloster Kinder*, Guttentag, Berlin.

Artuk, M. (1979) *Sinn und Zweck der Strafe und die Maßnahmen zur Sicherung und Besserung im türkischen Strafrecht*, Peter Hanstein Verlag, Königstein.

Artuk, M., E. (1998) 1926 Tarihli Türk Ceza Kanunu'nun Degistirilmesi Yönündeki Calismalar Hakkinda Düsünceler, *Istanbul Barosu Dergisi*, vol. 72, pp. 830–847.

Artuk, M. E. and Cinar, A., R. (2004) Yeni Bir Ceza Kanunu Arayislari ve Adalet Alt Komisyonu Tasarisi Üzerine Düsünceler, in Ergül, T. (ed.) *Türk Ceza Kanunu Reformu*, Ikinci Kitap, TBB Yayinlari, Ankara, pp. 43–45.

Aschrott, P., F. (1892) *Die Behandlung der verwahrlosten und verbrecherischen Jugend und Vorschläge zur Reform*, Liebmann, Berlin.

Aschrott, P., F. (1899) *Ersatz kurzzeitiger Freiheitsstrafen – eine kriminalpolitische Studie*, Richter.

Ashworth, A. (1992a) Sentencing Reform Structures in Tonry, M. (ed.) *Crime and Justice*, vol.16, pp. 180–241.

Ashworth, A. (1992b) Criminal Justice Act 1991: Part 2: Non-Custodial Sanctions, *Criminal Law Review*, April, pp. 242–251.

Ashworth, A (2002) European Sentencing Tradition: Accepting Divergence or Aiming for Convergence? in Tata, C. and Hutton, N. (eds.) *Sentencing and Society: International Perspectives*, Ashgate, Aldershot, pp. 225–226.

Ashworth, A. (2005) *Sentencing and Criminal Justice*, Cambridge University Press, Cambridge.

Ashworth, A. (2007) Sentencing in Maguire, M., Morgan, R. and Reiner, R. (eds.) *the Oxford Handbook of Criminology*, Oxford University Press, Oxford, pp. 991–1023.

Ashworth, A. and Player, E. (2005) Criminal Justice Act 2003: The Sentencing Provisions, *Modern Law Review*, vol. 68, no 5, pp. 822–838.

Atasoy, S, Baskan, M., T. and Ziyalar, N. (2006) Juvenile Justice in Turkey Friday, P. and Ren, X. (eds.) *Delinquency and Juvenile Justice in the Non-Western World*, Criminal Justice Press, Monsey.

Audit Commission (1996) *Misspent Youth: Young People and Crime*, Audit Commission, London.

Austin, J. and Krisberg, B. (1981) Wider, Stronger and Different Nets: The Dialectics of Criminal Justice Reform, *Journal of Research in Crime and Delinquency*, vol. 18, no 1, pp. 165–196.

Aybar. C. (1943) Türkiye'de Mahkumlar ve Suclar, *Siyasi Ilimler Mecmuasi*, pp. 604–642.

Aydin, M., A. (2009) *Türk Hukuk Tarihi*, Beta, Istanbul.

Azrak, A., Ü. (1962) Sosyal Devlet ve 1961 Türk Anayasasinin Sistemi, *Istanbul Üniversitesi Hukuk Fakültesi Mecmuasi*, vol. 27, no 1–4, pp. 208–224.

Baer, G. (1977) The Transition from Traditional to Western Criminal Law in Turkey and Egypt, *Studia Islamica*, vol. 45, pp. 139–158.

Bailey, J. (1987) *Delinquency and Citizenship: Reclaiming the Young Offender 1914–1948*, Clarendon Press, Oxford.

Ball, R., A. and Lilly, J., R. (1988) Home Incarceration with Electronic Monitoring in Scott, E., J. and Hirschi, T. (eds.) *Controversial Issues in Crime and Justice*, Sage, London.

Bamberger, G. (1917) *Geldstrafe statt Gefängnis*, Enke, Stuttgart.

Bannenberg, B. (1993) *Wiedergutmachung in der Strafrechtspraxis : Eine empirisch-kriminologische Untersuchung von Täter-Opfer-Ausgleichsprojekten in der Bundesrepublik Deutschland*, Forum, Bonn.

Bateman, T. (2001) Custodial Sentencing of Children: Prospects for Reversing the Tide, *Youth Justice*, vol. 1, no 1, pp. 28–39.

Bateman, T. (2005) Reducing Child Imprisonment: a Systemic Challenge, *Youth Justice*, vol. 5, no 2, pp. 91–104.

Battaglini, G. (1933) The Fascist Reform of the Penal Law in Italy, *Journal of Criminal Law and Criminology*, vol. 24, no 1, pp. 278–289.

Bauer, F. (1967) Das Strafrecht und das heutige Bild vom Menschen in Reinisch, L. (ed.) *Die deutsche Strafrechtsreform*, Beck, München, pp. 11–23.

Bauer, F. (1967) Die Reformbedürftigkeit der Strafrechtsreform, Gestern & Heute, München

Baumann, J. (1965) *Kleine Streitschriften zur Strafrechtsreform*, Verlag Ernst & Werner Gieseking, Bielefeld.

Baumann, J. (1967) Die reform des Allgemeinen Teils Eines Strafgesetzbuches in Reinisch, L. (ed.) *Die deutsche Strafrechtsreform*, Beck, München, pp. 56–71.

Baumann, J. (1968) *Beschränkung des Lebensstandards anstatt kurzfristiger Freiheitsstrafe*, Luchterland, Berlin.

Baumann, J. (1968) Konsequenzen aus einer Reformarbeit –Nicht Aufgenommene Vorschläge Für die Strafrechtsreform in Kaufmann, A. (ed.) *Gedächtnisschrift für Radbruch*, Vandenhoeck & Ruprecht, Göttingen, pp. 337–343.

Baumann, J. (1969) *Weitere Streitschriften zur Strafrechtsreform*, Gieseking, Bielefeld.

Baumann, J. (1980) Über die Denaturierung eines Rechtsinstituts (§59 StGB), *Juristische Zeitung*, pp. 464–469.

Baumann, J. (1988) Vollzugsgestaltung unter Schuldgesichtspunkten in Schwind, H.-D., Steinhilper, G. and Böhm, A. (eds.) *10 Jahre Strafvollzugsgesetz, Resozialisierung als alleiniges Vollzugsziel?* Kriminalistik-Verlag, Heidelberg, pp. 69–78.

Baumann, J., Brauneck, A.- E., Hanack, E.-W., Kaufmann, A., Klug, U., Lampe, E.-J., Lenckner, T., Maihofer, W., Noll, P., Roxin, C., Schmitt, R., Schultz, H., Stratenwerth, G. and Stree, W. (1966) *Alternativ-Entwurf eines Strafgesetzbuches Allgemeiner Teil*, Mohr, Tübingen.

Baumann, J., Brauneck, A.-E., Burgstaller, M., Eser, A., Huber, B., Jung, H., Klug, U., Luther, H., Maihofer, W., Meier, B.-D., Rieß, P., Riklin, F., Rössner, D., Rolinski, K., Roxin, C., Schöch, H., Springorum, H.-S. and Weigend, T. (1992) *Alternativ-Entwurf Wiedergutmachung*, Beck, München.

Baykal, S. (2002) Turkey-EU Relations in the Aftermath of the Helsinki Summit: An Analysis of Copenhagen Political Criteria in the Light of the Accession Partnership, National Programme and the Regular Reports, *Ankara Review of European Studies*, vol. 2, no 3, pp. 15–63.

Bayraktar, K. (1984) Ceza Hukukunda Suc Olmaktan Cikarma Akimi, *Istanbul Üniversitesi Hukuk Fakültesi Mecmuasi*, vol. 50, no 1–4, pp. 197–212.

Bazemore, G. (1996) Three Paradigms for Juvenile Justice in Galaway, B. and Hudson, J. (eds.) *Restorative Justice: International Perspectives*, Criminal Justice Press, Monsey, pp. 37–68.

Bazemore, G. and Colleen, M. (2002) Restorative Justice and the future of Diversion and Informal Social Control in Weitekamp, G., M. and Kerner, H.-J. (eds.) *Restorative Justice Theoretical Foundations*, Willan, Cullompton, pp. 143–176.

Beccaria, C. (1764) On Crimes and Punishments reprinted in 1995 in Bellamy, R. (ed.) *Beccaria On Crimes and Punishments and Other Writings*, Cambridge University Press, Cambridge.

Bellmann, E. (1994) *Die Internationale Kriminalistische Vereinigung* (1889–1933), Lang, Franfurt.

Berkes, N. (1964) *The Development of Secularism* in Turkey, McGill University Press, Montreal.

Birkmeyer, K. (1909) *Studien zu dem Hauptgrundsatz der Modernen Richtung im Strafrecht*, Engelmann, Leipzig.

Bishop, N. (1974) Aspects of European Penal Systems, in Blom-Cooper, L. (ed.) *Progress in Penal Reform*, Clarendon Press, Oxford, pp. 83–100.

Bishop, N. (1988) *Non-Custodial Alternatives in Europe*, HEUNI, Helsinki.

Blau, G. (1985) Diversion unter nationalem und internationalem Aspekt in Kury, H. (ed.) *Kriminologische Forschung in der Diskussion: Berichte, Standpunkte und Analysen*, Carl Heymanns, Köln, pp. 311–339.

Blau, G. (1987) Diversion und Strafrecht, *Jura*, vol. 9, no 1, pp. 25–34.

Blau, G. (1988) Die Entwicklung des Strafvollzugs seit 1945 – Tendenzen und Gegentendenzen in Schwind, H.-D. and Blau, G. (eds.) *Strafvollzug im Praxis*, 12th edition, de Gruyter, Berlin, pp. 17–29.

Bochel, D. (1976) *Probation and After Care: Its Development in England and Wales*, Scottish Academic Press, Edinburgh.

Bockelmann, P. (1951) Zur Reform des Strafensystems, *Juristische Zeitung*, pp. 494–498.

Bolle, P., H. and Yarsuvat, D. (2002) *Infaz Hukuku Alaninda Güncel Sorunlar ve Yeni Yaklasimlar*, Galatasaray Semineri Notlari, 4–7 Eylül 2002, Galatasaray Universitesi, Istanbul.

Bookbinder. P. (1996) *The Weimar Germany: the Republic of the Reasonable*, Manchester University Press, Manchester.

Böttcher, R. and Mayer, E. (1993) Änderungen des Strafverfahrensrechts durch den Entlastungsgesetz, *Neue Zeitschrift für Strafrecht*, vol. 13, no. 4, pp. 153–158.

Bottomley, K. (1984) Dilemmas of Parole in a Penal Crisis, *Howard Journal*, vol. 23, no 1, pp. 24–40.

Bottomley, K. (1990) Parole in Transition: A Comparative Study of Origins, Developments and Prospects for the 1990s, *Crime and Justice*, vol. 12, pp. 319–374.

Bottomley, K. and Pease, K. (1986) *Crime and Punishment: Interpreting Data*, Open University Press, Milton Keynes.

Bottoms, A. E. (1974) On the Decriminalisation of the English Juvenile Court in Hood, R. (ed.) *Crime, Criminology and Public Policy*, London, Heinemann reproduced in Muncie, J., Hughes, G. and McLaughlin (eds.) (2002) *Youth Justice Critical Readings*, Sage, London.

Bottoms, A., E. (1980a) *The Suspended Sentence After Ten Years: a Review and Reassessment*, University of Leeds, Centre for Social Work and Applied Social Sciences, Leeds.

Bottoms, A., E. (1981) The Suspended Sentence in England 1967–78, *British Journal of Criminology*, vol. 21, no 1, pp. 1–26.

Bottoms, A., E. (1987) Limiting Prison Use: Experiences in England and Wales, *Howard Journal*, vol. 26, no 3, pp. 177–202.

Bottoms, A., E. (1980b) An Introduction to 'the Coming Crisis' in Bottoms, A., E. and Preston, R., H. (eds.) *The Coming Penal Crisis: A Criminological and Theological Exploration*, Scottish Academic Press, Edinburgh, pp. 1–24.

Bottoms, A., E. (2004) Empirical Research Relevant to Sentencing Frameworks, Bottoms, A. and Rex, S. and Robinson, G. (eds.) *Alternatives to Prison: Options for an Insecure Society*, Willan, Cullompton, pp. 59–82.

Bottoms, A, Brown, P., McWilliams, B., McWilliams, W., Nellis, M. with Pratt, J. (1990) *Intermediate Treatment and Juvenile Justice: Key Findings and Implications from a National Survey of Intermediate Treatment Policy and Practice*, HMSO, London.

Bottoms, A., E. and Stevenson, S. (1994) What Went Wrong? Criminal Justice Policy in England and Wales 1945–1970 in Downes, D. (ed.) *Unravelling Criminal Justice*, Macmillan, Basingstoke, pp. 1–45.

Bottoms, A., E., Gelsthorpe, L. and Rex, S. (eds.) (2001) *Community Penalties: Change and Challenges*, Willan, Cullompton.

Bozkurt, G. (1992) Review of the Ottoman Legal System, *Ankara Üniversitesi Osmanli Tarihi Arastirma ve Uygulama Merkezi Dergisi*, vol. 3, pp. 115–128.

Bozkurt, G. (1996) Alman Arsiv Belgelerine Göre Alman Hukuku'nun Türk Hukuku'na Etkisi, *Ankara Üniversitesi Hukuk Fakültesi Dergisi*, vol. 45, no 4, pp. 29–40.

Braithwaite, J. (1989) *Crime, Shame and Reintegration*, Cambridge University Press, Cambridge.

Brake, M. and Hale, C. (1992) *Public Order and Private Lives: The Politics of Law and Order*, Routledge, London.

Brantingham, P., L. and Blomberg, T., G. (1979) Introduction in Brantingham, P. L. and Blomberg, T., G. (eds.) *Courts and Diversion*, Sage, Beverly Hills, pp. 7–14.

Brody, S., R. (1976) *The Effectiveness of Sentencing*, HMSO, London.

Brownlee, I. (1998) Community Punishment: A Critical Introduction, Wesley Longman, Harlow.

Brunner, R. and Dölling, D. (2002) *Jugendgerichtsgesetz*, de Gruyter, Berlin.

Büddemann, H. (1912) *Die Geldstrafe nach dem Vorentwurf zu einem Deutschen Strafgesetzbuch und dem Gegenentwurf* von Kahl, Lilienthal, Liszt, Goldschmidt, Erlangen.

Bundesministerium der Justiz (1986) *Neue ambulante Maßnahmen nach dem JGG, Bielefelder Symposium*, Bonn.

Bundesarbeitgemeinschaft für Straffälligenhilfe (1997) *Elektronisch überwachter Hausarrest – Alternativen zum Strafvollzug*, Bonn.

Bundesministerium der Justiz (1989) *Jugendstrafrechtsreform durch die Praxis*, Konstanzer Symposium, Bonn.

Burke, R., H. (2002) *An Introduction to Criminological Theory*, Willan, Cullompton.

Burnett, R. and Roberts, C. (eds.) *What Works in Probation and Youth Justice: Developing Evidence-Based Practice*, Willan, Cullompton.

Burney, E. (1985) All Things to all Men: Justifying Custody under the 1982 Act, *Criminal Law Review*, pp. 284–293.

Burney, E. (1985) *Sentencing Young People: what went wrong with the Criminal Justice Act 1982?* Gower Publishing, Aldershot.

Callies, R.-P. and Müller-Dietz, H. (2005) *Strafvollzugsgesetz*, 10th edition, Beck, München.

Carpenter, M. (1967) *Reformatory Prison Discipline*, reprinted from the 1872 edition, Patterson Smith, Montclair.

Cavadino, P. (1992) Reflections on the Criminal Justice Act 1991, Criminal Justice Matters, vol. 9, Autumn, p.7.

Cavadino, P. (1995) The Criminal Justice and Public Order Act 1994 and Young Offenders, *Youth and Policy*, vol. 48, pp. 71–83.

Cavadino, M. and Dignan, J. (1997) *The Penal System,* 2nd edition, Sage, London.

Cavadino, M. and Dignan, J. (2006) *Penal Systems: A Comparative Approach*, Sage, London.

Cavadino, M. and Dignan, J. (2007) *The Penal System*, 3rd edition, Sage, London.

Cavadino, M., Crow, I. and Dignan, J. (1999) *Criminal Justice 2000*, Waterside, Winchester.

Centel, N., Zafer, H. and Cakmut, Ö. (2005) *Türk Ceza Hukukuna Giris*, Beta, Istanbul.

Centel, N. and Zafer, H. (2006) *Ceza Muhakemesi Hukuku*, 4th edition, Beta, Istanbul.

Cin, H. and Akgündüz, A. (1989) *Türk Hukuk Tarihi*, vol. 1, Kamu Hukuku, Selcuk Üniversitesi Yayinlari, Konya.

Cinar, A., R. (2005) Yeni Türk Ceza Yasasi'nda Cezalar, *Kazanci Hukuk Dergisi*, pp. 40–65.

Clarkson, C., M., V., and Baker, E. (2002) Making Punishments Work? An Evaluation of the Halliday Report on Sentencing in England and Wales, *Criminal Law Review*, February, pp. 81–97.

Cocuklari Suc ve Suclulardan Koruma Vakfi (2002) *Cocuk Istismari ve Önleme Konulu Panel*, Istanbul.

Cohen, S. (1979) The Punitive City: Notes on the Dispersal of Social Control, *Contemporary Crises*, vol. 3, pp. 339–363.

Colak, H. and Altun, U. (2006) Kisa Süreli Hapis Cezalari, Secenekli Yaptirimlar ve Infaz Rejimleri, *Türkiye Barolar Birligi Dergisi*, vol. 67, Kasim-Aralik, pp. 163–229.

Coleman, J., C. and Warren-Adamson, C. (1992) *Youth Policy in the 1990s: The Way Forward*, Routledge, London.

Corden, J. and Nott, D. (1980) The Power to Defer Sentence, *British Journal of Criminology*, vol. 20, no 4, pp. 358–367.

Cordes, E. (1950) Fines and their Enforcement, *Journal of Criminal Science*, vol. 2, pp. 46–64.

Cornel, H. (1984) *Geschichte des Jugendstrafvollzugs*, Beltz, Weinheim.

Cosar, Y. (2005) Kentlesen Türkiye'de Cocuk Suclulugu, *Türkiye Barolar Birligi Dergisi*, vol. 56, pp. 281–325.

Council of Europe (1976) *Alternative Penal Measures to Imprisonment*, Strasbourg.
Council of Europe (1984) *Prison Information Bulletin*, vol. 2, no.3.
Council of Europe (1987) *Prison Information Bulletin*, vol. 6, no 9.
Council of Europe/European Committee on Crime Problems (1978) *Compensation for Victims of Crime*, Strasbourg.
Crawford, A. (1996) Alternatives to Prosecution: Access to, or Exits from, Criminal Justice in Young, R. and Wall, D., S. (eds.) *Access to Criminal Justice: Legal Aid, Lawyers and the Defense of Liberty*, Blackstone, London, pp. 313–344.
Crawford, A. (1997) *The Local Governance of Crime: Appeals to Community and Partnerships*, Clarendon Press, Oxford.
Crawford, A. and Newburn, T. (2003) *Youth Offending and Restorative Justice; Implementing Reform in Youth Justice*, Willan, Cullompton.
Crawford, A. and Burden, T. (2005) *Integrating Victims in Restorative Youth Justice*, Policy Press, Bristol.
Crawford, A. (2006) Institutionalising Restorative Justice in a Cold, Punitive Climate, in Aertsen, I., Daems, T. and Robert, L. (eds.) *Institutionalising Restorative Justice*, Willan, pp. 120–150.
Cross, R. (1971) *Punishment, Prison and the Public*, Stevens, London.
Crow, I. (2001) *The Treatment and Rehabilitation of Offenders*, Sage, London.
Cullen, F., T. and Gilbert, K. E. (1982) *Reaffirming Rehabilitation*, Anderson, Cincinnati.
Curran, D., J. (1988) Destructuring, Privatisation and Juvenile Diversion: Compromising Community-Based Corrections, *Crime and Delinquency*, vol. 34, no 4, pp. 363–378.
Cylotte, M. (1989) *The Crisis of Prison Overcrowding*, Social Work Monographs, Norwich.
Davidson, W. S., Redner, R., Amdur, R., and Mitchell, C. M., (1990) *Alternative Treatments for Troubled Youth: the Case of Diversion from the Justice System*, Plenum Press, New York.
Davies, M., Croall, H. and Tyrer, J. (2005) *Criminal Justice*, 3rd edition, Pearson Longman, Harlow.
Dean-Myrda, M., C. and Cullen, F., T. (1985) Panacea Pendulum An Account of Community as a Response to Crime in Travis, L., F. (ed.) *Probation, Parole and Community Corrections*, Waveland Press, Prospect Heights, pp. 9–29.
Delaquis, E. (1906) *Die Rehabilitation im Strafrecht*, Guttentag, Berlin.
Deleuze, G. (1992) Das elektronische Halsband, *Kriminologisches Journal*, vol. 24, pp. 181–186.
Demirbas, T. (2000) Hürriyeti Baglayici Cezalarin and Cezaevlerinin Evrimi in Naskali, G., E. and Altun, O., H. (eds.) *Hapishane Kitabi*, Kitabevi, Istanbul.
Demirbas, T. (2001) Af Tartismalari ve 4616 Sayili 23 Nisan 1999 Tarihine Kadar Islenen Suclardan Dolayi Sartla Saliverilmeye, Dava ve Cezalarin Ertelenmesine Dair Kanun, *Anayasa Yargisi*, vol. 18, pp. 87–97.
Demirbas, T. (2003) *Infaz Hukuku*, Seckin, Ankara.
Demirbas, T. (2005) *Ceza Hukuku Genel Hükümler*, Seckin, Ankara.
Demirbas, T. (2005) *Kriminoloji*, 2nd edition, Seckin, Ankara.
Demirbas, T. (2006) Ceza ve Güvenlik Tedbirlerinin Infazi Hakkinda Kanunun Genel Degerlendirmesi, *Ceza Hukuku Dergisi*, vol. 1, no 1, pp. 19–29.
Demirel, F. (2001) 1890 Petersburg Hapishaneler Kongresi, *Toplumsal Tarih*, no 89, pp. 11–14.
Denetimli Serbestlik ve Yardim Hizmetlerinden Sorumlu Daire Baskanligi (2007) *I. Ulusal Denetimli Serbestlik Konferansi*, Ankara
Denetimli Serbestlik ve Yardim Hizmetlerinden Sorumlu Daire Baskanligi (2008) *Uluslararasi Denetimli Serbestlik Hizmetlerinde Secenek Tedbirler Konferansi*, yayin no 17, Ankara.
Denetimli Serbestlik ve Yardim Hizmetlerinden Sorumlu Daire Baskanligi (2009) *Denetimli Serbestlik ve Yardim Hizmetlerinde 2 Yil*, yayin no 14, Ankara.
Denkschrift des Preußischen Justizministers (1933) *Nationalsozialistisches Strafrecht*, Dencker's Verlag, Berlin.
Deutsche Vereinigung für Jugendgerichte und Jugendgerichtshilfen (1981) *Die Jugendrichterlichen Entscheidungen- Anspruch und Wirklichkeit,* Schriftenreihe der Deutschen Vereinigung für Jugendgerichte und Jugendgerichtshilfen, Heft 12, Arbeitskreis III Diversion: Wege zur Vermeidung des Förmlichen Verfahrens, München, pp. 176–204.

Deutsche Vereinigung für Jugendgerichte und Jugendgerichtshilfen (1984) *Jugendgerichtsverfahren und Kriminalprävention*, Schriftenreihe der Deutschen Vereinigung für Jugendgerichte und Jugendgerichtshilfen, Heft 13, München.

Deutscherjuristentag (1992) Teil O Sitzungsbericht Über die Verhandlungen Der Abteilung Strafrecht ‚Empfehlen sich Änderungen und Ergänzungen bei den strafrechtlichen Sanktionen ohne Freiheitsentzug?' (16–17 September 1992), München, Beck.

Dickinson, E., R. (1996) *The Politics of German Child Welfare from the Empire to the Federal Republic*, Harvard University Press, Cambridge.

Dignan, J. (1999) The Crime and Disorder Act and the Prospects of Restorative Justice, *Criminal Law Review*, pp. 48–60.

Dignan, J. and Cavadino, M. (1996) Towards a Framework for Conceptualising and Evaluating Models of Criminal Justice from a Victim's Perspective, *International Review of Victimology*, vol. 4, pp. 153–182.

Dignan, J. with Lowey, K. (2000) *Restorative Justice Options for Northern Ireland: A Comparative Review*, Criminal Justice Review Commission/Northern Ireland Office, Belfast.

Doganay, G. (2002) *Zur Reform der Verwarnung mit Strafvorbehalt – Eine Darstellung und Kritik aktueller Änderungsvorschläge*, Shaker, Mainz.

Dolcini, E. and Paliero, E. (1990) Alternativen zur kurzen Freiheitsstrafen in Italien und im Ausland, *Zeitschrift für die gesamte Strafrechtswissenschaft*, vol. 102, no 1, pp. 223–246.

Dolde, G. (1999) Zum Vollzug von Ersatzfreiheitsstrafen: Eindrücke aus einer empirischen Erhebung in Feuerhelm, W., Schwind, H.-D. und Bock, M. (eds.) *Festschrift für Alexander Böhm zum 70. Geburtstag am 14. Juni 1999*, de Gruyter, Berlin, pp. 581–596.

Dolde, G. (1999) Vollzug von Ersatzfreiheitsstrafen –ein wesentlicher Anteil im Kurzstrafenvollzug, *Zeitschrift für Strafvollzug und Straffälligenhilfe*, no 6, pp. 330–335.

Dölling, D. (1992a), Die weiteren Entwicklung der Sanktionen ohne Freiheitsentzug im deutschen Strafrecht, *Zeitschrift für die gesamte Strafrechtswissenschaft*, vol. 104, pp. 259–289.

Dölling, D. (1992b) Der Täter-Opfer-Ausgleich – Möglichkeiten und Grenzen einer neuen Kriminalpolitischen Reaktionsform, *Juristen Zeitung*, pp. 493–499.

Dölling, D. (1998) Diversion in Elster, A., Lingemann, H., Sieverts, R. (eds.) *Handwörterbuch der Kriminologie*, de Gruyter, Berlin, pp. 275–287.

Dönmezer, S. (1943) Cocuk Suclulugu Nevi, Sebep ve Saikleri, *Siyasi Ilimler Mecmuasi*, vol.1, no 1, pp. 227–244.

Dönmezer, S. (1965) Cezalarin Infazi Hakkinda Kanun, *Istanbul Üniversitesi Hukuk Fakültesi Mecmuasi*, vol. 30, no 1–4, pp. 8–35.

Dönmezer, S. (1967) Cezalarin Infazi Hakkinda Kanun ve Bu Kanunla Ilgili Bazi Problemler Yargitay Kararlari, *Istanbul Üniversitesi Hukuk Fakültesi Mecmuasi*, vol. 32, no 1–4, pp. 22–33.

Dönmezer, S. (1974) Criminality in a Small Community of Rapid Urbanisation and Industrialisation (The Eregli Project), *Annales de la Faculte de Droit d'Istanbul*, vol. 22, no 4, pp. 55–71.

Dönmezer, S. (1981) Mukayeseli Hukukta Yasalastirma Egilimi ve Ilkeleri in *Atatürk'ün 100. Dogum Yildönümü Kutlama Calismalari, Kolokyumlar ve Tartismalar* (14 Ocak 1981), pp. 15–16.

Dönmezer, S. (1997) Sahsi Hürriyeti Baglayici Cezalarin Infazinda Milletlerarasi Standartlar in Adalet Bakanligi, *Türkiye'de Infaz Rejimi*, Ankara, pp.11–29.

Dönmezer, S. and Yenisey, F. (2001) Ceza Adalet Sisteminin Etkinligi, TESEV, Istanbul.

Downes, D. (1998) The Buckling of the Shields: Dutch Penal Policy 1985–1995 in Weiss, R., P. and South, N. (eds.) *Comparing Prison Systems: Toward a Comparative and International Penology*, Gordon & Breach, Amsterdam, pp. 143–174.

Downes, D. (2001) Mass Incarceration in the United States- a European Perspective, Garland, D. (ed.) *Mass Imprisonment- Social Causes and Consequences*, Sage, London.

Downes, D. and Hansen. K. (2007) Welfare and Punishment in Comparative Perspective in Armstrong, S. and McAra, L. (eds.) *Perspectives on Punishment: The Contours of Control*, Oxford University Press, Oxford.

Downes, D. and Morgan, R. (1997) Dumping the 'Hostages to Fortune'? The Politics of Law and Order in Post-War Britain in Maguire, M., Morgan, R. and Reiner, R. (eds.) *the Oxford Handbook of Criminology*, 2nd edition, Clarendon Press, Oxford.

Dreher, E. (1955) Die zweite Arbeitstagung der Großen Strafrechtskommision, *Zeitschrift für die gesamte Strafrechtswissenschaft*, vol. 67, pp. 77–107.

Dunbar, I. and Langdon, A. (1998) *Tough Justice: Sentencing and Penal Policies in the 1990s*, Blackstone, London.

Dünkel, F. (1983) Strafaussetzung zur Bewährung und Bewährungshilfe in Internationalen Vergleich: Ein Überblick in Dünkel, F. and Spiess, G., *Alternativen zur Freiheitsstrafe*, Max-Planck-Institut für internationales und ausländisches Strafrecht, Freiburg.

Dünkel, F. (1986) Alternativen zur Freiheitsstrafe im europäischen Vergleich in Ortner, H. (ed.) *Freiheit statt Strafe*, AS-Verlag, Tübingen.

Dünkel, F. (2002) Der deutsche Strafvollzug im internationalen Vergleich in the following link accessible: http://www.erato.fherfurt.de/so/homepages/janssen/scripte/strafvollzug/Strafvollzug_BRD.pdf (Acces Date March 2009).

Dünkel, F. (2004) Reducing the Population of Fine Defaulters in Prisons: Experiences with Community Service in Mecklenburg-Western Pomerania (Germany) in *Criminal Policy in Europe*, Council of Europe, Strasbourg, pp. 127–138.

Dünkel, F. and Pruin, I. (2009) Community Sanctions and the Sanctioning Practice in Juvenile Justice Systems in Europe in Junger-Tas, J. and Dünkel, F. (eds.) *Reforming Juvenile Justice*, Springer, Dordrecht.

Dünkel, F. and Rössner, D. (1991) Federal Republic of Germany in van Zyl Smit, D. and Dünkel, F. (1991) *Imprisonment Today and Tomorrow: International Perspectives on Prisoners' Rights and Prison Conditions*, Kluwer, Deventer, pp. 203–248.

Dünkel, F. and Spiess, G. (1983) *Alternativen zur Freiheitsstrafe: Strafaussetzung zur Bewährung und Bewährungshilfe im internationalen Vergleich,* Max-Planck-Institut für ausländisches und internationales Strafrecht, Freiburg.

Earle, R. and Newburn, T. (2002) Creative Tensions? Young Offenders, Restorative Justice and the Introduction of Referral Orders, *Youth Justice*, vol. 1, no 3, pp. 3–13.

Ebermayer, L. (1908) Welches Strafmittelsystem empfiehlt sich für das künftige Strafgesetzbuch? *Verhandlungen des 29. Deutschen Juristentag*, vol. 1, Berlin, Guttentag, pp. 259–312.

Erdem, M., R. (2000) Kisa Süreli Hürriyeti Baglayici Cezalarin Infazi ve Yeni Secenekler in Infaz Hukukunun Sorunlari, *Probleme des Strafvollzugsrechts*, 24/25.11.2000, Goethe Institut and Baskent Universitesi, Ankara, pp. 192–213.

Erem F. (1943) Türk Ceza Kanunu'nda Emniyet Tedbirleri, *Ankara Üniversitesi Hukuk Fakültesi Dergisi*, vol. 1, no 3, pp. 351–378.

Erem, F. (1970) *Ceza Usulü Hukuku*, Ankara Üniversitesi Hukuk Fakültesi Yayinlari, Ankara.

Ertosun, A., S. (2001) Ceza Infaz Sisteminin Sorunlari ve Cözüm Önerileri in *Infaz Hukukunun Sorunlari, Probleme des Strafvollzugsrechts*, 24/25.11.2000, Goethe Institut and Baskent Universitesi, Ankara.

Erwig, J. (1927) *Die Strafrechtliche und Strafprozessuale Bedeutung des § 27b des Reichsstrafgesetzbuches*, Janssen & Beine, Hüls.

Eser, A. (1973) Germany, *American Journal of Comparative Law*, vol. 21, no 2, pp. 245–262.

Eser, A. (1988) Hundert Jahre deutscher Strafgesetzgebung – Rückblick und Tendenzen in Dijk, J., M. and Stolwijk, S. (eds.) *Criminal Law in Action: An Overview of Current Issues in Western Societies*, Kluwer, Deventer.

Eser, A. (2001) Zur Entwicklung von Maßregeln der Besserung und Sicherung als zweite Spur im Strafrecht in Britz, G. (ed.) *Grundfragen des staatlichen Strafens*, Beck, München, pp. 213–236.

European Committee on Crime Problems (1967) *The Effectiveness of Punishment and Other Measures of Treatment*, Council of Europe, Strasbourg.

Evans, P. (1980) *Prison Crisis*, George Allen & Unwin, London.

Evans, R. and Ellis, R. (1997) *Police Cautioning in the 1990s*, Home Office Research and Statistics Directorate no 52, London.

Exner, F. (1931) *Studien über die Strafzumessungspraxis der Deutschen Gerichte*, Wiegandt, Leipzig.

Fachiotti, V. (2002) Alternatives to Imprisonment in the Italian Criminal Justice System, Albrecht, H.-J. and Kalmthout, A. (eds.) *Community Sanctions and Measures in Europe and North America*, Max-Planck-Institut für ausländisches und internationales Strafrecht, Freiburg, pp. 209–242.

Fairhead, S. (1981) *Day Centres and Probation*, Home Office Research Unit Paper No. 4, HMSO, London.

Farrington, D., P. and Bennett, T. (1981) Police Cautioning of Juveniles in London, *British Journal of Criminology*, vol. 21, no 2, pp. 123–135.

Farrington, D., Ohlin, L., E. and Wilson, J. (1986) *Understanding and Controlling Crime – Toward a New Strategy*, Springer, New York.

Fattah, E. and Peters, T. (eds.) (1998) *Support for Crime Victims in a Comparative Perspective*, Leuven University Press, Leuven.

Faugeron, C. (1991) Prisons in France: Stalemate or Evolution? in van Zyl Smit, D. and Dünkel, F. (1991) *Imprisonment Today and Tomorrow: International Perspectives on Prisoners' Rights and Prison Conditions*, Kluwer, Deventer, pp. 249–273.

Feest, J. (1990) "Behandlungsvollzug"- Kritik und vollzugspolitische Konsequenzen, *Juristische Arbeitsblätter*, vol. 22, pp. 223–227.

Feest, J. and Bammann, K. (2000) *Kommentar zum Strafvollzugsgesetz*, 4th edition, Luchterland, Neuwied.

Feest, J. and Weber, H.-W (1998) Germany: Ups and Downs in Resort to Imprisonment- Strategic or Unplanned Outcomes, in Weiss, R., P. and South, N. (eds.) *Comparing Prison Systems: Toward a Comparative and International Penology*, Gordon & Breach, Amsterdam, pp. 233–261.

Feld, B. (1987) The Juvenile Court Meets the Principle of the Offence: Legislative Changes in Juvenile Waiver Status, *Journal of Criminology and Criminal Law*, vol. 78, no 3, pp. 471–533.

Feld, B. (1993) Criminalising the American Juvenile Court, *Crime and Justice*, vol. 17, pp. 197–280.

Feld, B. (1998) The Juvenile Court in Tonry, M. (ed.) *The Handbook of Crime and Punishment*, Oxford University Press, New York, pp. 509–540.

Felisch (1893) Empfiehlt sich die Einführung von Verschärfungen der Freiheitsstrafen im Sinne des österreichischen Entwurfs? *Verhandlungen des 22. Deutschen Juristentag*, vol. 3, Berlin, Guttentag, pp. 1–42.

Feltes, T. (1982) Alternativen zur Freiheitsstrafe: Eine Europäische Bestandaufnahme in Sievering, U., O. (ed.) *Alternativen zur Freiheitsstrafe*, Haag & Herrchen, Frankfurt.

Feltes, T. (1985) Konfliktbereinigung zwischen Täter und Opfer: Institutionalisierung oder Reprivatisierung? in Janssen, H. and Kerner, H.-J. (eds.) *Verbrechensopfer, Sozialarbeit und Justiz: Das Opfer im Spannungsfeld der Handlungs- und Interessenkonflikte*, Deutsche Bewährungshilfe, Bonn, pp. 407–435.

Feltes, T. (1988) Kriminalität und soziale Kontrolle im 21. Jahrhundert – Ein futuristisches Szenario vor dem Hintergrund aktueller Entwicklungen, *Bewährungshilfe*, vol. 35, no 1, pp. 90–102.

Ferri, E. (1896) *Das Verbrechen als soziale Erscheinung: Grundzüge der Kriminal-Soziologie*, Wigand, Leipzig.

Ferri, E. (1901) The Positive School of Criminology reprinted in Grupp, S., E. (ed.) (1971) *Theories of Punishment*, Indiana University Press, Bloomington.

Feuerhelm, W. (1997) *Stellung und Ausgestaltung der Gemeinnützigen Arbeit im Strafrecht*, Kriminologische Zentralstelle, Wiesbaden.

Feuerhelm, W. (1999) Die gemeinnützige Arbeit im Strafrecht, *Neue Kriminalpolitik*, no 1, pp. 22–27.

Feurhelm, W. (1991) *Gemeinnützige Arbeit als Alternative in der Geldstrafenvollstreckung*, Kriminologische Zentralstelle, Wiesbaden.

Finger, A. (1904) *Lehrbuch des deutschen Strafrechts*, Heymann, Berlin.

Foucault, M. (1975) *Discipline and Punish: the Birth of the Prison*, Penguin, London.

Fox, L. W. (1950) The Criminal Justice Act and Prison Administration, *Journal of Criminal Science*, vol. 2 (a Symposium on the Criminal Justice Act 1948), Macmillan & St. Martin's Street, London.

Fox, L., W. (1952) *The English Prison and Borstal Systems*, Routledge & Kegan Paul, London.

Fox, D., Dhami, M., K. and Mantle, G. (2006) Restorative Final Warnings: Policy and Practice, *Howard Journal of Criminal Justice*, vol. 45, no 2, pp. 129–140.

Frankenberg, G. (1985) Critical Comparisons: Rethinking Comparative Law, *Harvard International Law Journal*, vol. 26, no 2, pp. 411–455.

Frede, L. (1932) *Die Beschlüsse der Internationalen Gefängnis-Kongresse* 1872–1930, Frommann, Jena.

Frehsee, D. (1987) *Schadenswiedergutmachung als Instrument strafrechtlicher Sozialkontrolle: ein kriminalpolitischer Beitrag zur Suche nach alternativen Sanktionsformen*, Duncker & Humblot, Berlin.

Frehsee, D. (1999) Restitution and Offender-Victim Arrangement within Criminal Law in Germany, *Buffalo Criminal Law Review*, vol. 3., no 1, pp. 235–259.

Freisler, R. (1934) Strafensystem in Grundzüge eines Allgemeinen Deutschen Strafrechts in Freisler, R. and Luetgebrune, W. (eds.) *Denkschrift des Zentralausschusses der Strafrechtabteilung der Akademie für deutsches Recht,* Decker, Berlin.

Freudenthal, B. (1907) *Amerikanische Kriminalpolitik*, Guttentag, Berlin.

Fritsch, M. (1999) *Die jugendstrafrechtliche Reformbewegung (1871–1923)*, ed iuscrim, Freiburg.

Frommel, M. (1991) Verbrechensbekämpfung im Nationalsozialismus in Stolleis, M. with Frommel, M., Rückert, J., Schröder, R., Seelmann, K., Wiegand, W. (eds.) *Die Bedeutung der Wörter – Studien zur europäischen Rechtsgeschichte, Festschrift für den Sten Gagner zum 70. Geburtstag*, Beck, München, pp. 47–64.

Frommel, M. (1999) Fahrverbot statt Freiheitsstrafe, *Neue Justiz*, vol. 1, p. 5.

Frommel, M. (1999) Alternative Strafen und Alternativen zum Freiheitsentzug, *Neue Kriminalpolitik*, no 3, pp. 9–13.

Gaes, G. (1985) The Effects of Overcrowding in Prison, *Crime and Justice,* vol. 6, pp. 94–146.

Galassi, S. (2004) *Kriminologie im deutschen Reich*, Steiner, Stuttgart.

Galatasaray Üniversitesi (2004) Türk Ceza Kanunu Tasarisi Hakkinda Galatasaray Üniversitesi'nin Görüsü in Ergül, T. (ed.) *Türk Ceza Kanunu Reformu*, Ikinci Kitap, TBB Yayinlari, Ankara, pp. 285–317.

Gallo, E. (1995) The Penal System in France: from Correctionalism to Manageralism in Ruggiero, V., Ryan, M. and Sim, J. (eds.) *Western European Penal Systems: A Critical Anatomy*, Sage, London, pp. 71–92.

Garland, D. (1985) *Punishment and Welfare: A History of Penal Strategies*, Aldershot, Gower.

Garland, D. (1988) British Criminology before 1935, *British Journal of Criminology*, vol. 28, no 1, pp. 131–147.

Garland, D. and Young, P. (1983) Towards a Social Analysis of Penality in Garland, D. and Young, P. (eds.) *The Power to Punish. Contemporary Penality and Social Analysis*, Heinemann, London.

Gazel, A., A. (2000) Tanin Muhabiri Ahmet Serif Bey'in Notlarinda Osmanli Hapishaneleri in Naskali, G., E. and Altun, O., H. (eds.) *Hapishane Kitabi*, Kitabevi, Istanbul, pp. 143–151.

Gelsthorpe, L. and Morris, A. (1994) *Juvenile Justice 1945–1992* in Maguire, M., Morgan, R. and Reiner, R. (eds.) *the Oxford Handbook of Criminology*, Clarendon Press, Oxford.

Gelsthorpe, L. and Morris, A. (2002) Restorative Justice, the Last Vestiges of Welfare in Muncie, J., Hughes, G. and McLaughlin, E. (eds.) *Youth Justice: Critical Readings*, Sage, London, pp. 238–254.

Gelsthorpe, L. and Padfield, N. (2003) Youth Justice: Discretion in Pre-Court Decision-Making in Gelsthorpe, L. and Padfield, N. (eds.) *Exercising Discretion: Decision-Making in the Criminal Justice System and Beyond*, Willan, Cullompton, pp. 29–49.

Gemalmaz, S. (1989) *The Institutionalization Process of the "Turkish Type of Democracy": A Politico Juridical Analysis of Human Rights*, Amac, Istanbul.

Gemalmaz, S. (2002) The Death Penalty in Turkey (1920–2001) Facts, Truths and Illusions, *Criminal Law Forum*, vol. 13, no 1, pp. 91–122.

Gennat (1905) *Das Strafensystem und seine Reform*, Mauke, Hamburg.

Georgi, P., G. (1914) *Die Reform der Geldstrafe im Vorentwurf zu einem Deutschen Strafgesetzbuch und im Gegenentwurf zu diesem Vorentwurf unter Berücksichtigung der veröffentlichen Beschlüsse der Strafrechtskommission*, Schulze, Meerane.

Gerber, H. (1994) *State, Society and Law in Islam: Ottoman Law in Comparative Perspective*, State University of New York Press, Albany.

Gerken, U. and Henningsen, J. (1987) Ersetzung der Ersatzfreiheitsstrafe durch freie Arbeit – Ein Betrag zur Diskussion um die Geldstrafe und ihre Surrogate, *Zeitschrift für Rechtspolitik*, vol. 20, pp. 386–390.

Germain, C. (1954) Postwar Prison Reform in France, *Annals of the American Academy of Political and Social Science*, vol. 293, pp. 139–151.

Gibson, B. (1990) *Unit Fines*, Waterside Press, Winchester.

Gibson, B. (1995) Young People, Bad News, Enduring Principles, *Youth and Policy*, vol. 48, pp. 64–70.

Gibson, B. and Cavadino, P. (2002) *Introduction to the Criminal Justice Process*, Waterside Press, Winchester.

Giller, H. (1999) From Centre Stage to Spear Carrier: The Repositioning of the English Juvenile Court, *European Journal on Criminal Policy and Research*, vol. 7, no 3, pp. 395–403.

Giller, H. (2004) *Final Warnings Interventions*, Youth Justice Board, London.

Gökcen, A. (1987) *Tanzimat Dönemi Osmanli Ceza Kanunlari ve Bu Kanunlardaki Ceza Müeyyideleri* (unpublished master thesis, University of Istanbul).

Gölcüklü, F. (1955) Ingiliz Adli Teskilati, *Ankara Üniversitesi Siyasal Bilgiler Fakültesi Dergisi*, vol. 10, no 1, pp. 160–185.

Gölcüklü, F. (1956) Acik Müesesseler, *Ankara Üniversitesi Hukuk Fakültesi Dergisi*, vol. 11, no 2, pp. 91–106.

Gölcüklü, F. (1962a) Ingiltere ve Gal Eyaleti'nde Hürriyeti Baglayici Cezalar ve Cezaevi Sistemleri, *Ankara Üniversitesi Hukuk Fakültesi Dergisi*, vol. 17, no 1, pp. 159–202.

Gölcüklü, F. (1962b) Türkiye'de Cocuk Suclulugu, *Ankara Üniversitesi Siyasal Bilgiler Fakültesi Dergisi*, vol. 11, no 3, pp. 151–181.

Gölcüklü, F. (1966) *Türk Ceza Sistemi (Hürriyeti Baglayici Cezalar)*, Sevinc Matbaasi, Ankara, pp. 46–60.

Goldschmidt, J. (1908) Strafen (Haupt- und Nebenstrafen) und verwandte Maßregeln in *Vergleichende Darstellung des deutschen und ausländischen Strafrechts*, Allgemeiner Teil, in Birkmeyer, K. (ed.) Vergleichende Darstellung des deutschen und ausländischen Strafrechts, Allgemeiner Teil, vol. 4, Liebmann, Berlin, pp. 81–506.

Goldson B. (2006) Penal Custody: Intolerance, Irrationality and Indifference in Goldson, B. and Muncie, J. (eds.) *Youth, Crime and Justice: Critical Issues*, Sage, London, pp.139–156.

Gönen, S., Y. (2000) Osmanli Imparatorlugunda Hapishaneleri Iyilestirme Girisimleri, 1917 Yili in Naskali, G., E. and Altun, O., H. (eds.) *Hapishane Kitabi*, Kitabevi, Istanbul, pp. 173–183.

Göral, S., Ö. (2007) 19. Yüzyil Istanbul'unda Suc, Toplumsal Kontrol ve Hapishaneler Üzerine Calismak in Levy, N and Toumarkine, A. (eds.) *Osmanli'da Asayis, Suc ve Ceza, Tarih Vakfi Yayinlari*, Istanbul.

Gove, W: (1980) The Labelling of Deviance: Evaluating a Perspective, 2nd Edition, Sage, Beverly Hills.

Graham, J. (1987) *The Declining Prison Population in the Federal Republic of Germany*, Home Office Research Bulletin, no 24, London, pp. 47–52.

Graham, J. (1990) Decarceration in the Federal Republic of Germany: How Practitioners are Succeeding Where Policy Makers Have Failed?, *British Journal of Criminology*, vol. 30, no 2, pp. 47–52.

Grau (1934) Verwarnung mit Strafvorbehalt in Gürtner, F. and Freisler, R. (1936) *Das neue Strafrecht - Grundsätzliche Gedanken zum Geleit*, 2nd edition, Decker's Verlag, Berlin, pp. 117–127.

Grebing. G. (1978) Die Geldstrafe in rechtsvergleichender Darstellung in Jescheck, H.-H. and Grebing, G. (eds.) *Die Geldstrafe im deutschen und ausländischen Recht*, Nomos, Baden Baden, pp. 1185–1357.

Green, P. (2000) Criminal Justice and Democratisation in Turkey: the Paradox of Transition in Green, P. and Rutherford, A. (eds.) *Criminal Policy in Transition*, Hart Publishing, Oxford.

Green, P. (2002) Turkish Jails, Hunger Strikes and the European Drive for Prison Reform, *Punishment and Society*, vol. 4, no 1, pp. 97–101.

Green, P. (2005) Disaster by Design: Corruption, Construction and Catastrophe, *British Journal of Criminology*, vol. 45, no 4, pp. 528–546.

Greer, D. (1996) *Compensating Crime Victims: a European Survey*, Max-Planck-Institut für ausländisches and internationales Strafrecht, Freiburg.

Gronemeyer, D. (2001) *Zur Reformbedürftigkeit der strafrechtlichen Fahrerlaubnisentziehung und des strafrechtlichen Fahrverbots*, Lang, Frankfurt.

Groß, A. (1907) Für den Bedingten Straferlass: Rechtsvergleichend-Kritische Untersuchung, A. Hödler, Wien.

Gruber, L. (1903) Die bedingte Verurteilung in Frankreich, *Gerichtssaal*, vol. 62, pp. 292–306.

Grünhut, M. (1948) *Penal Reform: A Comparative Study*, Clarendon Press, Oxford.

Günal, Y. (1965a) Yirmi Yildir Gerceklesmeyen Bir Tasari – Cocuk Mahkemeleri Kanunu Tasarisi, *Ankara Üniversitesi Siyasal Bilgiler Fakültesi Dergisi*, vol. 20, no 1, pp. 337–340.

Günal, Y. (1965b) Ceza Infaz Kanunu Tasarisi, *Ankara Üniversitesi Siyasal Bilgiler Fakültesi Dergisi*, vol. 20, no 2, pp. 889–901.

Günal, Y. (1967) Avrupa Ceza Hukukunun Birlestirilmesinin Türkiye ile Ilgisi, *Ankara Üniversitesi Siyasal Bilgiler Fakültesi Dergisi*, vo. 22, no 2, pp. 219–226.

Gürelli, N. (1965) Introduction for *Turkish Criminal Code*, The American Series of Foreign Penal Codes, Sweet & Maxwell, London.

Gürelli, N. (1983) The Recent Development of Turkish Criminal Procedure and the Practice of the Turkish Judiciary, *Annales de la Facultés de Droit d'Istanbul*, vol. 29, no 45, p. 6.

Gürtner, F. and Freisler, R. (1936) *Das neue Strafrecht - Grundsätzliche Gedanken zum Geleit*, 2nd edition, Decker's Verlag, Berlin.

Gutmann, H. (1909) *Die Natur der Geldstrafe und ihre Verwendung im heutigen Reichsstrafrecht*, Hirschfeld, Leipzig.

Güven, I. and Akco, S. (2004) Yeni Bir Dünya Icin Yeni Bir Dil Gerekir, *Türkiye Barolar Birligi Dergisi*, vol. 51, pp. 197–207.

Häger, J. (2006) vor § 40 bis 43 in Laufhütte, H. W, Rissing-van Saan, R. and Tidemann, K. (eds.) *Leipziger Kommentar*, vol. 2, pp. 836–952.

Haines, K. (1998) Some Principled Objections to a Restorative Justice Approach to Working with Juvenile Offenders in Walgrave, L. (ed.) *Restorative Justice for juveniles: Potentials, Risks and Problems for Research*, Leuven University Press, Leuven, pp. 93–113.

Haines, K. and Drakeford, M. (1998) *Young People and Youth Justice*, Macmillan, London.

Hale, C. (1989) Economy, Imprisonment and Punishment, *Contemporary Crises*, vol. 13, pp. 327–349.

Hale, W. (1994) *Turkish Politics and the Military*, Routledge, London.

Haleem, M., A., A. and Sharif, A., O. and Daniels, K. (2003) *Criminal Justice in Islam: Judicial Procedure in Sharia*, Tauris, London.

Hall, K. (1954) Die Freiheitsstrafe als kriminalpolitisches Problem, *Zeitschrift für die gesamte Strafrechtswissenschaft*, vol. 66, pp. 77–110.

Harding, J. (2003) Which Way Probation? A Correctional or Community Service? *Probation Journal*, vol. 50, no 4, pp. 369–373.

Harris, R. (1995) Probation round the World: Origins and Development in Hamai, K., Ville, R., Harris, R., in Hough, M. and Zvekic, U. (eds.) *Probation Round the World: A Comparative Study*, Routledge, London, pp. 25–67.

Hartmann, A. (1995) *Schlichten und Richten der Täter Opfer Ausgleich und das (Jugend-) Strafrecht*, Fink Verlag, München.

Hartmann, A. and Kilchling, M. (1998) The German Development of Victim-Offender Mediation in the German Juvenile Justice System from the Legal and Criminological Point of View, Walgrave, L. (ed.) *Restorative Justice for Juveniles, Potentials, Risks and Problems for Research*, Leuven University Press, Leuven, pp. 261–282.

Haverkamp, R. (2002) *Elektronischer überwachter Hausarrest*, edition iuscrim, Freiburg.

Hawkins, K. (1975) Alternatives to Imprisonment in McConville, S. (ed.) *The Use of Imprisonment: Essays in the Changing State of English Penal Policy*, Routledge & Paul, London, pp. 66–87.

Hawkins, R. and Tiedeman, G. (1975) *The Creation of Deviance*, Charles E. Merrill Publishing, Columbus.

Heilborn, P. (1908) Die kurze Freiheitsstrafe, reprinted in 1978, Scientia, Darmstadt.

Heinitz, E. (1958) Der Entwurf des Allgemeinen Teils des Strafgesetzbuches vom kriminalpolitischen Standpunkt aus, *Zeitschrift für die gesamte Strafrechtswissenschaft*, vol. 70, pp. 1–24.

Heinz, W. (1981) Entwicklung, Stand und Struktur der Strafzumessungspraxis, *Monatschrift für Kriminologie und Strafrecht*, vol. 64, no 3, pp. 148–173.

Heinz, W. (1982) Strafrechtsreform und Sanktionsentwicklung – Auswirkungen der sanktionenrechtlichen Regelungen des 1. und 2. StrRG 1969 sowie des EGStGB 1974 auf die Sanktionspraxis, *Zeitschrift für die gesamte Strafrechtswissenschaft,* vol. 94, no 3, pp. 632–668.

Heinz, W. (1990) Die Bedeutung des Erziehungsgedankens für Normsetzung und Normanwendung im Jugendstrafrecht der Bundesrepublik Deutschland in Wolff, J. and Marek, A. (ed.) *Erziehung und Strafe*, Forum, Bonn, pp. 28–49.

Heinz, W. (1992) *Diversion im Jugendstrafverfahren* der Bundesrepublik Deutschland in Heinz, W. and Storz, R., Bundesministerium der Justiz, Forum Verlag, Bonn.

Heinz, W. (1993) Neues zur Diversion im Jugendstrafverfahren- Kooperation, Rolle und Rechtsstellung der Beteiligten, *Monatsschrift für Kriminologie und Strafrechtsreform*, vol. 76, no 6, pp. 355–375.

Heinz, W. (1997) Entwicklungstendenzen und Reformstrategien im Jugendstrafrecht im europäischen Vergleich (in Deutschland) in Dünkel, F., van Kalmthout, A. and Schüler-Springorum, H. (eds.) *Entwicklungstendenzen und Reformstrategien im europäischen Vergleich*, Forum, Mönchengladbach, pp. 3–65.

Heinz, W. (2008) Sanktionierungspraxis in Deutschland, Internet Publication: accessible from the following link: http://www.uni-konstanz.de/rtf/kis/Sanktionierungspraxis-in-Deutschland-Stand-2006.pdf.

Helgerth, R. and Krauß, F. (2001) Der Gesetzentwurf zur Reform des Sanktionenrechts, *Zeitschrift für Rechtspolitik*, vol. 34, no 7, pp. 281–283.

Hellwig, A. (1921) *Die bedingte Strafaussetzung der Strafvollstreckung in Preußen und im Reich,* Müller, Berlin.

Hellwig, A. (1922) *Das Geldstrafegesetz vom 21 Dezember 1922*, Müller, München.

Hendrick, H. (2006) Histories of Youth Crime and Justice in Goldon, B. and Muncie, J. (eds.) *Youth Crime and Justice*, Sage, London.

Henze, M. (2007) Die internationalen Gefägniskongresse 1872–1935 in Keser-Biermann, S. and Overath, P. (eds.) *Die Internationalisierung von Strafrecht und Kriminalpolitik*, Berliner-Wissenschaft Verlag, Berlin, pp. 60–84.

Hermann, J. (1984) Diversion und Schlichtung in der Bundesrepublik Deutschland, *Zeitschrift für die gesamte Strafrechtswissenschaft*, vol. 96, no 2, pp. 455–484.

Hertwig, V. (1982) *Die Einstellung des Strafverfahrens wegen Geringfügigkeit – Eine empirische Analyse der Handhabung der § 153, 153a StPO in der staatsanwaltlichen und gerichtlichen Praxis,* Schwartz, Göttingen.

HEUNI (1985) *Criminal Justice Systems in Europe and North America*, Helsinki.

HEUNI (1989) *Changing Victim Policy: The United Nations Victim Declaration and Recent Developments in Europe* (Report on the Meeting of an ad hoc Expert Group Meeting, Helsinki 17–20 November 1988), Helsinki.

Heyd, U. (1973) *Studies in Old Ottoman Criminal Law*, Oxford University Press, Oxford.

Hirsch, H., J. (1978) Zur Behandlung der Bagatellkriminalität in der Bundesrepublik Deutschland, *Zeitschrift für die gesamte Strafrechtswissenschaft*, vol. 90, pp. 218–254.

Hirsch, H.-J. (1986) Bilanz der Strafrechtsreform in, H.-J., Kaiser, G. and Marquardt, H. (eds.) *Gedächtnisschrift für Hilde Kaufmann*, de Gruyter, Berlin, pp. 133–165.

Hirsch, H.-J. (1990) Wiedergutmachung des Schadens im Rahmen des materiallen Strafrechts, *Zeitschrift für die gesamte Strafrechtswissenschaft*, vol. 102, pp. 534–562.

Hoberg, J. (1910) *Ist die sachgemäße Ausgestaltung der Geldstrafe als Ersatz anderer Strafarten und zur Vermeidung kurzzeitiger Freiheitsstrafen für ein neues Strafgesetz zu Empfehlen?* Noske, Leipzig.

Hoegen, E. and Brienen, M (2000) *Victims of Crime in 22 European Criminal Justice Systems*, Wolf Legal Production in cooperation with the Global Law Association, Nijmegen.

Hoegner, H., W. (1911) *Die bedingte Strafaussetzung nach dem Vorentwurf (verglichen mit der bedingten Begnadigung)*, Schreiber, München.

Homann, C. (1984) Freiheitsentziehende Sanktionen und Haftplatzbedarf, dargestellt an der Entwicklung von Verurteiltenzahlen und Belegungszahlen der Gefangenen in den Justizvollzugsanstalten 1971 bis 1982, *Monatschrift für Kriminologie*, vol. 67, no 5, pp. 332–338.

Home Office (1957) *Alternatives to Short-Terms of Imprisonment* (A Report of the Advisory Council on the Treatment of Offenders, HMSO, London.

Home Office (1959) *Penal Practice in a Changing Society. Aspects of Future Developments* (England and Wales), HMSO, London.

Home Office (1964) *The War Against Crime in England and Wales 1959–1964*, HMSO, London.

Home Office (1965) *The Adult Offende*r, HMSO, London.

Home Office (1967) *Criminal Statistics England and Wales* 1966, HMSO, London.

Home Office (1969) *People in Prison (England and Wales)*, HMSO, London.

Home Office (1970) *Criminal Statistics England and Wales 1969*, HMSO, London.

Home Office (1977) *The Length of Prison Sentences* (Interim Report of the Advisory Council on the Penal System), HMSO, London.

Home Office (1979) *Criminal Statistics England and Wales 1978*, HMSO, London.

Home Office (1980) *Criminal Statistics, England and Wales 1979*, HMSO, London.

Home Office (1980) *Statistics of the Criminal Justice System England and Wales 1969–79*, HMSO, London

Home Office (1981) *Review of Parole in England and Wales*, HMSO, London.

Home Office (1981) *Criminal Statistics England and Wales 1980*, HMSO, London.

Home Office (1982) *Criminal Statistics England and Wales 1981*, HMSO, London.

Home Office (1991) *Crime, Justice and Protecting the Public*, HMSO, London.

Home Office (1996) *Criminal Statistics England and Wales 1995*, HMSO, London.

Home Office (1997) *No More Excuses: A New Approach to Tackling Youth Crime in England and Wales*, HMSO, London.

Home Office (2001) *Making Punishments Work* (Report of a Review of the Sentencing Framework for England and Wales), Home Office Communication Directorate, London.

Home Office (2007) *Sentencing Statistics 2005*, HMSO, London.

Hönicke, F. (1999) *Arbeitszwang als Kriminalrechtsreaktion, Gemeinnützige Arbeit in der Strafrechtspflege unter Art. 12 Abs. 2, 3 GG*, Florentz, München.

Hood, R. (1974) Criminology and Penal Change: A Case Study of the Nature and Impact of Some Recent Advice to Governments in Hood, R. (ed.) *Crime, Criminology and Public Policy*, pp. 375–417.

Hough, M. and Ashworth, A. (1996) Sentencing and the Climate of Opinion, *Criminal Law Review*, pp. 776–787.

Hough, M., Jacobson, J. ad Millie, A. (2003) *The Decision to Imprison, Sentencing and the Prison Population*, Prison Reform Trust, London.

Hoy, C. and Worrall, A. (2005) *Punishment in the Community: Managing Offenders, Making Choices*, Willan, Cullompton.

Hubrach, J. (2008) on Section 56, Laufhütte, H. W, Rissing-van Saan, R. and Tidemann, K. (eds.) *Leipziger Kommentar StGB*, 12th edition, vol. 4, pp. 1–106.

Hudson, B. (1993) *Penal Policy and Social Justice*, Macmillan, Basingstoke.

Hudy, M. (1998) *Elektronisch überwachter Hausarrest – Befunde zur Zielgruppenplanung und Probleme einer Implementation in das deutsche Sanktionensystem*, Nomos, Baden-Baden.

Hughes, G. (2001) Competing Logics of Community Sanctions: Welfare, Rehabilitation and Restorative Justice in McLaughlin, E. and Muncie, J. (eds.) *Controlling Crime*, Sage, London, pp. 257–302.

Hughes, G, Pilkington, A. and Leisten, R. (1998) Diversion in a Culture of Severity, *Howard Journal*, vol. 37, no 1, pp. 16–33.

Hünerfeld, P. (1978) Kleinkriminalität und Strafverfahren, *Zeitschrift für die gesamte Strafrechtswissenschaft*, vol. 90, pp. 905–926.

Hungerford-Welch, P. (2004) *Criminal Litigation and Sentencing*, Routledge, London.

Hutton, N. (2003) Sentencing Guidelines in Tonry, M. (ed.) *Confronting Crime*, Willan, Cullompton, pp. 112–139.

Icel, K., Sokullu-Akinci, F., Özgenc, I., Sözüer, A., Mahmutoglu, F., S. and Ünver, Y. (2000) *Yaptirim Teorisi*, Beta, Istanbul.

Ignatieff, M. (1978) *A Just Measure of Pain: the Penitentiary in the Industrial Revolution, 1750–1850*, Pantheon Books, New York.

Ignatieff, M. (1981) State, Civil Society and Total Institutions: A Critique of Recent Social Histories of Punishment, *Crime and Justice*, vol. 3, pp. 153–192.

Ince, H. (2008) Kisa Süreli Hapis Cezasina Uygulanabilecek Secenek Yaptirimlardan "Kamuya Yararli Bir Iste Calistirma" Yaptirimi, (Community Service Labour Programme, *sic.*), Adalet Dergisi, no. 30 accessible from: http://www.yayin.adalet.gov.tr/30_sayi%20i%C3%A7erik/H%C3%BCseyin%20%C4%B0nce.htm (Access Date: March 2010).

Istanbul Barosu (2006) Cocuk ve Genc Adalet Sistemi Sempozyumu – Türk Mevzuatinin ve Özellikle Cocuklari Koruma Kanununun Degerlendirilmesi, Istanbul.

Istanbul Barosu (2006) CMK Uygulama Servisi Faaliyet Raporu (01.06.2005–01.06.2006), Istanbul.

Istanbul Barosu Cocuk Haklari Merkezi (2006) *Cocuk Adalet Sisteminde Uzlaşma*, the report of the working group in 12. 05.2006, Istanbul.

Istanbul Üniversitesi (1972) Ceza Adalet Reformu Ilkeleri, Sempozyumu 24–26 Subat 1972, Sulhi Garan Matbaasi, Istanbul.

Jannsen, H. (1983) Diversion: Entstehungsbedingungen, Hintergründe und Konsequenzen einer veränderten Strategie sozialer Kontrolle, Oder: Es gibt viele zu Packen, tun wir es ihnen an in Kerner, H.-J. (ed.) *Diversion statt Strafe? Probleme und Gefahren einer neuen Strategie sozialer Kontrolle*, Kriminalistik Verlag, Heidelberg, pp. 15–54.

Jannsen, H. (1985) Diversion im Jugendstrafrecht als kriminalpolitische Alternative, *Kriminalistik*, vol. 39, no 4, pp. 208–212.

Jarvis, F., V. (1972) *Advise, Assist and Befriend: A History of Probation and After-Care Service*, National Association of Probation Officers, London.

Jescheck, H.-H. (1979) Die Krise der Kriminalpolitik, *Zeitschrift für die gesamte Strafrechtswissenschaft*, vol. 91, pp. 1037–1064.

Jescheck, H.-H. (1983) Die Freiheitsstrafe bei Franz von Liszt im Lichte der modernen Kriminalpolitik in Kohlmann, G. (ed.) *Festschrift für Ulrich Klug zum 70. Geburtstag*, Deubner, Köln.

Jescheck, H.-H. (1983–1984) (ed.) *Die Freiheitsstrafe und ihre Surrogate im deutschen und ausländischen Recht,* vol. 1–3, Nomos, Baden Baden.

Jescheck, H.-H. and Weigend, T. (1996) *Lehrbuch des Strafrechts*, 5th edition, Duncker & Humblot, Berlin.

Johnstone, G. (1999) Restorative Justice, Shame and Forgiveness, *Liverpool Law Review*, vol. 21, pp. 197–216.

Jones, S. (1983) Deferment of Sentence, An Appraisal Ten Years On, *British Journal of Criminology*, vol. 23, no 4, pp. 381–393.

Joutsen, M. (1991) Changing Victim Policy: International Dimensions in Kaiser, G., Kury, H. and Albrecht, H.-J., *Victims and Criminal Justice*, vol. 52/2, Max-Planck-Institut für internationales and ausländisches Strafrecht, Freiburg, pp. 765–797.

Julius, K.-P. (1999) Tagungsbericht, *Zeitschrift für die gesamte Strafrechtswissenschaft*, vol. 111, pp. 889–915.

Jung, H. (1998) Mediation/Paradigmwechsel in der Konfliktregelung, in Scwind, H.-D., Kube, E. and Kühne (eds.) H.-H. *Festschrift für Hans Joachim Schneider zum 70. Geburtstag am 14 November 1998*, de Gruyter, Berlin, pp. 913–926.

Jung, H. (1999) Die "European Rules on Community Sanctions and Measures" in Feuerhelm, W., Schwind, H.-D. und Bock, M. (eds.) Festschrift für *Alexander Böhm zum 70. Geburtstag am 14. Juni 1999*, de Gruyter, Berlin, pp. 69–79.

Junger-Tas, J. (1994) Alternative Sanctions: Myth and Reality, *European Journal on Criminal Policy and Research*, vol. 2, no 1, pp. 44–66.

Kahl, W., v. Lilienthal, K., v. Liszt, F., and Goldschmidt, J. (1911) *Gegenentwurf zum Vorentwurf eines Deutschen Strafgesetzbuchs*, Guttentag, Berlin.

Kaiser, G. (1977) Resozialisierung und Zeitgeist in Herren, R., Kienapfel, D. and Müller-Dietz, H. (eds.) *Kultur, Kriminalität und Strafrecht, Festschrift für Thomas Würtenberger*, Duncker & Humblot, Berlin, pp. 359–372.

Kaiser, G. (1979) Viktimologie an der schwelle der 80er Jahre –ein kritisches Resümee in Kirchoff, G., F. and Sessar, K. (eds.) *Das Verbrechensopfer*, Brockmeyer, Bochum, pp. 481–496.

Kaiser, G. (1980) *Kriminologie*, Müller, Heidelberg.

Kaiser, G. and Schöch, H. (2002) *Strafvollzug*, 5th edition, Müller, Heidelberg.

Kangaspunta, K., Joutsen, M. and Ollus, N. (1998) *Crime and Criminal Justice in Europe and North America 1990- 1994*, HEUNI, Helsinki.

Karaca, A. (2000) XIX. Yüzyilda Osmanli Devletinde Fahise Hatunlara Uygulanan Cezalar: Hapis ve Sürgün in Naskali, G., E. and Altun, O., H. (eds.) *Hapishane Kitabi*, Kitabevi, Istanbul, pp. 152–162.

Karpat, K., H. (1959) *Turkey's Politics: the Transition to a Multi-Party System*, Princeton University Press, Princeton.

Kaufmann, A. (1968) Die Dogmatik im Alternativ Entwurf, *Zeitschrift für die gesamte Strafrechtswissenschaft,* vol. 80, pp. 34–53.

Kausch, E. (1980) *Der Staatsanwalt, ein Richter vor dem Richter? Untersuchungen zu § 153a StPO*, Duncker & Humblot, Berlin.

Kawamura, G. (1998) *Gemeinnützige Arbeit in Bayern am Schnittpunkt von sozialer Arbeit und Justiz*, Georg-Simon-Ohm-Fachochschule, Nürnberg.

Kelk, C., Koffman, L. and Silvis, J. (1995) Sentencing Practice, Policy, and Discretion in Fennell, P., Harding, C., Jörg, N. and Swart, B. (eds.) *Criminal Justice in Europe: A Comparative Study*, Clarendon Press, Oxford.

Kensey, A. (2002) Community Sanctions and Measures in France in Albrecht, H.-J. and Kalmthout, A. (eds.) *Community Sanctions and Measures in Europe and North America*, Max-Planck-Institut für ausländisches und internationales Strafrecht, Freiburg, pp. 209–242.

Kensey, A. and Tournier, P. (1999) Prison Population Inflation, Overcrowding and Recidivism: the Situation in France, *European Journal on Criminal Policy and Research*, vol. 7, no 1, pp. 97–119.

Kern, E. (1927) *Zur Strafrechtsreform (1. Der Alkoholsverbrecher, 2. Der Gewohnheitsverbrecher und 3. Der Strafrichter im Dienst der Spezialprävention)*, Bensheimer, Mannheim.

Kerner, H.-J. (1983) Statt Strafe: Diversion, Zur Einführung in die Thematik in Kerner (ed.) *Diversion statt Strafe? Problems und Gefahren einer neuen strafrechtlicher Sozialkontrolle*, Kriminalistik Verlag, Heidelberg, pp. 1–13.

Kerner, H.J. (1986) Die Wiedereinsetzung des Opfers als Subjekt des (Straf-)Rechts in Janssen, H. and Kerner, H.-J. (eds.) *Verbrechensopfer, Sozialarbeit und Justiz: Das Opfer im Spannungsfeld der Handlungs- und Interessenkonflikte*, Deutsche Bewährungshilfe, Bonn, pp. 495–521.

Kesper-Biermann, S. (2007) Die Internationale Kriminalistische Vereinigung. Zum Verhältnis von Wissenschaftsbeziehungen und Politik im Strafrecht 1889–1932 in Kesper-Biermann, S. and Overath, P. (eds.), *Die Internationalisierung von Strafrecht und Kriminalpolitik*, pp. 60–84, Berliner-Wissenschaft Verlag, Berlin, pp. 85–107.

Kilchling, M. (2005) Victim-Offender Mediation with Juvenile Offenders in Germany in Mestitz, A. and Ghetti, S. (eds.) *Victim-Offender Mediation with Youth Offenders in Europe*, Springer, Dordrecht, pp. 229–257.

King, J., F., S. (1969) The Probation and After-Care Service, 3rd edition, Butterworths, London.

Kirchenheim (1890) Bedingte Bestrafung, *Gerichtsaal* vol. 43, pp. 51–69

Kirchoff, G., F. (1985) *Diversion im Jugendstrafrecht: Das STOP-Programm der INTEG nach zwei Jahren*, in Kriminologische Forschung in der Diskussion, Heymann, Köln, pp. 341–369.

Kitzinger, F. (1905) *Die Internationale Kriminalistische Vereinigung: Betrachtungen über Ihr Wesen und Ihre Bisherige Wirksamkeit*, Beck, München.

Kleber, H. (1933) *Die Ersatzgeldstrafe nach § 27b Strafgesetzbuch*, Tageblatt-Haus, Coburg.

Klee, P. (1904) Die bedingte Begnadigung in den deutschen Bundesstaaten unter rechtsvergleichender Berücksichtigung der bedingten Verurteilung des Auslands, *Zeitschrift für die gesamte Strafrechtswissenschaft*, vol. 24, pp. 69–87.

Klee, K. (1906) Die bedingte Begnadigung innerhalb der letzten sechs Jahre, *Zeitschrift für die gesamte Strafrechtswissenschaft*, vol. 26, pp. 458–487.

Klein, M. (1979) Deinstitutionalisation and Diversion of Juvenile Offenders: A Litany of Impediments, in Morris, N. and Tonry, M. (eds.) *Crime and Justice*, vol. 1, University of Chicago Press, pp. 145–201.

Kleve (1906) Das italienische Gesetz über die bedingte Verurteilung (Lex Ronchetti), *Deutsche Juristen-Zeitung*, vol. XI, no 4, pp. 237–241.

Koepsel, K. (1999) Jugendarrest – eine zeitgemäße Sanktionsform des Jugendstrafrechts? in, Feuerhelm, W., Schwind, H.-D., Bock, M. (eds.) *Festschrift für Alexander Böhm zum 70. Geburtstag am 14 Juni 1999*, de Gruyter, Berlin, pp. 619–634.

Koffman, L. (2006) The Rise and Fall of Proportionality: the Failure of the Criminal Justice Act 1991, *Criminal Law Review*, April, pp. 281–299.

Köhler, M. (2000) Reformen des strafrechtlichen Sanktionensystems, *Neue Kriminalpolitik,* no 2, pp. 10–11.

Köhne, M. (2004) Abschaffung der Ersatzfreiheitsstrafe, *Juristische Zeitung*, no 11, pp. 453–456.

Kommission zur Reform des strafrechtlichen Sanktionensystems (2000) Absclußbericht, accessible from the following link: http://www.bmj.bund.de/media/archive/137.pdf.

Köni, B. (1943) Ceza Hukukunda Tenkil ve Önleme Müessesesi, *Ankara Üniversitesi Siyasal Bilgiler Fakültesi Dergisi*, vol. 1, no 1, pp. 47–55.

Köni, B. (1956) Kriminoloji, *Ankara Üniversitesi Siyasal Bilgiler Fakültesi Dergisi*, vol. 14, pp. 76–90.

Kriegsmann, N., H. (1911) Begründung Denkschrift, Guttentag, Berlin.

Krisberg, B. (2004) *Juvenile Justice: Redeeming Our Children,* Thousand Oaks, California.

Krisberg, B. (2006) Rediscovering the Juvenile Justice Ideal in the United States in Muncie, J. and Goldson, B. (eds.) *Comparative Youth Justice Systems – Critical Debates*, Sage, London, pp. 6–18.

Krohne (1908) Welche Strafmittelsystem empfiehlt sich für das künftige Strafgesetzbuch? in *Verhandlungen des 29. Juristentag*, vol. 4, Guttentag, Berlin, pp. 199–245.

Kronecker (1893) Empfiehlt sich die Einführung von Verschärfungen der Freiheitsstrafen im Sinne des österreichischen Entwurfs, *Verhandlungen des 22. Deutschen Juristentag*, vol. 3, Guttentag, Berlin, pp. 43–92.

Kropp, C. (2004) Ist die Verwarnung mit Strafvorbehalt noch zeitgemäß? *Zeitschrift für Rechtspolitik*, vol. 37, no 7, pp. 241–242.

Kubink, M. (2002) *Strafen und ihre Alternativen im zeitlichen Wandel*, Duncker & Humblot, Berlin.

Kuhlen, L. (1988) *Diversion im Jugendstrafverfahren: rechtliche Probleme von Alternativen im Jugendstrafverfahren*, Müller, Heidelberg.

Kuhn, A. (1994) 'What can we do about prison overcrowding?' *European Journal on Criminal Policy and Research*, vol. 2, no 7, pp. 107–116.

Kuhn, A., Rudolph, M., Wandrey, M. and Will, H.-D. (1989) *"Tat-Sachen" als Konflikt. Täter-Opfer-Ausgleich in der Jugendstrafrechtspflege, Forschungsbericht zum Modelprojekt "Handschlag"*, Forum, Bonn.

Kümmerlein, H. (1944) *Reichsjugendgerichtsgesetz vom 6 November 1943*, Beck, München.

Kunter, N. (1949) Cocuk Mahkemeleri Kanunu Nasil Olmali? *Istanbul Üniversitesi Hukuk Fakültesi Mecmuasi*, vol. 14, pp. 55–95.

Kunter, N. (1950) Ceza ve Ceza Infazi Milleterarasi Onikinci Kongresi (La Haye, 14–19 Agustos 1950), *Istanbul Üniversitesi Hukuk Fakültesi Mecmuasi*, vol. 16, pp. 591614.

Kunter, N. (1951) Türkiye'de Suclulugun Ictimai Amilleri, *Ankara Üniversitesi Hukuk Fakültesi Dergisi*, vol. 8, no 34, pp. 98–121.

Kunter, N. and Yenisey, F. (2002) *Muhakeme Hukuku Dali Olarak Ceza Muhakemesi Hukuku*, 12th edition, Beta, Istanbul.

Kunz, K.-L. (1980) *Die Einstellung wegen Geringfügigkeit durch die Staatsanwaltschaft (§§ 153 Abs. 1. 153a Abs. 1 StP0*, Athenäum, Königstein.

Kurry, H. (1986) *Die Behandlung Straffälliger*, vol. 1, Duncker & Humblot, Berlin.

Kury, H. (1981) Diversion – Möglichkeiten und Grenzen am Beispiel Amerikanischer Programme in Kury, H. and Lerchenmüller, H. (eds.) *Alternativen zu klassischen Sanktionsformen*, Studienverlag, Bochum.

Kury, H. (1999) Zum Stand der Behandlungsforschung oder vom nothing works zum something works in Feuerhelm, W., Schwind, H.-D., Bock, M. (eds.) *Festschrift für Alexander Böhm zum 70. Geburtstag am 14 Juni 1999*, de Gruyter, Berlin, pp. 251–274.

Kürzinger, J. (1984) Die Freiheitsstrafe und ihre Surrogate in der Bundesrepublik Deutschland in Jescheck, H.-H. (ed.) *Die Freiheitsstrafe und ihre Surrogate im deutschen und ausländischen Recht*, pp. 1737–1938.

Lacey, N. and Zedner, L. (1995) Discourses of Community on Criminal Justice, *Journal of Law and Society*, vol. 22, pp. 301–325.

Lammasch, H. (1889) Empfiehlt sich die Einführung der bedingten Verurteilung (belgisches Gesetz vom 31 Mai 1888) in die Strafgesetzgebung der übrigen Länder und unter welchen Voraussetzungen? in *Mitteilungen der Internationale Kriminalistische Vereinigung*, pp. 34–43.

Lampe, E.-J. (1993) Wiedergutmachung als „dritte Spur" des Strafrechts? *Goltdammer's Archiv für Strafrecht*, vol. 140, pp. 485–494.

Lange, R. (1954) Neuaufnahme der Strafrechtsreform, *Zeitschrift für die gesamte Strafrechtswissenschaft*, vol. 66, pp. 167–170.

Lange, H. (1990) Geschichtliche Entwicklung, Nachkriegssituation und Aufbauphase der Gerichtshilfe in Kerner, H.-J. (ed.) *Straffälligenhilfe in Geschichte und Gegenwart*, Verlag Godesberg, Bonn, pp.107–136.

Lappi-Seppälä, T. (2001) Sentencing and Punishment in Finland: The Decline of the Repressive Ideal in Tonry, M. and Frase, R., S. (eds.) *Sentencing and Sanctions in Western Countries*, Oxford University Press, Oxford, pp. 92–150.

Laubenthal, K. and Baier, H. (2006) *Jugendstrafrecht*, Springer, Berlin.

Laubenthal, K. (2008) *Strafvollzug*, 5th edition, Springer, Berlin.

Laycock, G. and Tarling, R. (1985) Police Force Cautioning: Policy and Practice, *Howard Journal of Criminal Justice*, vol. 24, no 2, pp. 81–92.

Lazarus, L. (2004) *Contrasting Prisoner's Rights: A Comparative Examination of England and Germany*, Oxford University Press, Oxford.

Lemert, E. (1951) *Social Pathology – A Systematic Approach to the Theory of Sociopathic Behaviour*, McGraw-Hill, New York.

Lemert, E. (1967) *Human Deviance, Social Problems and Social Control*, Prentice Hall, New Jersey.

Lemert, E. (1981) Diversion in Juvenile Justice: What hath been wrought? *Journal of Research on Crime and Delinquency*, vol. 18, no 1, pp. 34–46.

Lerchenmüller, H. (1981) Bedeutung der Diversion zur Vermeidung von Prisonisierungsschäden in Kury, H. and Lerchenmüller, H. (eds.) *Alternativen zu klassischen Sanktionsformen*, Studienverlag, Bochum, pp. 127–161.

Levrant, S., Cullen, F. T., Fulton, B. and Wozniak, J., F. (1999) Reconsidering Restorative Justice: The Corruption of Benevolence Revisited? *Crime and Delinquency*, vol. 45, pp. 3–27.
Liepmann, M. (1909) *Die Kriminalität der Jugendlichen und ihre Bekämpfung*, Mohr, Tübingen.
Lilly, R., Cullen, F. and Ball, R., A. (2002) *Criminological Theory: Context and Consequences*, 3rd edition, Sage, London.
Lindenberg, M. (1999) Elektronisch überwachter Hausarrest auch in Deutschland? Kritische Anmerkungen für die Diskussion in der Praxis, *Bewährungshilfe*, vol. 46, no 1, pp. 11–22.
Lissner. P., H. (1935) *Historische Entwicklung der Begnadigung und ihrer Grenzen*, Zentraldruckerei, Berlin.
Lombroso, C. (1895) Atavism and Evolution, *Contemporary Review*, vol. 68, p. 4249 reprinted in Horton, D., M. and Rich, E., K. (2004) The Criminal Anthropological Writings of Cesare Lombroso published in the English Language, Mellen, Lewiston.
Lombroso, C. (1895) Criminal Anthropology: Its Origins and Application, *Forum,* vol. 20, pp. 33–49 in Horton, D., M. and Rich, E., K. (2004) The Criminal Anthropological Writings of Cesare Lombroso Published in the English Language, Mellen, Lewiston.
Lombroso, C. (1902) *Die Ursachen und Bekämpfung des Verbrechens*, Hugo Bermühler Verlag, Berlin.
Loos, F. (1990) Der Schuldgrundsatz als Sanktionslimitierung im Jugendstrafrecht in Wolff, J. and Marek, A. (ed.) *Erziehung und Strafe*, Forum, Bonn, pp. 83–91.
Loos, F. (1993) Zur Kritik des Alternativentwurfs Wiedergutmachung, *Zeitschrift für Rechtspolitik*, vol. 26, no 2, pp. 51–56.
Lösener, M., L. (1958) *Beitrag zum Problem der kurzen Freiheitsstrafen*, unpublished PhD Thesis, University of Cologne.
Mack, J. (1909) The Juvenile Court, *Harvard Law Review*, vol. 23, no 2, pp. 104–122.
Mahmutoglu, F., S. (2008) Das neue türkische Strafgesetzbuch, Allgemeiner Teil, *Annales de la Facultés de Droit d'Istanbul,* vol. 58, no.1–4, pp. 35–48.
Mahmutoglu, F., S. (2004) TBMM Adalet Komisyonu'nda Kabul Edilen Türk Ceza Kanunu Tasarisi Hakkinda Görüs in Ergül, T. (ed.) *Türk Ceza Kanunu Reformu*, Ikinci Kitap, TBB Yayinlari, Ankara, pp. 357–378.
Mair, G, (1991) *Part Time Punishment: The Origins and Developments of Senior Attendance Centre*, HMSO, London.
Mair, G. (2004) Diversionary and Non-Supervisory Approaches to Dealing with Offenders in Bottoms, A. and Rex, S. and Robinson, G. (eds.) *Alternatives to Prison: Options for an Insecure Society*, Willan, Cullompton.
Mair, G. (2007) Research on Community Penalties in Doing Research on Crime and Justice in King, R., D. and Wincup, E. (eds.) *Doing Research in Crime and Justice*, Oxford University Press, Oxford, pp. 399–430.
Mair, G. and Canton. R. (2007) Sentencing, Community Penalties and the Role of Probation Service in Gelsthorpe, L. and Morgan, R. (eds.) *Handbook of Probation*, Willan, Cullompton, pp. 248–291.
Mair, G. and Nee, C. (1990) *Electronic Monitoring: the Trials and their Results*, Home Office Research Study 120, HMSO, London.
Mannheim, H. (1939) *The Dilemma of Penal Reform*, George Allen and Unwin Ltd., London.
Mannheim, H. (1955) *Group Problems in Crime and Punishment and Other Studies in Criminology and Criminal Law*, Patterson Smith, Montclair.
Marks, E. and Rössner, D. (ed.) (1989) *Täter-Opfer-Ausgleich: vom zwischenmenschlichen Weg zur Wiederherstellung des Rechtsfriedens*, Forum, Bonn.
Marks, S., Hering, R.-D., and Rössner, D. (1993) *Täter-Opfer-Ausgleich im Allgemeinen Strafrecht – Theorie und Praxis konstruktiver Tatverarbeitung*, Forum, Bonn.
Marks, E., Meyer, K., Schreckling, J. and Wandrey, M. (1993) *Wiedergutmachung und Strafrechtspraxis*, Forum, Bonn.
Marshall, T., F. (1999) *Restorative Justice: An Overview*, Home Office Research, Development and Statistics Directorate, London.
Martinson, R. (1974) What works? – Questions and Answers about Prison Reform, *Public Interest*, vol. 35, pp. 22–54.

Masters, G. and Warner Roberts, A. (1999) Family Group Conferencing for Victims, Offenders and Communities in Liebmann, M. (eds.) *Mediation in Context*, Jessica Kingsley Publishers, London, pp. 140–154.

Mathiesen, T. (2000) *Prison on Trial*, 2nd edition, Waterside Press, Winchester.

Matthews, R. (1995) The Diversion of Juveniles from Custody: the Experience of England and Wales 1980–1990 in Albrecht, G. and Ludwig-Mayerhofer, W. (eds.) *Diversion and Informal Social Control*, de Gruyter, Berlin, pp. 83–104.

Matthews, R. and Young, J. (2003) *The New Politics of Crime and Punishment,* Willan, Cullompton.

May, T. (1991) *Probation: Politics, Policy and Practice*, Open University Press, Milton Keynes.

May, T. (1991) Under Siege: Probation in a Changing Environment in Reiner, R. and Cross, M. (eds.) *Beyond Law and Order: Criminal Justice Policy and Politics into the 1990s*, Macmillan, Basingstoke.

May, T. (1994) Probation and Community Sanctions in Maguire, M., Morgan, R. and Reiner, R. (eds.) *the Oxford Handbook of Criminology*, Clarendon Press, Oxford, pp. 861–887.

Mayer, H. (1962) *Strafrechtsreform für Heute und Morgen*, Duncker & Humblot, Berlin.

Mayer, M. (2003) The German Pilot Project: Potentials and Risks in Mayer, M., Haverkamp, R. and Levy. R. (eds.) *Will Electronic Monitoring have a Future in Europe?* edition iuscrim Freiburg, pp. 168–176.

Mayer, M. (2004) *Modellprojekt elektronisch Fußfessel – Studien zur Erprobung einer umstrittenen Maßnahme*, edition iuscrim, Freiburg.

Mayerhofer-Ludwig, W. (1995) Sentence without Conviction: Notes on Diversion from the Juvenile Court in the Federal Republic of Germany in Albrecht, G. and Ludwig-Mayerhofer, W. (eds.) *Diversion and Informal Social Control*, de Gruyter, Berlin, pp. 108–109.

McClintock, F., H. with Walker, M., A., and Savill, N., C. (1961) *Attendance Centres (An Enquiry by the Cambridge Institute of Criminology on the Use of Section 19 of the Criminal Justice Act 1948)*, Macmillan, New York.

McElrea, F., W., M. (1998) The New Zealand Model of Family Group Conferencing, *European Journal on Criminal Policy and Research*, vol. 6, no. 4, pp. 527–543.

McNeill, F. (2006) Community Supervision: Context and Relationships in Goldson, B. and Muncie, J. (eds.) *Youth, Crime and Justice: Critical Issues*, Sage, London, pp. 125–138.

McWilliams, B. (1981) The Probation Officer at Court: From Friend to Acquaintance, *Howard Journal of Criminal Justice*, vol. 20, pp. 97–106.

McWilliams W. (1983) The Mission to the English Police Courts 1876–1936, *Howard Journal*, vol. 22, pp. 129–147.

Meier, B.-D. (2000) Wiedergutmachung im Strafrecht? Empirische Befunde und kriminalpolitische Perspektiven in Bender, D. and Jehle, J.-M. (eds.) *Täterbehandlung und neue Sanktionsformen: Kriminalpolitische Konzepte in Europa,* Forum, Bonn, pp. 255–276.

Meier, B.-D. (2004) Restorative Justice – Bericht über Deutschland in Schöch, H., Jehle, J.-M. and Aebersold, P. (eds.) *Angewandte Kriminologie zwischen Freiheit und Sicherheit*, Kriminalistik-Verlag, Heidelberg, pp. 415–428.

Meier, B. (2006) *Strafrechtliche Sanktionen*, 2nd edition, Springer, Berlin.

Melossi, D. and Pavarini, M. (1981) *The Prison and the Factory: Origins of the Penitentiary System*, Macmillan, London.

Mener, H. (1892), Ist die bedingte Verurteilung im Strafrecht einzuführen?' *Verhandlungen des 21. Deutschen Juristentages*, vol.1, pp. 206–226.

Mengüc, A., R. (1968) *Ceza Infaz Hukuku ve Infaz Müesseseleri*, Cezaevi Matbaasi, Istanbul.

Mennel, R. (1972) Origins of the Juvenile Court: Changing Perspectives on the Legal Rights of Juvenile Delinquents, *Crime and Delinquency*, vol. 18, no. 1, pp. 68–78.

Mergen, A. (1967) Die Antwort der Gesellschaf auf das Verbrechen – Strafe oder Maßnahme in Reinisch, L. (ed.) *Die deutsche Strafrechtsreform*, Beck, München, pp. 40–55.

Messmer, H. and Otto, H.-U. (1992) (eds.) *Restorative Justice on Trial: Pitfalls and Potentials of Victim-Offender Mediation- International Research Perspectives*, Kluwer, Dordrecht.

Mestitz, A. (2005) A comparative perspective on Victim-Offender Mediation with Young Offenders throughout Europe in Mestitz, A. and Ghetti, S. (eds.) *Victim-Offender Mediation with Youth Offenders in Europe*, Springer, Dordrecht.

Meyer, K. (1919) Strafensystem und Geldstrafe, *Deutsche Strafrechts Zeitung*, vol. 6, no 7/8, pp. 242–243.

Meyer-Reil, A. (2006) *Strafaussetzung zur Bewährung – Reformdiskussion und Gesetzgebung seit dem Ausgang des 19. Jahrhundert*, LIT, Berlin.

Miehe, O. (1968) Anfänge der Diskussion über eine strafrechtliche Sonderbehandlung in Schaffstein, F. and Miehe, O. (eds.) *Weg und Aufgabe des Jugendstrafrechts, Wissenschaftliche Buchgesellschaft,* Darmstadt, pp. 22–27.

Miers, D. and Willemsens, J. (ed.) (2004) *Mapping Restorative Justice Developments in 25 European Countries*, European Forum for Victim-Offender Mediation and Restorative Justice, Leuven.

Millie, A, Jacobson, J. and Hough, M. (2005) Understanding the Growth in the Prison Population in England and Wales in Emsley, C. (ed.) *The Persistent Prison*, Francis Boutle, London.

Ministry of Justice (2007) Penal Policy: A Background Paper, accessible from the following link: http://www.justice.gov.uk/docs/Penal-Policy-Final.pdf.

Ministry of Justice (2010) *Sentencing Statitics 2008*, London.

Mitteilungen der Internationalen Kriminalistischen Vereinigung (1889) vol. 1, Guttentag, Berlin.

Mitteilungen der Internationalen Kriminalistischen Vereinigung (1891), vol. 2, Guttentag, Berlin.

Mitteilungen der Internationalen Kriminalistischen Vereinigung (1892), vol. 3, Guttentag, Berlin.

Mitteilungen der Internationalen Kriminalistischen Vereinigung (1899), vol. 7, Guttentag, Berlin.

Mitteilungen der Internationalen Kriministaltistischen Vereinigung (1897), vol. 5, Guttentag, Berlin.

Morgan, N. (1983) The Shaping of Parole in England and Wales, *Criminal Law Review*, pp. 137–151.

Morgan, R. (2003) Thinking about the Demand for Probation Service, *Probation Journal*, vol. 50, no 1, pp. 7–19.

Morgan, R. (2007) Children and Young Persons in Gelsthorpe, L. and Morgan, R. (eds.) *Handbook of Probation*, Willan, Cullompton, pp. 248–291.

Morgan, R. and Clarkson, C. (1995) The Politics of Sentencing Reform in Clarkson, C. and Morgan, R. (eds.) *The Politics of Punishment and Sentencing*, Oxford University Press, Oxford.

Morgan, R. and Newburn, T. (2007) Youth Justice in Maguire, M., Morgan, R. and Reiner, R. (eds.) *The Oxford Handbook of Criminology*, 4th edition, Oxford University Press, Oxford, pp. 1061–1099.

Morgenstern, C. (2007) Alternativen zur Freiheitsstrafe – Ursprung, Bedarf und Probleme, *Zeitschrift für Strafvollzug und Straffälligenhilfe*, vol. 56, pp. 248–252.

Morris, A. and McIsaac, M. (1978) *Juvenile Justice*, Heinemann, London.

Morris, A. and Giller, H. (1987) *Providing Criminal Justice for Children*, Edward Arnold, London.

Morris, A. and Gelsthorpe, L. (2000) Something Old, Something Borrowed, Something Blue, but Something New? A Comment on the Prospects for Restorative Justice under the Crime and Disorder Act 1998, *Criminal Law Review,* pp. 18–30.

Morris, A., Giller, H., Szwed, E. and Geach, H. (1980) *Justice for Children*, Macmillan, London.

Moxon, D, Sutton, M. and Hedderman, C. (1990) *Unit Fines: Experiments in Four Courts*, Research and Planning Unit Paper, Home Office, London.

Müller, R. (1975) Begünstigung der Steuer- und Wirtschaftstraftäter durch den Staat? *Zeitschrift für Rechtspolitik*, vol. 8, no 3, pp. 49–56.

Müller, C. (1997) *Das Gewohnheitsverbrechergesetz: Kriminalpolitik als Rassenpolitik*, Nomos, Baden-Baden.

Müller-Dietz, H. (1979) *Grundfragen des strafrechtlichen Sanktionensystems*, Decker, Heidelberg.

Müller-Dietz, H. (1999) Der Ort des Strafvollzuges in einem künftigen Sanktionensystem, Feuerhelm, W., Schwind, H.-D., Bock, M. (eds.) *Festschrift für Alexander Böhm zum 70. Geburtstag am 14 Juni 1999*, de Gruyter, Berlin, pp. 3–23.

Muncie, J. (1999) *Youth and Crime: A Critical Introduction*, Sage, London.

Muncie, J. (2004) *Youth and Crime: A Critical Introduction*, 2nd edition, Sage, London.

Muncie, J. and Hughes, G. (2002) Modes of Youth Governance: Political Rationalities, Criminalisation and Resistance in Muncie, J., Hughes, G. and McLaughlin, E. (eds.) *Youth Justice: Critical Readings*, Sage, London, pp. 1–18.

Muncie, J. and Sparks, R. (1992) Expansion and Contraction in European Penal Systems in Muncie, J. and Sparks, R. (eds.) *Imprisonment: European Perspectives*, Prentice Hall, New York, pp. 89–106.

Nelken, D. (1997) Understanding Criminal Justice in Maguire, M., Morgan, R. and Reiner, R. (eds.) *the Oxford Handbook of Criminology*, 2nd edition, Clarendon Press, Oxford, pp. 559–573.

Nelken, D. (2000) Just Comparing in Nelken (ed.) *Contrasting Criminal Justice*, Aldershot, Darmouth, pp. 3–22.

Nelken, D. (2007) Comparing Criminal Justice in Maguire, M., Morgan, R. and Reiner, R. (eds.) *The Oxford Handbook of Criminology*, 4th edition, Oxford University Press, Oxford.

Nellis, M. (1991) The Electronic Monitoring of Offenders in England and Wales, *British Journal of Criminology*, vol. 31, no 2, pp. 165–185.

Nellis, M. (2001) Community Penalties in Historical Perspective in Bottoms, A., E., Gelsthorpe, L. and Rex, S. (eds.) (2001) *Community Penalties: Change and Challenges*, Willan, Cullompton, pp. 16–40.

Nellis, M. (2004) Electronic Monitoring and the Community Supervision of Offenders in Bottoms, A., Rex, S. and Robinson, G. (eds.) *Alternatives to Prison: Options for an Insecure Society*, Willan, Cullompton.

Newburn, T. (2002) Young People, Crime, and Youth Justice in Maguire, M., Morgan, R. and Reiner, R. (eds.) *the Oxford Handbook of Criminology*, 3rd edition, Oxford University Press, Oxford, pp. 531–578.

Newburn, T. and de Peyrecave, H. (1988) *The Use and Enforcement of Compensation Orders in Magistrates' Courts*, Home Office Research Study no. 102, HMSO, London.

Newburn, T., Crawford, A., Earle, R., Goldie, S., Hale, C., Masters, G., Netten, A., Saunders, R., Hallam, A., Sharpe, K. and Uglow, S. (2002*) The Introduction of Referral Orders into Youth Justice System: Final Report*, Home Office Research Study no 242, Home Office, London.

Newman, G. (1999) *Global Report on Crime and Justice, United Nations Office for Drug Control and Crime Prevention Centre for International Crime Prevention*, Oxford University Press, New York.

Neziroglu, I. (2006) A Comparison of Law and Practice within the Turkish Prison System with Relevant International Prison Standards with Special Reference to F-Type High Security Prisons, *Turkish Studies*, vol. 7, no 3, pp. 421–450.

Nuhoglu, A. (1996) *Mukayeseli Hukukta ve Türk Ceza Hukuku'nda Özgürlügü Baglayici Emniyet Tedbirleri* (unpublished PhD thesis, Marmara University).

Nuhoğlu, A. (2005) Uzlaşma Bakımından Şikayete Bağlı Suçlar in Yenisey, F. (ed.) *Ceza Muhakemesi Hukukunda Uzlasma*, Arikan, Istanbul, pp. 281–284.

Nursal, N. and Atac, S. (2006) *Denetimli Serbestlik ve Yardim Sistemi*, Yetkin, Ankara.

Nüßlein, A. (1969) Freiheitsstrafen in Hessen 1969, Verl. Kriminalistik, Hamburg.

Nuttall, C., P. with Barnard, E., E., Fowles, A., J., Frost, A., Hammond, W., H., Mayhew, P., Pease, K., Tarling, R. and Weatheritt, M. (1977) *Parole in England and Wales*, Home Office Research Study no 38, HMSO, London.

Nutz, T. (2001) *Strafanstalt als Besseurungsmachine: Reformdiskurs and Gefängniswissenschaft*, Oldenbourg, München.

Nuvolone, P. (1954) *Probation and Related Measures in European Legal Systems: A Comparative Survey* in United Nations, European Seminar on Probation, 20–30 October 1952, United Nations Publications, London, pp. 15–32.

O'Brien, P. (1995) The Prison on the Continent: Europe, 1865–1965 in Morris, N. and Rothman, D. J. (eds.) *The Oxford History of Prison*, Oxford University Press, Oxford, pp. 199–226.

Oatham, E. and Simon, F. (1972) Are Suspended Sentences Working? *New Society*, no 3 (August), pp. 233–235.

Oberheim, R. (1985) *Gefängnisüberfüllung, Ursachen, Folgen und Lösungsmöglichkeiten in der Bundesrepublik Deutschland mit einem International Vergleich*, Lang, Frankfurt.

Oberwittler, D. (2000) *Von der Strafe zur Erziehung (Jugendkriminalpolitik in England und Deutschland 1850–1920)*, Campus, Frankfurt.

Oetker, F. (1922) Die Geldstrafe nach dem Strafgesetzbuch von 1919, *Gerichtssaal*, vol. 88, pp. 161–268.

Offner, J. (1896) Auf welche Weise kann der Vollzug der Freiheitsstrafen, insbesondere derjenigen von der kurzen Dauer, wirksamer gestallt werden? in *Mitteilungen der Internationalen Kriminalistischen Vereinigung*, vol. 5, pp. 195–203.

Oldfield, M. (1993) Assessing the Impact of Community Service – Lost Opportunities and the Politics of Punishment in Whitfield, D. and Scott, D. (eds.) *Paying Back Twenty Years of Community Service*, Waterside Press, Winchester, pp. 30–50.

Önder, A. (1974) Der Einfluss des deutschen Rechts auf das türkische Strafprozessrecht, *Annales de la Facultés de Droit d'Istanbul,* vol. 38, pp. 367–385.

Önder, A. (1981) Die türkische Strafprozessordnung, *Annales de la Facultés de Droit d'Istanbul*, vol. 44, pp. 178–196.

Ortner, H. (1986) Ambulante Alternativen – Die Begleitmusik des Strafvollzugssystems? Anmerkungen zu einer neuen Doppelstrategie in Ortner, H. and Maelicke, B. (eds.) *Freiheit statt Strafe*, 2nd edition, AS-Verlag, Tübingen, pp. 187–195.

Örücü, E. (1999) Turkey: A Survey of the Public Law Framework, *European Public Law*, vol. 5, no. 1. pp. 30–41.

Ostendorf, H. (1997) Die elektronische Fußfessel – Wunderwaffe im Kampf gegen die Kriminalität, *Zeitschrift für Rechtspolitik*, vol. 30, no 12, pp. 473–476.

Ostendorf, H. (2007) *Jugendstrafrecht*, 4th edition, Nomos, Baden-Baden.

Özay, I., H. (1998) A Republic with Double Constitution, *Annales de la Facultés de Droit d'Istanbul, vol.* 48, pp. 101–109.

Özay, I., H. (2002) Democracy without "Demos": Namely "*Cracy*", *Annales de la Facultés de Droit d'Istanbul,* vol. 51, pp. 137–146.

Özbek, V., Ö. (1999) *Ceza Hukukunda Suctan Dogan Magduriyetin Giderilmesi*, Seckin, Ankara.

Özbek, V., Ö. (2006) *Ceza Muhakemesi Hukuku*, Seckin, Ankara.

Özbudun, E. (2000) *Contemporary Turkish Politics: Challenges to Democratic Consolidation*, Lynne Rienner Publishers, London.

Özgenc, I. (2004) Suc ve Yaptirim Teorisine Iliskin Yeni Gelismeler Isiginda Türk Ceza Kanunu Tasarisi in Ergül, T. (ed.) *Türk Ceza Kanunu Reformu*, Birinci Kitap, TBB Yayinlari, Ankara.

Özok, S. (2004) Barolarin Cocuk Hareketindeki Rolü (Bir Örnek: Kocaeli Barosu Cocuk Haklari Komisyonunun Calismalari), *Türkiye Barolar Birligi Dergisi*, vol. 51, pp. 208–212.

Öztürk, B. (2001) Ist das Legalitätsprinzip zu halten, und welche rechtstaatliche Anforderungen haben für das Opportunitätsprinzip zu gelten? Aus türkischer Sicht in Hirsch, E., J.(ed.) *Krise des Strafrechts und der Kriminalwissenschaften?* Tagungsbeiträge eines Symposiums der Alexander von Humboldt Stiftung, Bonn Bad Godesberg (1–5 October 2000), Duncker & Humblot, Berlin.

Paley, J. and Thorpe, D. (1974) *Children: Handle with Care* (A Critical Analysis of the Development of Intermediate Treatment), National Youth Bureau, Leicester.

Parliamentary All-Party Penal Affairs Group (1980) *Too Many Prisoners*, Barry Rose Publishers, Chichester.

Parsloe, P. (1978) *Juvenile Justice in Britain and the United States The Balance of Needs and Rights*, Routledge & Kegan Paul, London.

Pavarani, M. (1994) The New Penology and Politics in Crisis, the Italian Case, *British Journal of Criminology,* vol. 34, special issue, pp. 49–61.

Pavlich, G. (2002) Deconstructing Restoration: the Promise of Restorative Justice in Weitekamp, E. and Kerner, H.-J. (eds.) *Restorative Justice Theoretical Foundations*, Willan, Devon, pp. 90–109.

Peachey, D., E. (1989) The Kitchener Experiment in Wright, M. and Galaway, B. (eds.) *Mediation and Criminal Justice: Victims, Offenders and Community*, Sage, London.

Pears, E. (1872) *Prison and Reformatories At Home and Abroad: The Transactions of the International Penitentiary Congress*, Longmans, London.

Pease, K. (1975) *Community Service Orders*, Home Office Research Study no 29, HMSO, London.

Pease, K. (1980) Community Service and Prison: Are They Alternatives? in Pease, K. and McWilliams, W. (eds.) *Community Service by Order*, Scottish Academic Press, Edinburgh.

Pease, K. (1985) Community Service Orders in Tonry, M. and Morris, N. (eds.) *Crime and Justice*, vol. 6, pp. 50–94.

Pelikan, C. and Trenczek, T. (2008) Victim Offender Mediation and Restorative Justice: the European Landscape in Sullivan, D. (ed.) *Handbook of Restorative Justice*, Routledge, London, pp. 63–90.

Penfold, C., Hunter, G. and Hough, M. (2006) The Intermittent Custody Pilot: A Descriptive Study, Home Office Online Publication, accessible from the following link: http://www.homeoffice.gov.uk/rds/pdfs06/rdsolr2306.pdf (Access Date: October 2009).

Peters, K. (1960) *Grundprobleme der Kriminalpädagogik*, de Gruyter, Berlin.

Peters, J. (2000) *Die Entwicklung von Sanktionspraxis und Strafrechtsreform 1871 bis 1933 – eine Rechtshistorische Untersuchung unter besonderer Berücksichtigung der Reformmodelle zur Freiheitsstrafensubstitution*, Shaker, Aachen.

Peters, E., M. (1995) Prison before the Prison: The Ancient and Medieval Worlds in Morris, N. and Rothman, D. J. (eds.) *The Oxford History of Prison*, Oxford University Press, Oxford, pp. 3–47.

Peukert, D., J., K. (1986) *Grenzen der Sozialdisziplinerung* (Aufstige und Krise der deutschen Jugendfürsorge von 1878 bis 1932), Bund-Verlag, Köln.

Pfeiffer, C. (1983) *Kriminalprävention im Jugendgerichtsverfahren – Jugendrichterlichen Handeln vor dem Hintergrund des Brücke-Projeckts*, Heymann, Köln.

Pfohl, M. (1983) *Gemeinnützige Arbeit als strafrechtliche Sanktion* (eine Untersuchung unter Berücksichtigung der britischen Community Service Order), Duncker & Humblot, Berlin.

Pickford, J. (2000) A New Youth Justice for A New Century in Pickford, J. (ed.) *Youth Justice, Theory and Practice*, Cavendish, London.

Pilgram, A. and Steinert, H. (1986) Plädoyer für bessere Gründe für die Abschaffung der Gefängnisse und für Besseres als die Abschaffung der Gefängnisse in Ortner, H. and Maelicke, B. (eds.) *Freiheit statt Strafe*, 2nd edition, AS-Verlag, Tübingen, pp. 196–217.

Pin, X. and Lombard, F. (2001) Frankreich in Eser, A., and Walther, S. (eds.) *Wiedergutmachung in Kriminalrecht: Internationale Perspektiven*, Max-Planck-Institut, Freiburg, pp. 1–127.

Pistorius, E. (1934) *Die bedingte Strafaussetzung im Jugendgerichtgesetz*, Nolte, Düsseldorf.

Pitts, J. (1986) Thinking About Intermediate Treatment, *Youth and Policy*, no 17, pp. 1–8.

Pitts, J. (2003) Changing Youth Justice, *Youth Justice*, vol. 3, no 1, pp. 5–20.

Pitts, J. (2005) The Recent History of Youth Justice in England in Bateman, T. and Pitts, J. (eds.) *The RHP Companion to Youth Justice*, Russel House Publishing, Dorset, pp. 2–11.

Pointing, J. and Maguire, M. (1988) Introduction: the Rediscovery of the Crime Victim in Maguire, M. and Pointing, J. (eds.) *Victims of Crime: A new Deal?*, Open University Press, Milton Keynes.

Polk. K. (1987) When Less Means More: An Analysis of Destructuring in Criminal Justice, *Crime and Delinquency*, vol. 33, no 2, pp. 358–378.

Pratt, J. (1986) Diversion from the Juvenile Court: A History of Inflation and a Critique of Progress, *British Journal of Criminology*, vol. 26, no 3, pp. 212–233.

President's Commission on Law Enforcement and Administration of Justice (1967) *The Challenge of Crime in a Free Society*, U.S. Government Printing Office, Washington.

Prison Reform Trust (1990) *Tackling the Fine Default*, London.

Radbruch, G. (1952) *Entwurf eines Allgemeinen Deutschen Strafgesetzbuches*, Mohr, Tübingen.

Radzinowicz, L. (1961) *In Search of Criminology*, Heinemann, London.

Radzinowicz, L. and Hood, R. (1990) *The Emergence of Penal Policy in Victorian and Edwardian Penal Policy*, Clarendon Press, Oxford.

Radzinowicz, L. (1991) Penal Regressions, *Cambridge Law Journal*, vol. 50, pp. 422–444.

Ranft, O. (2005) *Strafprozessrecht*, 3rd edition, Richard Boorberg Verlag, Stuttgart.

Raynor, P. (2001) Community Penalties and Social Integration: 'Community' as Solution and as Problem in Bottoms, A., E., Gelsthorpe, L. and Rex, S. (eds.) (2001) *Community Penalties: Change and Challenges*, Willan, Cullompton, pp. 183–199.

Raynor, P. and Vanstone, M. (2002) *Understanding Community Penalties. Probation, Policy and Social Change*, Open University Press, Buckingham.

Raynor, P. (2007) Community Penalties: Probation 'What Works' and Offender Management in Maguire, M., Morgan, R. and Reiner, R. (eds.) *the Oxford Handbook of Criminology*, 4th edition, Oxford University Press, pp. 1066–1099.

Redondo, S., Sanchez-Meca, J. and Garrido, V. (2002) Crime Treatment in Europe: A Review of Outcome Studies in McGuire, J. (ed.) *Offender Rehabilitation and Treatment: Effective Programmes and Policies to Reduce Re-offending Crime*, John Wiley, Chichester.

Reeves, H. and Wright, M. (1995) Victims: Towards a Reorientation of Justice in Ward, D. and Lacey, M. (eds.) *Probation Working for Justice*, Whiting and Birch, London, pp. 73–85.

Reichjustizsamt (1909) *Vorentwurf zu einem deutschen Strafgesetzbuch* and *Vorentwurf zu einem deutschen Strafgesetzbuch Begründung (Allgemeiner Teil)*, Guttentag, Berlin.

Reichsjustizministerium (1921) *Entwürfe zu einem deutschen Strafgesetzbuch,* vol. 1: Entwurf der Strafrechtskommission (1913), Berlin, de Gruyter.

Rentzmann, W. and Robert, J. P. (1986) *Alternative Measures to Imprisonment*, Council of Europe Publishing, Strasbourg.

Rex, S. (2005), Reforming Community Penalties, Sage, London.

Rietsch (1934) Strafensystem in Gürtner, F. (ed.) *Das kommende deutsche Strafrecht*, Vahlen, Berlin.

Roberts, J. and Smith, M., E. (2004) Custody Plus and Custody Minus in Tonry, M. (ed.) *Confronting Crime: Crime Control Policy under new Labour*, Willan, Cullompton, pp. 182–210.

Rolinski, K. (1981) Ersatzfreiheitsstrafe oder Gemeinnützige Arbeit, *Monatsschrift für Kriminologie*, vol. 63, no 1/2, pp. 52–62.

Rosenfeld, E. (1890) *Welche Strafmittel können an die Stelle der kurzzeitigen Freiheitsstrafe gesetzt werden?* Guttentag, Berlin.

Rössner, D. (1985) Eine konstruktive Alternative zu Geld- und Freiheitsstrafe, *Bewährungshilfe*, vol. 32, no 2, pp. 105–110.

Rössner, D. (2000) Ergebnisse und Defizite der aktuellen TAO-Begleitforschung. rechtliche und empirische Aspekte, in Gutsche, G. and Rössner, D. (eds.) *Täter-Opfer-Ausgleich*, Forum Verlag, Godesberg, pp. 7–40.

Rothman, D. (1971) *The Discovery of the Asylum: Social Order and Disorder in the New Republic*, Little Brown, Boston.

Rothman, D. (1980) *Conscience and Convenience: the Asylum and its Alternatives in Progressive America*, Little Brown, Boston.

Roxin, C. (1969) Franz von Liszt und die kriminalpolitische Konzeption des Alternativentwurfs, *Zeitschrift für die gesamte Strafrechtswissenschaft*, vol. 81, pp. 613–649.

Roxin, C. (1987) Die Wiedergutmachung im System der Strafzwecke in Schöch, H. (ed.) *Wiedergutmachung und Strafrecht,* Symposion aus Anlass des 80. Geburtstages von Friedrich Schaffstein, Fink, München, pp. 37–55.

Roxin, C. (1991) Zur neueren Entwicklung der Kriminalpolitik in Stolleis, M. with Frommel, M., Rückert, J., Schröder, R., Seelmann, K., Wiegand, W. (eds.) *Die Bedeutung der Wörter : Studien zur europäischen Rechtsgeschichte (Festschrift für Sten Gagnér zum 70. Geburtstag)*, Beck, München, pp. 341–356.

Roxin, C. (1992) Zur Wiedergutmachung als einer„Dritten Spur"im Sanktionensystem in Arzt, G., Fezer, G., Weber, U., Schlüchter, E. and Rössner, D. (eds.) *Festschrift für Jürgen Baumann zum 70. Geburtstag 22 Juni 1992*, Gieseking Verlag, Bielefeld, pp. 243–254.

Roxin, C. (2006) *Strafrecht Allgemeiner Teil*, vol. 1, 4th edition, Beck, München.

Ruggiero, V. (1998) The Country of Cesare Beccaria: the Myth of Rehabilitation in Italy Weiss, R., P. and South, N. (eds.) *Comparing Prison Systems: Toward a Comparative and International Penology*, Gordon & Breach, Amsterdam, pp. 207–232.

Ruggles-Brise, E. (1911) An English View of the American Penal System, *Journal of Criminal Law and Criminology*, vol. 2, no 3, pp. 356–369.

Ruggles-Brise, E. (1925) *Prison Reform at Home and Abroad: A Short History of the International Movement since the London Congress 1872*, Macmillan, London.

Rusche, G. and Kirchheimer, O. (1939) *Punishment and Social Structure*, Columbia University Press, New York.

Ruscheweyh, H. (1918) *Die Entwicklung des deutschen Jugendgerichts*, Dietsch & Rückner, Weimar.

Rutherford, A. and Morgan, R. (1981) *No More Prison Building*, Howard League for Penal Reform, London.

Rutherford, A. (1984) *Prisons and Process of Justice*, Heinemann, London.

Rutherford, A. (1989) The Mood and Temper of Penal Policy, *Youth and Policy*, no. 27, pp. 27–31.

Rutherford, A. (1996) Principled Pragmatism in Rutherford, A. (ed.) *Transforming Criminal Policy*, pp. 85–123.

Ryan, M. and Sim, J. (1998) Power, Punishment and Prisons in England and Wales 1975–1996 in Weiss, R., P. and South, N. (eds.) *Comparing Prison Systems: Toward a Comparative and International Penology*, Gordon & Breach, Amsterdam, pp.175–206.

Saglam, M., Y. (2000) Infaz Hukukunun Sorunlari in Izmir Barosu, *Yargi Reformu Sempozyumu* (5–8 Nisan 2000), pp. 746–754.

Sahin, C. (1998) Ceza Muhakemesinde Uzlasma, *Selcuk Üniversitesi Hukuk Fakültesi Dergisi*, Professor Süleyman Arslan Armagani, vol. 6, no 1–2, pp. 221–297.

Saleilles, R. (1911) *The Individualisation of Punishment*, reprinted in 1968, Patterson Smith, Montclair.

Sancar, M. and Atilgan, E., Ü. (2009) *"Adalet Biraz Es Geciliyor..." Demokratiklesme Sürecinde Hakimler ve Savcilar*, TESEV, Istanbul.

Sanders, A. (1989) The Limit to Diversion from Prosecution, *British Journal of Criminology*, vol. 28, no. 24 pp. 513–532.

Saner, Y. (2007) Osmanli'nin Yüzlerce Yil Süren Cezalandirma ve Korkutma Refleksi: Prangaya Vurma in Levy, N and Toumarkine, A.(eds.) *Osmanli'da Asayis, Suc ve Ceza, Tarih Vakfi Yayinlari*, Istanbul, pp. 163–189.

Sarihan, S. (2002) Türkiye'deki Cezaevleri Sorunu ve Tarihsel Gelisimi in Istanbul Barosu Cezaevleri Calisma Grubu, *Cezaevleri Sempozyumu* (29-30 Haziran 2002), pp. 28–37.

Sarri, R. (1983) Paradigms and Pitfalls in Juvenile Justice Diversion in Morris, A. and Giller, H. (eds.) *Providing Criminal Justice for Children*, Edward Arnold, London, pp. 52–73.

Schädler, W. (1983) Das Projekt „Gemeinnützige Arbeit" die nicht nur theoretische Chance des Art. 293 EGStGB, *Zeitschrift für Rechtspolitik*, vol. 16, no 1, pp. 5–10.

Schädler, W. (1985) Der "weiße Fleck" im Sanktionensystem: Ein Beitrag zur Diskussion um Geldstrafe, freie Arbeit und Ersatzfreiheitsstrafe, *Zeitschrift für Rechtspolitik*, vol. 18, no 7, pp. 186–192.

Schädler, W. (1988) The Interest of the State in the Effectiveness of Alternatives to Imprisonment in HEUNI, *Alternatives to Custodial Sanctions* (Proceedings of the European Seminar held in Helsinki, Finland, 26–28 September, 1987), Helsinki.

Schädler, W. and Wulf, R. (1999) Thesen zur Erprobung der elektronischen Überwachung als Weisung und elektronischer Hausarrest, *Bewährungshilfe*, vol. 46, no 1, pp. 3–10.

Schaffstein, F. and Beulke, W. (2002) *Jugendstrafrecht*, 14th edition, Kohlhammer, Stuttgart.

Schall, H. (1985) Die Sanktionsalternative der gemeinnützigen Arbeit als Surrogat der Geldstrafe, *Neue Zeitschrift für Strafrecht*, no 3, pp. 104–111.

Schall, H. (1988) Auf der Suche nach strafrechtlichen Modifikationen und Alternativen, *Bewährungshilfe*, vol. 35, no 4, pp. 433–447.

Schlömer, U. (1999) Die Anwendbarkeit des elektronisch überwachten Hausarrests als Bewährungsweisung nach geltendem Recht, *Bewährungshilfe*, vol. 46, no 1, pp. 31–43.

Schmidt, E. (1935) Zum internationalen Kongreß für Strafrecht und Gefängniswesen: Die internationalen Gefängniskongresse, *Zeitschrift für die gesamte Strafrechtswissenschaft*, vol. 55, pp. 177–200.

Schmidt, E. (1952) Eröffnungsansprache auf der Tagung der Arbeitsgemeinschaft zur Reform des Strafvollzuges, *Zeitschrift für die gesamte Strafrechtswissenschaft*, vol. 64, pp. 1–16.

Schmidt, E. (1957) Kriminalpolitische und Strafrechtsdogmatische Probleme in der deutschen Strafrechtsreform, *Zeitschrift für die gesamte Strafrechtswissenschaft*, vol. 69, pp. 359–396.

Schmidt, E. (1965) Einführung in die Geschichte der deutschen Strafrechtspflege, 3th edition, Vandenhoeck & Ruprecht, Göttingen.

Schmölder, R. (1894) Die verwahrlosten Kinder und die jugendlichen Verbrecher, *Der Gerichtsaal*, vol. 49, pp. 157–201.

Schmölder, R. (1902) *Die Geldstrafe (Vortrag gehalten auf der 74. Jahresversammlung der Rheinisch-Westfälischen Gefängnisgesellschaft in Düsseldorf am 15 Oktober 1902)*, Griebsch, Hamm.

Schneider, I. (1995) Imprisonment in Pre-Classical and Classical Islamic Law, *Islamic Law and Society*, vol. 2, no 2, pp. 157–173.

Schneider, U. (2001) Gemeinnützige Arbeit als "Zwischensanktion", *Monatschrift für Kriminologie und Strafrecht*, vol. 84, no 4, pp. 273–287.

Schöch, H. (2008) On Section 61 in Laufhütte, H. W, Rissing-van Saan, R. and Tidemann, K. (eds.) *Leipziger Kommentar StGB*, 12th edition, vol. 3, pp. 215–402.

Schreckling, J. (1991) *Täter-Opfer-Ausgleich nach Jugendstraftaten in Köln – Bericht über Aufbau, Verlauf und Ergebnisse des Modellprojekts„Waage"*, Bundesministerium der Justiz, Bonn.

Schull, K. (2007) Tutuklu Sayimi: Jön Türklerin Sistematik Bir Sekilde Hapishane Istatistikleri Toplama Calismalari ve Bunlarin 1911–1918 Hapishane Reformu Üzerine Etkileri in Levy, N. and Toumarkine, A. (eds.) *Osmanli'da Asayis, Suc ve Ceza, Tarih Vakfi Yayinlari*, Istanbul.

Schur, M., E. (1973) *Radical Non-Intervention* (Rethinking the Delinquency Problem), Prentice Hall, London.

Scot, D. (2007) The Changing Face of the English Prison: A Critical Review of the Aims of Imprisonment in Jewkes, Y. (ed.) *Handbook of Prisons*, Willan, Cullompton, pp. 49–72.

Seebode, M. (1999) Problematische Ersatzfreiheitsstrafe in Feuerhelm, W., Schwind, H.-D. und Bock, M. (eds.) *Festschrift für Alexander Böhm zum 70. Geburtstag am 14. Juni 1999*, de Gruyter, Berlin, pp. 519–552.

Sen, H. (2007) Osmanli'da Hapishane Mefhumu, Levy, N. and Toumarkine, A. (eds.) *Osmanli'da Asayis, Suc ve Ceza, Tarih Vakfi Yayinlari*, Istanbul, pp. 200–211.

Sentop, M. (2004) *Tanzimat Dönemi Osmanli Ceza Hukuku*, Istanbul.

Sesar, K. (1994) Overcrowding – Not only Crisis in the Custodial System, *European Journal on Criminal Policy and Research*, vol. 2, no 4, pp. 107–116.

Sessar, K. (1985) Über das Opfer: Eine viktimologische Zwischenbilanz in Vogler, T. with Herrmann, J., Krümpelman, J., Moos, R., Triffterer, O., Leibinger, R., Schaffmeister, D., Meyer, J., Hünerfeld, P. and Behrendt, H.-J. (eds.) *Festschrift für Hans-Heinrich Jescheck*, vol. 2, pp. 1137–1157.

Sessar, K. and Hering, E. (1985) Bedeutung und Reichweite Pädagogisch Gemeinter Verfahreneinstellungen durch den Jugendstaatsanwalt: Das Beispiel des„Lübecker Modells" in Kury, H. (ed.) *Bedeutung und Reichweite Pädagogisch Gemeinter Verfahreneinstellungen durch den Jugendstaatsanwalt: Das Beispiel des„Lübecker Modells"*, pp. 371–415.

Seuffert, H. (1892) Ist die bedingte Verurteilung im Strafrecht einzuführen?', *Verhandlungen des 21. Deutschen Juristentages*, vol. 1, pp. 227–258.

Shapland, J. (2003) Restorative Justice and Criminal Justice: Just Responses to Crime in von Hirsch, A., Roberts, J., V., Bottoms, A., Roach, K. and Schiff, M. (eds.) *Restorative Justice and Criminal Justice: Competing or Reconcilable Paradigms?* Hart Publishing, Oxford, pp. 195–218.

Shapland, J. and Maguire, M. (1990) The Victim Movement in Europe in Lurigio, A., J., Skogan, W., G. and Davis, R., C. (eds.) *Victims of Crime: Problems, Policies and Programmes*, Sage, Newbury Park, pp. 205–225.

Sichart (1904) Die Freiheitsstrafe im Anklagestande und ihre Verteidigung, Winter, Heidelberg.

Sim, J. and Fitzgerald, M. (1982) *British Prisons*, 2nd edition, Blackwell, Oxford.

Sim, J., Ruggiero, V. and Ryan, M. (1995) Punishment in Europe: Perceptions and Commonalties, in Ruggiero, V., Ryan, M. and Sim, J. (eds.) *Western European Penal Systems: A Critical Anatomy*, Sage, London, pp. 1–23.

Singer, S., I. (1996) *Recriminalising Delinquency*, Cambridge University Press, Cambridge.

Sipahi, A. (2006) *The Labour-Based Prisons in Turkey (1933-1953)* (Unpublished master study, University of Bogazici).

Smith, K. and Keenan, D., J. (2004) *Smith & Keenan's English Law*, Pearson, Harlow.

Snacken, S. and Beyens. K. (1994) Sentencing and Prison Overcrowding, *European Journal on Criminal Policy and Research*, vol.2, no 1, pp. 84–99.

Society for the Improvement of Prison Discipline and for the Reformation of Juvenile Offenders (1832) *The Eighth Report of the Committee of the Society for the Improvement of Prison Discipline and for the Reformation of Juvenile Offenders*, J. and A. Arch, London.

Softley, P. (1978) Compensation Orders in Magistrates' Courts, Home Office Research Study 43, HMSO, London.

Softley, P. (1978) Compensation Orders in Magistrates' Courts, HMSO, London.

Sofuoglu. E. (2000) Osmanli Hapishanelerinde Islah ve Firar Tesebbüsleri in Naskali, G., E. and Altun, O., H. (eds.) *Hapishane Kitabi*, Kitabevi, Istanbul, pp. 163–172.

Sokullu-Akinci, F. (2005) Criticism of the Provisions of the New Turkish Criminal Code, Concerning Restorative Justice, *Annales de la Facultés de Droit d'Istanbul*, vol. 54, pp. 3–10.

Sokullu-Akinci, F. (2006) No Midnight Express: Prison Reform of Turkey on the Way to Europe, *Annales de la Facultés de Droit d'Istanbul*, vol. 56, no 1–4, pp. 61–91.

Sonnen, B.-R. (1981) Die §§ 45 und 47 JGG- Eine Betrachtung der Anwendungspraxis und der Möglichkeiten Deutsche Vereinigung für Jugendgerichte und Jugendgerichtshilfen (ed.) *Die Jugendrichterlichen Entscheidungen – Anspruch und Wirklichkeit*, München, pp. 177–190.

Soothill, K. (2007) Prison Histories and Competing Audiences 1776–1966 in Jewkes, Y. (ed.) *Handbook of Prisons*, Willan, Cullompton, pp. 27–48.

Soyaslan, D. (2001) Af, *Anayasa Yargisi*, vol. 18, pp. 412–436.

Sözüer, A. (2004) Toplumsal Degisim Sürecinde *Türk Ceza Kanunu Reformu* in Ergül, T. (ed.) Türk Ceza Kanunu Reformu, Birinci Kitap, TBB Yayinlari, Ankara, pp. 33–49.

Sözüer, A. (2007) Die Reform des türkischen Strafrechts, *Zeitschrift für die gesamte Strafrechtswissenschaft*, vol. 119, no 3, pp. 712–749.

Sözüer, A. (2008) Das neue türkische Strafgesetzbuch in Tellenbach S. (ed.) *Das neue türkische Straf- und Strafprozessrecht*, Berliner Wissenschaftsverlag, Berlin, pp. 11–40.

Sparks, R. (1971) The Use of Suspended Sentences, *Criminal Law Review*, pp. 384–401.

Sparks, R. (2002) Prisons, Punishment and Penality in McLaughlin, E. and Muncie, J. (eds.) *Controlling Crime*, Sage, London, pp. 201–256.

Speis, F. (2008) *Gemeinnützige Arbeit als selbstständige Hauptsstrafe im Erwachsenenstrafrecht*, Kovac, Hamburg.

Spierenburg, P. (1996) Four Centuries of Prison History: Punishment, Suffering, the Body, and Power in Finzsch, N. and Jütte, R. (eds.) *Institutions of Confinement: Hospitals, Asylums, and Prisons in Western Europe and North America, 1500–1950*, Cambridge University Press, Washington, pp. 17–38.

Stammberger, W. (1963) Die Geschichte der Strafrechtsreform bis zum Strafgesetzbuchentwurf 1962 in *Probleme der Strafrechtsreform*, Schriftreihe der Friedrich-Naumann-Stiftung zur Politik und Zeitgeschichte, Stuttgart, pp. 11–29.

Stapenhorst, H. (1993) *Die Entwicklung des Verhältnisses von Geldstrafe zu Freiheitsstrafe*, Duncker & Humblot, Berlin.

Statistisches Bundesamt (1998) Rechtspflege, Fachserie 10, Reihe 3, Metzler Poeschel, Stuttgart.

Statistisches Bundesamt (1999) Rechtspflege, Fachserie 10, Reihe 3, Metzler Poeschel, Stuttgart.

Statistisches Bundesamt (2000) Rechtspflege, Fachserie 10, Reihe 3, Metzler Poeschel, Stuttgart.

Statistisches Bundesamt (2001) Rechtspflege, Fachserie 10, Reihe 3, Metzler Poeschel, Stuttgart.

Statistisches Bundesamt (2002) Rechtspflege, Fachserie 10, Reihe 3, Metzler Poeschel, Stuttgart.

Statisticsches Bundesamt (2003), (2004), (2005), (2006), (2007), and (2008) are available in electronic format in the following address http://www.destatis.de (Access Date: March 2010).

Stenner, D. (1968) *Die kurzfristige Freiheitsstrafe und die Möglichkeiten zu ihrem Ersatz durch andere Sanktionen*, Kriminalistik-Verlag, Hamburg.

Stephenson, M., Giller, H. and Brown, S. (2007) *Effective Practice in Youth Justice*, Willan, Cullompton.

Stern, V. (1989) *Bricks of Shame: Britain's Prisons*, Penguin, London.

Stöckel, H. (2002) Strafen mit Fantasie: Zur Frage neuer Sanktionen im Strafrecht in Dölling, D. and Ebb, V. (eds.) *Festschrift für Karl Heinz Gössel zum 70. Geburtstag am 16 Oktober 2002*, Müller, Heidelberg.

Stöckel, (2007) Gedanken zur Reform des Sanktionenrechts in Helgerth, R., Konig, P. and Schöch, H. (eds.) *Recht gestalten- dem Recht dienen*, de Gruyter, Berlin, pp. 329–344.

Stone, N. (1994) The Suspended Sentence Since the Criminal Justice Act 1991, *Criminal Law Review*, pp. 399–408.

Strafrechtsausschuss des Deutschen Antwaltvereins (2000) *Reform des strafrechtlichen Sanktionensystem*, Deutscher Anwaltverlag, München.

Stree, W. (2006) On Section 42 in *Schönke/ Schröder Strafgesetzbuch Kommentar*, 27th edition, Beck, München.

Streng, F. (2000) Entwicklung neuer Sanktionsformen in Deutschland in Jehle, J.-M. and Bender, D. (eds.) *Täterbehandlung und neue Sanktionsformen: Kriminalpolitische Konzepte in Europa*, Forum, Bonn, pp. 207–233.

Streng, F. (2002) *Strafrechtliche Sanktionen*, 2nd edition, Kohlhammer, Stuttgart.

Sutherland, E., H. (1934) The Decreasing Prison Population of England, *Journal of Criminal Law and Criminology*, vol. 24, pp. 880–900.

Tak, P., J., P. (1986) Community Service Orders in Western Europe in Albrecht, H.-J. and Schädler, W. (eds.) *Community Service: a New Option in Punishing Offenders in Europe*, Max-Planck-Institut für ausländisches und internationales Strafrecht, Freiburg.

Tallack, W. (1889) *Penological and Preventive Principles*, reprinted in 1984, Garland Publishing, New York.

Taner, T. (1953) *Ceza Hukuku Umumi Kisim*, 3rd edition, Ismail Akgün Matbaasi, Istanbul.

Taner, T., Dönmezer, S., Gökay, F. K., Findikoglu, Z. F., Kunter, N., Sensoy, N., Erman, S., Karaorman, T. N. (1951) The Prevention and Treatment of Juvenile Delinquency in Turkey, *Annales de la Faculte de Droit d'Istanbul*, no 1–4, pp. 1–42.

Tanör, B. (1986) Iki Anayasa (1961–1982), Beta, Istanbul.

Tas-Junger, J. (1994) *Alternatives to Prison Sentences: Experiences and Developments*, Kugler Publications, Amsterdam.

Taylor, R., Wasik, M. and Leng, R. (2004) *Blackstone's Guide to the Criminal Justice Act 2003*, Oxford University Press, Oxford.

Teeters, N., K. (1949) *Deliberations of the International Penal and Penitentiary Congresses: Questions and Answers, 1872–1935*, Temple University, Philadelphia.

Tellenbach, S. (1997) Türkei in Eser, A., Überhofen, M. and Huber, B. (eds.) *Korruptionsbekämpfung durch Strafrecht*, Max Planck Institut für ausländisches und internationales Strafrecht, Freiburg, pp. 617–653.

Tellenbach, S. (2005) *Zum neuen türkischen Strafgesetzbuch*, pp. 76–93 in KAS-Auslandsinformationen, accessible from the following link: http://www.kas.de/wf/doc/kas_6625-544-1-30.pdf.

Tezcan, D. and Erdem, M., R. (2004) Dokuz Eylül Üniversitesi Hukuk Fakültesi'nin TCK Tasarisi Hakkindaki Raporu in Ergül, T. (ed.) *Türk Ceza Kanunu Reformu*, Ikinci Kitap, TBB Yayinlari, Ankara.

Thomas, D. (2003) Judicial Discretion in Sentencing in Gelsthorpe, L. and Padfield, N. (eds.) *Exercising Discretion: Decision Making in the Criminal Justice System and Beyond*, Willan Publishing, Cullompton, pp. 50–73.

Thorpe, D. (1982) Intermediate Treatment: Problems of Theory and Practice in Bailey, R. and Lee, P. (eds.) *Theory and Practice in Social Work*, Basil Blackwell, Oxford, pp. 78–97.

Timasheff, N., S. (1943) Part II: *Probation in Continental Europe, Latin America, Asia, and Africa*, Fordham University Press, New York.

Timasheff, N., S. (1941) *One Hundred Years of Probation, 1841–1941*, Part I: Probation in the United States, England and the British Commonwealth Countries, Fordham University Press, New York.

Tonry, M. (2004) *Punishment and Politics: Evidence and Emulation in the Making of English Criminal Control Policy*, Willan, Cullompton, pp. 92–146.

Tonry, M., H. (2006) *Thinking About Crime: Sense and Sensibility in American Penal Culture*, Oxford University Press, Oxford.

Tonry, M. and Lynch, M. (1996) Intermediate Sanctions, *Crime and Justice*, vol. 20, pp. 99–144.

Toroslu, N. (1987) *Nasil Bir Ceza Kanunu*, V Yayinlari, Ankara.

Toroslu, N. and Ersoy, Y. (2004) Kanunlasmamasi Gereken Bir Tasari in Ergül, T. (ed.) *Türk Ceza Kanunu Reformu*, Ikinci Kitap, TBB Yayinlari, Ankara, pp. 1–20.

Tournier, P. (1994) The Custodial Crisis in Europe: Inflated Prison Populations and Possible Alternatives, *European Journal on Criminal Policy and Research*, vol. 2, no 4, pp. 89–100.

Trager, L. (1911) Die Geldstrafe als Hauptstrafe, *Gerichtssaal*, vol. 78, pp. 241–330.

Trenczek, T. (2003) Within or outside System? Restorative Justice Attempts in the Penal System in Weitekamp, E., G. and Kerner, H.-J. (eds.) *Restorative Justice in Context: International Practice and Directions*, Willan, Devon, pp. 272–284.

Tuncay, M. (1997) *Cagdas Türkiye* (1908–1980), Cem Yayinevi, Istanbul.

Turhan, F. (2006) Yeni Türk Ceza Kanununa Göre Cezalarin Ertelenmesi ve Uygulanmasinda Ortaya Cikan Bazi Sorunlar, *Erzincan Üniversitesi Hukuk Fakültesi Dergisi*, vol. 10, no 3–4, pp. 27–54.

Turhan, F. (2007) Yeni Türk Ceza Kanununda Güvenlik Tedbiri Olarak Hak Yoksunlugu ve Yasakliligin Hukuki Niteligi, Kapsam ve Kosullari Üzerine Bir Degerlendirme, *Ceza Hukuku Dergisi*, vol. 2, no 4, pp. 171–196.

Türk Kriminoloji Enstitüsü (1948) *Türkiye'de Adam Öldürme Cürmü Mahkumlari Hakkinda Kriminolojik Istatistik*, Hüsnütabiat Matbaasi, Istanbul.

Tutt, N. and Gelsthorpe, L. (1986) The Attendance Centre Order, *Criminal Law Review*, pp. 146–153.

Ücok, C. (1947) Osmanli Ceza Kanunnamelerinde Islam Ceza Hukukuna Aykiri Hükümler, *Ankara Üniversitesi Hukuk Fakültesi Dergisi*, vol. 4, no 1–4, pp. 48–73.

Ücok, C., Mumcu, A. and Bozkurt, G. (1999) *Türk Hukuk Tarihi*, Ankara.

United Nations/Department of Economic and Social Affairs (1951) *Probation and Related Measures*, United Nations Publications, New York.

United Nations/Department of Social Affairs (1954) *Practical Results and Financial Aspects of Adult Probation in Selected Countries*, United Nations Publications, New York.

Ünver, Y. (2002) Einige strafrechtliche Probleme über Kinder und Jugendliche in der Türkei, *Annales de la Facultés de Droit d'Istanbul,* vol. 34, no 51, pp. 193–214.

van Dijk, J. (1979) *The Extent of Public Information and the Nature of Public Attitudes Towards Crime in Public Opinion and Crime and Criminal Justice* (Reports presented to the Thirteenth Criminological Research Conference, 1978), Council of Europe, Strasbourg, pp. 7–39.

van Dijk, J. (1988) Ideological Trends within the Victims Movement: An International Perspective in *Victims of Crime: A new Deal?* in Maguire, M. and Pointing, J. (eds.) *Victims of Crime: A new Deal?,* Open University Press, Milton Keynes, pp. 127–137.

van Dijk, J. (1993) More than a Matter of Security: Trends in Crime Prevention in Europe in Heidensohn, F. and Farrel, M. (eds.) *Crime in Europe*, Routledge, London, pp. 27–42.

van Kalmthout, A., M. (1989) *Sanction Systems in the Member-States of the Council of Europe*, Kluwer, Deventer.

van Kalmthout, A. and Dünkel, A. (2000) Ambulante Sanktionen und Maßnahmen in Europe, *Neue Kriminal Politik*, vol. 12, no 4, pp. 26–30.

van Swaaningen, R. and Beijerse, J. (1983) From Punishment to Diversion and Back again: the Debate on Non-Custodial Sanctions and Penal Reform in the Netherlands, *Howard Journal*, vol. 32, no 2, pp. 136–156.

van Swaaningen, R. and de Jonge, G. (1995) The Dutch Prison System and Penal Business Management in Ruggiero, V., Ryan, M. and Sim, J. (eds.) *Western European Penal Systems: A Critical Anatomy*, Sage, London, pp. 26–27.

van Zyl Smit, D. and Dünkel, F. (1991) *Imprisonment Today and Tomorrow: International Perspectives on Prisoners' Rights and Prison Conditions*, Kluwer, Deventer.

van Zyl Smit, D. and Snacken, S. (2009) *Principles of European Prison Law and Policy*, Oxford University Press, Oxford.

Vanstone, M. (1993) A "Missed Opportunity" Reassessed: the Influence of the Day Centre Experiment on the Criminal Justice System and Probation, *British Journal of Social Work*, vol. 23, pp. 213–229.

Vanstone, M (2004) *Supervising Offenders in the Community: a History of Probation Theory and Practice*, Ashgate, Aldershot.

Vass, A. (1990) *Alternatives to Prison- Punishment, Custody and the Community*, Sage, London.

Vass, A. and Weston, A. (1990) Probation Day Centres As An Alternative to Custody: A Trojan Horse Examined, *British Journal of Criminology*, vol. 30, no 2, pp. 189–206.

Verrest, P. (2000) The French Public Prosecution Service, *European Journal of Crime, Criminal Law and Criminal Justice*, vol. 8, no 3, pp. 210–244.

Vito, G., F. and Wilson, D., G. (1985) *The American Juvenile Justice System*, Sage, London.

Volk, K. (2002) Strafprozessrecht, Beck, München.

von Hentig, H. (1955) *Die Strafe*, vol. 2, Die modernen Erscheinungsformen, Springer, Berlin.

von Hirsch, A. (1986) *Past or Future Crimes*, Manchester University Press, Manchester.

von Hirsch, A. and Ashworth, A. (1997) Recognising Elephants: the Problem of the Custody Threshold, *Criminal Law Review*, pp. 187–200.

von Hirsch, A. and Wasik, M. (1988) Non-Custodial Penalties and the Principle of Desert, *Criminal Law Review*, September, pp. 555–572.

von Lilienthal, K. (1912) *Der Streit um die Strafrechtsreform* (Akademische Rede zur Erinnerung an den zweiten Gründer der Universität), Hörning, Heidelberg.

von Liszt (1882/3) *Der Zweckgedanke im Strafrecht*, reprinted in 2002, Nomos, Baden.

von Liszt (1905) *Strafrechtliche Aufsätze und Vorträge*, vol. 1 and 2, de Gruyter, Berlin.

von Liszt, F. (1908) *Lehrbuch des deutschen Strafrechts*, 16/17th edition, Guttentag, Berlin.

von Liszt, F. (1908) Bedingte Verurteilung und Bedingte Begnadigung in *Vergleichende Darstellung des deutschen und ausländischen Strafrechts* in Birkmeyer, K. (ed.) Vergleichende Darstellung des deutschen und ausländischen Strafrechts, Allgemeiner Teil, vol. III, Liebmann, Berlin, pp. 1–91.

Vormbaum, T. (2009) *Einführung in die moderne Strafrechtsgeschichte*, Springer, Berlin.

Vormbaum, T. and Rentrop, K. (2008) *Reform des Strafgesetzbuches*, Wissenschaft's Verlag, Berlin.

Vosgrau, R. (1990) Elektronische Überwachung: Auf dem Weg zur Abschaffung von Freiheitsstrafen oder on die totale Kontrolle, *Bewährungshilfe*, vol. 37, no 2, pp. 166–168.

Voß, M. (1986) *Jugend ohne Rechte*: die Entwicklung des Jugendstrafrechts, Campus-Verlag, Frankfurt.

Voß, M. (1987) Verwahrvollzug – Behandlungsvollzug. Der strafrechtliche Gebrauch der Freiheitsstrafe im Zuge ihrer Veränderten Ansprüche. Zugleich eine Kritik der Kurzstrafenkritik in Sievering, U., O. (ed.) *Problem Strafhaft- Alternative Sanktionen*, Haag & Herchen, Frankfurt, pp. 224–253.

Wach, A. (1890) *Die Reform der Freiheitsstrafe: Ein Beitrag zur Kritik der bedingten und unbestimmten Verurteilung*, Duncker & Humblot, Leipzig.

Wach, A. (1899) Die bedingte Verurteilung, *Deutsche Juristen-Zeitung*, vol. 4, no 6, pp. 117–120.

Wach, A. (1900) Die bedingte Verurteilung vor dem Reichstag, *Deutsche Juristen-Zeitung*, vol. 5, no 4, pp. 81–84.

Walgrave, L. (2001) On Restoration and Punishment: Favourable Similarities and Fortunate Differences in Morris, A. and Maxwell, G. (eds.), *Restorative Justice for Juveniles: Conferencing, Mediation and Circles*, Hart Publishing, Oxford, pp. 17–37.

Walker, N., D. (1965) *Crime and Punishment in Britain*, Edinburgh University Press, Edinburgh.

Walker, N. (1972) Crime and Penal Measures in Halsey, A., H. (ed.) *Trends in British Society since 1900*, Macmillan & St. Martin, London.

Walter, M. (1985) Wandlungen in der Reaktion auf Kriminalität. Zur kriminologischen und insbesondere dogmatischen Bedeutung von Diversion, *Zeitschrift für die gesamte Strafrechtswissenschaft*, vol. 93, pp. 32–68.

Walter, M. (1990) Der Erziehungsgedanke im Jugendstrafrecht – Abschied oder Reformulierung in Wolff, J. and Marek, A. (ed.) *Erziehung und Strafe*, Forum, Bonn, pp. 51–61.

Walter, M. (1999) Elektronisch überwachter Hausarrest als neue Vollzugsform, *Zeitschrift für Strafvollzug*, vol. 48, pp.287–295

Walter, M. (2001) Strafvollzug – Ende der Resozialisierung? in Bieschke, V. (ed.) *Strafvollzug im Wandel*, Kriminologische Zentralstelle, Wiesbaden, pp. 25–38.

Walther, S. (2004) Communication over Confrontation: Modern Criminal Procedure in Transformation in Eser, A. and Rabenstein, C. (eds.) *Strafjustiz im Spannungsfeld von Effizienz und Fairness*, Duncker & Humblot, Berlin, pp. 367–379.

Ward, R., W. and Ward, M., S. (1993) *Community Sentences: Law and Practice,* Blackstone, London.

Wasik, M. (1991) 'Non-Incarcerative Sanctions in England, *Federal Sentencing Reporter*, July/August 1991, pp. 42–44.

Wasik, M, (1992) Sentencing: a Fresh Look at Aims and Objectives in Stockdale, E. and Casale, S. (eds.) *Criminal Justice under Stress*, Blackstone, London, pp. 119–141.

Wasik, M. (2004) What Guides Sentencing Decisions in Bottoms, A. and Rex, S. and Robinson, G. (eds.) *Alternatives to Prison: Options for an Insecure Society*, Willan, Cullompton, pp. 290–312.

Wasik, M. and Taylor, R. (1994) *Guide to the Criminal Justice Act 1991*, 2nd edition, Blackstone, London.

Wayne, L. (1993) The History of Change in Whitfield, D. and Scott, D. (eds.) *Paying Back Twenty Years of Community Service*, Waterside Press, Winchester.

Webber, G. (1957) Recent Trends in Criminal Justice, *Current Legal Problems*, vol. 10, pp. 127–151.

Weigend, T. (1980) Continental Cures for American Ailments: European Criminal Procedure as a Model for Law Reform, *Crime and Justice*, vol. 2, pp. 381–428.

Weigend, T. (1982) Neoklassismus – Ein Transatlantisches Missverständnis, *Zeitschrift für die gesamte Strafrechtswissenschaft*, vol. 94, pp. 801- 814.

Weigend, T. (1984) Viktimologische und kriminalpolitische Überlegungen zur Stellung des Verletzten im Strafverfahren, *Zeitschrift für die gesamte Strafrechtswissenschaft*, vol. 96, pp. 761–793.

Weigend, T. (1989) *Deliktsopfer und Strafverfahren*, Duncker & Humblot, Berlin.

Weigend, T. (1989) Privatgefängnisse, Hausarrest und andere Neuheiten, *Bewährungshilfe*, vol. 36, pp. 289–301.

Weigend, T. (1992) *Sanktionen ohne Freiheitsentzug, Goltdammer's Archiv für Strafrecht*, vol. 139, pp. 345–367.

Weigend, T. (1997) Das Opportunitätsprinzip zwischen Einzelfallgerechtigkeit und Systemeffizienz, *Zeitschrift für die gesamte Strafrechtwissenschaft,* vol. 109, no 4, pp. 103–121.

Weigend, T. (2001) Sentencing and Punishment in Germany in Tonry, M. and Frase, R. (ed.) *Sentencing Sanctions in Western Countries*, Oxford University Press, pp. 189–221.

Weigend, T. (2006) Criminal Law and Criminal Procedure in *Elgar Encyclopaedia of Comparative Law*, Smits, J. (ed.), Edward Elgar Publishing, Cheltenham, pp. 214–227.

Weitekamp, E., G. (2001) Mediation in Europe: Paradoxes, Problems and Promises in Morris, A. and Maxwell, G. (eds.) *Restorative Justice for Juveniles*, Hart Publishing, Oxford, pp. 145–160.

Weßlau, E. (1999) In welche Richtung geht die Reform des Sanktionensystems, *Strafverteidiger,* vol. 19, no 5, pp. 278–287.

Whitehead, P. (1990) *Community Supervision for Offenders*, Gower, Aldershot.

Whitehead, P. and Statham, R. (2006) *The History of Probation: Politics, Power and Cultural Change*, 1876–2005, Shaw & Sons, Crayford.

Whitfield, D. (1997) *Tackling the Tag: the Electronic Monitoring of Offenders*, Waterside Press, Winchester.

Wiener, M, J. (1994) *Reconstructing the Criminal: Culture, Law and Policy in England, 1830–1914*, Cambridge University Press, Cambridge.

Wilkitzki, P. (2006) Vom Beruf unserer Zeit zur Sanktionenreform, *Goltdammer's Archiv für Strafrecht*, vol. 153, pp. 399–402.

Wilkiztki, P. (2000) Neue kriminalpolitische Akzente in Deutschland in Jehle, J.-M. and Bender, D. (eds.) *Täterbehandlung und neue Sanktionsformen*, pp. 447–454.

Willis, A. (1977) Community Service as an Alternative to Imprisonment, *Probation Journal*, vol. 24, 120–122.

Willis, A. (1986) Alternatives to Imprisonment: an Elusive Paradise in Pointing, J. (ed.) *Alternatives to Custody*, Blackwell, Oxford, pp. 18–38.

Wines, E. C. (1873) *Report on the International Penitentiary Congress of London* (held July 3–13, 1872), Government Printing, Washington.

Wise, E., M. and Maitlin, A. (1978) *The Italian Penal Code*, Rothman, Colorado.

Witmer, H., L. (1927) The History, Theory and Results of Parole, *Journal of Criminal Law and Criminology*, vol. 18, no 1, pp. 47–61.

Wittsam, K. (1998) *Elektronischer Hausarrest? Zur Anwendbarkeit eines amerikanischen Sanktionsmodells in Deutschland*, Nomos, Baden-Baden.

Wolf, J. (1986) Die Entwicklung der Gesetzgebung im Jugendstrafrecht, *Zeitschrift für Rechtssoziologie*, vol. 7, pp. 123–142.

Wolf, J. (1992) *Jugendliche vor Gericht im Dritten Reich – Nationalsozialistische Jugendstrafrechtspolitik und Justizalltag*, Beck, München.

Wolters, G. (2002) Der Entwurf eines "Gesetzes zur Reform des Sanktionenrechts", *Zeitschrift für die gesamte Strafrechtswissenschaft*, vol. 114, pp. 63–87.

Worrall, A. and Hoy, C. (2005) *Punishment in the Community: Managing Offenders*, Making Choices, Willan, Cullompton.

Würtenberger, T. (1965) Kriminologie und Strafrechtsreform in Gedanken zur Strafrechtsreform in Heinitz, E., Würtenberger, T. and Peters, K. (eds.) *Gedanken zur Strafrechtsreform*, Schöningh, Paderborn, pp. 21–38.

Yenisey, F. (1984) Die Entwicklungen im türkischen Strafrecht von 1960 bis 1983, *Zeitschrift für die gesamte Strafrechtswissenschaft*, vol. 96, pp. 212–240.

Yenisey, F. (1992) Juvenile Delinquency in Turkey in Messmer, H. and Otto, H.-U. (eds.) *Restorative Justice on Trial*, Kluwer, Dordrecht, pp. 409–415.

Yenisey, F. (1997) Zum türkischen Straf- und Strafprozessrecht: Entwicklungen zwischen 1983 and 1995, *Zeitschrift für die gesamte Strafrechtswissenschaft*, vol. 109, pp. 212–240.

Yenisey, F. and Nuhoglu, A. (2006) *Muhakeme Hukuku Dali Olarak Ceza Muhakemesi Hukuku*, Kunter-Yenisey, 15th edition, Beta, Istanbul.

Yesilada, B. (2002) Turkey's Candidacy for EU Membership, *Middle East Journal*, vol. 56, no 1, pp. 94–111.

Yildiz, A., K. (2005) Uzlasma – Sikayet Iliskisi in Yenisey, F. (ed.) in Yenisey, F. (ed.) *Ceza Muhakemesi Hukukunda Uzlasma*, Arikan, Istanbul, pp. 259–280.

Yildiztas, M. (1991) *Mütareke Döneminde Suc Unsurlari ve Istanbul Hapishaneleri* (unpublished master thesis, Istanbul University).

Young, P. (1976) A Sociological Analysis of the Early History of Probation, *British Journal of Law and Society*, vol. 3, no. 1, pp. 44–58.

Young, W. (1979) *Community Service Orders: the Development and Use of a new Penal Measure*, Heinemann, London.

Young, W. (1986) Influences upon the Use of Imprisonment: A Review of Literature, *Howard Journal*, vol. 25, no 2, pp. 125–135.

Young, R. (2001) Just Cops Doing 'Shameful' Business?: Police-led Restorative Justice and the Lessons of Research in Morris, A. and Maxwell, G. (eds.) *Restorative Justice for Juveniles*, Hart Publishing, Oxford, pp.195–226.

Young, W. and Brown, M. (1993) Cross National Comparisons of Imprisonment in Tonry, M. (ed.) *Crime and Justice*, vol. 17, pp. 1–49.

Young, R. and Goold, B. (1999) Restorative Police Cautioning in Aylesbury – from Degrading to Reintegrative Shaming Ceremonies, *Criminal Law Review*, pp. 126–138.

Young, R. and Hoyle, C. (2002) New Improved Police-Led Restorative Justice? Action Research and the Thames Valley Police Initiative in von Hirsch, A., Roberts, J., Bottoms, A., E., Roach, K. and Schiff, M. (eds.) *Restorative Justice and Criminal Justice: Competing or Reconcilable Paradigms*, Hart Publishing, Oxford.

Yücel, M., T. (1987) Hürriyeti Baglayici Cezaya Alternatifler: Dünyadaki Görünüm, Adalet Dergisi, vol 78, no.1, pp. 95–100.

Yücel, M., T. (1977) Ceza Infaz Kurumlarindaki Gerilim ve Secenek Yaptirimlar, *Adalet Dergisi*, vol. 68, no 5–6, pp. 325–335.

Yurtcan, E. (1980) Child in Turkish Criminal Law and Criminal Procedure Law, *Annales de la Facultés de Droit d'Istanbul,* vol. 27, no 43, pp. 237–242.

Zedner, L. (2002) Dangers of Dystopias in Penal Theory, *Oxford Journal of Legal Studies*, vol. 22, pp. 341–366.

Zehr, H. (1990) *Changing Lenses: A New Focus for Crime and Justice*, Herald Press, Scottdale.

Zipf, H. (1966) *Die Geldstrafe*, Luchterland, Berlin.

Zucker (1892) Noch ein Wort zur Frage der sogenannte bedingte Verurteilung, *Gerichtssaal*, vol. 47, pp. 255–263.

Zvekic, U. (1994) *Alternatives to Imprisonment* (United Nations Interregional Crime and Justice Research Institute), Nelson-Hall Publishers, Chicago.

Zweite Landesversammlung der Gruppe Deutsches Reich der IKV (Bericht) (Report) *Zeitschrift für die gesamte Strafrechtswissenschaft*, vol. 11, pp. 21–38.